GOD'S OTHER
A London

Vernal W. Scott

BORN AT ST MARY'S HOSPITAL, London, Vernal Scott is an ex-man of faith, diversity and human rights consultant, 'McKenzie Friend' in family court, zestful keynote speaker, media commentator, and facilitator of workshops dealing with the issues raised in this, his distinctive debut. He also provides confidential advice and support to public and private individuals dealing with sexuality, 'coming out', equality issues, and sexual health, including HIV. He has made an impressive contribution to both public and voluntary sectors over the past three decades and speaks with considerable authority on an extensive range of topics. In the mid-80s he launched the People's (multi-cultural) Group at the London Lesbian & Gay Centre, and later founded the Black Communities AIDS Team. In 1987 he was appointed Head of HIV services for Brent, and in 2003, he joined Islington as Head of Equality and Diversity. Vernal remains a leading voice on equal life chances and is rightly acknowledged on both Black and LGBTQ History websites.

Rising above the fiercely competitive market of new books and authors, Vernal has written the only self-published title to be shortlisted for the 2014 Polari First Book Prize. An astonishingly soulful and candid account of a bespoke London life, his book has won rave reader reviews and recommendations by WH Smith and notables such as Peter Tatchell, Lord Paul Boateng and Sir Nick Partridge. Written with tears and humour, his story reflects on UK Black culture, 'coming out', the "AIDS war years", troubled fatherhood, "damaging religion", and much more. His readings have generated capacity engagements at venues as diverse as the London School of Economics, King's College London, South Bank University, St Martin in the Fields, St Anne's Church Soho, Brighton Pride Literature Festival, and the Royal Festival Hall. He has made television chat, Attitude magazine, and appears in an extensive bio-pic on the life of Whitney Houston. This admirable author and his courageously different book shine a very very special light.

© Copyright Protected Material

All rights reserved. This work - text and pictures - is owned by the author, Vernal W. Scott. Permission is required before any of the content is shared or duplicated, however, short excerpts may be used for book reviews and promotional purposes only.

For bookings, permissions, interviews and media related enquiries, please contact Vernal Scott: vernalscott@gmail.com

Please connect via Facebook, LinkedIn, You Tube, and Twitter.

All Rise!

"Our journey is not complete until our gay brothers and sisters are treated like anyone else under the law. For if we are truly created equal, then, surely, the love we commit to one another must be equal as well." - **Barack Hussein Obama**

Dear Mr President, Sir, thank you for your love, exemplary leadership, commitment to decency, equality and inclusion, and your natural gift to unite rather than divide. You never promised or delivered perfection, but you are so much better than the detestable baby-caging personality defect that has followed you. May yours and Michelle's years ahead be full of happiness and love, but may you also remain a visible and vocal beacon of hope on the world stage to help us through the inevitable challenges ahead. Despite his racist obsession in seeking to erase you and your legacy from the history books, the inept 45th President of the now divided States will ultimately find that he cannot erase, equate to, or buy, your talent or class. Trump openly refers to torch-bearing Nazi-like haters as "very fine people"; banned brave patriotic transgender military personnel who, unlike him, are willing to spill blood for their country; and cares more for Russian dictator Putin than the bloodied hourly victims of America's incessant suicidal orgy with guns. His chaotic presidency was only made possible because of the Republican Party's willingness to unashamedly prostitute itself to him for payment in the form of power without dignity, and together, instead of draining the Washington DC swamp, they have formed new lows. I believe that time will reveal him to be the enemy of his own country and its allies, and turncoat to his loyal "anything but another black..." white voters. All decent people must pin our uneasy optimism to the glorious certainty that his tenure is time-limited and will one day come to an end. Let's count the days.

Love back! Vernal x

"If heaven is a homophobic place, then I'd prefer to go to the other place." - **Desmond Mpilo Tutu**

LGBTQ Pride

"Love doesn't discriminate, people do! Love is an experience of the heart, and it is at this level that heterosexual, bisexual, gay, lesbian, and transgender people are exactly the same. The physicality or mechanics of how we love may be different, but the integrity, passion and value of the love that we feel, is the same. Our journey as LGBTQ people has often been dangerous and bloody, but also, heroically courageous and rewarding. Our sense of pride was earned fighting for the simple freedom to live and love as we truly are, and that fight continues within our families, places of work and worship, and the Russias, Jamaicas and Ugandas of the world. The essential visibility offered by LGBT History Month, Black Pride and Gay Pride, undoubtedly saves lives by raising the self-esteem of the fearful, isolated, and victimised. These annual events also help to celebrate the countless positive contributions that we make to this awesome but oh so fragile gift called life.

To deny rather than enjoy our true sexuality is to initiate a corrosion of the human spirit and life's potential joys, but fear should never be permitted to dictate the gender of the consenting adults we love; only the heart, human attraction and integrity should do that. An authentic life path may not be easy, but its challenges and opportunities help to reveal and refine who we were born to be. To free ourselves from the dusky closet of guilt and shame is a declaration of self-love and self-respect, and an assertion of our resolve to live happy dignified lives. So, in freedom from fear and with pride in my authentic stride, I declare that I am what I am and there is much to celebrate."

Vernal Walter Scott

Love/Hate

Our sexuality is said to be a human complexity, but the real complication lies with those who perceive and treat us unfairly. Ignorance and fear are usually redressed by education, human empathy, and being awake in the present and not the past. Lots of communication and some R-E-S-P-E-C-T help, too! Hate, however, is malicious. We don't become a victim of hate because of our sexuality, colour, gender identity, HIV status, religion, or any other personal or human characteristic; we are solely victimized because of the warped mind of the perpetrator; who can wound and kill, but will always be denied the integrity of their victim.

Death is life's ultimate and inescapable act of equality. Its inevitability ensures that the ashes of those who hate will one day blow in the wind, equal to their victims'. The perpetrator's hateful mind is a cesspool of aggregated fear, bias, ignorant assumptions and prejudices that have either been learned or are based upon deceased past events that have nothing to do with their latest victim. Their mind shit readily contaminates new experiences and people by seeking or inventing reasons to hate rather than love anything or anyone 'different'. However, they will inevitably become soiled by the sewage of their own thinking, indeed, they already are; hateful minds live tarnished lives, as there is no joy in propagating hate. By embracing difference and remaining consciously present and open, we promote our personal growth and free ourselves from the prison that is the hateful or ignorant mind. This moment has only just been born; it has no past, bias or reason to fear or hate. It does, however, offer us the opportunity to love one another, as one human family. To love is why we exist; let's not complicate or contaminate it. Love, that's all! Vernal x

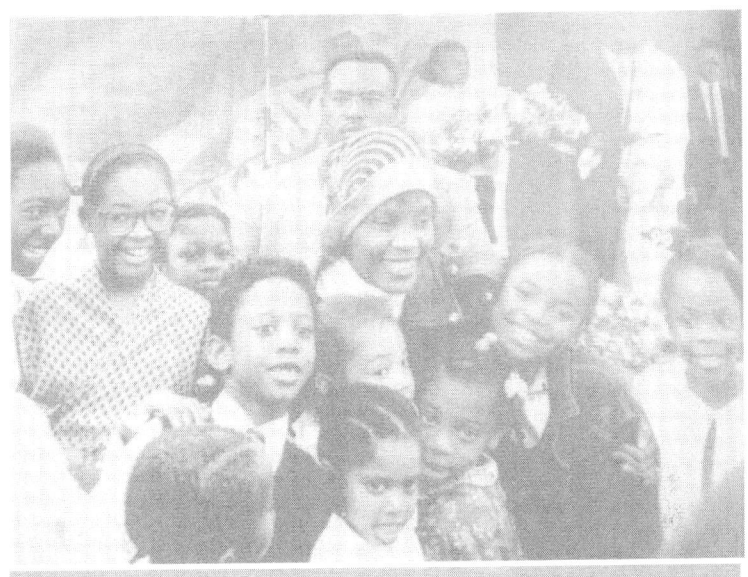

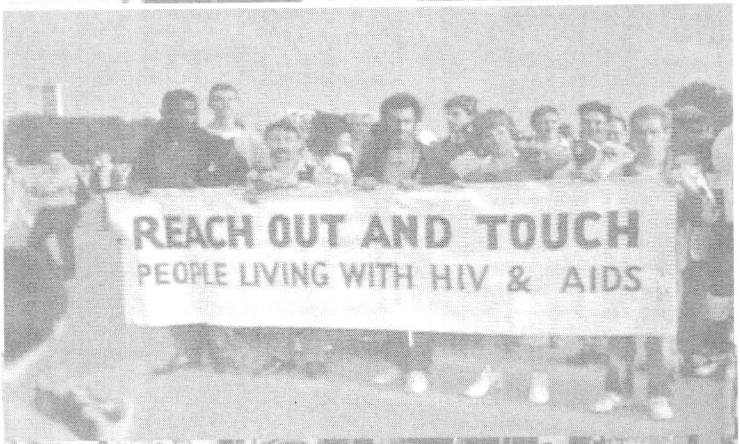
REACH OUT AND TOUCH
PEOPLE LIVING WITH HIV & AIDS

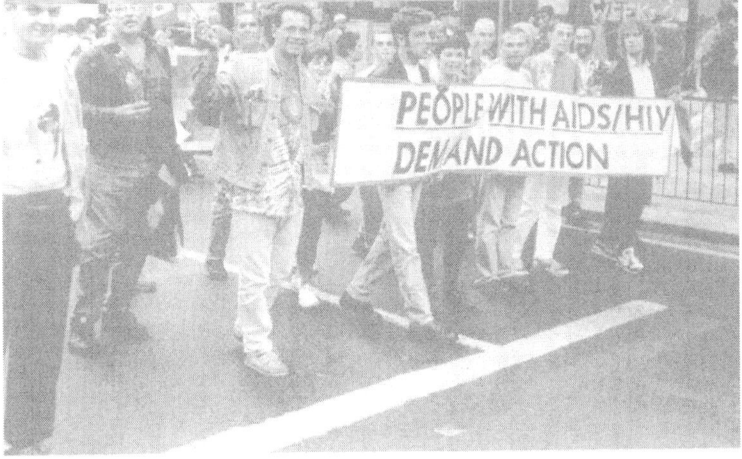
PEOPLE WITH AIDS/HIV
DEMAND ACTION

Table of Contents

1. Forewords
2. Dedication and Appreciation
3. Prologue
4. The Beginning: From May Pen to London
5. Hey, What's My Name?
6. Don't Mess With My Mum!
7. Lord, Me Dutchy Pot Bon Up!
8. Love Is a Song
9. Our Palace As A Refuge
10. Mum Goes Missing
11. Young Boy, You're Too Girlie-Girlie!
12. Bingo! Spend, Spend, Spend!!!
13. Sleeping with Strangers
14. My First Love?
15. Hey, Batty Man!
16. The Disco Kid Will Survive
17. Divorce: Doreth vs Skippy
18. Obeah Spells and Evil Hands
19. Ghosts and Demons
20. From the Knife to Life
21. I Am What I Am and It's Raining Men!
22. Black Men Loving Black Men
23. 'Born Again' - Thanks to Exegesis!
24. Love To Love You, Mr Shakespeare!
25. The People's Group
26. HIV and AIDS – My Purpose!
27. I'm Coming Out!
28. Homeless

29. Knocking on Doors
30. Police! Under Homophobic Attack
31. Brent HIV Centre - Meeting the Challenge
32. He Ain't Heavy, He's My Brother!
33. That's What Friends Are For
34. News of the World: 'Sex on the Rates!'
35. California Dreaming
36. Reach Out and Touch with Sister Whitney
37. Saying Goodbye to Love
38. Heartmenders - Princess Diana and Dionne
39. A Conveyor Belt of Death and Dying
40. Tribute to My Brother
41. We Will Survive
42. Facing the Facts: My HIV Test
43. I Want To Be a Daddy
44. Evangelist Sister Scott Meets Jesus
45. Who's the Daddy?!
46. Brother Leo and the Lord's Prayer
47. Black Beautiful and Traumatized
48. High Court Showdown: A Fight For Justice
49. A Milestone of Joy and Pain
50. Goodbye Sister Whitney, Hello Kids!
51. Cancer Scare!
52. I've Got Work to Do
53. Ahh Men: The Circumcision of Religion
54. Words of Love & Light For My Daughter
55. Contact the author Vernal W. Scott
56. God's Backroom Disco Classics: Burn Baby, Burn!

1. FOREWORDS

Lord Paul Boateng

THE GLOBAL HIV/AIDS PANDEMIC'S impact on Africa is well documented, but less well known is its effect on the continent's wider diaspora. Vernal Scott seeks to redress this omission in this moving and deeply personal memoir, which deserves attention beyond the usual readership of such works, however insightful and well written they might be. This autobiography is an account of the public and personal dimensions of the human disaster that is HIV/AIDS, and much much more. The book also tells the story of an 'out' young gay black man during a period when the pandemic raged and we, as black people in London, were struggling to come to terms with both the impact of the virus on the community and burgeoning demands for gay rights.

As British Member of Parliament for the London Borough of Brent at that time, I represented the most racially diverse constituency in Europe. It was during this time that Vernal first came to my attention as an energetic and highly effective black health activist. I was a Patron of the London Lighthouse, Britain's first HIV/AIDS hospice. My wife and I lost a neighbour to the virus, and, subsequently, my youngest son's godfather, the well-known and much loved Caribbean cook, Mr Butters. This was in the early days of the AIDS crisis, when nobody was quite sure what we were dealing with. Fear of the disease gripped whole communities, and people were very reluctant to talk about it. Vernal tells the story of those times, as he does his own life, with searing honesty. His story does not always make for comfortable reading; homophobia and racism are ugly things. I wish we could say they had been overcome but unfortunately we can't. They continue to exist, not only in society at large, but also within the black community itself. The fact that we have made some progress is in no small part due to the courage and persistence of people like

Vernal Scott. The struggle for a caring and inclusive society, in which people are judged by the content of their character rather than by the colour of their skin, by their gender, or sexual preferences, is an on-going one. The reality is that blacks and gays are not immune from exhibiting bigotry themselves, even as they are the subjects of precisely the same narrow-minded thinking and behaviours. Vernal tells this side of the story as he sees it. I witnessed what he was up against as a Health Minister at an early stage of my early career in Government, seeing otherwise excellent organisations utterly fail to reach out to black gay men or African refugee women. These groups were too often unseen, or portrayed in ways that tended to perpetuate old stereotypes. The churches, (as Vernal, too, observed from the standpoint as a believer), were often keener to display the stern judgment of man than the tender loving care of Jesus towards the sick and the marginalised.

This book is the story, too, of Vernal as a father in a very modern kind of family: one of multiple parents, but clearly much loved, and well cared-for children. Vernal's writing reveals the complexities of these relationships; all is not always well, and there are difficulties that persist, but what shines out is a determination that loving and nurturing relationships should be permitted to flourish. This speaks very much, to my mind, to the on-going and at times acrimonious debate about the nature of marriage. I have no doubt that the legislation currently proposed will pass into law, but I suspect that we still have a way to go before there is full acceptance and equality. The story and tempo of Vernal Scott's life, its joyfulness, challenges and love, and the history of the black community in London at this time, is compellingly told in this book. It is surely a story that is worth the telling. I wish it, and its author, every success.

Paul Boateng
The Rt Hon The Lord Boateng PC DL
The House of Lords,
London, SW1A OPW
United Kingdom

Sir Nick Partridge

WHEN I TURNED THE LAST PAGE of Vernal Scott's remarkable, moving, sobering and powerful book, I was struck by how rarely we tell our own stories and how much is lost as a consequence. The past fifty years has seen seismic changes in our attitudes to sex and sexuality, family and parenting, race and racism, faith and community. We have all lived through this and many of us have campaigned and contributed to achieving change in brave, varied and imaginative ways. Very few have done so with such depth, breadth and determination as Vernal. His story speaks to all of us, reminding us of our tumultuous times and challenging us to do still more.

The impact of AIDS in the 1980's changed and redefined many of our lives and took the lives of far, far too many of our family and friends. Vernal describes this clearly, passionately and personally, reliving the pain, loss and anger and, most importantly, the extraordinary, compassionate, loving and dramatic response from those on the side of the angels. Through the Reach Out and Touch Vigil in 1991, Vernal gave us a passionate and vibrant expression of this response, dramatically supported by his own personal angel, Whitney Houston.

Today, HIV continues to devastate the black community both nationally and globally. In every country around the world, black gay men are at greater risk of HIV than any other community and bear a greater burden of infection. In far too many countries, rates of HIV infection among black gay men are rarely even collected, let alone safer sex and condom programmes provided or basic care and support given. Vernal's story shows how different this could and should be. This book is much more than a memoir – it is a call to renewed action.

Sir Nick Partridge,
Chief Executive, Terrence Higgins Trust

Peter Tatchell

VERNAL SCOTT HAS WRITTEN a very moving, powerful testimony that chronicles his personal journey as a black gay man, spanning five decades. Through his story, we get an insight into many of the tribulations and triumphs of the black and gay communities, traversing racism, homophobia, religion and HIV/AIDS.

This book is, at times, painful and shocking in its exposure of raw prejudice; while in other moments we see wonderful altruism, compassion, wisdom, tenderness, solidarity and understanding. There is also quite a lot of fun, including entertaining recollections about various disco divas.

I worked with Vernal when he organised the Reach Out & Touch Vigil in Trafalgar Square in London in 1991, to show support for people living with HIV/AIDS and to challenge the ignorance and intolerance that was, in those days, often blighting their lives. "Carry a flower in remembrance, support and unity", the flyer urged.

His superb organisational skills ensured a stunning event, which was capped by a wonderful speech from Whitney Houston. Moreover, the whole front section of the square was a riotous rainbow of flowers in commemoration of those who had died, and in solidarity with those who were defiantly surviving and thriving with HIV/AIDS. It was a spectacularly uplifting and beautiful experience, which was reflective of Vernal's guiding vision and spirit.

All these years later, HIV/AIDS is still with us, with 34 million people living with the infection worldwide. Most of them are in poor countries with little or no access to the latest medicines. Much remains to be done to ensure global equity of support and treatment for people with HIV. Even in the UK, the battle against HIV is far from won, with thousands of new infections every year - especially in the gay and black communities - plus continued inadequate HIV education in schools and no high-profile media campaign to inform the public.

Being a person of faith has been central to Vernal's life and activism. He tells his story of negotiating between his religion and his sexuality; an experience that is often difficult, even traumatic, for some LGBT people. Unlike some other religionists, his Christian beliefs have cemented his commitment to equality and diversity. He is not the only one. Although organised religion is the single biggest global threat to human rights - especially the human rights of women and LGBT people - some religious figures have taken a strong, commendable stand for universal equality; notably Archbishop Desmond Tutu in South Africa and Bishop Christopher Senyonjo in Uganda.

In his prologue, Vernal mentions on-going challenges regarding the continued criminalisation of LGBT people in 80% of Commonwealth nations; comprising more than half of all the countries in the world that still outlaw same-sex relations. Six Commonwealth countries stipulate life imprisonment, and in regions of two member states, Pakistan and Nigeria, sharia law prescribes the death penalty. The struggles against institutional homophobia, biphobia and transphobia in the Commonwealth is part of the wider, barely begun, struggle for global LGBT freedom. I very much hope to see Vernal contribute to positive change globally, perhaps in conjunction with the Peter Tatchell Foundation and international LGBT movements.

Urgent action is necessary to counter the homophobic backlash in about 20 countries; including Uganda, Russia, The Gambia, Brunei, Cameroon, Egypt and Nigeria. Ours is a global freedom movement and there can be no let up until every LGBT person on this planet has equality and acceptance.

Here in the UK, we've made great progress in terms of legal rights and public attitudes - mostly quite recently, since the late 1990s. Historic anti-gay laws, some of them dating back centuries, have been progressively repealed. This great reform movement culminated in the legislation of same-sex civil marriage in England and Wales in 2013. But the battle for marriage equality began way back in 1992, when the LGBT group OutRage! organised five same-sex couples to file applications for a marriage licence at Westminster Register Office in London. The launch of the Equal Love campaign in 2010 reignited the campaign for marriage equality; including an application to the European Court of Human Rights to overturn the twin legal bans on same-sex civil marriages and opposite-sex civil partnerships.

Although the Marriage (Same-Sex Couples) Act is an important advance - signifying that LGBT relationships are, in principle, on a par with opposite-sex ones - it is not true equality. Same-sex marriages are legalised under a new law that is completely separate from the 1949 Marriage Act. Separate is not equal.

There are six shortcomings in the new legislation:

Rightly or wrongly, the existing grounds for the annulment of a marriage - non-consummation and adultery - do not apply in the case of same-sex marriages.

The Church of England is explicitly banned from performing same-sex religious marriages, even if decides that it wants to.

The special requirements for the conduct of religious same-sex marriages are much harsher than for opposite-sex marriages in places of worship. In the case of small religious denominations that share premises with other faith groups, all the sharing faith organisations have to give their permission for the conduct of same-sex marriages in the premises. This means that anti-gay marriage churches that share premises with pro-gay marriage churches have an effective veto over the latter's right to conduct same-sex marriages.

Pension inheritance rights are fewer on death of a same-sex marriage spouse. The surviving partner is not entitled to inherit the full value of their pension if it was begun prior to 1988 (only the value of contributions since 1988 can be inherited). There is no such sweeping limitation in the case of surviving partners in opposite-sex marriages. They can inherit the full value of their deceased partner's pension from the year they first started contributing, which may be as far back as 1970 or earlier.

Trans people - especially those already in marriages or civil partnerships - get a raw deal. Among other flaws, married transgender people will need their spouse's written permission before they can get a gender recognition certificate. This amounts to a 'spousal veto' over a trans person's life.

The legislation does not repeal the ban on opposite-sex civil partnerships ie. straight couples continue to be banned from having a civil partnership, even though the government's own public consultation on equal marriage found that 61% of respondents supported the right of heterosexual couples to have a civil partnership if they desire one. Only 24% disagreed.

Much still needs to be changed, in the UK and worldwide.

This book is Vernal's story. Read, learn and then join us - help make change happen.

Peter Tatchell

Director, Peter Tatchell Foundation
www.PeterTatchellFoundation.org

2. DEDICATION AND APPRECIATION

My special thanks to Lord Paul Boateng, Sir Nick Partridge, and Peter Tatchell, for their very kind words and life-long commitment to making this world a better place. Special thanks also to Dr James 'Jim' Doherty PhD for his time and encouragement with this book. My eternal gratitude to Archbishop Carl Bean, Bernie Grant MP, Professor David Divine, Adrienne Barnett QC, David Kerr, and Daniel Williamson, for being in the right place at the right time.

To the most joyous, talented and generous Georgios Kyriacos Panayiotou, known to the world as George 'Listen Without Prejudice' Michael. He was the silent angel behind the UK HIV/AIDS challenge and trusted me with his secret and cash of approximately £45,000. I thank and love you, George! You turned a different corner this last Christmas 2016, but have faith that there will be no careless whispers; you are a true hero and real freedom is now yours. Vx

To HRH Diana, Princess of Wales, and her son, HRH Prince Harry for their inspiration and courage in helping to confront prejudice and remove HIV stigma. To Nelson 'Freedom' Mandela, President Barack Obama, Michelle Obama, Desmond Tutu, Bayard Rustin, James Baldwin, Justin Fashanu, Simon Watney, Christopher Spence MBE, Sir Elton John, Tony Whitehead, Bill Buckley, Ken Livingstone and Lord Norman Fowler.

To the leading ladies of my life: my beloved mother, Doreth May (Eubank) Scott, my gorgeous daughter – Lil' Rose May Scott, Doreene May Blackstock, Veronica 'Beverley' Scott, Gloria Gaynor – the Godmother of Disco, Dionne Warwick, Sister Whitney Houston, and Robyn Crawford, her personal friend and public 'Assistant'.

To family: Dad, Aunt Edna, Blackstock family, Aunt Mercy, Aunt Vera, brothers Bunny and Leo, Joy and sons, Valerie, Jazz, Spencer 'Sizza Hands', Nyisha, Samantha, Andrew and

Emma Scott, Mitchell, the Toussaint family, Donna Wilde, Uncle Sonny, Everton, and Timothy Speid.

This book is dedicated to the memory of my friends and relatives taken by AIDS; far too many of you. Your courage and dignity inspires me still, and together we've proved that love is stronger than death. I'd like to take this opportunity to express my heartfelt appreciation to the many doctors, nurses, volunteer 'buddies' and community workers, who went beyond themselves to care for our loved ones with skill, compassion and a smile. You are evidence that angels on Earth are real.

My book is also dedicated to the memory of Dwayne Jones, Eric Lembembe, Matthew Shepard, Dexter Pottinger, and those mass slaughtered in Orlando on 12th June 2016. They can't be replaced, but all victims of anti-gay and internalized hate around the world can rest knowing that they did not die in vain. My book is further dedicated to those of us damaged by religious shame and guilt. We shall overcome.

In memory of the great man pictured here, **Terry Uhr.** Worthy of my tears. Rest in peace and love, my dear friend. Thank you for the memories. V x

To friends, key acquaintances and notable others: Murvyn Doctrove, Dirk Pfannenschmidt, Robert Taylor, Paul Thurlow, Gord Ray, Lloyd Johnson, Dr Yansie Rolston PhD, Clyde Mullings, Dave Loweirnely, Christian John Wikane, Ian Worrell, John, Raymond Kernaghan, Colin Clark, Leigh Chislett, Adam Fletcher, Steve Ball, Malcolm Allan, Charles Maude, Christopher Stanislaus, Jean Gibbs, Martin O'Toole, Angelo Andreuchetti, Beverleigh Forbes, Mal Mace, Jonathan Grimshaw, James Oyeniyi, Shivananda 'NAZ' Khan OBE, Cyril Husbands, Yvonne McCalla Sobers, Graham Sykes, Derek St Louis, Chris Brownlie, Paul Davies, David Stuart, Jide Macaulay, Ade 'the Quest' Adeniji, Giles Addison, Nick Frank, Kim Coe, Sylvester (James), Phyll Opoku-Gyimah, CJ White, Keith Carabello, Carolyn Solomon-Pryce, Gerson Samuel Nason, David 'soulmusic.com' Nathan, Franklin Makin, Kevin Jones, George Bellinger, Craig Harris, Maurice Tomlinson, Ronan de Burca, Paul Carswell, Marlon 'Booker Prize' James, David P Martin, Trevor Moore, Geoff Hopping, Nigel Sheldrick, David, Margaret, Marcia Ore, Jaime Sylla Paredes, Jeremy Tuck, Mehboob Dada, Aisha Khan, Jeff Sawyerr, Stephen Brown, Aaron Cini, Rasheed 'Soul Trader' Agunlaru, Gamal Turawa, Phillip Lingard, Peter Kenny, Ted Brown, Dirg Aaab-Richards, Paul Burston, Matt Cain, Vg Lee, Phill Wilson MA, Reggie Williams, Bisi Alimi, Marc Thompson, Peter Staley, Garry Brough, Oliver Berman, Paul Harris, Guy Andrews, Paul Boakye, Dennis Carney, Elizabeth F Obisanya, Tim Batho, Shena Winchester, Richard Chadwick, Savi Hensman, Dr Antoine Rogers, Dr Robert Berkeley, Rikki Beadle-Blair, Juliette Foster, Phil Willcox, Tristram Wyatt, Mark Phillips, Brian Levett, Kevin Sell, Dugan Warn, Rev Vincent Manning, Conroy Winter, Essex Hemphill, E. Lynn Harris, Joseph F. Beam, John Teamer, Richard Torne, Patrick King, David Atkinsanya, Rev Edward Collier, David 'DC' Larue, Glen Stobbart, Angelina Namiba, Stephen Duffy, Paul Giaconne, David Furness, Jamie Hamilton, Tashini Neita Jones, Darrell Hope, Martin Phillips, Rev Father Steve Gayle, Simon White, Wijay Pitumpe, Philip Lightowlers, Prof. Kevin Fenton, Stephen Fry, RuPaul, Sir Ian Mckellen, Jeremy Corbyn MP, Trojan Gordon, Richard Beaven, (continued...)

3. PROLOGUE

MY LIFE'S PATH AS A BLACK GAY MAN, ex-man of faith, and Londoner, has led to experiences, both darkly challenging and intensely exhilarating, that I feel compelled to share. I hope I haven't been too explicit for your tastes, but my intention isn't to shock; I needed to be totally open and honest about life's peculiar fusion of disparate components, which, for me, include: unrequited love; prejudice and hate; disease, death and dying; sex, sexuality and 'coming out'; religion-fuelled self-harm; lesbian and gay baby-making; family court; domestic violence; child chastisement/abuse; even the supernatural. All potentially depressing stuff, so you'll be heartened to know that there are occasional reasons to belly laugh in here too.

I Am What I Am has long been my personal feel-good disco anthem. I relate emphatically to the song's self-affirming lyrics, which celebrate a strident pride in self-identity and authenticity, and an unyielding defiance in demolishing the self-hating closet. I learned the hard way that my authenticity is priceless and should never be negotiable; my attempt to deny it very nearly killed me. Having survived the related trauma of my teenage years, I later decided that I wasn't going to be yet another gay man to 'play the part' and enter into a heterosexual relationship to try and hide the truth about my sexuality and conform to the expectations of family, community and God. Such strategies often have disastrous consequences, especially when the pretty bride discovers that her handsome hubby can't perform sexually; has secreted gay porn on his phone or computer, and/or; has brought home a sexually transmitted infection, such as HIV, as a result of his cheating with other men. LGBTQ people must be enabled by society (and our families) to be our natural selves, or we all pay an avoidable high price. The 2016 Orlando nightclub mass shooting was a grotesque example of internalized self-hate made manifest in bloody terror and horror. However, there are millions of other personal tragedies that you and I will never hear about, but they keep local morticians busy.

Like the life-draining closet, yesterday has the potential to become a decaying prison for fools; we can acknowledge it without living in it. Being 'out' and living in the present – the gift of this moment, is where I need to be. The past – the good, bad, and however recent, is still the past; it is deceased, and just like other people's expectations of me (and my sexuality) I cannot and must not be bound by it. So, I say, COME OUT, COME OUT wherever and whoever you are and free yourself from your mind's chains to yesterday. Claim your power by getting in the driver's seat in 'the now'; much inner peace and self-respect awaits. *Major wink* to legendary crooner Johnny Mathis, athletes Jason Collins, Colin Jackson, and Michael Sam, actors Jodi Foster and Neil Patrick Harris, singers George Michael, Sir Elton John, Will

Young, Frank Ocean, and Sam Smith, journalists Anderson Cooper and Don Lemon, and the inspirational Stephen Fry and John Amaechi OBE. Their courageous visibility undoubtedly helps to lift low self-esteem and reduce the high suicide rate of mostly younger LGBTQ people who struggle to accept their sexuality, as I did. Yes, LGBTQ visibility and positive role models save lives! Congratulations, too, to the person reading this book who is living in truth. We really can let go of the energy-sapping burden of being someone we are not, and plan for a happier, more fulfilling future based upon the honesty and integrity of who we really are. In my own experience, the fear became pride, as the post 'coming out' storms passed and the sun glowed brighter than ever before. I'm in control now and my life's agenda is set by me. My attitude is simple: if others (family, friends etc.) are unhappy with my natural sexuality, then that's their issue, not mine; they need the help, not me! Sing: "Life's not worth a damn, 'til you can shout out, I AM WHAT I AM!"

The non-bigoted will know that love is an experience of the heart, and it is at this level that heterosexual, bisexual, and gay people are exactly the same. The physicality or mechanics of how we love may be different, but the integrity, passion and value of the love that we feel, is the same. So, if there is equality in love, there should, of course, be equality in marriage. The long-embedded hetero-centric doctrine and its mission to deny equal status to same-sex lovers has been drummed into us all from birth and any proposition that same-sex love has any real value is viewed with utter contempt by those maintaining its ghastly hypocrisies. If, in a fair and just society, loving relationships, marriage and tax breaks are good for heterosexuals, then they must be good for gays and lesbians, too. To belittle our love for each other and deny us the legal status and dignity of marriage because we happen to be of the same sex, isn't just prejudicial and dehumanizing to us, but it also creates a less happy and cohesive society for everyone else. The idea that only opposite genders are capable of any deep, physically-expressed love, is among the biggest falsehoods ever told, as is the assertion that the doctrine is justified because it ensures the reproduction of the human species. Our reproduction is of course important, but we don't all need to do it, but if we choose to, then lesbians and gay men are good at that too! As I mentioned earlier, we cannot make ourselves heterosexual if that isn't our natural orientation, nor should we have to pretend to be in order to be treated with the equality and dignity we all deserve. The assumption that being heterosexual is right and anything other than that is wrong is, itself, wrong. There needn't be any losers where love is concerned, as there is enough for people of all sexualities to enjoy. Fact: Love isn't prejudiced, people are. Heterosexuals have nothing to fear or sacrifice because of same-sex marriages; their own marriages aren't about to suddenly collapse. Really! We all win when we are free to live and love as we truly are. Lesson: love and let love.

Sexual orientation is a blend of emotional, romantic, sexual or affectionate attraction or feelings towards another person. Sexual orientation is not just about sex or sexual activity. For many of us, sexual orientation can also be fluid over time and in different contexts, and may not be 'labelled' at all; e.g. 'gay', 'straight', or otherwise. Self-perceived sexual identity is a subjective view of one-self and is about whom a person is, not what they do. A person can have a sexual identity and not be sexually active. When haters attack, it isn't because of our sexuality; it is because of their ignorance, prejudice or personal hang-ups. Be proud of your sexual orientation, whatever it is.

Gay or LGBTQi+ people, like heterosexuals, contribute to life on this earth in pedestrian and, sometimes, unique and wonderful ways. We are doctors and lawyers, teachers and builders, mothers and fathers, sisters and brothers, neighbours, young and old, rich and poor, employed and unemployed, disabled, non-disabled, black, brown, and white. We have the strengths, and of course, the frailty of any other human being. However, it is the irrational hatred and prejudice aimed at us that sets us apart from the rest of society. I am a holistic multi-faceted person, and although my sexuality is an important component of who I am, it's not all that I am. My ability to contribute to society isn't constrained by my sexual orientation, but by the ignorance and prejudice of others. Exorcising my internalized homophobia was a long and prickly process; on a subconscious level, I had bought into the corrosive lie that gay people are all about sex and that our relationships weren't capable of 'real love'. Heterosexual love was celebrated as 'the norm' everywhere I looked; from literature and the printed press, to film and music. The absence of gay love in these and similar media, helped to paint a picture of us as a flawed sub-culture of abnormal people. The only time we were heard of was in the context of sleazy public toilet arrests, press 'outings', or a fatal disease. Heterosexuals enjoyed 'relationships' while gays could only manage something less wholesome-sounding called 'lifestyles'. 'Heterosexual sex' was supposed to be productive (e.g. children come from it) and clean, while 'gay sex' was just plain "dirty". Sex between consenting gay men was illegal until the fairly recent past. Just the idea of it fired up the warped imaginations of sex-obsessed bigots, who publicly condemn "unnatural" gay men for enjoying sex that they well know many 'straight' men enjoy too, if only on the 'Down Low' or behind the walls of a prison before returning home to their wives and girlfriends. Fact: the vagina is tight but an ass is tighter, or so they tell me **cough!!!** My tongue in cheek (!!!) jesting aside, straight men have long enjoyed anal sex with their wives and girlfriends and they didn't wait to get to prison to try it out. Not all gay men have anal sex, but limiting gay men to any sex act is yet another attack upon us as the holistic people that we are. The emphasis on anal sex is the bigots' not so subliminal PR effort to associate gay men with faecal matter (shit!) and deny our ability to love, as well as our true sexual repertoire, which is as extensive as it is natural. Yes, I said it; gay sex is natural! Every human being must deal with faecal matter, but at least gay men know how to 'prepare' themselves so that it doesn't become part of the sexual experience. Yes, human bodily waste is best avoided, but contact with it won't make you grow a third eye. Sexual activity enjoyed by heterosexuals and LGBTQ people is natural to the diverse spectrum and polarity of the human condition and experience. The only freaks of nature are those who resist this truth and who won't accept the fact that the laws of nature are not like human laws. Natural laws are *observed regularities* with plenty of exceptions and anomalies that fall both within and outside of our personal likes, dislikes, values, needs, and desires. Our disliking or applying a human law to something that is naturally occurring for the individual or between consensual adults won't make it unnatural to them or cause it to go away. Only failure and misery will come of such attempts. Further bias against gay people is evident when it is said that heterosexuals seeking to better their lives have a 'vision', while gay people seeking to do the same have an 'agenda'. I had to work hard to dismantle these deeply embedded heterosexist/hetero-centric lies, but I eventually arrived at a place within myself where I no longer felt dirty, and self-love was my new permanent and graceful reality.

Given its varied content, some of which is alluded to in this prologue, my book may well be a challenge to categorize, but it's not religious. Lord, no! As you will later see, my original choice of book title was inspired by a somewhat uncomfortable comment made by my street-preaching evangelical mother. I had long identified as a Christian, but writing this very book provoked me to finally detach myself from the destructive ancient holy myths and religious supernatural noise that inspires modern-day hate and division between people who would otherwise embrace one another. I am now happily godless and free of all holy trappings, although love remains my reason and passion. I consider myself a Naturalist, although I could live with being referred to as a Humanist or New Atheist, of the admittedly over-complicated homo-rainbow kind, naturally!

It is my long held view that sexual activity between consenting adults, of whatever sexuality, is no one else's business, including gods, of whatever religion. Our penises, vaginas, nipples, butts, ears, lips and every other erogenous zone exist to be enjoyed without guilt, shame, or fear. Only an odd god would spend his time looking down from heaven at what I do with my penis while millions of adults and children regularly die of war, terror, starvation, preventable disease, and natural disasters. That would be a very odd god, indeed! The very existence of such dreadful misery is all the evidence that my rational mind needs to dismiss the primitive and illogical notion that our world is supervised by an invisible heroic intervening god of love and healing. Please!

We appear to have come into existence by a fluke chance lottery win of the universe, or was it a cosmic burp? Either way, imagined gods had nothing to do with it. Our evolutionary development has been a case of the survival of the fittest, in competition with other earthly species. It just isn't cogent that a conscious all-perfect all-powerful higher 'intelligence' created an endless universe just for us to occupy the equivalent of a spec of cosmic dirt within it, which is itself riddled with imperfections; from our troublesome tonsils and appendix, to cancers, volcanos, earthquakes, and parasitical worms that gorge on the eyes of babies from the inside out. No, Earth was not created with selfish humans or any other species in mind, and we will all be gone as soon as the seemingly oblivious universe does something else with the space that we currently occupy. To further make my point, there are significant parts of this planet where humans would perish in a matter of seconds, either because of a non-conducive natural environment, or due to other dangerous life forms. So, the natural universe and not some supernatural god is how we've come to exist. We are no longer primitive people and should have long ago placed our holy books about gods and miracles on the same shelves as books about the Tooth Fairy, Santa, and Harry Potter. I confidently predict that day of awakening will come, even if its arrival is still some centuries away. I took a ride on my personal time machine and now reside on Planet Reality with a few other lucky ones.

In my earlier years I worried about coming out as a gay man, and then later, as a *Christian* gay man. I feared criticism and condemnation from all sides; evangelical bigots, and bewildered, largely atheist, gays. Of course, religion doesn't make you a bigot, because once you are educated and experience the true facts about LGBTQ people you can only remain so out of choice. Despite the passing of time and changes in anti-discrimination laws, people like me remain a target for religious haters, who use Holy Scripture to justify our oppression and that of others considered 'different', but the day will come when hate dressed up as religion will be subject to legal consequences. Holy bigots will increasingly be revealed as impotent in dealing with life's real challenges: domestic and gang violence, drug abuse, increasing knife and gun crime, unemployment, poverty, incessant hopelessness, and horrendously high suicide rates. The pulpit prophets of profit will be forced to go out and get a real job instead of living off the poor and vulnerable. For too long they have picked *à la carte* from scripture to suit their own prejudices, ultimately choosing to gorge themselves on an unhealthy diet of constipation-inducing ignorance and hatred, especially concerning homosexuality. Jesus said nothing about homosexuality but they choose to ignore this. Further, they never mention that he spent his adult life in the company of twelve men whom he *loved* and avoided sexual relationships with women. Shhh, quiet now!

To oppose religion or dare to withdraw from it (apostasy) in parts of today's world is to take your life into your hands. This very day, as I write, there are news reports of three atheists who were viciously hacked to death in separate attacks on the streets of Pakistan due to the perpetrators' objection to any open stance against religion. There are further reports, this time from Iraq, of the on-going persecution of gay and bisexual men by the self-anointed blood-gushing Islamic State, who lure men from the relative safety of their closets into an extremist 'honey trap'. Victims soon find themselves shackled and flung to their deaths from roof tops. If still alive after crashing to the ground, they are then finished off with rocks and stones thrown by frenzied crowds keen to participate in the slaughter of men who only yesterday were their peaceful neighbours. This barbaric behaviour is directly inspired by early century Holy Scriptures, which sanctions the stoning of adults and children considered to be 'different'. 21st century adherents are in no position to claim any moral supremacy over anyone else, because their faith is founded on the blood of innocent people. To live by 'the word' of the world's most popular religions would be to live an unconscionably brutal existence, underpinned by fear and opportunistic death, hence the emergence of today's 'moderates', who are forced to abandon the word as originally written in order to fit into the norms and expectations of a modern (decent!) society.

Whether peaceful or of a blood-letting iteration, religion is a choice which still enjoys legal protection not afforded to 'I was born this way' sexual orientation. This is of course a grotesque act of prejudice. Man created God, not the reverse. In fact, we created a few of them. An acknowledgement and belief in a particular *Supreme Being* is dictated by our birth culture, hence the diverse range of different faiths and gods around the world. Related Holy Scriptures were similarly created by primitive early century men with no knowledge of today's science. Despite feeble efforts by our politicians to convince us otherwise, representations of religion, God and terror have become inextricably and permanently linked. In my near-final chapter, 'Ahh Men: The Circumcision of Religion', I take a look at the Bible and religion as they relate to people like me, and share how, in the process of writing, my eyes were opened to my own self-deception about the so-called 'good book'. Indeed, by the time I'd complete it, my perception of and relationship with my God would be forever changed.

The internalized shame and guilt propagated and implanted by religion erodes our self-esteem, damages our mental health, and even leads to suicide. This is especially true in respect of LGBTQ people. Trust me, I really can preach about this. Whoops! Having freed my mind from the entrapment of Christianity, my honesty and integrity then enabled me to see that only a non-existent or impotent God of love would do nothing to prevent the pointless suffering of his so-called children over the centuries, continuing to this very day. There is no hope of things changing, either. To continue to believe in God, despite life's harsh reminders of his absence, would be to engage in a kind of spiritual masturbation; pleasuring oneself with fantasies of an imaginary supernatural lover, whose prowess can stimulate his indoctrinated believers, from the seamstress in Jamaica to the President of the United States, to an orgasmic "Hallelujah!" whilst remaining completely invisible to them. I shall return to these issues later in the aforementioned chapter. For now, if you just happen to be searching for the meaning of life, then I am happy to confirm that you have picked up the right book, although your heart will probably already know the answer. To love is why we exist: give it to get it! Religion isn't needed as a context, where the faithfully blind, out of fear rather than love, try but mostly fail to comply with illogical ancient scriptures that even the most conformist of sheep or bewildered visiting aliens would be compelled to question. No, love doesn't need religion; religion needs love and a great dose of integrity, too!

My work is mostly concerned with diversity, inclusion, and sexual health. I also provide confidential support to individuals dealing with 'coming out'/sexuality, HIV-related issues, and gay-parenting. I act as a 'McKenzie Friend' in Family Court, and give talks and facilitate workshops on the issues contained in this book. I am mostly known for my work with people with HIV and AIDS during what I refer to as the war years of the '80s and '90s, but you may have come across my later work on the wider equality and diversity agenda. Perhaps you've never come across me at all, until now, and I very much hope that you will find my book and experiences worthy of your time. In addition to this book, you may occasionally find me on the radio or television as a news commentator, and like most people these days, my profile can be found on Linked In, Facebook, You Tube, and Twitter.

Perhaps you've chosen my book because you relate to how I self-identify, and we have shared experiences. Or perhaps you're curious to peep into the window of a life that appears to be markedly different from yours. Whatever your reason for choosing my book, thank you, from my heart to yours. Pop icon George Michael once urged us to listen to his music without prejudice. I have a similar request, which is that you please read my book with your heart. By putting finger to keypad and telling my personal story, I have inevitably touched upon the stories of my mother and father, and other important people in my life; people who are unlikely to have their story told elsewhere, but who have contributed, positively or negatively, to the man that I am today. They all have some relevance here.

The process of writing proved intensely cathartic for me. At times, I found myself laughing out loud at sweet memories, and then convulsing with what felt like tears of blood, when the darker ones proved too painful to deal with; there was too much pain, too much fear, and far too much dying. Surprisingly, perhaps, I was most tearful when I came to realise that I still mourned the loss of my innocence as a little boy. I had been a lonely shy child, who desperately sought approval, acceptance and love, but who instead, experienced rejection, and physical and emotional torment at the hands of those to whom I looked for comfort. My emerging sexuality only served to compound my predicament, and I lived with an ever-present fear of what dreadful event might happen next. I was always afraid back then, and constantly strategizing about how best to get through each cloudy day and dreadful night. As you will see, I ultimately took desperate action, when the fear that had become characteristic of my teenage years became too much for me, but I survived! Writing brought back the magnitude of my childhood fear, and re-living it was debilitating to the point of causing me to cease writing for weeks on end. However, if you are reading my book, then you have the evidence in your hand that I was able to get on with it in the end. Writing was integral to my healing.

A lasting symptom of the damage caused by my childhood was that I would later struggle to love myself and overcome a haunting feeling that there was something wrong with me and that I wasn't really capable or worthy of love. Self-love usually promotes high self-esteem and overall well-being, but when it is itself damaged, the exterior 'all is well' appearance becomes a mask for inner troubles which manifest themselves in addictions, depression, poor decision-making and self-destructive habits and patterns of behaviour. Some of my similarly afflicted gay brothers seek fake healing in the form of potentially destructive bareback 'chemsex' chill parties, however, my sticky plaster healing was in the form of *bling* (money, cars, gadgets etc.) and emotionally vacant sexual quickies, which could never reach or heal my festering internal wounds. My healing would eventually come, not from drugs, religion or counselling, but by my active engagement in the present moment. By doing so, I set myself free from the chains of past hurt. I cannot heal myself in the past as it no longer exists, but I am undamaged in the present, and by staying consciously awake in the present – the now – I do not relive past pain.

As you will see, I am very human, and sometimes, plain stupid. Even Stevie Wonder could see that only disaster would come of my chosen path into fatherhood, but I wilfully adopted his blindness in order to realise a dream that quickly became a living nightmare. That part of my story should serve as a red alert warning to all desperate wanna-be gay fathers, but more on that later. For now, I would only add that I remain frustrated with the lie that heterosexual (married) couples make better parents than gays. Just a quick audit of child care homes and the thousands of children that occupy them should make even the most blinkered of bigots think again. Children need loving, capable parents, of whatever sexuality. Fact: being born heterosexual doesn't automatically make you a capable parent.

Lord Norman Fowler was Secretary of State for Health in Mrs Thatcher's government. His national campaign, 'AIDS – Don't Die of Ignorance', remains etched in my memory, for reasons both good and bad. Some say that our respective books complement each other and I strongly agree.

1st of Dcember is World AIDS Day, but every day is World AIDS Day for people directly affected by the big disease with the little name. I later share my personal and professional experience of the truly catastrophic human tragedy of AIDS, and its impact upon both heterosexual and gay communities during the height of the crisis here in the UK, when I was Head of HIV Services at a London borough. For far too many of us it was like living through an unacknowledged bloody war, and my own family and friends would not escape its terrifying and merciless advance. The ultimate virus of equal opportunity, HIV (and AIDS) had no respect for race, nationality, wealth, location, education, sexuality, religion, age, or marital status. Just being human made you eligible. At the time of writing this book, some thirty plus years after its devastating arrival, the Foundation for AIDS Research, and Public Health England, respectively, reported the shocking worldwide and UK statistics as follows:

- 35 million people are currently living with HIV

- 3.3 million of them are under 15 years old
- 2.3 million people were newly infected in 2012
- 260,000 of them were under 15 years old
- Every day nearly 6,300 people contract HIV – nearly 262 every hour
- 1.6 million people died of AIDS in 2012
- 210,000 of them were under 15 years
- To date 75 million people have contracted HIV and
- 35 million have died of related symptoms

In 2013 there was an estimated 107, 800 people living with HIV in the UK. The overall prevalence was 2.8 per 1,000 population aged 15-59 years. 42% were diagnosed late. About a quarter (24%, 26,100) of those living with HIV are unaware of their infection and may unwittingly pass it on to sexual partners. 6,000 people were newly diagnosed with HIV infection in 2013 – 54% of them were non-UK born. 41% of new infections were in black and ethnic communities. AIDS related symptoms were reported in 320 people.

Gay and bisexual Men

In 2013 an estimated 43,500 gay/bi men were living with HIV in the UK; this is equivalent to 59 per 1,000 MSM aged 15-59 years or 1 in 17. HIV prevalence was higher in London where 1 in 8 were living with HIV, compared to 1 in 26 outside London. 3,250 gay/bi men were newly diagnosed with HIV, and an estimated 7,200 (16%) of them are HIV positive but currently undiagnosed. 31% were diagnosed late. By 2015 the trend of new infections would decrease significantly, thanks to effective treatments and prevention campaigns.

Heterosexual men and women

59,500 people living in the UK with HIV in 2013 acquired their infection through heterosexual contact. A worrying

58% were diagnosed late. An estimated 57% of all infections among heterosexual men and women were probably acquired in the UK, while the proportion of UK-acquired infections has almost doubled over the last decade, up from 32% in 2004. 38,700 black-Africans were HIV positive, and this group constitutes two-thirds (65%, 38,700) of all heterosexual people living with HIV. The proportion of late diagnoses was particularly high among black-African (66%) and white (61%) followed by black-Caribbean (59%) heterosexual men. Among women, the proportion diagnosed late was highest among black-African (57%), followed by black-Caribbean (48%) and white (42%) women.

At the time of writing there had been approximately 22,000 HIV/AIDS related deaths in the UK and our annual spend on related treatment and care is in the region of one billion pounds. An effective prevention campaign would be considerably cheaper in the long term, but successive UK governments have wilfully buried their heads in the sand to that fact. The level of new infections should be unacceptable to any conscious and responsible government, and yet a national HIV prevention campaign hasn't been active in the UK since Mrs Thatcher's tenure at Number 10 back in the 1980s. If the statistics in this book fail to ignite prompt and on-going action, then, frankly, I don't know what will. Sexual health awareness should start in school, not STI clinics. Hey government, are you listening yet? Wake the hell up! Until science produces a definitive answer, education and changes in behaviour must deliver the cure that we are still seeking. Once again, let's start in school.

Upon its arrival in the 1980s, AIDS produced the equivalent of a jackpot lottery win for the world's undertakers and millions of broken hearts for the survivors, whom, like wounded but determined soldiers, fought the greatest battle of our lives. However, we were never as brave as those who had no choice but to face death at a time when life should have been their only focus. They were so very very brave.

The life-long pain we feel for those we've lost is powerful confirmation that love is more abiding than death. In conflict with this knowledge, I often struggle to find words that adequately convey the gravity of our losses; frankly, an endless primeval howl of agony would be more fitting. We sorely miss the arms that used to hold us; the smiles that used to greet us; the lips that used to kiss ours; the feet that used to walk and dance with ours; and the dreams for two that became torment for the one left behind. Here we are in this modern age of tablets and smartphones and I cannot get myself to dispose of my faux leather-bound phone book from the 90s, because it contains hand-written names far too precious for a dustbin. The wonderful men behind those names, my dear friends, were silenced in their prime by the coldest of cold callers, and my enduring commitment to them compel me to keep my old book close to my heart, even though the numbers within it have long been disconnected; like their former owners, cut off from the gift that was once happy, healthy, abundant life. Many of you reading this book will relate to my experience and we stand together as we remember.

HIV doesn't discriminate, people do. I organised the Reach Out and Touch UK HIV/AIDS Vigil in remembrance, support, and unity with the men, women and children behind the dreadful statistics. You'll meet some of those people in these pages; up close and painfully personal. I will forever remember them... always! Regrettably, due to the stigma and prejudice that is still associated with HIV and AIDS, I've decided to change some names to protect the individuals and families concerned. However, there are no fictional characters or situations in this book; just real men, women and children, and our very real lives.

I was fortunate to cross paths with legends such as Princess Diana, Whitney Houston, Gloria Gaynor, Dionne Warwick, Luther Vandross and others, and hope that you enjoy the many previously unpublished pictures, especially those of a very happy and vibrant Whitney in London. The beautiful lady did more than sing great songs, and my book reminds the world that she was also a commendable humanitarian. The mega star, encouraged by Robyn Crawford, her long-time private 'companion' and public 'Assistant' supported me when I needed her most, along with Dionne, her equally wonderful cousin and fellow humanitarian. In fact, few did more than Dionne and our beloved Princess Diana to combat the public hysteria and stigma associated with AIDS. Let this book be a timely reminder.

A stroll with Whitney in London's Hyde Park

My joyous embrace in Whitney's arms at Reach Out and Touch

I took Whitney's early passing very personally indeed; I knew things were bad, but not that bad! I was equally affected by her mother's apparent repulsion at the much touted rumour that her world famous daughter may have had a lesbian or bi-sexual past. This behaviour was particularly ugly in the midst of the death of someone such as Whitney, whose sole artistic purpose was to challenge hate and generate "nothing but love," for and between all people, regardless of their sexuality or any other personal characteristic. Love was her mission.

I was interviewed for an extensive UK-produced television bio-drama to be broadcast in August 2015, called Whitney and Bobby: Addicted to Love. Featuring original footage of Whitney at Reach Out and Touch and starring the excellent actress Shena Winchester as the singer, I am seen explaining that Whitney paid the ultimate price for turning away from her authenticity in order to appease religious homophobic bigotry and the heterosexist expectations of the black community. That bigotry and her unwise decision to collude with it, sowed the seed for her premature demise way before her ruinous drug use ever did; her usage was an external symptom of immense inner pain, brought about, not only by the denial of her true sexuality, but the permanent separation from Robyn, her one true love. The two women met as teenagers and had already been together for ten years by the time I'd meet them in late 1991. A more fitting title for the television biopic would have been, Whitney and Robyn: The Love That Dare Not Speak its Name! Other than our meeting, the momentous year would see Sister Whitney learning the lines for her sensational debut as an actress in the Bodyguard. It was also the year in which she allowed a certain male singer to enter into her life and shatter Robyn's 'together-forever' dreams. The rest is tragic history.

Prejudice, especially when it emanates from those who are supposed to love us unconditionally, can lead to self-loathing and self-destructive behaviour. Whitney's situation was of course further complicated by her unsurpassed fame and fortune, but given the awful, uncompromising reality of her early death, I would offer, as sensitively as I can, that it would be preferable to most loving parents to have a happy and thriving lesbian daughter over a deceased drug addict. Rest in peace, Sister!

My mother used to say "those who feel it know it," and she was right. Many equality challenges have been won, including important changes in legislation, but others remain outstanding. The business (economic) case, the social justice case and the moral case for greater equality are clear, but equality and community cohesion aren't just about affording respect to 'difference' and how well we get on with each other; it's about how well we do when compared to each other. This is particularly relevant when looking at health, education, and socio-economic experiences and outcomes. Yes, the equality and diversity agenda is much more than training, policies and processes, as important as the delivery and close examination of those things are; it's about real men, women, and young people and us making tangible improvements to their life chances and outcomes. I'm all for equality in taxes, love, marriage, and just about everything else, but there is much work to do before we can all live in dignity and experience equal life chances. The June 2017 victims of the Grenfell Tower fire tragedy lived in London's wealthiest borough but clearly did not experience health and safety outcomes equal to their better off neighbours. Prison sentences for those responsible will hopefully follow, although no form of justice can bring back the precious loved ones lost.

Advances in equality and diversity outcomes are incremental, and there isn't really an 'end' point, because there is always some kind of injustice to put right, or an actual or potential inequality to deal with. We have to keep our eyes open and remain motivated and intolerant to inequality.

The Equality Act 2010 offers protection in respect of the following equality characteristics (or strands): age, disability, gender, race, religion, marital or civil partnership status, maternity or pregnancy, sexuality. Of these, disability needs much greater attention at a micro level than it gets. There is physical impairment; hidden impairment (MS, HIV, cancer, diabetes etc.); sensory impairment (hearing and sight); and mental health and learning impairments, respectively. Each one requires and deserves individual attention. People with impairments are holistic as well as sexual beings, and are only made 'disabled' by debilitating environmental obstacles and ingrained negative attitudes held by the general public and service providers. Oh, while I'm at it, the gay community and black community are as guilty as any other for holding views which exclude rather than include disabled people and this mess needs to stop.

Despite the appearance of progress in recent years, the glass ceiling for women remains pretty solid. Similarly, gays and lesbians, despite considerable legal changes in their favour, still need a breakthrough regarding negative attitudes. On the 5th February 2013, and again on the 20th and 21st May 2013, the House of Commons voted in favour of same-sex marriage. On 15th July 2013, I joined a couple of hundred happy campaigners outside the House of Lords in unrelenting heatwave temperatures, as peers voted the same way. Peter Tatchell and Lord Norman 'Don't Die of Ignorance' Fowler were there too. The peer had previously voted in favour of Clause 28 – the UK's anti-gay legislation, but later had a welcome change of heart. Marriage equality was finally a reality in the UK – even if the detail still showed at least five lingering inequalities. The substantive war had been won and we had good reason to celebrate. The Marriage (same-sex couples) Bill went on to receive Royal Assent the following day. This was of course a momentous giant step forward, and yet, homophobia remains a living reality in the lives of too many gay people, resulting in low self-esteem, risky behaviour and suicide. I just hope real change won't be dependent on the gay equivalent of the Stephen, Doreen and Neville Lawrence tragedy. Their experience confirmed current challenges regarding racism are the same as they were in the sixties and seventies; it's just that the *window dressing* is different.

I thought that I would find refuge from racism in the gay community, but this was not to be the case. Despite our shared history of oppression, including being subjected to legalised discrimination, some ignorant white gay men and lesbians still find reason to discriminate against black people; encountering them is like being hit by racist bad breath gurgled in rainbow-coloured mouth wash. The leaders of the UK LGBT movement decided that Marriage Equality was the pressing priority. Of course they did; they are mostly, if not all, white. If they were black or from another ethnic minority group, then they would have, without hesitation, prioritised an anti-racism drive. Rallying behind a whites-only 'rainbow' flag and boasting salaries way above average, our representatives appear to suffer collective amnesia; conveniently forgetting that black LGBT people, through our earlier Civil Rights (and Stonewall!) struggles, helped to create the template and foundation for the later equality achievements upon which they now stand

and assume credit. Their memory lapse is compounded by a lack of empathy with today's black LGBT experience, and with an air of misplaced arrogance, they now see us, the original trail blazers, as annoyingly inferior noise. I strongly suspect that they would prioritise becoming the first LGBT passengers on a return flight to the moon before dealing with racism in the gay community; because eradicating its putrid stench will require an unpleasant look in the mirror and an acknowledgement that they are part of the problem. Oh yes, they will give the impression of 'solidarity' by funding *soft* events, like the annual UK Black Pride party; oblivious to their own ignorance and perpetuation of a common racist stereotype: 'All black folk can do is dance.' And while we're busy dancing we won't be bothering them with our futile requests for a place at the decision-making table: 'Yes, Master, you enjoy the cake and we will hope for the crumbs – after we party!' If our leaders don't want to come across as self-serving, as they currently do, then they would ensure black and minority ethnic representation at the top table. Our lack of representation is not an accident or matter of fate; it's a choice by those already there. Also, talking about racism within the gay community isn't a distraction, as some at the top table think; it's essential to our future cohesion as a community to have these now long overdue conversations. If it's okay to discuss 'black homophobia' – not that homophobia has a colour – then it must be okay to discuss the gay community's racism. We need responsible, conscientious and inclusive leadership, as well as agendas that reflect the experiences and aspirations of all the LGBT community; plans should seek to add black substance to the 'rainbow', not more rhetoric. And we won't be fooled by *window dressing,* either; it is not enough to just have Black, Asian and Latino LGBT people adding to the colour scheme in the meeting room when the key decisions have already been made over tea at Carluccio's in Hampstead. We must be key decision-makers, too. Frankly, I believe there is something quite odd, or even shameful, in our achieving marriage equality before we've dealt with racism within our own community. Let me be clear;

marriage equality is indeed a just cause, but it has an air of privilege to it, especially when racism is your everyday living reality.

To my black LGBTQ sisters and brothers, we are only limited by the constraints of our own thinking; let's think (and act) big! We must break out of the limitations of the 'sexuality closet' and take our place as leaders in education, business, politics, media, medicine, the arts, IT, sport, and more. Playing small lacks ambition and belies our true potential; our hearts and experience will tell us that only frustration will come from winning a place at a table headed by others. Let's start with ambitious thoughts, trusting allies and a plan. If we fail then let's try again.

Okay, it's about that time of year again when the homosexual elite, mentioned above, dish out the LGBTQ Community Awards and print the names of the Top 100 most influential inside their grossly incestuous line of vision. Among 'the chosen ones', the ethnic minority faces will, as always, be very few, but it's not because we're low in number or haven't made a positive difference where it matters; our back-breaking contributions simply fall below the radar of the gay media and those responsible for deciding what 'success' or 'important contribution' look like; as I said earlier, if it ain't white then it ain't right – for them! If you are black, then the organisers may well send you an invite anyway, just to ensure that there's a *splash of colour* among the sea of white faces at their champagne-gushing award dinners. Now, as tempting as it might be, I must warn you that there are inherent risks involved in accepting such invitations. Because black faces are so rarely seen at these events, upon your very dignified arrival, kitted out in traditional dress to make your ethnic point, you shouldn't be too surprised if you find yourself promptly wrestled to the ground by overly-suspicious muscle-bound security men with voices pitched higher than Smurfette's. They will discover soon enough that the worrisome 'protruding lump' is all you, baby; even if you are forced to hide your crashing disappointment that it is your sizeable rear rather than your front that caught their eye. If not tackling you, then in their state of ingrained unconscious bias, they'll automatically direct you to the person responsible for staffing the event; of course, as a black person you must be there to either cause trouble, wait on tables, or clean up after the elite have gone home with their gleaming golden gongs. In all seriousness, I'm sure that you'll be escorted to your table just like everyone else. However, once seated, your eyes will naturally be drawn to that exclusive elitist menu, and when their fuzziness adjusts to the semi-darkness, you'll realise that it doesn't say Neville Cousins, as first thought, but Nouvelle Cuisine, darling! To your absolute horror, the 'set main' and only dish for meat lovers is some ghastly roasted wild baby pink pigeon from some unpronounceable God-forsaken place that you've never heard of and will definitely never visit if you dare taste it. Other guests will assume that you are simply saying grace under your breath, when in fact you'll be praying for God to inflict instantaneous heart failure upon you before you are forced to 'look the part' and actually eat it. Advice: poke it to make sure it's dead before you put it into your mouth, just in case the overly-keen to impress chef decided to take 'rarely done' to a new grotesque extreme; first impressions can be very deceiving with these oh so posh menus! Once you pluck off the decorative but very real feathers, you might then pluck up the courage to take a bite. Within a millisecond of doing so you will be wishing for your usual jerk on rice; someone really should tell the *choice* chef that there is more to 'flavouring' food than garlic, more garlic, topped with something else that tastes like yet more garlic. Every subsequent dreadful munch of the hideous thing in your mouth will bring you closer to dropping your feigned act of approval and pick up the phone to call the police; this unprovoked assault against your black taste buds must be a breach of one race law or another. As for your black digestive system; when at 3am the next morning you find your backside Siamese-twinned to your toilet bowl trying to expel the culinary poop you ate only hours earlier, you will contemplate the *never again* high price you are paying for having turned your back on good old reliable Colonel Sanders. Lesson: bin the invitation if it arrives and stay home. But if you must be the black face at an LGBT awards dinner, bring some jerk or KFC in your bag and slip it onto the plate when nobody's looking. There, sorted!

Okay, okay! The entire last paragraph was my lamentable attempt at making light of a woefully unfunny subject. Major fail, I know, but I reserve the right to stalk anyone who dares to jest in a similar way, especially if they're white, cook weird shit and try to pass it off as even vaguely edible.

All joking firmly aside, London's 'queer spaces', comprising of trendy eateries, cosy places to drink, and sweaty night clubs in the hubs of Soho, Vauxhall, and Old Compton Street, have either been deliberately or unwittingly 'whitewashed' to mirror white-run gay publications. So much so, that it truly catches my eye when I spot a black face in the gay media; they are usually limited to the clubbing or paid escorts sections at the back. It's the same with social settings; if I see a black face, I automatically do a double-take to make sure my eyes aren't deceiving me. I had to do just that and stop myself from exploding in anger when Mother Nature forced me to visit the basement toilets in a popular Old Compton Street establishment. Standing there in the airless underground human waste facility and resurrecting an image offensively reminiscent of dutiful black slave servants from another century, referred to at that time as 'house niggers', were two miserable though oddly-smiling middle-aged African men. Boasting crisp white shirts and pressed black trousers better suited to a quality restaurant, the two men struck me as uncomfortably self-conscious, or even embarrassed. I didn't at all expect to see staff in the toilets, and once I was over the surprise, the fact that they were black disturbed me greatly. I didn't want or need them to be there, and they didn't want to be there either; yet here they were. I felt as uncomfortable as they looked, but my need for bladder relief stopped me from turning around and walking out. It was unspoken between us, but something about our past humiliations and sufferings as black people was brought bang into the present by the men's placement as workers in the toilets and this was somewhat exacerbated by the awkward silence in the tight space, interrupted only by grunts, the occasional cough and loo flushing noises from men using the cubicles. The African workers' uncertain gestures revealed a nervousness underpinned by an intrinsic knowing that they were born into the world for something better than this: overseeing the washing of ribs and scampi-tainted hands, applying soap, and offering paper towels in the hope of winning the spare coins of the indifferent white gay men who frequent the facilities and who would never acknowledge the two if they later saw them on the street. Deemed far 'too black', old, and un-pretty for above-ground bar work, in their sullied wisdom, the venue management believed that these men's attributes could only be fitting for the same environment as the unremitting stinking shit and piss from the innards of their paying customers. At least the black shoeshine men of the past mostly had the benefit of outside city air in which to carry out their work and were assured of a few coins for their prideful skill in bringing about a leathery sheen where there was once none. There was no such privileged conditions for our two modern-day equivalents, who must feel like bargain–basement prostitutes; having to give of themselves in a sloppy environment whilst never being certain of any monetary reward beyond the minimum wage offered by their pimp-like manager upstairs, who expects them to give their all. His goal is simply to engineer happy returning customers, and in his unflushed toilet-bowl for a brain, he thinks they are more likely to do so if they know that they'll be pampered by his resident black servants below stairs. This white manager is wise to his own racist game and is acutely aware that 'white servants' would erode the sense of privilege that he wishes to bestow upon his cash-laden white customers; only black skin could deliver that desired outcome. If the majority of his customers were black then the entire situation would not arise, because they would not want to see other blacks in such demeaning jobs, as I didn't, and the white manager would find employment elsewhere where the majority of customers share his skin colour and expectations. As captives of their circumstances, the African men concerned here probably live in cramped over-occupied accommodation on the edges of the city, and are willing to do desperate things to survive. And whilst they do not have visible chains around their necks or ankles, they are implacably bound by a very human need to feed and house themselves and possibly wives and children too.

I was to later learn that other gay venues also employ black African men in the same roles; roles that are consistently too low for white hands to grasp. So here we have it; unpleasant black history repeating itself in modern gay London Town. Could it get any worse? Keep reading!

Further to my original point, the not so subliminal message in gay social settings is: whites = money and blacks don't! So, denied the social opportunities that whites take for granted, black LGBT people, like a sub-class below a sub-class, must go elsewhere to find people who look 'like them'. If we do venture into the hubs, black gay men are more often than not perceived as eye-candy fetish-material, and/or hyper-exotic sex toys; not as holistic people. We are seen as somewhat subservient; designed to please white men in the bedroom, on the dance floor, in the kitchen, or on stage as their entertainers. Like unseen ghosts, we are present but frighteningly invisible where matters of significance are being dealt with; because we are seen as powerless, unimportant, void of intellect, low in economic status, and by implication, takers rather than givers – outside of the bedroom where we are expected to 'perform!' We are even considered to be worthless by some who believe that our inclusion and visibility tarnish rather than enhance the ambience of the 'gay life' they want to project. Is the solution really to relegate us to unnecessary toilet duties in dusky basements? Well, apparently so!

It is patently clear that the various identities and stereotypes of black gay men have not made the progress enjoyed by our white counterparts in recent years and our struggle to be seen and appreciated for the talent and potential we possess feels like an endlessly lonely one; we remain marginalized, minimized and traumatized. Left in the hands of the current leadership, any optimism for change may as well be buried with the Titanic, as we continue to watch white gays openly and repeatedly perpetuate the same caustic prejudices and attitudes towards blacks that they rightly object to when they are the victims of it. This should be shamed, condemned, and redressed, but will it be? Other than Peter Tatchell, I can't think of many white gay men who fight for equality across racial lines. Conversely, to our detriment and maybe to his too, the constant recycling of Peter in the media plays into the perception that black gay men don't exist or can't articulate the relevant issues. We would have much to say, if only we were asked. I am personally very knowledgeable about worldly matters beyond my sexuality and race: ask me about Islamic State in Iraq and Syria; politics in America, Russia or Nigeria; the economic prowess of China; the silent war in the Ukraine; or the Unconscious Bias influencing management decisions from Australia to London. That's who I am; I am not just a walking colour or sexuality. I don't want to participate at the top table because of those factors; I want to participate because I have a brain, ideas, and abilities that can help move us forward as one community. My intellect and abilities are replicated and improved upon many times over in my fellow black and gay brothers and sisters; just ask them. Challenge: drop the bias and open your mind; the reality may surprise you.

Racism isn't just a word; it's an experience. It scars to the very soul and carries an impact akin to the death of someone close; you will forever relive the time and place of its occurrence, especially, how it made you feel; the hurt and damage to your dignity and self-esteem. A white gay man cannot comprehend, or more importantly, feel the experience of being black and gay and the 'double-minority' status and discrimination that come with it; although some believe that they do; citing their sexuality as substantiating evidence. A black gay man will be racially profiled by the police in the street or by staff at a department store, and then be treated with suspicion or even hostility when trying to get into a gay bar. If allowed inside: SHAAZAM!!! Like magic, he's suddenly invisible. The black gay man can now expect to grow a full beard from nothing while waiting to purchase his well-deserved drink. Ignoring him is a not so subtle hint from behind the bar that they are wise to his criminal intent: trying to buy while Black! You're the wrong colour in the wrong bar, Bro! The hint feels like a hammer blow as his patience morphs between undeserved embarrassment and anger. They'll proceed to serve everybody but *him* until it is beyond obvious that he will not give up. Experience will have taught the black gay man that white people find innovative ways of expressing the derogatory intent behind the word nigger without actually saying it; it would have been nice if the barman had placed the change into our hero's open hand, as he did the previous white customer, instead of throwing it onto the bar in a not so subliminal insult, but at least the wait to be served is at last over. The black gay man knows that he must never give in to racism when he comes across it, as he inevitably will. Hell, he can't even get away from it when on-line, as some 'contact' websites come as close to overt racism as skin itself. Advertisers stating "No Asians or Blacks" are more common than the black gay man would prefer to see, whether he's interested in white guys or not. Everyone is entitled to their 'preferences', but some ads frequently cross the line with wording such as, 'Too much black flesh makes my skin crawl' or 'Asians smell', and 'Blacks are too stupid to date'. Anyway, with a drink at last in his hand, and having regained his former visibility, the black gay man is now seemingly elevated from skunk to spunk and must skilfully navigate through the sudden wave of white guys who are making a deliberate beeline in his direction. They are keen to be the first to pop that old familiar question: "Are you selling, mate?" Yes, my Brother; you've just been hit with that infuriatingly common assumption; you're a black man, and therefore, must be a walking portal for drugs and other illegalities. As for racist sexual stereo-typing; well, the night is still young! Oh, here it is! The white guy who's been checking out the front of your pants really isn't interested in your name; your cock size will do. Yes Brother, you have yet another assumed role to fulfil before the night is through, 'top' man!

On one hand, white gay men say that their sexuality enables them to empathise with the black experience, and yet, on the other, they say my race isn't a relevant factor and that I have a 'chip' on my shoulder. Well, let me state loud and clear: my race is always relevant; I can't make it invisible like I can my sexuality. And, if I have a chip on my shoulder, guess who put it there? Another oh too common assertion by white gay men is: "Look, I date black men, so I'm not racist, see!" Blissfully unaware that their obnoxious arrogance has polluted the very relationship that they are talking about, guys like that would benefit from stepping back a little bit and acknowledge that owning an Aretha Franklin or Bob Marley CD doesn't make him black or eradicate his racism. Dating black men doesn't do it either. Really! Being an *armchair* black man doesn't cut it. When white men can carry the experience and burden of walking in this skin shade, then I might sit up and listen. White folk need to understand that my path has different obstacles and challenges than theirs. It's less about blame and more about sharing knowledge and mutual understanding about our differences, similarities, feelings, and actual experiences. By the way, fella, after your black lover delivers what is expected of him tonight and thrills you to the point of orgasmic bliss, you will notice that he will yet again hum himself to sleep with that familiar song that you just can't seem to name. No, no, no, silly! It's not 'Endless Love'; it's called, 'What Have You Done for Me Lately?'

I have witnessed abhorrent displays of prejudice, including the use of offensive language such as 'nigger', on more than one occasion in London gay venues. This is unacceptable, or should be! One memorably infuriating incident saw a black man, in spite of his vehement protest of innocence, be forcibly ejected out onto the street after he was falsely accused by a white man of stealing his pack of cigarettes. The red-faced accuser later found the unopened packet on his own person. In another London bar, the staff was happily handing out jelly babies, when an over-excited Caucasian patron seized the container, loudly proclaiming, "I want a nigger one!" On yet another occasion, an Asian friend and I made our way into a popular bar on London's Old Compton Street, and heard a Caucasian man sitting at the bar announce our arrival with, "Oh, here come the niggers". No action was taken by staff against any of the above vile offenders. However, this was not the case when a particularly nasty incident occurred at the gay-friendly King William pub on Hampstead High Street. In an unprovoked verbal assault, a white man with excrement for brains, openly mocked a suit-clad black man, who was simply enjoying a summer drink, like the rest of us. "Oh my God, you look like a damn gorilla!" the offender bellowed, to the obvious embarrassment of his target and the people he was with. The previously bustling pub was suddenly silenced. If that wasn't bad enough, the offender, with a discernible German accent, then distorted his face and began making loud animal-like grunting noises, aimed towards his remarkably composed victim. Other patrons, myself included, looked on in horror at what was unfolding before us. For a moment, I expected to be next. Thankfully, on this occasion, the well-proportioned barman was having none of it, and in commanding voice, told the despicable excuse for a human being that his behaviour would "NOT BE TOLERATED!!!" I of course would have been much happier to have seen him ejected, right on his racist face.

Finally, another vital area where we see the unconscious or deliberate bias of our community is when it comes to public demonstrations. We'll see many many hundreds of chanting white LGBT people and even the odd celebrity household name turn out for demonstrations against Putin's crack down on gay people in (white) Russia, but you can count them on one hand when it comes to demonstrations against the same or worse injustices in (black) Jamaica or Uganda. Obvious rhetorical question: isn't injustice against black gays abroad just as wrong and objectionable as injustice against white gays abroad? This is powerful evidence that apartheid didn't die in South Africa; it simply packed its bags and relocated to LGBT UK.

So, what's being done about the racism in the gay community? Well, not very much, it would appear. Stonewall, the leading LGBT rights organisation in the UK, is to be commended for much of its work to date, including the production of a report in 2012 highlighting the experiences of black LGB people. But, frankly, it could have been written twenty years earlier, as the issues have not changed substantially in that time. It is proof that Stonewall suffers from a solely 'academic' appreciation of racism, which holds no credibility under objective scrutiny. Noticeably and worryingly, nowhere in the report does it acknowledge racism in the (white) gay community, and I mean nowhere! This non-acknowledgement of in-house racism is regrettable 'white-washing' nonsense, but it's no surprise. They just don't get it: there is little point in promoting my rights as a *gay* man – or even my right to marry – whilst ignoring my experience of racism as a *black* gay man. As I've made clear, colour matters in the gay community, as in the wider world; people will always see skin colour well before they see sexuality. There are some signs that Stonewall wishes to build upon the report, and, despite enormous reservations on the part of many in the black gay community, myself included, this is to be welcomed. I will want to be as supportive as possible, but action speaks louder than tired rhetoric. I will also support other human rights organisations, such as the Peter Tatchell Foundation, who seem much more willing to see racism as the priority that it should be. Racism in the gay community is particularly repugnant and should never be tolerated by any decent individual or organisation, especially the Stonewalls.

To ignore it could be interpreted as complacency or even collusion.

This acknowledgment of the distinct experience of black gay men is made more urgent by the fact that they are disproportionately represented in new HIV statistics in the UK, and present late for diagnosis and treatment. There is little evidence that their needs are being prioritised by leading organisations, such as the Terrence Higgins Trust (THT) and Gay Men Fighting AIDS (GMFA). I have a great deal of respect for the work of these organisations, but this apparent apathetic response to the needs of the black gay community is ominously similar to my experiences at the height of the AIDS crisis of the 1980s, so I would like to believe they are just running a little late, and that plans are being devised as I type to ensure history doesn't repeat itself. I am ready to assist if needed. The needs of black communities must not be an after-thought or add-on, but an integral part of core planning and service delivery of all modern organisations.

HIV-related discrimination also persists in the gay community, leading some men living with the virus to try to escape rejection by lying. On some 'contact' websites, it's increasingly common to find some arrogant advertisers describing themselves as "disease-free", which must be pretty devastating reading for those living with the virus. This is confirmation that people with HIV are being defined solely by their positive status, which is wrong: people with HIV are still holistic people and should not be thought of as a walking disease risk. What really matters is whether someone is into safer sex, not what their HIV status is. Either way, there is absolutely no reason to discriminate, or to make someone feel less attractive because they have HIV. As I write this book, HIV statistics for gay men are on the rise, and the reasons appear complex. I share my thoughts and related experience later in the book, but the message, in brief, for all sexually active people, especially gay men, remains: get tested and practice safer sex, always!

The black community has got its own burdens and peculiarities. A lingering burden is the gross racial bias by police, both unconscious and blatantly deliberate, in the stopping and searching of black youth in London on 'suspicion' of crime committed or intended. Such dehumanizing searches never happen to white guys in the Square Mile of the City, where they walk unfettered while committing financial criminality using the latest portable gadget. Some of our internal idiosyncrasies involve blacks disliking others because they're "not black enough", or because they're Jamaican, African, Mixed, or their skin tone is too dark or too light, or even because one "sounds like a white man". Boy, have I heard that before! As a closeted teenage schoolboy, I remember my dear mother telling me never to come home with a girl who had a darker complexion than mine. Needless to say, I never did, but for reasons quite unrelated to my mother's highly inappropriate colour bar. I preferred men, but shhhh, don't tell my mum! Come election time, like entranced zombies drawn to the irresistible scent of warm human blood, most black folk feel compelled to cast their vote for Labour (or Democrats in the USA) without giving a single thought to the potential merits of voting otherwise. It was British Labour Prime Minister Tony Blair who, without reservation, gave police all the stop and search powers they were seeking, but it was a subsequent Conservative government that acknowledged the unacceptable racial bias evident in the implementation of the policy. They appear determined to claw those powers back. This example demonstrates that auto-pilot voting for Labour (or any political party) isn't about being black; it's being plain stupid. But am I ready to vote Conservative? Hmm, I will vote for the ideas, issues, and policies that I believe are the correct ones, whichever party offers them. That said, if knife crime predominantly affects black youth then they should be stopped and searched more than others. That's my considered view. Racism, sexism, and anti-gay prejudice are undoubtedly a reality, but identity politics risks self-victimisation to the point of making us blind to facts over fiction and undermine our potential to succeed in the future based on our actual talent rather than shade of skin. We cannot live in the past, and must, therefore, let go of past hurt and injustices. This doesn't mean we forget, but that we consciously move on. No, we are not all born victims or experience racism, but we can foolishly adopt that excuse if we want to live mediocre or worthless lives. Let's open our eyes and minds; there is more than one way to be black. Let's refuse to collude with the limited category of the skin. This is 2016 and victimhood doesn't cut it. It only facilitates the appeal to white majority communities of the Donald Trumps and UKIPs of the world.

I have similar frustrations with the wider Black community's British colonial-influenced auto-pilot hating of gays, lesbians and trans people, which is no less senseless. However, I was to be disappointed if I thought that my experience of racism as a black gay man would enable partnership working on the issue with my black heterosexual counterparts. Their ingrained homophobia and anti-gay tribal stance would kill off that idea, literally. Indeed, just the mere suggestion prompted some hideous monster to post a 'doctored' picture of me on Facebook, complete with a super-imposed bloody bullet wound to my head. The police were concerned enough to investigate the incident, but my cyber assailant was just one of many in the straight black community who feel strongly that being gay is a 'White man's thing' and is a symptom of my blackness having been diluted and corrupted by them. A deranged Jamaican woman sent me this message via the web:

'Vernal Scott, you fool, you psychopath, you condemned demon sent on Earth. You rapist, go to hell. You demon from the pit of hell, one day you shall die like the boy in the video, and I hope yours is more painful. *(16-year old feminine/Trans youth Dwayne Jones was shot, hacked, and stabbed to death in Jamaica by a mob of hate-filled criminals.)* You have brought shame to humanity and you have caused so much pain through your fake teachings. You shall know no peace. Everything you do in life shall be against you for supporting evil. You will regret your actions; you and your minions, demon Vernal Scott!'

Such foul messages are an almost daily occurrence for me, and for the record, I have never raped anyone or engaged in underage sexual activity of any kind. In their vicious short-sightedness, the authors are evidently more ready to see black gays and lesbians as another problem rather than as allies in the fight against racism. Their rigorously maintained denial of gayness as a natural, intrinsic and valid part of black cultural identity, not only hinders the progress of the entire black community, but also generates internalized homophobia within us as Black LGBTQ individuals. As a result, our relationships with each other is undermined by a sense that our blackness means we are not good enough for love, and therefore, the real prize is white; the same whites who could very well treat us like disposable sexual fodder. It is my considered view that the black community will never make any real progress until it deals with its self-loathing, which, among other symptoms, include learned anti-gay hate. The annual UK black Pride festival is part of our healing process, but we should learn to love ourselves enough to celebrate who and what we are every day. That means coming out of the closet and healing our inner pain and/or addictions by accessing counselling services; educating ourselves beyond 'bling' and achieving our career aspirations; and, of course, consciously enjoying great sex with reduced harm: fuck, test, treat (to) prevent! Oh, and before our church leaders start praying for God to expel the demon of homosexuality from our community, they should prepare themselves for depleted congregations and choirs, missing cooks, and disappeared family members – who are all gay and living in the holy closet. This tired, self-defeating hate is BS and needs to stop; at home, in church, and in the wider black community. Hey, I think I hear an Amen! Oh, it's coming from behind that closet door.

If there is a hidden group experiencing regular discrimination, then, in my experience, it is fathers. Too many of them find out the hard way that the 'private (secretive)' UK family court system is heavily biased towards mothers. Campaigning groups such as Families Need Fathers and Fathers4Justice exist for good reason, and change is long overdue. Due to our system, I am only able to allude to a little of my own experience in this book, but I can confirm that miscarriages of justice occur often, and fathers pay the fiscal and emotional price. My heart goes out to every broken-hearted father who leaves court with nothing but legal bills in his hands, but I implore them, don't give up! Let the passing of time be part of your strategy, and be assured that your children will come to you one day – they did not choose to be fatherless. We have seen historic change in the UK on issues such as sexuality and same-sex marriage, and this is absolutely right, but it's also right to ensure loving and committed fathers are no longer excluded from their children's lives because of hostile mothers and incompetent work by officers of the court. I hope David Cameron demonstrates the same leadership on this issue as he did regarding same-sex marriage, because thousands of children and their perfectly decent fathers need a high profile champion.

We need courageous and moral leadership in Commonwealth Nations. They should once and for all dispose of outdated laws and penal codes inherited from colonial days; laws that are no longer in place in the countries that influenced or even authored them; the same countries that now take advantage of significant 'pink' (gay) buying power.

Commonwealth HQ with **Peter Tatchell.** London, 23 April 2013

In forty-two of the Commonwealth's fifty-four member states, homosexuality is a criminal offence, and as Britain is at the heart of the Commonwealth, it must continue to show leadership on discrimination issues by condemning sister nations where homosexuality remains a criminal offence. Silence on these issues could be interpreted as collusion. I am reminded at this point of the tremendous courage of Maurice Tomlinson, a Jamaican-born gay man who has decided to challenge the country's 1864 anti-sodomy laws in court. Courage and visibility are crucial to the success of any struggle, and I wish him well. The evidence for his case is stark, if the justice system wishes to see it!

Maurice Tomlinson, a champion of change in Jamaica

The Commonwealth's collective institutions produced its own evidence in 2011, which showed that where homosexuality had been decriminalized, HIV infection rates had fallen. In Caribbean countries where homosexuality is not against the law, one in every fifteen men who have sex with other men is infected with HIV, however, where it is criminalized, the rate of infection is one in four. The region has the highest rate of HIV transmission outside of sub-Saharan Africa, with gay/bi men being the most affected group. It is estimated that 33 percent of gay/bi men in Jamaica are HIV infected. The country is one of eleven in the region where homosexuality (through anti-sodomy laws) is illegal. This 'illegal' status directly undermines the effectiveness of prevention initiatives aimed at 'at risk' groups.

Nations in Africa and the West Indies have a history steeped in the slave trade, and their cultures are deeply scarred by the agony which it inflicted over five hundred years. Many of these countries have ageing or inadequate infrastructure, and a paucity of industry and employment, again thanks to colonialism. As these nations celebrate fifty or so years of independence, they lack, and have persistently lacked, capital for economic development, which is the only way that they will raise living standards. In other words, many of the economic strategies that they have tried, in the course of a half-century of self-government, have failed; and they need to think innovatively about how they will attract investment, and sources of revenue in an ever-more competitive world. Their economies still suffer the effects of colonialism, and their citizens, at home, or abroad, have almost certainly experienced racial discrimination at one time or another. If the British Empire was "the white man's burden", the throttled economies it left behind, and the racism (and homophobia) it enshrined, has been the black man's. It is, however, a depressing fact of human nature that to be a victim of discrimination is no inoculation against turning one's hatred upon other groups. Abhorrence of anything to do with homosexuality in many of these countries is deep and abiding. Perversely, the persecution of gays, some of the most vulnerable members of these societies, is revered as a symbol of manliness, and fervidly associated with righteousness against sin.

Imagine, for a moment, the Caribbean. Here you have a scattering of islands, verdant oases in a turquoise sea; and just a stretch of water, or short plane flight away, you have the United States. A land of 350 million comparatively prosperous inhabitants, *scores millions of whom are gay*. The islands, with their golden beaches, lush mountains, and laughing waterfalls, must embrace change if they are to ever to break free from deprivation and take advantage of pink money.

Gays and lesbians tend to have a higher proportion of their income considered as 'disposable'. American gays and lesbians, for example, spend approximately $790 million a year on travel and other lifestyle choices; funds that could be spent, if the circumstances were right, in countries needing new roads, schools, hospitals and a general economic boost. The previously homophobic political leadership in Sydney, London, Paris, and Madrid, understand that homophobia not only stifles life, but it also undermines wealth. These governments now grasp the lucrative pink money prize, while mostly black countries bury their heads in the past and lose out on billions of dollars because of it.

Black leaders should embrace the new age; where love, of whatever sexuality, is welcomed, and hatred of (gay) love, is made illegal. Sadly, The Charter of the Commonwealth, inaugurated on 11 March 2013 by Queen Elizabeth II, regrettably failed to require forty or more Commonwealth nations to address, and redress, their State-sponsored violence against homosexual and transgender people. It was a missed opportunity, but as an equality and diversity consultant, I remain keen to work with African and Caribbean Commonwealth nations on related issues, so they *do the right thing* by their own people; by making moral, legal, and social-justice changes. The change must be genuine in order for gay money to begin to flow; gay men and women will not be fooled by pretty window dressing. Change can be achieved without a need for the countries concerned to compromise on their *values and traditions;* but, as a minimum, it must ensure the freedom and safety of gay and transgender residents and visitors, and start with the decriminalization of homosexuality where this has not yet been done.

Commonwealth leaders can turn around local attitudes to homosexuality by demonstrating how a greater tolerance of gays would enhance personal, local and national prosperity. Gay tourism will stimulate business, and create opportunities for enterprising young and older people alike. A thriving gay-friendly tourist industry will increase tax revenues; meaning more money for roads, schools, and hospitals. The most resistant islander, who comprehends that those impeccably-dressed same-sex pairs of visiting men and women, positively impacts his household economy, will soon alter his views. People understand (the value of) money; they have it or they don't, but most spend their lives seeking more of it. Money is useful, whether it's green, pink or otherwise.

I am not pretending entrenched attitudes and prejudices are easy to change. It will take years of effort through tough resistance, but change will eventually happen where the seed of will and intention has been planted; Gandhi, Martin Luther King, and Nelson Mandela prevailed against more formidable odds.

Until real change takes place, gay people may want to think twice about spending our cash in countries where homosexuality remains a crime and our brothers and sisters experience unrelenting discrimination. Yes, we can now marry in London, but we'd be unwise to spend our honeymoon in the following locations (amongst others!):

Antigua and Barbuda: 15 years in jail

Barbados: Life in prison

Dominica: Ten years jail or sectioning

Grenada: Ten years jail for men

Guyana: Life in prison

Jamaica: Ten years' hard labour for men

Kenya: 14 years jail

Malaysia: 20 years jail

Mauritius: Five years jail

Morocco: Three years jail

Saint Kitts and Nevis: Ten years jail for men

St Lucia: Ten years jail for men

St Vincent and the Grenadines: Ten years jail

Seychelles: 14 years jail

Solomon Islands: 14 years jail

Singapore: Two years jail

Trinidad and Tobago: 25 years jail

Tunisia: Three years jail

United Arab Emirates: death penalty and deportation

Uganda is another country where a life sentence is the punishment for being gay. You can even find yourself in prison for failing to report someone who is gay, or for providing services to a gay person.

What's striking about this list is the high proportion of Muslim nations, and countries with black-majority populations, particularly Caribbean ones, that feature on it. As a gay man of Jamaican heritage, I have first-hand experience of the venom of particular cultures towards homosexuality, but it is self-defeating, because talented, bread-winning native gays, either opt to leave for more gay-friendly countries, or stay and succumb to illness, disease or homophobic assault.

I of course totally deplore the mortal plight of gays in the Muslim world - Iraq, Iran, and Saudi Arabia - no less vigorously than I do anywhere else, however, it is the African and Caribbean countries that I believe my background and experiences give me special licence to speak out. There are, however, a number of prominent black men and women, who are likely to be listened to well before I am. President Barack Obama is one such person. His daily working at the White House with openly gay people (and their children), exposed him to the facts instead of misinformation, and this caused him to change his mind from non-support of same-sex marriage to being fully supportive of it (and gay families). I also appreciate now ex British Prime Minister, David Cameron, for his dogged determination and public support of same-sex marriage, despite spitting opposition from many within his own party. On 4th June 2013, a historic moment in time, the House of Lords overwhelmingly voted in large numbers in support of his stance. World leaders failing to demonstrate the same courage forfeit the right to call themselves such. All leaders should embrace the facts rather than the myths and lead for all their people. That would be the right thing to do, socially, morally and economically. I say morally, because that is what we are dealing with here; the moral courage and decency to stand up for (adult) love in all its forms, over ignorance, hate, and prejudice. Despite their vigorous assertions, self-serving political or religious diehards are not entitled to claim ownership of morality or what constitutes love, and will no longer be allowed to force LGBTQ love to wither and die in the silence of the closet. Their superiority complex is as repugnant as it is flawed. It is they who belong in a closet, and preferably a sealed one. Fact: LGBTQ love is part of the 'new normal', and our love is worthy, right, and good. We have rewritten the outdated moral template that was designed to exclude us and have set a new inclusive standard of our own, based upon the principle of dignity in love for all. We now claim the new moral higher ground.

By writing this book I am standing up for love and the freedom to love, whatever our sexuality. It is testament that I was here, was true to myself, and left something of value behind. I hope that my story will inspire people to abandon the closet and embrace their authenticity as the gift that it is. If I am really lucky, then these pages will also stimulate constructive discussion and spur change around the globe, especially in the religion-heavy Jamaicas, Ugandas, Zimbabwes and Nigerias, and everywhere where ignorance, inequality and misinformation currently remain a reality. Yes, this book does indeed have a purpose or two.

I could go on forever about my thoughts on this subject or that, but it's now time to put away my soap box and share my personal story; my journey so far, although you will soon see that it is *our* story. So, imagine that I'm opening up to you over an extra-shot skinny latte in a cosy café somewhere in North London. You will hear about births and deaths, joy and pain, successes and mistakes, hopes and aspirations. You will hear about courageous men and women who fought, not just one of the cruellest illnesses of modern times, but unprecedented prejudice, loathing, and on-going stigma. You will hear about sex and violence, tears and laughter, lessons lost and lessons learned; including a wonderful truth: death is incapable of defeating love. The lows will probably shock you, but I count myself amongst those who were not built to break. By building our lives on a foundation of self-love and integrity, we will remain optimistic and unshaken through the occasional storm. In my case, a thumping dose of disco music helps, too! Let's start with that timeless feel-good classic and personal favourite. Sing it, Gloria!: 'I am what I am...'

4. THE BEGINNING: FROM MAY PEN TO LONDON

IN THE EARLY 1940S a young boy and girl gleefully played together amongst the fruit trees and sugar cane plants of May Pen, a tiny, sun-scorched town set in the near-inaccessible Jamaican countryside. The dusty rural gardens rang with the sound of their calls: her high-pitched and exaggerated "Skip-peeey!" and his enthusiastic response, "Dor-Dor!" The more juicy mangoes he could reach for her, the more she called his name in ecstatic gratitude. She was hooked on that particular fruit, and this particular boy.

The great-great-grandchildren of former slaves, they spent as much time together as possible. He was Desilver Augustus Scott, nicknamed 'Skippy', a red-skinned, sports-crazy boy. She was Doreth May Eubank (pronounced Dorrett), an irrepressible, beautiful and decidedly feminine girl, and a little taller than her beau; she could reach for her own mangoes, but that would be missing the point; they must be handled by Skippy, first! She loved sewing and singing and playing her piano almost as much as playing around in the bush with Skippy, and won a scholarship for her musical talents. Her distraction by and love for Skippy would mean that she would never pursue her gift in a formal manner, but she would sing whenever the feeling to do so took her. Her heavenly voice would win the heart of anyone fortunate enough to hear it.

The children's respective families lived opposite each other, in tiny wooden homes not unlike today's garden sheds, with no electricity or running water. Skippy's family grew so large that his parents, Vernal Walter Scott and Ambrose Amanda Robinson, built a second home next door in order to accommodate their six girls and six boys. The boys slept in one and the girls in the other, top to tail, three at the top of the bed and three at the bottom. Skippy was one of Ambrose Amanda's children with Vernal – she had divorced her first husband in order to start a new family with Vernal. Across the dirt track, Doreth's siblings had similar gender-assigned sleeping arrangements, but they could all be accommodated in one house with their parents, Dadou and Elizabeth. Everybody, including her children, referred to Elizabeth as Aunty Bet, and Doreth was the apple of her father's eye.

Despite the appearance of poverty, both the Scott's and the Eubank's were actually doing very well in an environment where most families were dirt poor and daily living was rough. Both families owned extensive land and one even owned the local post office. These were happy, proud families; everybody had clean homemade or hand-me-down clothes, and went to bed bathed, and with a full tummy. Church, growing and selling their own food, and singing and playing were the usual weekly activities. With no radio, families made their own entertainment, with improvised instruments and dancing. Yes, these were happy families. Still, they had an appreciation for the opportunities that a good education could provide in creating a better future; schooling was therefore the number one priority for both sets of parents. Christianity underpinned their values, and church was hands down the most important event of the week.

In the blink of an eye the no-longer-shy Doreth and ever-frisky Skippy became teenage lovers; he was to be her first and last, but sadly, she wasn't his, in either respect. In her late teens/early twenties she twice became pregnant by him, and gave birth to two sons. The first was Aldred, the second, Earl; in the peculiar Caribbean fashion, where almost nobody seems to go by their given name, the boys were nicknamed 'Leo', and 'Bunny', respectively. Tragically, and to the shock of their young, unmarried parents, both boys were born with haemophilia – they were 'bleeders', as such children were called. This was not an uncommon condition in May Pen, because of the history of deliberate in-breeding perpetrated by slave owners, who had no consideration for the health implications of the practice. The affliction was not diagnosed early on, but became apparent only when children's usual rough-and-tumble cuts and bruises did not heal. Bunny was frail and particularly badly affected by frequent bleeds, which would cause him extreme discomfort and pain throughout his life.

Doreth and Skippy, who at the time remained living in their respective parental homes, knew very little about how to care for their sick children, but Doreth did her best with help from her mother and sisters. A disappointed Dadou, who had hoped for better for his daughter, kept out of it. Skippy didn't take fatherhood too seriously and carried on playing the local stud and bad boy. His minor offences eventually landed him in trouble with local police.

Doreth and Skippy began to think about their future, and following discussions with their respective parents, they decided to join other young 'Windrush' couples and seek a new, and hopefully, more prosperous life in England. The UK government was actively recruiting Jamaicans to work on London Transport Services.

Skippy left first, arriving in London in 1954. His ship sailed to Italy, and from there, he and his fellow Jamaican adventurers took a series of trains and ferries to England. Once in the capital city, the handsome young man soon found lodgings and secured a job as a bus conductor for London Transport, working the number 16 route from Cricklewood to Victoria Station. He stayed in touch with his parents and Doreth by letter, though his missives neglected to mention the many young black ladies, married and single, he was meeting on the bus. Many of them would visit his room at the end of the working day.

In 1956, Doreth borrowed some old suitcases, left her two small sons behind with her parents and sisters, and boarded a ship to join Skippy in chilly London. Edna, Doreth's younger sister, and her husband, Neville, would follow three years later, and settle in Coventry; for the time being, Edna became principal carer for Bunny and Leo, as Aunty Bet became increasingly frail.

The summer, after joining Skippy in his room at Barnsdale Road, Doreth gave birth to Arlene, who, continuing the Jamaican nickname tradition was dubbed 'Jan'. Jan had a lighter complexion than that of his sons back in Jamaica, and this made her the instant favourite of her father. Her arrival prompted the still-unmarried couple to find larger accommodation, which they moved into in 1958, just before the birth of their second daughter, Veronica, nicknamed 'Beverley', in June. The non-self-contained apartment in the substantial four-story house at Lowfield Road in South Hampstead, shared with three other Jamaican families, would be home for the next six years.

Skippy soon dropped his job as a conductor, and secured better paying work as a driver, delivering kosher meat across the city. He was determined to get his family out of rented accommodation. Doreth shared his ambition, and worked full time as a machinist; she was second to none with her ability to turn plain cloth into beautiful garments. The couple saved every penny they could, and often spoke about wanting to buy their own home.

Though two of her children were still in Jamaica, Doreth's strong traditional Christian values caused her to become increasingly embarrassed that she had had four children out of wedlock, and she began to insist that Skippy put a ring on her finger, "otherwise there would be no more children or living together in sin", as she put it.

Skippy, whose freedom and playboy image were seriously threatened by Doreth's demands, reluctantly agreed. The couple married in 1961, but by this time Doreth, who had recently suffered a miscarriage, was again pregnant with what would be the couple's last child. Unfortunately for Doreth, marriage did not prevent Skippy from continuing to have affairs with other women. He later told a close friend that he didn't really love Doreth at the time of their marriage. His later behaviour would make me wonder whether he had ever loved her at all.

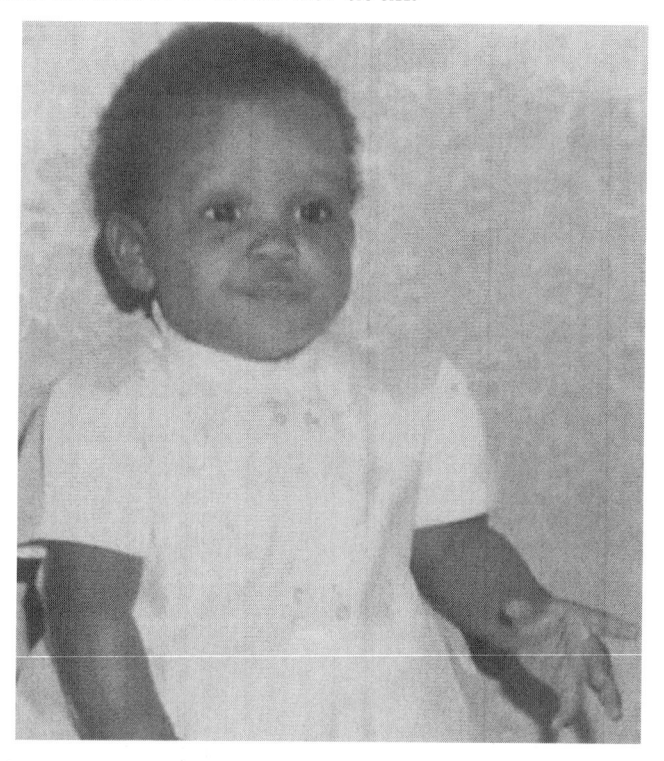

Doreth gave birth to her fifth child on 16th November 1961 – a mid-to-light-skinned boy, whose resemblance to Skippy became a talking point for all who came to see the bright-eyed new baby. Yes, it was me, and my big arrival into the world. My mother told friends that mine was the most painful of her five deliveries, and would often thereafter refer to me as "that big-head boy". Skippy decided to call me Vernal Walter Scott, after his own father, and I wonder to this day why his first-born sons, Bunny or Leo, weren't afforded that privilege.

The couple was especially pleased to learn that I did not have haemophilia, like my two brothers, who remained in Jamaica, and whom I wouldn't meet for some years to come. Unbeknownst to anyone at this time, my sister, Jan, like our mother, carried the haemophilia gene, and might pass it on to future children.

But although I was born healthy, I was only home for a short while at our poorly-heated Lowfield Road home before I was rushed back into hospital with pneumonia. My parents were beside themselves when doctors told them that I was gravely ill. They were unprepared for the news that the doctors suspected that I had been subjected to physical child abuse. In a panic, Skippy explained that the cuts and bruises on my face and body were caused by other children living in the house. The hospital at King's Cross was unconvinced and decided to supervise my recovery for a period longer than the original diagnosis required.

Doreth's faith in the power of prayer gave her a sense of comfort and strength; strength she shared with Skippy. It was touch and go, but I made it – God had a mission or two for me yet. I was to be troubled by a thunderous cough for years to come, especially during the winter months, which gradually lessened, although now and again, when I have a particularly bad cold, it returns and with a rib-shattering presence. As for the suspicion of abuse, I can only assume my father was right and that my siblings and others were perhaps a little too aggressive when playing with me.

Once returned to the family home, my father wouldn't let me out of his sight and would pack his little bundle of joy into his car and take me everywhere with him. My mother was annoyed as she was left alone to care for Beverley and

Jan while Dad and I enjoyed our love-in. I was his pride and joy; his son, his healthy son!

Still, one of my earliest memories is of my mother, not my father. She was wheeling me in a pushchair down Lowfield Road, towards some shops that have long since disappeared. I must have been about three. In my fragmentary recollection, I can remember that it was very cold and grey, but not much else. I even think my coat and hat were grey. I can remember my fascination with the cracks in the pavement, as they disappeared beneath the wheels of my pushchair.

My parents continued to work hard and eventually saved enough money for a down payment on a house at 13 Kingsley Road, Kilburn. Kingsley Road was, an ordinary street of terraced houses that became Willesden Lane at one end, and Priory Park Road at the other. They paid a deposit of one thousand, two hundred pounds, for the three-bedroom, three-reception house, which cost a total of five thousand pounds. I was about four years old when my sisters and I ran about the empty house that was shortly to become our home, and it wasn't too long before we had moved in.

Although the street was mostly populated with home-owning white families, the Scotts were not the only black family on Kingsley Road. Marlon, of a similar age and soon to be my best friend, lived at number 19 with his very nice parents, his older brother, Sam, his baby brother, George, and four pretty sisters. Angela Brown and her over-strict Jamaican parents lived opposite our house at number 24, and my first Asian friend, and footballing pal, Michael Ali, lived immediately next door to us at number 15. In later years he and I were to spend many hours kicking an airless football around Kingsley Road, trying to avoid the dog mess as we did so. When dusk fell, his mother would often threaten to take a strap to him if he didn't, "Get inside, now!"

My mother and Michael's did not get on at all, yet they would always exchange bland niceties if they had the bad luck to be on their respective doorsteps at the same time. Once inside the house, my mother would mutter some kind of insult under her breath, such as, "... your food stink like I don't know what! You see dem damn Indian people deh." Yes, my mother could bitch with the best of them, and she was good at it too! She did not like Angela Brown's mother either, to whom she referred as "that spy across the road there".

The problem was that the Kingsley Road ladies spent too much of their time peeping through their pristine-white net curtains at each other. My mother could hold a five-minute conversation with her back to you, while she peeped out at the neighbours at the same time. She was particularly scathing whenever she would spot a single middle-aged Jamaican woman who lived in rented rooms half way down Kingsley Road: "Look at her", my mother would hiss, "She doesn't know man." I later came to realise that this was a *'Jamaican'* way of suggesting the woman concerned was lesbian and my mother obviously did not approve. I also got the impression that Mum and Angela's mother would sometimes be peeping at the same time, because now and again – no doubt when their sneaking eyes met, Mum would quickly pull back the curtain and kiss her teeth in Jamaican fashion, saying: "You see that damn spy across the road there. That spy!" There could, of course, be no acknowledgement that my mother was guilty of the same thing – who would dare tell her so? Somehow she felt she was the self-appointed queen of Kingsley Road, and as such was justified in spying on other people, especially characters as patently suspicious to Mum's way of thinking, as Mrs Brown and Mrs Ali.

To help meet the bills, my parents took in an older Jamaican woman called Eugenie as a lodger. However, the arrangement came to a crashing end when voices inside the rampaging woman's head told her to systematically smash up my mother's ornaments. It was all very scary to my young eyes and a bad start to our lives at 13 Kingsley Road. Anyway, my parents soon cleaned up and aimed to carry on.

5. HEY, WHAT'S MY NAME?

I DIDN'T LEARN that my name was Vernal until the day I started school. My first lesson! This was because my immediate family had always referred to me as 'Ian' (and they still do to this very day).

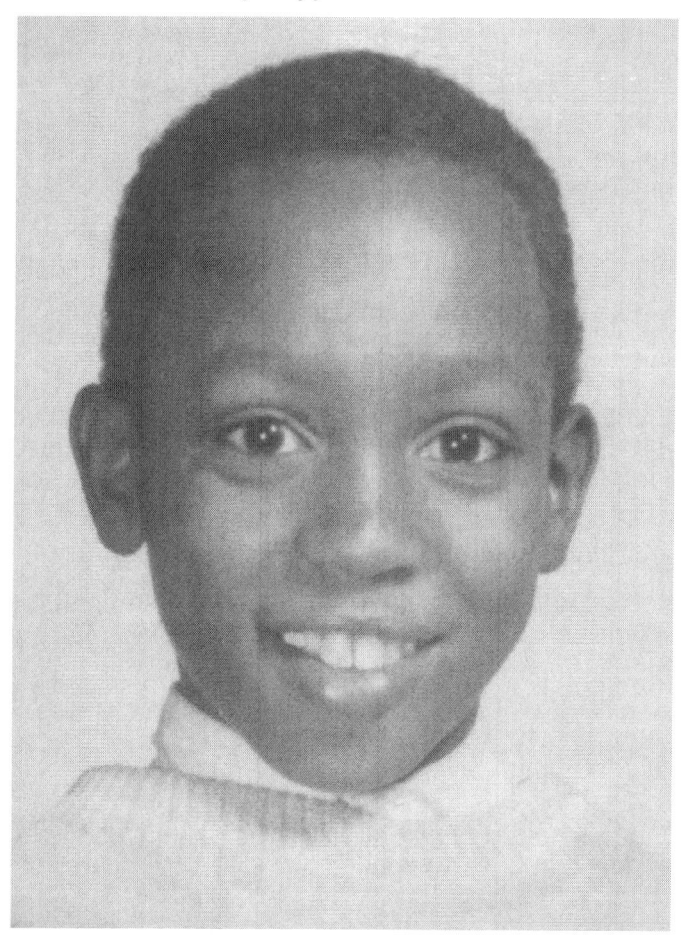

The discovery of my true name came as quite a shock to my small, five-year-old system on my first day at Kingsgate Primary School, West Hampstead. I clung to my mother's hand as she rushed me through the busy streets on the fifteen-minute walk to school. Upon arrival, I felt overwhelmed with anxiety at the sight of what seemed like a million parents and an even greater number of similarly petrified children. Everybody exchanged uncomfortable smiles as a multi-racial collection of parents and children had their first encounter with the all-white school staff.

A kind-faced middle-aged white woman crouched down in front of me, but then looked up and addressed her question to Mum: "And what's this handsome young man's name then?"

To my complete amazement, my mother, in her most posh, Jamaican-tinged English accent, responded: "His name is Vernal."

I immediately looked up at my mother and sought to correct her: "No, Mum, my name is Ian!"

Mum's fake smile disappeared as she looked sternly down at me. "Your name is Vernal, you hear me, boy!"

Now standing, the teacher smiled down at the puzzled expression on my face. My confusion deepened as the two women moved on to exchange necessary information about me, and the school. My mind struggled to come to terms with why my mother had just lied about my name. *Vernal? Vernal! But my name is Ian,* I repeated to myself. It simply made no sense to me at all.

I felt as if I was being abandoned as my mother said a hurried goodbye that rainy day; so much so that I wanted to run after her. I didn't have the courage to do so, though mostly because I feared her reaction. She didn't even look back at me as she walked away. I could see some kids receiving kisses from their parents, but none of that for me! My mother and father did not do kisses, or even hugs; it just wasn't their style. I guess they felt that they did their part in raising their kids, and there was no need to go over the top with all that huggy-kissy stuff.

That afternoon I found myself isolated in the school playground, feeling far too shy to join my fellow pupils, some of whom I now realise were probably just as scared as me. I don't know whether it was the intimidating situation, or the shock of being told by my mother that I was not who I thought I was, but my tummy started to heave, and before I could so much as swallow, my mouth opened up and an Exorcist-like arc of projectile vomit spouted from my mouth onto the grey concrete, and my freshly polished brown shoes. Any chance of making friends evaporated after the other kids witnessed my display of instant muck. *So this is what embarrassment feels like,* I thought, as children gathered around to stare and point at my nauseating technicolor production before them. The rest of my first day at Kingsgate Primary passed in a dismal blur.

On returning home, I immediately ran to tell Dad, not about my new found regurgitative talents, but that Mum had made up a new name for me. He laughingly explained, "No, Vernal is your real name, Old Soldier". He carefully explained that, like 'Old Solider', 'Ian' was a nickname. "When you were born, my best friend was a white man called Ian. We called you Ian to honour my friend. But your name is Vernal, after your grandfather – he's a very proud man."

I soon began to appreciate my real name, and 'Ian' became relegated for use by immediate family only, though Grandad Vernal had died before I even knew what a grandparent or pride was. In fact, I would never meet any of my grandparents. Nor would I discover anything about my dad's white friend, the real Ian, who remains a mystery to this very day.

6. DON'T MESS WITH MY MUM!

MY MOTHER WOULD TAKE NO PRISONERS if someone crossed her. One hot summer's day, during one of her window-spying sessions she spotted an elderly white neighbour allowing her dog to do its business outside our house. My mother had seen this happen before and had convinced herself that this was a deliberate act of disrespect and decided enough was enough. In a flash she exchanged her old slippers for black street shoes, hurried down the stairs, and flew out of the front door with a look of murderous intent in her eyes. I followed from a safe distance as she headed down Kingsley Road in pursuit of the old lady, whose dog was now making use of a lamp-post.

"Aye! Aye!! Aye!!! Hello… hello!!!" my mother shouted as she caught up with the woman. Even the dog looked up to see what was going on. "Don't you ever bring your darg to shit outside my house again. Do it outside yours." Mum spat out.

The startled elderly woman opened her mouth wordlessly, but my mother hadn't finished: "If you do it again, I'm going to put your face in it." With that, she turned on her heels, and left the woman standing there with her mouth agape.

Finally coming to her senses, the woman shouted after my mother: "I'm going to tell my husband about you."

Without looking back, my mother responded: "Yes, you bring him. I will take that stupid dog and beat both you and him with it!" There was then a final sucking of teeth to seal the threat and the incident was over as quickly as it had begun. I ducked behind a parked car as my steaming mother headed back up the street and returned to her palace and old slippers. Moments later and she was singing the house down as if nothing had happened.

My football and the pavement outside our house were going to be free from dog mess from here on; the old woman and her cowardly husband kept their distance. There was no need for a dog whisperer; just call my mother. I was so very proud of her that day, but a little frightened of her too. She was fearless.

My parents had to deal with overt racism from white people when they arrived in the UK in the mid-1950s, and although my mother did not refer to the dog-fouling incident as such, I am confident that is how she saw it; that's certainly how it must have felt. The dog owner felt it appropriate to allow her pet to repeatedly defecate outside our home; a black family's home, and my mother both mentally and emotionally had connected this to past insults. She had become a hard-working, home-owning member of British society, and yet this white woman brought her 'shit' to our doorstep-- in an attempt to remind my family (as my mother saw it) that we were just that, shit!

My father would never have done what mother had. It wasn't his style. His attitude was that dogs need to shit, so what's the big deal? He did, however, give tacit approval to my mother's actions by saying nothing about the matter. Later on in life he would tell me that he was one of the original Notting Hill rioters - in the early 1960s, though he didn't go into any detail about what he got up to. Caribbean youth of my dad's generation trying to settling in England felt angry enough to throw stones at the police because of harassment and blatant discrimination. When similar riots later flared up in English cities in the early 1980s, my father would be a sympathetic spectator. He knew what the rioters were angry about because he was once in their shoes.

My mother's fight against bigotry didn't involve sticks and stones; she was more subtle and graceful. She demonstrated that she was at least as good as members of the white population by the manner in which she lived; with self-respect, poise and dignity. The dog incident brought out her rarely seen 'black' side; by which I mean her fierce determination to defend her dignity and rights against those who sought to demean her because of the colour of her skin. On this occasion my mother wasn't bothered about being posh; she was simply a black Jamaican woman protecting her pride and her family.

I just hoped Mrs Brown saw my wonderful super-mother in action on that glorious day.

Dad was hardly home as he held down two jobs in order to make the mortgage payments. During the day he delivered meat to butcher shops across north London, and at night he worked in a plastics factory in Slough that made moulded parts for cars. When he arrived home he frequently brought the stress of his day with him, and the family would invariably wait tensely, trying to work out what sort of mood he was in. Dad would always head to my mother's sewing room first to say "Hey, Dor-Dor" before plonking himself in front of the TV and switching the channel to whatever he wanted to watch. It didn't matter if we were already watching something – the TV was his and we didn't argue. Occasionally, he would arrive in a playful, even frisky mood, and touch or indeed grope my mother from behind, causing her to giggle like the little schoolgirl she once was. She would put on a false protest: "Skippy, leave me alone, you hear? Ha ha haaa..." - her giggles belying her demand. Her deep love for her handsome husband showed itself in these rare moments of spontaneous affection. He could do no wrong as far as she was concerned.

Dad didn't do much once he was home other than watch TV with its three black and white channels, read his newspaper, eat his food and take involuntary naps when he could no longer keep his eyes open. He on occasion would help Jan with her homework, but that was pretty much it. It seemed that no sooner had he arrived home, that he was getting ready to leave again for his night job. It was only at the weekends that he got a chance to enjoy time at home.

I was responsible for preparing Dad's overnight work bag. He would send me to the corner shop to buy the snacks that would get him through the night. A couple of tins of Green Giant sweet corn were always in there, as well as his favourite drink, vitamin-rich Nutriment. After his fitful nap in front of the TV, he'd sling the bag over his shoulder, straighten his cap, and off he'd go for his next shift. His brown-beige cloth cap was his constant companion, even at home. He must have been self-conscious about his bald head. Come to think of it, I don't recall my dad ever having hair on the top of his head; he had always been bald. Looking just like him, as I did, I feared that one day my precious curly afro would follow his down the bathroom plug hole. I hated it when people, especially in the black barber shops that Dad would drag me to, predicted that this was indeed my fate: "Yes, man, de bwoy ah go ball, jus' like 'im father. See de line deh!" It was if they had identified the mark of the Devil, right there on my scalp.

I guess Dad was a typical Jamaican man of his generation and background: he was raised hard and only knew how to behave hard. He was a proud man and he made himself appear bigger than his five-foot-six inches with an exuberant laugh, broad gestures, and a determined, almost macho stride – he always took the stairs two steps at a time. To his friends he was a lively, gregarious man, but at home, behind closed doors, my dad became increasingly moody and intimidating. The days when we were inseparable had passed and I drew ever closer to my feminine mother.

Perhaps it was the pressure of living in British society, but my father tended to save his laughter for strangers and passers-by, and his frowns and anger for us. He had a quick, hot temper that took me by surprise – he was playful one minute and then deadly serious the next, with a look in his eye that seem to say, "If you mess up, I'm going to break bones you didn't even know you had, and that's just for starters!"

Dad increasingly used his hand or belt instead of words to convey his unhappiness with whatever it was we had done wrong. Because of his volatility, my siblings and I would sit quietly in the tiny dining-cum-TV-room and not say a single word while he was in there with us. We were frightened of him; or at least, I was. If we dared to interrupt the sound from the TV with our whispering he would erupt with, "Shut... I bet I'll smash you to atoms in here!" He threatened to smash us to atoms quite a lot. That threat and his smoke-reddened eyes served notice that we would have to creep about for the rest of the day or pay sorely if we irritated him.

Occasionally his playful side would emerge, but this only caused further anxiety. In the middle of sipping his hot tea that had been whitened with the obligatory overdose of Carnation Milk, or watching something less than exciting on the TV, Dad would cause us to jump out of our skin by suddenly thumping his fists onto the dining table and shouting something bizarre such as, "I want a lion fe buy!" He would then turn to me with a sincere expression and ask in a pitiful tone: "Old Soldier, you know where I can find a good lion fe buy?"

I, of course, had to humour him with a polite, but nervous, response: "Er, maybe they have a spare one at the zoo?"

He would then react with incredulity and reject the only suggestion I had to offer. "What? You mean to tell me that you call yourself a man and you don't know where I can get a good lion to buy? Well, well, well, bwoy!"

A grin would eventually steal across his face and he'd fall into loud laughter. Trying to make myself invisible was my immediate strategic thought, but there was to be no escape while Dad was in such a heightened happy mood. He'd continue: "So, Old Soldier, you know what a British cat say when him hungry?" My obvious and very innocent response was of course, "Me-owww." Then, with yet another devilish grin on his face, he asked, "And you know what a Jamaican cat say when him hungry?" I could only think of repeating the same answer, because I thought all domestic cats made the same sound wherever they were in the world. However, my belly-tickled father knew better, and with the same incredulity as before, he sought to put me right: "No, no, no, man! A Jamaican puss only say one thing, you know!" Throwing his head back, he delivered his killer line: "Me-raaaasss!!!" With his impersonation of a strange sounding feline ringing in our ears, Dad was hysterical and laughing the roof off at his own joke. I could see from her much more subdued chuckles that Mum was impressed with that one. Just as I realised that a fabricated need to use the toilet would facilitate my escape, Dad hit me with another of his self-amusing party tricks. He let out a loud fart, and with a typical smirk, asked: "Hey boy, can you name that tune?" On another occasion, he did the same *trick* when I was walking up the stairs behind him. When he turned around to see what effect he'd had, I hurriedly raised my hands in the air, as if in fear of being robbed at gun point. My Dad was so tickled by my spontaneous collusion with his nonsense that his own laughter knocked him completely backwards onto the steps. With his uncontrollable laughter now causing tears to fall from his eyes, Dad turned over and crawled up the remainder of the steps. To amuse him further, I dropped onto my knees and followed behind him. We were both laughing when we reached the top, but my mother's stern expression made it obvious that she was anything but impressed with her husband and youngest child behaving like two fools in her presence.

Yes, Dad had a good sense of humour, but only so long as he was the one telling the jokes. Perhaps it was because my sisters were older, but he never bothered them with such foolery. We soon cottoned on that whenever he behaved in this way he was in a good mood, and if we were feeling brave enough, we might even suggest he give us a little pocket money. The old one penny coins with dates such as 1936, 1931, or even earlier would set my imagination racing, almost as fast as my legs could race my shadow to the nearest sweet shop.

When he wasn't angry or oddly playful, Dad was distant, and interacting less and less with my mother or with us, preferring instead to give his attention to the television or the *Daily Mirror* newspaper. He developed some annoying habits, like shaving at the dining table using a plastic basin filled with hot water and a small hand-held mirror, and picking his teeth with a snapped match stick and spitting the bits onto the carpet, driving my mother crazy as he did so. "Dirty habit," she would mutter under her breath.

Another favourite pastime was cutting corns from his toes while watching television. Shows such as Love Thy Neighbour, riddled with racially offensive language such "Nig-nog", were popular viewing, and Dad laughed along with the rest of the country. Following his do-it-yourself pedicure he would then summon either one of my unhappy sisters to fill a bowl with warm water and bathe his feet: "Come wash me foot fe me, gal!" he would command and then sit back with his Golden Virginia roll-up cigarettes and his whiskey or tea to enjoy some more TV. Whichever of my two sisters had the 'foot task' for that particular day, her close-to-tears face made it clear that she hated every second of it, but we all knew that only a death in the family (meaning their own) could rescue them from the dreaded chore. Thankfully, this was a task my father never asked me to do. Apparently such humiliations were the preserve of my sisters.

There were no family outings for us, and I mean none! There were no trips abroad, to the seaside, out to dinner, to the movies, or even to a local park. None! Television's Wish You Were Here? series was the closest we ever got to a beach. Not even the popular Notting Hill Carnival with its redolent with the culture of my parents' Caribbean home could motivate them to take us out. They were completely oblivious to the concept of spending quality family time together. If a lack of funds was the cause behind us being house-bound, that doesn't explain why we couldn't have a day out at the seaside or a park.

The closest thing to a family outing that I can recall, was a visit to Madame Tussauds with my mother and her favourite cousin, Aunt Vera, who also came to the UK in the 1950s. The two women had been skin-close since they were kids back in Jamaica. Like my mother, Vera had a medium-light complexion, curly-permed hair, was sexy-slim and very pretty with it. Belying her raucous laughter, she was the sort of fiery Jamaican woman who would repay you with a good slap if you dared to insult her youthful appearance by offering her your seat on a packed tube train. Huh, how very dare you! Vera worked on London Transport, but topped up her income by dressing ladies' hair on the side – and she was good at it, too! She did a fantastic job on my mother's hair most weekends, by using additional hair pieces to give her a regal top-knot look; fitting for any glam-puss magazine front cover, or even better, Skippy's happy eyes.

As we made our way around the wax models of the Hollywood stars and royalty, Mum and auntie were too preoccupied to hear my increasingly urgent pleas to use the toilet. The result, of course, was a pair of wet pants. To hide their embarrassment at what I had done, the women forced me to walk a couple of steps behind them. Perhaps it was felt that staying at home in future was what I deserved after my piddling display of appreciation for our one and only outing.

Considering that we spent most of our time at home, the few occasions that Dad would take Mum to a *'big people's* reggae dance' caused great excitement in the house. It always seemed like a great state occasion. I was amazed by my mother's Cinderella-like transformation; from a drab housewife to the most glamorous beauty that God had ever put on this Earth. She was classy and stunning; with jet-black hair, complete with the essential top knot, light-brown skin, a pretty beauty spot on her right temple, bright red nails, all squeezed into the latest dress that she had created for herself. Sister Jan would say, "You look lovely, Mummy," and my proud father would look up at her – for she stood a couple of inches taller than him – and add, "Yes, man; beautiful, man!" My mother's gushing red-lipstick smile said it all; she knew she looked sensational. A compliment from her adored husband was all she ever craved for her efforts. She clearly loved him with all her heart, and appreciated his simple but emphatic approval. It was all for him, the man she loved; her Skippy. They would step out the door and I wouldn't see them again until I awoke the next morning.

My mother had a great sense of self-respect and took pride in her appearance. Truth be told, she had posh pretensions. Image was everything. She knew she was black, of course, but she didn't want to be what she considered to be 'too black'; she was a lady, even if she was a black one. In her view, there was classy black and there was common black. Occasionally, she would make disparaging remarks about fellow Jamaicans, whom she would refer to as "typical black"; usually because of their less-than-smart appearance or inability to demonstrate a convincing command of 'proper' English, like she could, or both.

Indeed, my mother didn't want to look or sound 'black' at all. At home she was more relaxed about giving the Jamaican in her free rein, but never in public, and certainly not when answering the phone. When the phone rang, she would automatically restrain the *patois* so that when she picked up the receiver she would greet the caller with a contrived English accent better suited to Buckingham Palace than 13 Kingsley Road: "Good afternoon, may I help you?" This was, of course, completely hilarious to us kids. We would make fun of her by mimicking her posh voice. In good humour she would laugh along with us, but only after she'd hung up the phone.

My dear mother felt that fitting in meant looking and sounding 'proper' English, which, unfortunately, stirred a preoccupation with skin complexion. When I hit my teens, she warned me, "Never bring home a girl who is darker than you". Her determination to be as 'white' as possible drove her to buy skin products that had the effect of lightening her skin, or at least that's what the products promised. She called a particular favourite product, 'skin toner'. I'm not sure that it worked; I certainly didn't notice her skin getting any lighter. She ignored advice that such products could be harmful; feeling that the prize of fairer skin was worth the risk.

Despite her effort to look and sound the part, my mother rarely went out for any reason, other than to get her hair done at Aunt Vera's in Ruislip, or to do the weekly shopping at Safeway on Kilburn High Road. The only other regular treat was bingo, which she absolutely loved. On an average day you would find her at home in her favourite flower-patterned tie-head and worn-out slippers, busy cooking, cleaning and sewing. As well as making clothes for herself and other females in the family, she sewed blouses, dresses, trousers and bikinis for a local clothing manufacturer in the Finchley Road.

It is Mum's singing that most stands out in my memory; as she cleaned she sang, and by the end of her performance, every speck of dirt would have been removed from her personal concert hall. Hers was a clear, faultless, Sarah Vaughan-like voice that was truly fit for the radio. Even though she wasn't attending church at this time, she would stick to a fairly limited repertoire of religious songs that she had learned in church as a girl back in Jamaica – 'Amazing Grace', How Great Thou Art', or her favourite, 'Precious Memories', which she would sing almost every day: "Precious memories, how they linger, how they ever flood my soul..." There was only one problem: she could not quite pronounce the 'c' in "precious", so it came out sounding something like "preshush". We were greatly amused by her efforts to get it right, but no matter how much she tried, she just could not pronounce that damn 'c' as it should have been. I would find myself quietly singing along in the background, as if trying to *will* her to get that 'c' right, and yes, I could hold a note too! Indeed, later on in life, I would admit to myself that I should have been a singer, but it would be a career move that I would never have the courage to pursue. The perfect duo: Doreth and Son.

Dad could also sing, although the quality of his over-confident efforts never quite matched my mother's polished performance. He would come out with something from a Shirley Bassey or Tom Jones songbook, and just a line, never more than that. It was as if he just wanted to remind us that he was home and awake. Sometimes, after a drink or two...or three...he would get carried away and sing while slowly gyrating his hips. Throwing his empty arms around the waist of some large invisible woman and with a lurid, sickly expression of love on his boozed-out face, he would pause to kiss her before continuing to woo her with his increasingly unstable feet. It was a truly embarrassing sight, and I'm sure his unseen dance partner was as glad as me when it was all over. She may have been invisible but I could still sense her utter relief, the poor woman!

It was a good thing that my mother could sing solo, because future events would threaten to make her precious Skippy the invisible one.

7. LORD, ME DUTCHY POT BON UP!

My mother was at her culinary best on Sundays. She would start at first light, cooking our traditional rice and peas, and roasting a tasty chicken that had been caked in curry and black pepper seasoning from the night before. Sunday 'dinner' would always be cooked by eleven thirty a.m.; I still don't know why – just Jamaican tradition, I suspect. 'Dinner' would then be served in the afternoon and be washed down with Mother's Mum's delicious pineapple and milk smoothie whose secret ingredient was a sprinkling of nutmeg. I'd have drunk buckets of that stuff if she'd only let me.

Her Saturday chicken and vegetable soup was another big winner with us. It was full of voluptuous dumplings, sweet potato, soft carrots and yam, and I couldn't get enough of it. I could see memories of her homeland, and perhaps of Aunty Bet's cooking, creep across her face as she dropped the ingredients into the cooking pot. Mum knew I coveted an extra dumpling or two, and she would tease me with comments such as, "You must have dumpling mouth, boy!" A tin of Campbell's chicken soup served as a base, which she would dress up with a touch of thyme, the compulsory black pepper, mixed seasoning and salt. Sometimes she would use Campbell's chicken noodle soup, but I always got the impression that my mother had picked these cans up by mistake. Either way, the soup was truly delicious. I'd be licking my lips in anticipation of a second helping, and yes, more dumplings, please!

During the week, Mum served up Jamaican fare, such as curried goat, pig or cow foot, and ackee and salted fish. When Mum was in a hurry, we would have to settle for corned beef and rice, but even that was made tasty by adding onions and spices. On rare occasions, we would be treated to snacks such as beef patties or salt-fish fritters, and at Christmas, we would feast on red snapper and turkey. I wasn't keen on everything my mother would cook, though. I definitely drew the line at dishes such as cow tongue. Not for me, thank you very much! There was one isolated occasion when Dad treated us to Chinese food. My eager mouth watered as he dished out the exotic takeaway, comprising of moist noodles, roast duck, and sweet and sour prawns. We were soon tucking in; well, all apart from my mother, who reluctantly placed the unusual looking food into her suspicious mouth. Then all hell broke loose when Dad said the food tasted great, "even though Chinese people often cook cat and dog meat instead of de real thing". Well, I didn't know my mother was capable of moving so fast, but in a flash, she had raced from the table into the bathroom, where we could hear her heaving, coughing and spitting to get whatever the animal product was out of her sorry mouth. In the meantime, Dad casually took her plate and emptied it into his, while continuing his unappetizing charges: "Yes man, dem Chinese people eat all kinda ting: puss, rat, snake - all kinda thing! But it taste good, boy!" finishing with a loud laugh. We didn't really believe him, but Mum obviously did.

Sunday mealtimes were an occasion. Sometimes my father, sitting at the head of the table opposite Mum, would wear a suit jacket just for the meal. Mum would proudly lay a delicious-smelling roast chicken on the dinner table and my father would ceremoniously cut into the bird, before sharing out the generous portions with relish. He would always make sure that I was well looked after, plunking a sizable chunk of meat on my plate. "There you go, Old Soldier," he would say, flashing those perfect teeth of his in a smile. My mother would help herself, but only after everyone else had been given their share. Dad would tuck in, Mum would laugh obediently at his jokes, Jan would eat quietly and Beverley would tease me for topping my rice and peas with onions and juices from the roasting pan: "Urgh, look at those horrible onions on Ian's plate, they look like worms, urgh!"

Mother didn't bother too much with dessert, but when she did, it was vanilla or strawberry ripple ice cream with a dollop of fruit salad. Very Jamaican! It was only later on in life that my mother started baking gorgeous cakes, filled with rum or wine. Even if her efforts at icing were a complete disaster to look at, the cakes themselves were the best on Earth. Her diversification into cake-making contributed to the expansion of her waistline, but she was still gorgeous, and she knew it, and besides, she knew Dad loved his women on the larger side.

There was one problem with my mother's cooking; she would frequently get so absorbed in her sewing whilst listening to her favourite Jim Reeves albums that she would forget about the food cooking in the kitchen. On smelling the burning, she would race her own shadow through the house to save her pitiful creation. "Quick, quick," she would shout as we leapt out of her way. Then came the predictable woeful words as she examined the blackened contents of the dutchy pot: "Lord, me pot burn up – again!" Dad would usually be oblivious to the latest kitchen drama and have his eyes glued to TV news or sport. It was us kids that would dissolve in laughter. Even my mother would be forced to laugh at her hapless self, but not before putting her head through the serving hatch and warning us to "shut up". Even then I was certain that I could hear her giggling along with us. Once served, we were sometimes left wondering whether the meal was fish, pork, or chicken. The charred remains were still edible, just about, but it was a taste of my childhood that was mostly happy and full of laughter.

8. LOVE IS A SONG

I WAS IN ST MARY'S HOSPITAL with my pitiful self, having broken my leg during a school football game. At the end of visiting hours on the children's ward a few floors up from where I had been born only a few years earlier, my mother looked on uncomfortably as other, mostly white mothers, kissed their sick children good night. Her woeful expression told me that she was trying to awaken something of her rarely seen tactile nature, in order to deliver what was surely expected of her. Then, wearing something of a contrived smile, and keen to get the ghastly task over with, Mum swooped down, aiming her lips at my cheek. I felt the breeze, but no kiss; she had completely missed her stationary target. It was an awkward and embarrassing moment for us both, as my maternal hawk paused to calculate whether to try her torturous act again. As for me, I wanted to escape our mutual plight by diving under the covers, but before I could action the thought, Mum's second attempt hit the mark, and without a word of goodbye, she hastened from the ward faster than a frightened hare.

That is the one and only memory I have of my mother voluntarily kissing me; forced to do so because of peer pressure and needing to *look* the part. There was a previous occasion when she refused to help me out of the bath. As I feared, my wet feet slipped off the edge and I fell to the sodden floor, face first. As my chin hit before the rest of me, my front teeth penetrated my tongue, leaving what would be a life-long reminder.

Oh, poor me. Poor Mum. I guess it was a blessing that she didn't work as a carer with the elderly or infirm; that would not have been a good career choice! She was absolutely lovely but just not very tactile; she demonstrated her love for her family through her cooking, sewing and singing – especially her singing. Through her songs, I knew she was saying *I love you, big-head boy.* If she was going to be touchy-feely, then that would be behind closed bedroom doors with her husband.

Still, I would grow into an adult without experiencing hugs or kisses from either of my parents, which is perhaps why I would later seek affection from strangers and people who were not always good for me. The utter lack of physical warmth in my formative years rendered me as uncomfortable as my mother in attempting to give or receive affection and led me to spend much of my life feeling that I was not worthy of love. I mean, if my parents couldn't demonstrate love towards me then how the hell could anyone else? The feeling of not being good enough for love would follow me like an invisible Siamese twin; socially, at work, and at home - wherever home would be. My chances to love and be loved would constantly be undermined by my sense of mistrust, unworthiness and suspicion. 'Ian', that little un-hugged boy within me could never quite believe it to be true whenever love was offered, even though love was all he craved.

Out of St Mary's and back home, my naughty behaviour sometimes provoked my mother's anger, but there was always something soft and sweet behind her threats to roast me "like pork", such as when I would *'borrow'* the lubricating oil that she had purchased for her industrial sewing machine – a heavy duty piece of equipment that was as noisy as a speedboat. The trouble is that my Dad had bought me an awesome bright-red 'Chopper' bicycle, which was every boy's dream at the time. Its wheels just happened to like the same oil as her sewing machine and my bike was more important, of course it was. My overuse of the oil meant there was very little left when I sneakily returned the can to its place near the back of her sewing machine where it lived. My mother suspected that her dwindling oil was greasing the wheels of my pride and joy, and despite my protestations of innocence, she knew I was lying. I had a feeling that she really didn't mind at all, but would have preferred that I had asked rather than to steal and then lie about it. Anyway, she never did make a Sunday roast of me, and two minutes after sternly questioning me, she would be singing the house down: "Precious Lord, take my hand, lead me on, let me stand..."

These were the good times at 13 Kingsley Road; times when I knew security and love through my mother's lilting tones. I didn't know it then, but darkness was on the way, and her joyous singing would turn to weeping.

My parents had a small group of friends who would pop into the house on a regular basis as they were passing by. We saw a lot of Miss Evelyn, a short, dark-skinned Jamaican-born woman who lived somewhere in Neasden with her three teenage kids – two boys and a girl. There was the jet black, camp, large, and flamboyant Mr Thomas, who seemed to eat nothing but garlic for breakfast, judging by his breath, which tarnished his appeal to the level of a bloody drive-by shoot out. He really belonged on stage, as his booming voice demanded—and got—everyone's attention. There was also Mr Hector, a quiet, serious man in a gangster hat, who always ended up in a huge argument with my dad about something or other. One of them had to be right, and they would get very animated, before Mr Hector would return to his taciturn self, and slink out of the front door.

Dad's best friend and confidante was an older Jamaican man, who came to visit so often you'd be forgiven for assuming he was part of our immediate family. We called him Uncle Sonny; my sisters and I formed the habit of referring to most black adult visitors to the house as 'uncle' or 'aunt', even if they weren't. I guess it was our way of showing respect. Uncle Sonny and his family still lived in the basement rooms at 41 Lowfield Road, my family's first lodgings in London, where the two men had met before my birth. They remained inseparable after my family moved to Kingsley Road. It was unsaid in words, but my Dad and Uncle Sonny shared a brotherly love for one another.

Dad would often affectionately refer to Sonny as 'Money' or 'Sunshine'; the former description because he was lucky at card games, and the latter because the house was always happier when he was there. He was a tall, dark-skinned, paper-thin man, with a jovial demeanour and an ever-present smile. He always told jokes, and though I often did not understood them, I laughed along with him just to show my appreciation of his kindness which sometimes included him giving me his spare coins from his pocket. This was a real boon as Dad rarely gave me any pocket money; like a scene from Mission Impossible, I would have to wait until my father was asleep and raid his pockets without stirring him. Well, someone had to fund my craving for custard tarts and sherbet fountains. Oh yes, and my Love Hearts.

It was my job to keep the tea flowing as the two men entertained each other with their take on whatever was on the TV. I would hand Sonny his cup of tea with just the right amount of Carnation milk and remain rooted to the spot, until he'd take that first important sip. "Ahhhhhhh," he would sigh, with a satisfied expression on his face. Only then would my feet become unstuck and allow me to resume my place on the floor at the back of the room, where I would sit until their cups needed a refill. I was secretly quite proud that my tea won his approval.

The only tense moment that I can recall between the two friends happened when Sonny visited the house while my mother and father were having an argument about something trivial. He jokingly took my mother's side, but my dad took it badly, telling him, "Listen, don't come to my house and come between me and my wife, you hear!" Uncle Sonny laughed it off, but Dad continued to grumble. Ten minutes later, though, the two men had their shoes off, and were laughing and drinking in front of the TV once more.

Sonny came to the house most days – weekend afternoons and weekday evenings, and he wouldn't leave our house until well after midnight on most nights; after endless tea and roll-up cigarettes, a little booze, and my Dad giving up the struggle to stay awake in front of the then meager choice of three TV channels. Sometimes sleep would overtake them both and we would find them the next morning, fast asleep with their heads on the dining table. We found this hilarious. Even my mother smiled at the sight of them; she didn't seem to mind having her bed to herself all night, and evidently Sonny's wife, Dotty, felt the same way. At least my mother knew Skippy was home and wasn't out playing elsewhere.

Occasionally, Mr Hector and Mr Thomas would join Dad and Sonny to debate the issues of the world in our smoke-filled dining/TV room. My mother would leave the men to it and just keep on sewing on her machine, leaving me to carry out the tea duties. Sometimes the discussions became quite heated. My dad would have to be right about everything (I think I picked up some of his bullishness in my adult life). Whenever he was losing an argument he would assert himself even more: "Look, man, don't come into my house and tell me no rubbish, you hear?" He got his information from the *Daily Mirror*, the TV news, and the car radio, and once he had made up his mind, no one was going to tell him anything different. His voice was usually the loudest to be heard, and therefore the most convincing, or so he thought. But the deceptively quiet Mr Hector was not to be made to look a fool, and he gave as good as he got.

Hector: "No, man, is the Russians who will start World War Three."

Dad: "That is rubbish, man! Listen, don't come to me house and argue with me. Is China who people must afraid of. Dem build all kinds a nuclear weapon which will wipe out everybody else in minutes, man!"

Hector: "No, man! Ah who tell you dat? Me say, is the Russian's dem!"

Uncle Sonny, meanwhile, would be so completely engrossed in football on the TV that his entire body would assume the role of the player with the ball. I could be walking by his chair, and in his unconscious trance-like state, Sonny's feet would suddenly jet out and make all the moves, as if he was on the actual field and tackling his way past the opposing team. Whilst his feet had the invisible ball, his mouth was the mouthpiece of the head coach; frantically (and loudly!) steering his star player, himself, to the net. In a move of my own, and to escape becoming his unwitting ball, kicked and maimed for life to the back of our TV screen-come-net, I'd skilfully skip over his jolting feet and take my place on the floor at the back of the room. My sisters and I thought Sonny was hilarious, but we muffled our giggles so as to not attract attention to ourselves. Irritating children were not to be seen or heard from when the menfolk were at their footie, unless we were on tea-making duties; which involved manoeuvring hot beverage past adult kicking feet and risk wearing instead of serving it.

The men could argue for hours, and often did, while slowly drinking themselves into a stupor. Some of their conversations left me petrified about the world outside our house and the evil that men seemed capable of committing against each other. Later, lying in bed, I would worry about whether the Chinese or Russians were going to allow me to live to the morning or nuke me into nothingness in the middle of the night. But the conversations weren't all doom and gloom. The men were also appreciative of the occasional glimpse of female cleavage on the TV screen. Philadelphia's singing trio, the Three Degrees, was especially popular, followed by LaBelle. Dad also had a soft spot for Shirley Bassey. "Yes maaan!" the men would approvingly bray in one united semi-drunk voice.

The women of the family appreciated the cut of a well-turned out man, too. While the men were out, I can recall hearing my mother and Aunt Vera watching TV, making reference to the "front" on Errol Brown, lead singer of Hot Chocolate, giggling in strong approval: "Look pon da front deh! Hey heeeey!" My mother had a way of repeatedly pouting her lips, just to cement the point.

9. OUR PALACE AS A REFUGE

For a while Aunt Vera lived in a spare room downstairs in our house. She had three kids and a husband of her own but was experiencing marital problems, so she left them behind in Ruislip and came to live with us for respite. Vera had access to her own toilet and kitchen, but had to share our family bathroom on the first floor.

I really loved Aunt Vera. She was always sweet, good-humoured and kind to me (well, apart from at the waxwork museum, that is!). Like my mother, Vera was a strong and very proud woman who shared my mother's high sense of self-respect. Physically, she had the same light skin and good looks of my mother, but she was not quite so pretty. In my eyes, no one was as beautiful as my sweet mother.

The cousins would spend much of their time in the sewing room (which doubled as my bedroom at night), chatting and whispering about 'grown-up issues' while my mother stitched away and I drifted in and out. Sometimes, when my mother left her sewing to check on dinner, Aunt Vera would follow, and the two women's gossip and howling laughter would spill out of the kitchen. When their chat became too loud for my dad to hear the television, he would simply shout "Shuuu...!" at them at the top of his voice. He never completed the word; the first threatening sound was supposed to be enough. He did the same to us kids when we were too loud around him, coupled with a terrifyingly long stare that said, *My belt will be next, if you don't obey.* I would button my lip, and avert my eyes from his death-ray gaze; but after some time, when I found the courage to glance in his direction again, I would find he was still glaring at me.

But Aunt Vera was not the kind of woman you could tell to shut up, and on one such occasion she came into the TV/dining room and, with hands on hips, stood in front of the TV and stared my dad down. "Look, Skippy, is me you tell fe shut up? You are so damn rude!" She flicked her curly perm to accentuate her point. "Woman, move out the way, you hear!" was his feeble response, picking his teeth and spitting the loosened food to the floor at the same time. They were not in public now, so there were no posh English accents to be heard, just raw "back home" Jamaican dialect. My aunt stared at him and claimed victory with some exaggerated sucking of teeth. She swaggered back to the kitchen, where the two women carried on as before, but deliberately louder this time. Dad accepted defeat; he knew better than to get into an argument with two fiery Jamaican women. They soon disappeared back into the sewing room to chat for the rest of the afternoon.

Vera and Mum loved Dad really, and he knew it, and he loved them too, in his own tarnished macho way. He may not have been king of England but he was king in his own house – with an occasionally bruised ego, thanks to Aunt Vera's bravery. I was good at being invisible at such tense moments in Kingsley Road.

Aunt Vera definitely had her fiery side. I recall one occasion when Sam, her husband, visited in the hope of reconciling with her, bringing two of their kids with him. Vera lost her cool, grabbed one of my mother's glass candlesticks, and cracked it over Sam's head, causing blood to spurt from the wound onto the hallway carpet; which, thankfully, was as red as the blood that hit it. Derek, their young son, was in hysterics as he tried to separate his battling and bloody parents. I just stood, in shock at the violence that had erupted from my darling Aunt Vera. Mum and Dad soon succeeded in separating the quarrelling pair, and I retreated behind the sofa. I didn't see Vera again until the next day, when, on seeing me, she gave me the same sweet smile with which she always greeted me.

Vera eventually moved out and went back to live with Sam, or that's the impression I got from overhearing adult gossip. But that wasn't the end of the drama at 13 Kingsley Road; in fact, it was only the beginning.

Our family next gave refuge to Pat, who was married to Byron, one of my dad's five, now UK-based, brothers. She and their two young daughters had moved into our house after a falling out with Byron.

Aunty Pat was very different in appearance to my mother or Vera. She was short, fat and very dark-skinned, and she wore a rather obvious tight-fitting curly black wig. She also wore skirts that were a little too short for my mother's liking, and had an unfortunate habit of sitting in a somewhat mannish pose, with her legs apart. It was not a pleasant sight at all, and I could tell that my mother was less than happy by the way in which she tried to avoid looking in Pat's direction. As young as I was, I can recall thinking that my mother would never sit like that! My mother was a lady.

Depressed, Pat sat eating green grapes by the bucket load and spitting the seeds into the palm of her hand. Sometimes she would start laughing, then she would start crying again for no obvious reason, as far as I could tell. My mother would just continue sewing and ignore Pat's mood swings while her little daughters played together at her bare feet. I was far too young to understand why Pat was so changeable with her moods, so I kind of ignored her too.

One day, Uncle Byron arrived. Red-skinned, he was very similar looking in complexion to my dad, but unlike my dad he had a full head of hair, and was taller and thinner with a neat jet-black goatee to complete his look. He was dressed smartly, in a blue suit and tie. He had come to try to reconcile with his wife, or so we thought.

Pat reluctantly left the safety of the room she shared with her daughters and my mother's old defunct sewing machine, and agreed to speak with a pleading Byron in the hallway at the top of the stairs. The house was quiet enough at first, but after a short while, voices became disconcertingly raised. Dad went to see what was happening between his brother and his wife, only to find Byron man-handling her.

With Dad's help, a tearful Pat tried to extract herself from Byron's grasp. My sisters and I looked on from the safety of the TV/dining room as the warring couple's petrified daughters ran to save their mother. An infuriated Byron appeared to retreat slightly after Dad successfully pried his hands off Pat, scolding him in the process. But in a flash, my uncle revealed that he had more than a nice shirt under his suit jacket – he pulled out a kitchen knife from his breast pocket and made a determined thrust in the direction of Pat's stomach.

I nearly wet myself with fear at the sight of the frantic commotion of the three tussling adults and their two now-hysterical little girls. Pat's screams were equally hysterical as my dad wrestled the six-inch blade away from his maniacal brother. "God, him want fe kill me! Lord help me!" Pat yelled before collapsing with her terrified girls to the floor.

My mother flew to the aid of Pat and her girls, as Dad bundled his younger brother down the stairs and out the front door, cursing at him all the way. "You fucking mad? You bring knife come into my house! Come out and don't come back with your fuckries!" That meant unacceptable nonsense, in *black* language.

To see such violence within my home, acted out by people to whom I was related, people whom I loved... that was truly a scary day in my young life. At least *my parents* were kind to each other, I reassured myself.

10. MUM GOES MISSING

ANOTHER PARTICULARLY SCARY DAY arrived when I awoke to find that there was no breakfast on the table and my mother was nowhere to be seen. It soon transpired that she had left in the night to live at Aunt Vera's house following a heated argument with my dad; she had, in fact, done 'an Aunt Vera!' Despite my early years, I knew my mother would not leave my sisters and me without good reason, and that something quite serious must be behind her actions. Beverley and Jan whispered away between themselves but I remained in the dark about the reason for Mum's flight. What was obvious was that Dad was stomping around the house in a hostile mood, muttering unintelligibly to himself – and of course I did not dare ask him anything.

I thought about my missing Mum every second of the few days that she was away before she returned one night while Dad was out on his night shift. I was over the moon to see her and she had clearly missed us too, even though, in her style, there were no hugs or kisses. She cooked us some food – never mind that Dad had already done that before leaving the house only half an hour or so earlier. She also tidied up, and then said to Jan and Beverley, "Now you keep this house clean while I am away." My heart sank. She did not intend to stay.

After an hour watching TV with us she said she had to go, but I really didn't want her to and said so. Perhaps without thinking she decided to take me with her, and it wasn't long before I was being tucked into bed next to my mother at Aunt Vera's. I was so very pleased to be with my mother.

The morning came quickly, but instead of my mother or Vera coaxing me awake, I found myself being hoisted out of the warmth of the bed and into my dad's angry arms. He put me over his shoulder and grabbed my clothes with his free hand as he hissed and cursed his way out of Vera's house into the cold morning air. What an awakening! I saw my mother standing with her cousin by the front door, but she said nothing as Dad all but threw me and my clothes into his car, which already had its engine running. He was soon sitting in the driver's seat with his foot on the pedal. As he sped away, like a scene from a kidnapping movie, he turned to me with a cigarette in one corner of his mouth and said in no uncertain terms: "If you ever leave the house with someone you don't know again, I will give you the hiding of your damn life." I was too cold and fearful to say anything other than a meek, "Okay." I don't think he saw my tears.

My mother returned home a few days later and life seemed to carry on as before. I never did learn what had caused the brief break-up. Unfortunately, permanent marital disasters lay ahead.

11. YOUNG BOY, YOU'RE TOO GIRLIE-GIRLIE!

I WAS NOW ABOUT SEVEN YEARS OLD. Seldom seen or heard, my principal characteristics were my small frame and painfully shy nature. There was a sense that I was always looking up from under everyone's feet.

Dad was mostly out at work, so I spent my time with Mum and my sisters. Perhaps it was due to my predominantly female environment that I too displayed the occasional feminine or camp mannerism. But I was just a child - happy, carefree me, and wasn't at all aware of what such behaviour might imply in respect of my possible sexuality. I certainly had no idea what words like sexuality, gay or homosexual meant. Such adult subjects did not yet register with me.

Despite my young age and genuine innocence, there were signs that Dad had begun to worry about my possible sexuality. On a vividly memorable day, I was at home tucking into my lunch: delicious buttered mash potato and overdone, slightly tough-to-chew, steak. Mum and I both looked up from our plates when we heard the front door open. Dad had unexpectedly returned home from work. We held our breath in curious anticipation as, in his patent style, he stomped his way up the stairs and into the room where we were eating. He didn't say hello, but just stood in the doorway looking in my direction, with a curious, almost bemused expression on his face. Mum asked what he was doing home at this time, but Dad didn't reply. Instead, in a quick fluid movement, he reached into his breast pocket and retrieved what looked like a colour magazine. He then strode over to where I was sitting and placed it, front cover up, on the table beside my plate.

I'm not sure what I expecting to see, but my potato-filled mouth ceased chewing as my little brain began to register what was pictured: an array of topless white women with very large breasts, happily strutting their stuff and smiling up at me. I felt as though a bolt of lightning had hit me, causing my skin to peel from top to toe onto the wine-red carpeted floor under my feet, exposing my naked inner self.

Frozen to my seat, I had no idea what to say or do to escape this terrible assault upon my person at the hands of my own father. So I just sat and gazed down at the paper-bound ladies gazing up at me.

Crashing into my dumbfounded senses, my incensed mother rose to her feet shouting: "Skippy, what the hell do you think you're doing!"

He again completely ignored her, and continued to peer down at me, as if trying to assess my reaction to his surprise lunchtime gift from hell. My state of acute embarrassment left me ready to combust into flames. Dad, clearly dissatisfied by my un-macho response, leaned over my shoulder so that he could thumb through the pages whilst monitoring my expression. This was sex education Jamaican style, and he hadn't finished with me yet. He became more frantic as he struggled to locate an image that would generate excitement rather than fear on his young son's face: blonde girls, Asian girls, black girls, all smiling up at me. Of course, none of their floppy bits produced the reaction he was hoping for.

My eternity of shame continued with the turn of each page and the revelation of yet another scary female body. Perhaps the eternity was only a matter of seconds, but it sure felt like hours, and in front of my beloved mother, too! I couldn't imagine her naked, and didn't ever want to think of her that way.

Finally, Dad thumped his hand down on the table and declared: "Yes man. Mi bwoy like the girls dem... yes, man!"

How on Earth he could have come to that conclusion was way beyond me. I quietly prayed never to see another naked woman again, at least not in front of my parents. No, not at all!

A short second or two later and Dad left the house as quickly and unexpectedly as he had arrived, taking his top shelf smut with him. With the emphatic words, "Lord, have mercy", Mum retook her seat and resumed eating. My mouth still had food in it, but it wasn't capable of speaking, chewing, or anything else. I felt dead; I was deceased and my corpse was still sitting at the family dinner table with a knife and fork in my immobile hands. My eyes remained fixed on the spot where Dad's girly magazine had only moments earlier stolen my previously keen appetite. I swore to myself that if I ever heard his unexpected footsteps again, it would be my cue to run and hide under anything big enough to accommodate my small being.

Thanks to my dad, as far as I was concerned, all women could keep their clothes on forever, and in all circumstances; even at the beach or when taking a bath. I wasn't interested in seeing them naked; not now, not ever! Not that I was thinking of men or boys either; I was a child, and a desire to see people naked wasn't yet part of my thinking. Give me a football, model car or gun, or even a doll, but spare me the naked people thing!

What on Earth made Dad do that? Perhaps he knew something I didn't, or at least, he suspected it. All I knew was that I'd rather swap my eyes for Stevie Wonder's than look through a girlie magazine in front of my parents again. My parents were very private about their own sex lives, and frankly, I was glad of that fact. I didn't want to know what they did in the privacy of their bedroom, thank you very much!

Looking back, my worried Dad had obviously made an association between my mannerisms and possible sexuality. But if he was really honest, he would have to admit that he was actually worried about himself, and the dent to his macho man pride for having produced a sissy for a son. Any son of his had to follow in his stomping footsteps, and this included lusting after smiley topless women. *Sorry Daddy, but it ain't happening!*

I guess I should be grateful he hadn't presented me with a magazine full of naked men. Now that might have been interesting, especially if it excited me in a way the girlie magazine didn't. Once my saliva hit my plate of mash, it would have provided the confirmation that Dad had been dreading; he had indeed produced a filthy homosexual for a son. Of course, the sight of my gushing mouth would have also marked the beginning of my life as the youngest child living on the streets of London. There would be no homosexuals of any age living at 13 Kingsley Road, not under my Dad's roof!

My dawning homosexuality would never be acceptable to either of my parents. I was gay, either by birth or nurture, and in the years ahead my parents would be forced to revisit their feelings on the subject.

12. BINGO! SPEND, SPEND, SPEND!!!

I LOVED TO ROLLER SKATE AS OFTEN AS I COULD, that was until I made a complete fool of myself by wearing them on a shopping errand for Mum. As I perused for the items on the list in my hand, I lost my balance and crashed into the neatly arranged shelves. After struggling to my feet-on-wheels amongst the scattered groceries on the floor, I beat a hasty retreat towards the exit, as the enraged shop keeper shouted after me to "Get out and don't come back. You stupid, stupid...!" My dad and Uncle Sonny, on the other hand, loved to gamble. At one point they set up a gambling den in a spare room in our house, but Mum was having none of it. On a few occasions the two men bundled me into the back of Dad's car, on our way to one of their favourite gambling dens, somewhere in Harlesden, if I recall correctly. I would sit quietly at the back of the smoke-filled room, as the gaggle of Jamaican men cursed their way through the win-or-lose card game: "Blood claaaaat, man"... "You too damn teef"..."Kiss my ass, you fu..." It all sounded very serious to me, but I think I detected a good dose of subliminal humour, belying the wry threats to cut off each other's balls and slash each other's throats: "Raaas claaat man, I bet I cut you throat in here!"

It certainly looked like a lot of money was at stake; but then again, any money in note form was a lot to my young eyes. Some of the men would slip me a few coins, which I gratefully accepted, even if I struggled to say "thank you very much" through my smoky coughs and sleepy eyes. As the minutes turned into hours, and despite the noise, I'd eventually fall asleep at the back of the room.

My mother wasn't shy of the odd flutter herself. She had three great passions in life: my father, mangoes and bingo, in that order! As well as her bingo evening during the week, she followed the horses on a Saturday morning. I would always have to get up early on a Saturday morning to go and buy the *Daily Mirror*, which listed the races for the day on the back pages. When it was the Grand National, all the kids would be able to bet on our favourite horses, which was great fun. Red Rum proved lucrative for us all, and my one-pound winning meant the world to me: sweets galore!

Our lives changed significantly on a cold winter night when my mother returned home from her regular bingo night at the Rank State building on Kilburn High Road, which was just a ten-minute walk up the road from our house. She had won the jackpot of five thousand pounds! This was a gigantic sum of money back in 1968. My father was out at his night job, so my mother had only the lodger downstairs to tell. I learned of it the next day.

Soon there were not one, but two new cars outside. Dad had given Mum driving lessons, and she passed her test first time around. His car was a blue Morris, and she now the proud new owner of a white Ford Cortina. There were new curtains at the windows and new luxury carpet throughout the hallways. My mother also purchased a bright orange and green living-room set, which was reserved for her front lounge that no one other than very special guests could enter. That was Mum's 'show-off' room. It even had a mini bar, stocked with all kinds of alcoholic drinks that no one was allowed to touch.

The other main expenditure was a holiday to Jamaica, which, sadly, didn't include my sisters and me. Mum and Dad dropped us of in Coventry to stay with her sister, Aunt Edna, Uncle Neville, and their seven children, and they promptly jumped on a plane to visit family "back home", as my mother put it. I'd heard a lot about Jamaica, and about my grandparents, but couldn't really imagine a country that was always hot, and where my mother could eat mangoes off the trees in the garden. I knew reggae music came from there, though, and I loved reggae.

This was my first separation from Mum and Dad, and they were going to be gone for an eternity of five weeks. As my parents drove away, Aunt Edna sensed my anxiety, and did her best to make me feel at home. She succeeded, and my cousins with their odd Midlands accents and I were soon running all over the small but happy house, laughing and giggling as we did so. They really did sound strange to me, but they were all friendly and equally intrigued by my London accent. They were all much younger than me, except bubbly Doreene, who was nearly my age. Together with her siblings, Elaine, Florence, Tracy, Maxine, Calvin and Phillip and my sisters, we spent most of the hot summer school recess playing in their narrow turfed garden whilst Uncle Neville was at work or in front of the TV. Aunty cooked non-stop and was always offering me something to eat; some fruit, a piece of cake or a fried dumpling, which I gulped down in the hope of being offered even more. Aunt Edna soon became my new best friend. Her delicious cooking and the company of a slew of cousins made me forget my worries about my parents' absence.

The family home backed onto an alley, which ran the length of the street. At its end was a noisy railway depot, protect by railings, which I could have squeezed through if I was so tempted. I was fascinated by the rust-riddled coal carts lumbering to and fro and I dreamt about whence they had come and where they might be going. Doreene introduced me to a small sweet shop, where I spent what little money I had on sherbet fountains and rhubarb and custard boiled sweets, by the pocketful. I was very happy indeed. Doreene and I formed a bond that summer, which the passing years would not tarnish.

When a tanned and gleaming Mum and Dad returned to collect us, they brought a case full of Jamaican fruit, together with stories about their holiday. Mum chuckled as she insisted that the mangoes were not for sharing, but then that's exactly what she did with Aunty Edna and Uncle Neville's family. I could tell that she was very happy to be reunited us, as we headed down the M1 motorway towards 13 Kingsley Road. It was good to be back in my own room and own bed that night, but most especially, it was good to see my darling Mum again.

13. SLEEPING WITH STRANGERS

I WAS ABOUT EIGHT and completely astonished upon hearing the news that I had two older brothers, and that, thanks to the bingo win, they were going to come over from that faraway place that I'd always heard of called Jamaica.

"I didn't know I had two brothers!" I told Dad.

"Not one, but two?" I asked my mother.

"Yes, two," she replied with a laugh.

I was truly fascinated. What would they would be like? Would they be big like Dad, or small like me?

In what seemed like days rather than weeks, Dad was on his way to collect them from Heathrow. A few hours later, there they were, standing at the front door with their battered brown leather suitcases in hand, looking up the stairs at me and my sisters. My two brothers had arrived!

We peeped down at our strange-looking siblings from the top of the stairs and whispered to each other about which one might be Bunny or Leo. My sisters and I cleverly guessed that eleven-year-old Bunny was the smaller of the two and that thirteen-year-old Leo must be the big one. They looked nothing like my sisters and I – they were very dark skinned and wore what to me looked like 1950s gangster hats and suits.

My big brothers stood in the open doorway for what seemed like ages without saying a word. They looked so nervous that I thought they were going turn and run. They were in a new country and about to head into an unfamiliar house, which must have been very scary for them.

Finally, Mum told my petrified brothers to come inside. The two boys came in, and under Mum's direction, took their suitcases upstairs. They were soon standing on the upstairs landing with my sisters and me, looking down at the red carpet beneath their shiny black shoes. They still said nothing. Dad closed the front door and made his way upstairs and introduced us, laughing as he did.

My two new older brothers opened up their respective cases, to reveal virtually no clothes, but loads of fruit that they'd picked before flying. Some of them were new to me-guineps, breadfruit, and sugar cane; and mangoes, which I already knew. I was uncomfortable around my brothers, but I certainly liked their goodies, especially the juicy guineps. My mother pounced on the mangoes. "I could eat these all day and night," she laughed. Bunny and Leo just stood frozen, silent.

My parents had no concept of the value of bonding, and did nothing to help my brothers and the rest of the family get to know one another. Over dinner, my impossibly shy older brothers spoke just enough for me to ascertain that they had heavy Jamaican accents. When bedtime came around, I was suddenly aware that I would be sharing my bedroom – and its one double bed – with these two silent strangers. I was understandably reticent, but my mother ignored my anxiety and told me told me to "get in the middle". She then simply turned out the light and shut the door behind her. I was petrified. I was used to sleeping alone and now I was the filling in a sandwich. As hard as I tried, it was impossible to not touch one of them, although I did my best to avoid doing so.

Bunny and Leo were enrolled in a special school because of their haemophilia, and were collected by a special Brent Council school bus every morning. All the children on it had an impairment of one kind or another. Bunny was particularly badly affected and suffered swollen knees and other ailments almost daily. Leo's symptoms were less chronic.

I very much wanted my brothers to like me, but the more I tried, the less they seemed to. Bunny was my main tormentor. He hated me and told me that at every opportunity, with words and with his fists. Leo also hated me, but was less vicious in the expression of his distaste.

Looking back, part of the cause may have been the chronic pain that Bunny had to live with, caused by his haemophilia. He would scream the house down some nights. His agony was beyond any assistance my mother could give. Dad was nowhere to be seen; abandoning Bunny to the care of Mum. Perhaps Bunny needed to lash out, to put the pain onto someone else. Perhaps he saw me, his younger, lucky-by-birth, pain-free brother and hated me for it. He was determined to get me to share his pain.

Bedtimes were the worst. My brothers did their best to make sure my nights were a living hell: I was crushed, poked, pinched and worse. I tried to tell Mum, but she just brushed me away. I don't recall Dad being around much and I wouldn't have dared complain to him anyway. I was alone in my misery.

My sisters soon turned against me as well, perhaps because they believed it the only way to survive our hateful older siblings. With the words "Mummy's Pet" ringing in my ears, I was ambushed, kicked and punched by all of them. I would run to my mother, but too afraid to really complain, I tried instead to remain close to her feet at all times; like petrified new-born zebra, afraid of being tonight's meal. I would be so close to my mother, that she would shuffle her feet to regain a little space from me. I think my Mother believed her kids were just playing, but there was no fun in it for me. This was unrelenting torture.

I thought she had woken up to the gravity of the situation on the night when I was kicked so hard that I bled from my rear end. In pain, I ran crying to my mother, clasping my painful backside in my little hands. She pulled my pants down and looked, then shouted "Are you going to kill him?" as my siblings dispersed. But Mother's instruction that they leave me alone only served to fire them up for the next onslaught. It was if they had some kind of bet between themselves about who could inflict the most damaging assault against my person. Bunny won most nights, with Beverley and Jan competing for second place.

That same night, after heading to bed and nervously attempting to take my usual place in between my malicious brothers, out of nowhere, Bunny suddenly grabbed my head and smashed it with full force against the wall. I can still remember the terrible cracking sound and the hot shooting pain across my scalp. I ran screaming from the room, trying to find my mother in the darkness. I never found her. Perhaps she was too tired to respond, or too tired to care. I decided to make my way back to my torture chamber after deciding the dark was scarier than my now giggling brothers. As I sheepishly crept in between them, their giggles turned to laughter. I cried. They pinched me. I cried some more.

I fell asleep, eventually, but it was long after they both did. I was truly afraid of them, especially Bunny.

The sexual games started some time later. I didn't enjoy them and didn't tell anyone about them either. It wasn't anything heavy, but mostly involved petting and body rubbing. I knew it was naughty, but I was too frightened to object. This form of contact was better than being pinched or slapped. Mercifully, it never became more serious than that.

One afternoon after school, I just couldn't face going home to suffer more torture at the hands of my siblings, so I decided to visit my old house in Lowfield Road, West Hampstead, which was still owned by my parents' former landlords, the Bent family. They were pleased to see me and I forgot about time as I happily played games with them into the early evening. Uncle Sonny and his family lived in the basement, but I didn't see them that evening.

It was about 7pm when Dad phoned to find out if I was there and sent Leo to collect me. As we walked a silent fifteen minutes to Kingsley Road, the only comment my older brother made was a warning: "Dad is going to kill you." In response, my stomach knotted up with worry, but I was somewhat unsurprised. I last saw Dad the night before, when, to make everybody laugh, I had the spontaneous crazy idea to put on my mother's black night dress and run around the house imitating her singing. My foolery had everyone laughing, as intended; everyone that is apart from Dad. Before I could even think of complementing the shimmering dress with my mother's heels, I somehow sensed his disapproval, and turning to investigate my hunch, my eyes caught his; all I could see was contemptuous bloody malice looking back at me; a previously unseen evil which silenced my laughter and proceeded to penetrate to my very soul. Inhaling and exhaling without blinking an eye, the emitting smoke from Dad's roll-up seemed to signal my imminent demise, together with that of my never to be repeated amateur drag act. I felt like I was caught up in the intensity of a classic Clint Eastwood western; trapped in the breathless moments just before the lethal gun fight would condemn his inferior bullet-holed enemy to the dust. My feet only regained their freedom after Dad, without saying a word, got up and left the room; on his way, I was certain, to dig my grave. I couldn't understand what it was that I'd done to deserve his unspoken threat, but there was no doubt that I had crossed, however unwittingly, a forbidden line.

Once home, Leo and I entered our bleakly-lit house. Dad, looking distinctly ominous, was waiting for me on the upper landing. His belt was already in hand and seeing it prompted my tears; I knew that its presence had only one purpose and that my explaining myself was an option that was not on offer. Leo quickly disappeared out of sight, as if fearful of becoming trapped by the black magic pull of Dad's unforgiving gaze. I was already a victim of its magnetic force when I took a cue from his silence that I must do what was expected of me and begin my ascent of the sixteen steps towards the dark greeting that he was determined to bestow upon me. Climbing Mount Everest barefoot would have felt less daunting a task, but as I mounted the first step I knew that my fate would be so much worse if he had to come down to me. Dad was well aware of the psychological power in his stance; my torturous ascent towards him cloaked in the air of my imminent demise was a deliberate and integral part of the punishment he believed I deserved. Like an innocent but condemned man on his way to meet his executioner, my reluctant feet carried the weight of my burden but couldn't help but collude with my doom; their faltering could delay but not prevent my inevitable end awaiting me at the top of the stairs. As I laboured further upwards towards Dad's unblinking smoke-reddened eyes, the disturbed tone and incremental volume of my crying was yet another unconscious but similarly doomed strategy to win his pity, but we both knew that my tears would drown me before they could ever save me. I was now only a step or two away from the belt that would not rest tonight until it had tasted my young flesh. A seventeenth step would have provided refuge for another precious second or two, but its cruel non-existence delivered me sooner rather than later to my dreaded expiration location. Reaching him, my desperate eyes searched Dad's face in the hope that I might find a late sign of sympathy, or even reprieve, but there was to be none. Before my foot could even touch the upper landing, my father launched into the most vicious and merciless beating of my life. His loyal belt rained down again and again upon me as I fell to the floor in searing pain. Using my hands as a shield proved pathetically futile in protecting me from the incessant onslaught of stinging leather. Dad was determined to hurt me as much as he could, and he succeeded. I was certain that my skin was on fire as I rolled around trying to put out the invisible flames. My writhing, screaming and begging garnered no compassion from him. No one came to help me, not even my beloved mother. It seemed that God and everyone below him had abandoned me to my father's frenzied assault. When his right hand got tired, he swapped his belt to his left and kept on going; strike, after strike, after strike. Now curled in a ball at his feet, I stopped resisting and submitted to the fact that I was going to die, but just as I was beginning to accept that this was indeed my end, I heard my mother's assured intervening voice say: "Skippy! Are you going to kill him?" With that, Dad recovered his sanity. He ceased his onslaught and stepped over and away from the sobbing dishevelled heap that was once me, his young son. My execution was over. I was still sobbing five minutes later when I heard Mum call to me from the kitchen: "Ian, come for your dinner, boy!" I was now expected to resume life as if my horrid beating hadn't happened. My mind would query why my mother hadn't intervened sooner than she did, but my mouth said nothing. The truth was obvious; she approved of it, at least until it got out of control.

Although other beatings preceded and followed that one, this particular beating stood out for the sheer viciousness and loss of control exhibited by my father. He went beyond 'corporal punishment'; way beyond. On appearance, surely all he was trying to say, albeit through his inappropriate language of parental violence, was that he got worried when I failed to come home on time; I mean I wasn't out robbing old ladies or contaminating baby food. And perhaps if he had known why I didn't want to come home in the first place, he would have whipped my siblings instead. But I suspect this would have made little difference to him, because the lesson that Dad was trying to teach me had nothing at all to do with my being late. Even if I'd arrived home earlier than expected he would still have whipped the skin off my body. As far as he was concerned, I had given him all the reason he needed the night before when I'd donned my mother's night dress. In the innocence of my amateur drag act, I'd somehow stripped him of his manhood and therefore had to be punished for having done so. His girlie magazine prank of some months earlier was a serious sign that he was concerned about my possible sexuality. My daft drag act was confirmation that drastic action must be taken to get me to man-up.

The beating of my life was intended to restore his manhood, exorcise his disgust, and cure my sissy-gay persona. As young as I was, and even though I couldn't articulate it back then, I knew what he did to me was wrong, but as my father he could get away with assaulting me in a manner that would see him locked up if we had been unrelated. He'd crossed a forbidden line, not me; a line from child chastisement to child abuse, or even criminal assault; but he was my father and so it was okay? No it wasn't! Like many other self-justified perpetrators of domestic crime of his culture and time, he was a Jamaican man and he took pride in allowing his belt to do his talking. He expected to get away with it and he did.

If I thought the subsequent passing days would thaw his anger towards me, then I was wrong. Dad saw me out playing street games with other Kingsley Road children; he had returned from work earlier than expected and was wearing a seriously pissed off expression on his face. Without a word of hello, he grabbed me by my wrist and hauled me up the street towards our house. The other kids knew I was in severe trouble, and so did I, of course, but they could only watch as I was led away. Mrs. McKenzie at number 19 was out tending to her front garden. She called out at my Dad, saying: "Ah Mr Scott, don't do it. Don't do it!" She had read his intentions just by looking at him. With that, Dad laughed embarrassingly in her direction, released his grip and proceeded to stop and chat with her. Relieved, I hastened the few doors home and made myself scarce. Thank you Mrs. McKenzie, because you saved my hide that day. The plight of abused children everywhere would be very different if they all had conscientious, intervening neighbours like her.

Writing this chapter forced me to relive part of my childhood that I very very much wanted to bury with the passing years, but the tears that fell onto my keyboard tell me how very raw the memory still is. Some forty-plus years after the events I describe, I can still feel those stinging lashes and the harrowing fear which accompanied them. And while time would heal my bruised skin, nothing on Earth could repair the emotional gulf that would forever separate me from my father. His willingness to beat me confirmed that we were 'father and son' by blood and name alone; love was manifestly absent in this relationship; at least on his side of it. However, despite this acknowledgement by me, I was destined to be plagued well into my adulthood by a longing to be loved and held by him, but his mind would never allow his macho arms to be so gentle...so fatherly. He found wielding his strap easier than allowing himself to display the characteristics that most of us would associate with a 'loving parent'. Perhaps he would have found me easier to love if I did go out and rob old ladies or commit other crimes, but he couldn't, or didn't want to love a son he saw as effeminate.

I had to face it; my father, the man who was supposed to love me the most had wilfully damaged me the most, at least emotionally. By so consciously separating himself from me, both physically and emotionally, I would go through my life separating myself from other people: Vernal Scott, the eternal one-man show was born not of my mother, but of my father. Being single and separate was safe for the adult me. As for enduring loneliness; well, when seen in the context of my childhood it feels like a welcome gift.

My siblings took a cue from that beating and later subjected me to humiliating beatings of their own whenever my parents were out of sight. I don't recall being hit by Leo much, but Bunny, Beverley and Jan got stuck in. They would gang up on me and take great pleasure in seeing who could hurt me the most. I tried not to complain to my mother, but she knew something was wrong and repeatedly warned them to leave me alone. They didn't.

One night my brothers and sisters stood by and cheered and laughed as I was being beaten up on our doorstep by other neighbourhood kids. My nine-year old body did its best to fight back, but I was no fighter. "Hit him again", shouted my happy siblings in excited unison, as I struggled to protect my bruised face from a bigger boy's consistent blows. When I found the courage to peek at him from behind the pathetic shield of my hands, I got the impression that the boy felt somewhat sorry and didn't really want to hurt me, but he felt obliged to please his audience by putting on a convincing show. So, like a showman boxer in the ring, and despite the confined space of the doorstep, the dark skinned boy shuffled his feet and sought to land slick but increasingly softer blows. In quick succession he struck my face, body, head, before going into random mode, thus making it impossible to predict where I was going to be hit next. The cheers soon confirmed him as the undisputed king of Kingsley Road's mock ring, as I retreated indoors, feeling hurt and humiliated. I was now used to such feelings, so I didn't cry or complain, even though I wanted to do both. At least it was all over – for tonight.

Tears were not going to rescue me. I accepted my daily existence of kicks, punches, bruises, sexual games, dinner and school. I felt like the loneliest boy in the world and knew that I had little option but to put up with my situation. I was deeply afraid of the people around me and didn't know what to do to get them to like me, let alone love me. The only time anyone touched me was to hurt or abuse me.

Number 13 Kingsley Road was my prison. I recall regularly sitting on the stairs, halfway up and halfway down, contemplating the agony that was my young life. I'd sit there for ages looking at the door that led to freedom. *"Where would I go?"* I would muse to myself. Even though the door wasn't locked and I had no chains around my ankles, I'd decide to stay with the hell that I knew rather than risk the unknown. My existence was tough at home, but somehow I was convinced that it would be even harder out there – a child against the world. Plus, what would happen if I left and it didn't work out? I would then have to return home to my father's belt. I knew nothing of social services or child care homes, but even if I did, would I have had the courage to call them?

I got excited and thought life was getting better the day Bunny told me he wanted to play with me. He called me into the room in which my mother was sitting sewing, which was now our bedroom, and gestured that I sit with him near the paraffin heater. Mum had her back to us and was getting on with her sewing and singing to herself. Bunny told me that he was going to throw a coin into the air, and if I caught it first I could keep it. I couldn't believe it. He had only moments earlier said, "I'd rather play with a dog than you!" Now he was saying that he was going to count to three, but I had to close my eyes first. "And don't peep!" he instructed me. I wouldn't dare. I did as instructed, but wondered why it was taking him so long to start counting. After about thirty seconds he started to count, and after three, I opened my eyes and plunged out my hand and successfully grabbed the coin before he did, only to yelp in agony and drop it. In the time I had been wondering about the delay in his counting, Bunny had put the coin on the heater. He looked at me and then looked pointedly at Mum, who was still sewing away, oblivious to what had just happened behind her back. Bunny then simply slipped out of the room. I looked at the palm of my sore hand and could clearly see the outline of the coin in my skin. I didn't dare complain.

In between the kicks and punches, my siblings would allow me to enjoy music with them on the old gram. Every West Indian household had a gram vinyl record player. We would dance to tunes like Millie Small's 'My Boy Lollipop' and the Soul Children's hit 'The Sweeter He Is' and pop tunes like 'Sugar Sugar'. But it was Aretha's 'Rock Steady' that I loved most. Despite my misery, that song always made me feel better. I'd try to impress everyone by dancing and trying to match Aretha's high notes. Jan also loved that tune and would dance and move her hips from side to side in line with Aretha's soulful instructions. When I could, I'd flip the record over to hear Aretha sing 'Oh Me Oh My, I'm a Fool for You Baby'.

I loved Aretha's voice and could escape the misery of the house listening to her – at least in my mind. I knew it wouldn't last; when they got bored, my siblings would throw me out of the room and leave me to languish in the hallway alone until they were ready to administer another beating. But for those precious moments, when I was dancing, I was free.

14. MY FIRST LOVE?

AT THE AGE OF TEN, I BECAME INFATUATED with a pretty girl at school called Sandra. She was milky coffee black and skinny-thin. Yellow ribbons were regularly intertwined with her plaits. Tragically, her cute looks were severely undermined by her unfortunate smile, which was sprinkled with odd looking teeth and somewhat reminiscent of a 16th century graveyard. Our love affair consisted of smiling and giggling with each other. Just a little glance at each other would cause us to run in the opposite direction in fits of irrational laughter. If we bumped into each other again, we would promptly repeat our mutual foolery. I think we kissed only once – and it was my very first. The experience made me think I was smooching decomposing road kill; it wasn't pleasant! Ah, but I did like Sandra, despite her Hammer Horror kiss. Giggles and an occasional hug would have to suffice in this, my first love affair.

I was now part of a small group of football-crazy friends; Greg, Stephen, Leno, Martin and Mohammad. None of us were good enough to make the school team, but we didn't care about that. My enthusiasm for the game stopped short of buying football cards and going to games with my dad. Huh, I never went anywhere other than a barber shop or a smoky gambling den with my dad. School and football were a good distraction from home. Unlike other children, my parents never attended parents' evenings or school plays; I guess they were too busy working. My siblings were all attending classes for older children or secondary school. Bunny and Leo continued to attend special school for no other reason than their haemophilia.

My other love at the time was my PE teacher, Mr Arnold. I suspected that I was his too! There was something going on between the two of us, even if I was too young to really understand it. One day I headed for the cloakroom to collect my anorak before heading home; yes, I had one of those and I loved it too, especially when it was sodden-wet from a heavy rainfall. I felt a hand on my shoulder and turned to see Mr Arnold smiling down at me. In a moment he'd dropped to his knees (he was a good six feet tall, but around my height on his knees) and pulled me to his chest in a full embrace. I didn't understand what was happening and didn't say anything, I was too shocked. His hand came up and stroked the skin on my face. "You're so soft," he said wonderingly. I plucked up the courage to push him away then and I ran home without even putting my coat on.

Although I had run away from him, I was secretly intrigued by what had happened and part of me wanted it to happen again. It felt nice to be held so warmly and be touched by someone in a way that wasn't violent. I guess I liked it.

Despite my running away, Mr Arnold didn't cease in his affections towards me, not one bit, but in a way, I didn't want him to stop. I got some kind of delight from looking across the school hall during morning assembly and finding Mr Arnold looking warmly at me from behind his big black-rimmed glasses, giving me his brilliant smile. Yes, I did like it, even if I wasn't supposed to.

One day I was asked by my classroom teacher to deliver a sealed envelope to Mr Arnold in his classroom upstairs. I nervously took it and made my way up the stairs to where his class was on the first floor. On reaching his room, I peered through the glass panel on the door and tapped before entering. His pupils were just settling in and paid little attention to me, but Mr Arnold's mouth was agape when he saw it was me. I approached quickly and handed him the envelope and then speedily hurried out. But after closing the door behind me, I sensed that he would still be getting his last glimpse of me, so I peered back through the glass and there he was, smiling at me. I don't know what made me do it, but I stuck two fingers up at him, in a defiant 'fuck off' sign and ran off. I didn't see him again until the next day when he was the supervising teacher in the playground. While he kept an eye on me, he didn't try approaching. I kept myself busy playing football with the other boys, but I kept an occasional eye on him too, and yes, he was still smiling at me.

I would forever associate Mr Arnold with the songs, 'Hold Your Head Up' by Argent, and Isaac Hayes' 'Theme Form Shaft', perhaps because they were popular at the time and I kept hearing them on the radio.

He carried on touching and smiling lovingly at me whenever he could. I was aware that he was married to a beautiful Caucasian woman with long black hair, who frequently came to meet him after school. Even though they held hands as they strolled away from the school, this did not prevent him from looking over his shoulder at me, flashing that comforting smile.

Of course his behaviour was inappropriate; despite my young age, I knew that much. His touching, as far as I can remember, never involved my genitals and I have no idea if he got a sexual thrill from what he was doing. I had zero interest in sex at that age and knew nothing much about what it involved. Looking back, I can say that he was definitely *inappropriately* affectionate; a line had been crossed that shouldn't have been. However wrong it was, he successfully replaced Sandra in my heart, even if he didn't deserve it. The inappropriate Mr Arnold had become a secret but welcome distraction from the ongoing nightmare at home, and my little heart had to thank him for that.

15. HEY, BATTY MAN!

IT WAS AROUND THE TIME of my 10th birthday and when one of my mother's close friends left London to set up home in New York, our household gained a new member: her teenage son, Neville. The tall black teenager moved into the downstairs back bedroom that I now shared with Bunny – Leo now had his own room and even had a job at a local button factory. My brother and I slept on the double bed, while Neville slept on a folding single.

Neville turned out to be a frisky teenager with a big ego, whose passions were reggae and showing off his penis to anyone who would care to look at the foot-long thing. I recall one night, when Bunny was playing reggae tunes to some local friends he'd made, Neville stood up and took out his cock and introduced it to everyone. They all laughed, apart from Bunny. Two of the other boys soon had their dicks out too and were laughingly comparing their respective sizes. Bunny wasn't impressed and told them in no uncertain terms to stop it. I said nothing and did nothing other than try to be invisible.

Yes, Neville won that particular competition. And he seemed to think that gave him a gift with the opposite sex. The problem was Neville had a body odour issue. He was too busy chasing girls to bathe. He even tried it on with my sisters. I can clearly recall Beverley telling him to "Get lost and grab a bath". When he made advances to a neighbour's equally frisky teenage daughter, though, he succeeded. The first time I woke up and found them screwing, I was rather perturbed. Bunny was looking on and giving them directions, but when he realised I was awake, he hit me in the head and told me to "Keep quiet and mind your business". I did, but not before seeing Neville's bottom rising and falling on top of the squealing black girl; someone whom my sisters and I knew well. After that, I just pretended I was asleep whenever she crept through our ground floor bedroom window for a repeat session with smelly Neville.

Neville didn't leave his amorous advances to the girls. Late one night I thought Bunny was getting into the bed, but it wasn't him at all, it was Neville. He climbed on top of me and started thrusting and gyrating his hips. At first I tried to get away, but then I gave up the fruitless exercise and lay there as he carried on doing his thing. This began to happen regularly – whenever Bunny stepped out of the room, Neville would try to get on top of me.

My little world shattered when I came to realise that Bunny knew exactly what had been happening. He didn't try to protect me, but instead laughed with my abuser. I overheard him joking with Neville about it. I felt dirty and ashamed, far too ashamed to tell anyone. "That little batty man," I heard my brother say. Even though some years had passed since his arrival from Jamaica, Bunny still had not warmed to me at all, even though by now he'd stopped hitting me.

As if things weren't bad enough, I wandered into my mother's bedroom one afternoon and she looked at me with a big grin that made me expect something warm and welcoming to come out of her mouth, but instead she chuckled and said, "Hey batty man, you want something?" Instead of being protected, I was being mocked and laughed at by the person I loved and needed the most. Until then my mother had been my rock and the only source of genuine care and affection in that house. But my rock had fallen and crushed me into a million pieces.

'Ian' was dead. I was a walking corpse. A sense of shame engulfed my every waking moment and I felt as if everyone knew I was a dirty batty man and was mocking me about it. No one tried to rescue me. No one cared. I was really alone now and totally vulnerable to the humiliations inflicted by the people around me. Neville picked up on this and started to pick on me too. One night, to the applause of my siblings, he picked me up, took me into the bathroom, stuffed my head into the toilet and flushed it. I didn't cry and I didn't complain. I walked the line of shame and then went and sat on the stairs; halfway up and halfway down as the laughter carried on above my sodden head.

Hughy, a cousin on my dad's side who was about the same age as Leo, visited one hot summer's day. I was keeping a low profile as usual, out of the way of the people around me. The heat eventually caused everyone to make their way out onto the street. Marlon, my neighbour and friend, passed by and asked me to go to the shops with him. We were nearly at the top of Kingsley Road when, at the top of his voice, I heard Hughy shout out, "Ian, how's your bum today?" I died again as everyone around him laughed. Marlon hadn't made out the insult and I wasn't about to explain it to him. When we returned from the shops ten minutes later, I said goodbye to Marlon and shamefacedly squeezed past the throng of people laughing and chatting outside our house. I then sought out a corner where I could become invisible.

That night, I recited a prayer that had become my morbid mantra: "God, please take (kill) me if I'm a bad sinner, *before I reach twelve.*" This very dark prayer was influenced by my mother, who told me that "after a child reaches twelve he is no longer a child in the eyes of God and will burn in eternal hell fire if he commits a sin". Her words stuck in my brain.

I was just one of billions of God's children to be terrorized out of our minds by scary Bible stories about sin and hell fire. Praying for my own death seemed much less scary than punishment in a lake of flames, especially, as my mother stressed, "It will be ten times hotter than normal earthly fire, boy!"

My little inexperienced mind compounded my torture. Why was I a batty man? How did it happen and when? Did it happen at my conception or arrive with my birth? Perhaps I caught it like I catch a cold. Maybe Mr. Arnold caused it to happen when he held me? Perhaps it happened with a random thought in my head or an odd combination of beats of my heart. Surely God didn't do it... or did he? Not according to the Bible!

I was as baffled as I was tormented. I didn't want to be this way, of that I was certain...but I was. Later on in life I would have to conclude that if I didn't choose my sexuality then it must have chosen me.

For now, at least, I believed I was on my way to the lake of eternal hell fire; my fear and terror of it was very real. An early death was not so unattractive, if it meant that I would be spared. I was petrified of God and yet I was supposed to love him, or else!

When I look back on my plight, I realise that it was most cruel of my mother to fill my head with such dark thoughts; but she believed in the word of God and I believed in her. I guess she was just as frightened as me; too frightened to question Bible scripture or the damage that it was doing to us. "The Bible was the word of God himself", she would say, and no one was supposed to question it. That's how she was raised and how she was raising her children.

I needed to pray harder: "Oh God, please, please, please help me! God, are you really there? Please help me. I don't want to be a sinner. I don't want to burn in hell fire! God, please!"

16. THE DISCO KID WILL SURVIVE

A LOT HAD HAPPENED in the last couple of years. I now attended Brondesbury and Kilburn High School in northwest London. I had moved on from Kingsgate school and the attention of Mr Arnold. I did see him in the street near my new school one day and he stopped dead in his tracks. He smiled his old smile at me, but I turned around and went another route home. I would never see him again, even if a curious part of me very much wanted to.

At home, my siblings had also moved on from bullying me. I had my own bedroom again, and Bunny was living downstairs in his own room. Despite his haemophilia, causing him painfully swollen joints, he had lots of girlfriends coming and going all the time. Beverley remained in the house too, but Leo moved out, and in his place, my eldest sister, Jan, returned home. She'd become a troubled teen and my parents hoped a stay with Aunt Edna in Coventry would turn her around. Instead, she got pregnant, aged sixteen, and came back home with her baby son, JJ. He was delightful. Thankfully, Mum and Dad, despite signs of serious strains in their marriage, accepted the situation for what it was. Unfortunately, like his uncles, Bunny and Leo, JJ too had haemophilia.

At school, I was gaining a sense of self through engaging with the arts. I was not known for my academic ability. I detested maths, but was more than competent in English, especially creative writing – that was my forté. After writing a number of poems that won the approval of my teacher, my confidence grew. One poem I wrote was titled 'Sex Me', and it caused my teacher's eyebrows to rise off his head. It was about a teenage boy having sex with a man for the first time. It got top marks, even though my teacher made no comment about why he had scored it so highly. All he did say was, "Keep writing, Vernal, keep writing!" I was also good at History, Economics and Biology. Above all, I thoroughly enjoyed drama and any opportunity to dance.

My closest school friends were Terry, Fred and Burch, all of Jamaican parentage. There was also David, who was Chinese, and Marius, who was Cypriot. They were all quite affectionate towards me, but in a totally non-sexual manner. We all shared a love of music and chased and dating girls. My dating of girls was out of a necessity; to fit in, rather than a genuine interest; even though I really tried hard to be genuine with them. By the age of fourteen, my fantasies and desires evolved to guys rather than girls, although I would keep such secrets to myself. Marius was very attractive and great fun to be with, and yes, I fancied him, but I could hardly admit it to myself at the time. We were all very 'straight' in our outlook on life and girls. That was the game, and I was playing my part the best I could. I'm sure some had suspicions about me; I was just a little too 'arty' to be completely *straight*, and my obsessional love affair with disco music was a giant clue for anyone *in the know*.

I mostly opted out of playing football during breaks, and instead, usually hang out with the girls and gossiped about rubbish. No one questioned my sexuality until a fellow female pupil sniffed me out. We'd had an argument about some trivial matter, and her response was to call me a "batty man". I was mortified and felt as if she had stripped and paraded me naked around the playground. She kept on: "Queer...poofter..." She even accused my then girlfriend of being a lesbian for going out with me. I felt that my secret was out, even if I remained firmly locked within my personal closet. I wanted to die. The same pupil would name-call for the remainder of my time at Brondesbury and Kilburn high school. Her teasing caused me to become introspective and mindful of any overt 'gay' behaviour that I might be displaying. I had to macho-up to survive, but my attempts to do so where often undermined whenever I'd hear that disco beat: I didn't care what I looked like, I just had to dance. When the music would end, I tried to become all butch again.

My discovery of disco happened one magical day in December 1974. I was at home in bed with chicken pox, scratching furiously whenever I could escape the beady eyes of my mother, who kept putting her head around the door and shouting, "Stop it!" At least my radio offered some respite from the dual irritation of itching and maternal injunctions. I reached out to turn up the volume, when I heard a familiar song; it was 'Never Can Say Goodbye'. Here it was being sung by a woman with a vibrant, compelling voice over a happy, danceable rhythm. The song had been completely transformed from its original Jackson Five arrangement as a ballad. I sat up straight in bed, and within a moment, I was on my feet on top of the sheets, dancing frantically, as if my spotty condition was a distant memory. An equally enthused Tony Blackburn, the Radio One DJ, announced the sensational singer as "Gloria Gaynor!" That was it for me. I was to be forever hooked on that singer, that version of a wonderful song, and the thumping new musical genre that Gloria and her producers, Meco Monardo, Tony Bongiovi, and mixer, Tom Moulton, had introduced to the world called Disco.

Lorna, my girlfriend at the time, bought me the LP as a late birthday gift in early 1975. I preferred the record to kissing Lorna, although she was very cute. Gloria's music was sizzling hot and demanded all my attention. The medley on side one was unbelievably exciting to my ears and feet. I would listen and dance while looking at the picture of Gloria in her black negligee on the back cover. I was obsessed with her. I invited my school friends' home so we could listen to Gloria and act like we were her band: Fred on drums, Burch on guitar, Terry on bass and me on percussion and backing vocals. We were the best band in town and Gloria was fortunate to have us behind her.

Everyone at school came to associate me with disco music and killer dance moves. I just had to hear the beat and I'd be up and dancing with everyone crowding around to watch. If there was a school play or improvisation involving music and dance, I would be in there somewhere, dancing my butt off and loving every second of it. With the beat in my ears and every part of my body in motion, I was transported to disco heaven. In the words of Sister Sledge, I was the greatest dancer.

Even though my very first vinyl 45 purchases as a boy were Roberta Flack's haunting 'Killing Me Softly' ballad, and Bobbie Houston's (no relation to Whitney) blistering reggae version of Bread's classic, 'I Want to Make It with You', disco had become my sanctuary; it was *my music*!

A whole stream of divas would follow Gloria into my pantheon of disco demi-goddesses, such as Donna Summer, Linda Clifford, Loleatta Holloway, Grace Jones, Carol Douglas, Amii Stewart, and honorary cross-dressing gay diva, Sylvester and his Two Tons o' Fun – latterly known as the Weather Girls of 'It's Raining Men' fame. Many others would hit with one song and then fade into insignificance, such as Karen Young with 'Hot Shot', and Linda Carr with 'Highwire'. I often wondered how someone with as much talent as Linda could deliver one mega hit and then appear to fall off the face of the Earth. Not even modern internet searches could lead me to where she is today.

Donna Summer grew in popularity as a disco star with the film Thank God It's Friday. Many considered her to be the new Queen of Disco, but my dancing feet were bored by seventeen minutes of her moaning and groaning through songs like 'Love to Love You Baby' and 'Try Me I Know We Can Make It'. However, 'I Feel Love, 'McArthur Park', 'Last Dance', and her brilliant Bad Girls album, was all the proof I needed that she could sing as well as fake discofied orgasms. My poor gospel-loving Mum could just about tolerate loud disco music booming from my bedroom, but Donna's disco orgasms were the last straw: "Lord, have mercy! Boy, turn off that dirty woman!" she'd shout.

The ladies were the big disco stars. Jamaican born Grace Jones was the new darling of the disco scene in 1977, with a hit called 'I Need A Man'. She didn't have the greatest voice, but what she couldn't do with that, she made up for with her outrageous wardrobe and behaviour. Loleatta Holloway, a former gospel singer, also hit the disco charts in 1977, with a huge smash called 'Hit and Run'. The superior singer was able to hold spine tingling notes longer than a freight train, whilst simultaneously injecting them with her patent gospel overtones. Her church subsequently ejected her from their pews, citing her venture into disco as 'sinful', but the gay disco crowd was very happy to welcome her. In 1978, Linda Clifford stormed to the top of the disco chart with her electrifying album, 'If My Friends Could See Me Now'. The title cut, previously recorded by Shirley McClain for her film, Sweet Charity, was the campest disco fest to ever hit my Saturday night radio. I loved every morsel of it. Linda's explosive vocals gave me the impression she was getting paid by the word; the entire LP was a disco fan's ball. First Choice, the Ritchie Family, and Sister Sledge, were huge stars, too. Disco also had a number of male stars, such as Sylvester, Cerrone, and the Village People, but it was the ladies of the beat who were the real superstars.

So, by the close of 1978, Gloria had lots of competition for her official disco queen crown. Having survived a horrendous stage accident which threatened to end her career, Gloria, wearing a post spinal surgery back brace, went into the studio. Fittingly, given her predicament, and whether by coincidence or fate, the title of this particular studio session was a song that would start life as a B-side single, called 'I Will Survive': three little words that would have great meaning to me and millions of others across the world. The A-side was Substitute, a cover of Clout's UK hit.

Gloria had enjoyed a number of hits following Never Can Say Goodbye – Reach Out, I'll Be There, How High The Moon, If You Want It, Do It Yourself, Walk On By, This Love Affair – but I Will Survive wasn't just another disco recording. Love Tracks, the platinum-selling album which featured the iconic track and Gloria's sixth album for Polydor, wasn't just another disco album. There was something more than that going on within the grooves; it was a magic that was unique to the singer. I must have been amongst the first to buy it. In fact, all my scarce pocket money went on records and articles on disco music. I'd cut them out and put them in a scrapbook I called my Disco Bible. I would also trawl through newspapers of all kinds, just to see if there was any reference to the music I loved.

Gloria, with considerable DJ and public support, pressured Polydor Records to flip the single and make I Will Survive the A-side. The company agreed, but this didn't prevent one record reviewer from writing: "Polydor is beginning to work on I Will Survive, but it really isn't anything special and the company would be better advised to go for something new." The rest is pop history. The song was soon sitting at the top of disco and pop charts around the world. The self-affirming lyrics, coupled with Gloria's assured delivery, tapped into a universal human experience that everyone could relate to; in our (failing) relationships, at work, in health, and in life in general. The bar-setting song went on to win a Grammy and a further nomination for 'Record of the Year'. It was to become disco's greatest ever hit. When it left the number one spot on the US pop chart, it returned there just a week later, as if to reinforce the point; survival of the fittest! Here at home, it sat at the number one spot for an entire month.

My love of disco was becoming a practical problem, too. To my ears, disco was meant to be heard and heard loud. My feet were made to dance to it. No one in my household liked my choice of music and would constantly shout for me to "turn it down!" If that wasn't bad enough, over a period of months my mother observed the complete destruction of my bedroom carpet; my dancing wore it down to the bare threads. My poor mother didn't know what to do with me, but I didn't care. I just kept on dancing...and dancing...

I would find out about new dances, like the hustle, the bus stop, the freak, and the bump, from television. There was no MTV in those days, so the clues came from TV's only music programme, *Top of the Pops*, especially when it showed clips from the black American TV show, *Soul Train*. Those brief but precious clips were magic to my eyes and feet, as I tried out the moves in my bedroom. By the time I was done, I wasn't copying anyone else; I had my own rhythm and style.

Disco music was my escape. It set me free from all the trouble and misery at school and at home. Mum and Dad were beginning to have frequent arguments, and some were violent. Chic sang 'Dance, Dance, Dance' and I did. I didn't have to think or remember; just dance to the happy beat. Any pocket money I could get out Dad or Mum went on the latest cuts from Billboard's Top 20 Disco Action Chart, which appeared in *Black Echoes* music newspaper every week. I didn't know at the time that the chart was compiled according to what was most popular in gay discos, but this makes sense now. Gays and disco go together like roofs on houses.

I Will Survive wasn't the only dance hit from Love Tracks. Accompanying it to the number one spot on Billboard's Disco Chart of 1979 was the gloriously funky Anybody Wanna Party?, an impassioned reworking of Goin' Out Of My Head, and the storming, I Said Yes. The LP also contained ballads, such as the beautifully intimate Please Be There, and the compelling mid-tempo swayer, You Can Exit. The latter, delivered in a sophisticated whisper-like vocal, finds Gloria telling her egotistical lover with a misplaced superiority complex: "I know you're fine, yeah, but so am I. You can exit, anytime!" Totally exquisite! The rich diversity of the album helped it ease into the top five of Billboard's Pop, and a world tour followed, including dates set for London. This disco kid had to be there to see the true Queen.

It was April 1979 and I managed to save up enough money to buy two of the cheaper tickets to see Gloria Gaynor at the London Palladium. Jan agreed to come along with me. When we got to the theatre, I was quick to notice, even if Jan didn't, that Gloria attracted a lot of gay people; they were everywhere I looked. The disco superstar had sold out four nights and a matinee, the latter being all I could get tickets for. The seats were way up with the gods, but it was very exciting, especially as it was my first ever live concert and the first opportunity to see my idol in the flesh.

When Gloria took to the stage, I nearly passed out. Jan just looked green from our vertiginous position; afraid of toppling over the small balcony and becoming Gloria's unwitting *surprise* guest. Gloria, however, looked and sounded amazing. It was great to finally see her live. She sang all her hits: 'How High the Moon', 'Reach Out I'll Be There', 'Never Can Say Goodbye', 'Anybody Wanna Party', 'After the Loving', 'Casanova Brown' and 'Every Time You Make Love to Me'. But most of the audience was there to hear her perform her current number one smash single, 'I Will Survive', and the house duly erupted when she hit us with those immortal opening words: "At first I was afraid..." I was on my feet and in disco heaven. It was the happiest day of my teenage life.

When I got home Mum startled me when she rushed into my bedroom, looking quite agitated, to ask, "Did she sing *that* song?"

"You mean I Will Survive?" I asked, in my puzzlement.

"Yes, that one." She said, intensely.

"Yes, Mum, she did. Of course she did." I replied.

She simply said "Good, good" and turned and left my room.

Poor Mum. She was clearly having yet another difficult day grappling with the reality that her marriage to Dad was over. In recent weeks, she had skillfully altered Gloria's hit to say: "I will survive, as long as I have God above I know I'll stay alive." But the truth was that she missed her Skippy and I would later wonder whether she could survive without him.

'I Will Survive' became Gloria's very worthy signature tune, and other than making her a very wealthy woman, the timeless hit would, in later years, be voted number one in VH1's all-time Disco 100. It would also feature in countless films, documentaries and TV shows. At the time of writing this book, the song had been recorded over two hundred times by a diverse array of singers, including the wonderfully 'out' and proud Mr Johnny Mathis, Gladys Knight, Billie Jo Spears, Lonnie Gordon, REM, Cake, Eartha Kitt, Diana Ross, Shirley Bassey, and the Queen of Soul herself, Aretha Franklin. Despite these offerings, the song remains 'The Gloria Gaynor song'. The version recorded by Chantay Savage, would be the only one to win Gloria's approval, "because she made it different". Fellow disco diva Donna Summer included 'Survive' in her personal 'all-time top 10', saying, "It helped me get through those difficult times". Her producer, Giorgio Moroder, cited the song as "disco's greatest ever recording". To top it all, February 2012 saw the song formally inducted into the Grammy Hall of Fame and its original singer completed a tour of Italy, attracting in excess of 20,000 fans. Evidence, if any was needed, that the great lady has indeed survived and people still want to hear her sing 'that song'. I guess we're all survivors, of sorts.

I had my first opportunity to meet Gloria in 1985, at her opening of a night club in North London. I waited ages to get my nervous-self close to her, but when my idol turned and said a warm "Hello there!" my stricken mouth opened up and nothing came out. Not a single word. But despite my embarrassing sudden speech impediment, the smiling diva snuggled close to take a picture with me. My friend Leon was behind the camera, and he remarked about our Colgate smiles.

A second opportunity presented itself years later in 1998, when Hans Spaarnay, her former Euro fan club president, arranged for me to meet the star after her performance at the GAY night club, formerly Bang!, my gay club debut as a teenager. I was there only months earlier to meet the amazing Loleatta Holloway, who greeted me with a kiss, full smack on my stunned lips. I was still in recovery mode when the bubbly singer took to autographing my records and scrap book. There was no indication of her gospel roots during her performance, especially during Love Sensation, her signature song, when she got on her knees and simulated oral sex with her microphone. *You wouldn't catch Gloria doing anything like that*, I told myself.

I turned up at GAY alone and enjoyed Gloria's somewhat understated performance from the wings. When it was over, and in line with previously agreed arrangements, Jeremy Joseph, the club's DJ, escorted me up to Gloria's dressing room. I took a deep breath as he opened the door to let me in. Gloria wasn't alone; in fact the room was full of media and PR people. I soon spotted her down at the far end of the room, sitting on the edge of her dressing table happily chatting away with another recognizable soul legend, Candi Staton. Both ladies looked my way as I approached. I gave them both a kiss and warm hug. This time when I opened my mouth to speak, I found my voice. "Gloria," I said, as if making an important announcement to the lady and the room, "I love you!"

Gloria chuckled lovingly and said, 'Hey, I love you too, Vernal. We hugged again. I heard Candi say, "Oh, how sweet."

"How are you doing?" Gloria asked.

"Great!" I replied, handing her a compilation of her music that I'd put together on my computer.

"A very professional job it is, too!" she complimented me.

She donned reading specs to inspect the tracks of my creation. "Oh, I love this," Gloria enthused, as she read through the track listing. "Did you do the artwork too?" she queried, but I let my smug grin reply for me.

Without looking up, the disco legend told me she had work for me to do: "Vernal, I want you to find one of my old tracks. It's called, Come Tonight". She then quickly explained to Candi that she had recorded the song in dimmed studio lights but never owned a copy of it.

Like a happy puppy, I rose to the challenge: "I have it at home and will get it to you, through Hans", I enthused back. My queen smiled, approvingly.

We then exchanged other niceties about my love of her and her music. I soon realised other GG groupies were waiting to meet the queen, so we took a quick picture together, and after hugs and kisses, I said goodnight to both ladies. I then floated out of the building and above the clouds all the way home.

I had finally met my childhood idol and could not have been happier. Nothing in this world could have removed the smile from my face that night.

I would meet up with glorious Gloria many times over the years ahead; in London, Denmark, Holland and her home soil of New York. On every occasion I found her to be warm, graceful and compassionate; giving much of her time and resources to the fight against cancer in children. And she isn't just a legend with a distinctive history in music; she's also got considerable intellect, as evidenced by her qualification as a psychologist and the ability to talk about a wide range of worldly subjects, with an informed and articulate tongue.

When the disco boom came to an end, Gloria, like Donna Summer, became a 'born again' Christian. She is deeply passionate about her love for Jesus Christ, her first love. Like most *decent* Christians, this enhances her love of her multitude of gay fans, not the reverse. There was, however, a memorable moment when she appeared to face a dichotomy regarding an invitation to attend the then forthcoming 'wedding' of Hans, her gay former European fan club president and his life partner of fifteen years. In the end, the happy ceremony went ahead in The Hague, but Gloria was busy *surviving* elsewhere. I attended with Dirk, a very handsome German friend I was dating at the time.

On a memorable occasion, Gloria and I were speaking on the phone and she suddenly shared her fears for me: "You don't have to have sex, Vernal," came the unexpected comment. I later assumed this was Gloria's way of expressing her worry about the perils of HIV; the concern of a caring friend? For the life of me, I can't recall how the subject even came up, but she prayed for me at the end of that conversation and it was much appreciated.

More recently, I asked Gloria to contribute a foreword for this book. It was an opportunity, I thought, for her to make public her thoughts, feelings and beliefs about (her interpretation of) Christianity, as it relates to gay people.

Sadly, she was too busy with one exciting project or another: a new book of her own called We Will Survive, a TV reality show, a project for teen parents, an on-going fund raising initiative for children with cancer, and more. If that wasn't enough, she remains in high demand to perform her hits around the globe; from London to Sydney, and just about everywhere in between. Time hasn't slowed the Godmother of Disco down, and I can't imagine it ever will. Gloria was born to survive and to perform, and whatever her faith-based reservations, it is not a barrier to the love she feels for all her fans, gay or otherwise.

Over the years, I developed an appreciation for a wide range of music; from the wonderful jazz sounds of Sarah Vaughan, Ella Fitzgerald, Nancy Wilson and George Benson, to the rock and pop sounds of Tina Turner, the Eagles, Scott Walker, Michael Bolton and Cher, the soul of Aretha Franklin and the Four Tops, the country sounds of John Denver, and the gospel of Tramaine Hawkins, The Brooklyn Tabernacle Singers, Kirk Franklin, and Mary Mary. However, despite its fake demise at the hands of the racist and homophobic Disco Sucks movement, the genre would forever provide the 'pick-me-up' soundtrack to my life.

My all-time disco playlist, the dancing soundtrack to my life – and that of just about every other gay man – appears at the end of this book.

17. DIVORCE: DORETH VS SKIPPY

BY 1976 MY PARENTS WERE CONSTANTLY at each other's throats, as their fractured marriage slipped beyond the point of repair. Months earlier, the amateur detective in my mother, probed her suspicion that her Skippy had been cheating with a series of women. It turned out, according to her evidence, that he'd been utterly rampant.

I innocently drew Mum's attention to one of his lovers when I mentioned that I'd seen a "big black woman getting into Dad's car at a bus stop on Willesden Lane". Later, as Mum screamed at Dad, he looked at me with daggers in his eyes and I realised I was meant to keep my mouth shut about such sightings. I had unwittingly broken some kind of unspoken code. Then there was the barber's wife. I'd been totally clueless that while her husband was busy cutting my hair downstairs, my dad was upstairs having adult fun with his wife. The first I knew of it was when Dad and I had to find another barber at short notice, because my crafty mum, in an earlier anonymous phone call, blew the whistle on that extra marital romp. However, to her embarrassment, and despite having disguised her voice, the barber promptly called her back to query whether she had just called him. Her emphatic but lame denial would not win her an Oscar.

Mum, with a number of successes under her belt, and still honing her skills as an amateur sleuth, continued tracking down Dad's lovers, one after the other. One winter night, she bungled me in her car and drove me to an address in north London and demanded: "Go knock on that door. Your father is in there with one of his women." I didn't argue, I just got out and did as I was told. Eventually, a very elderly hearing-impaired Caucasian man opened his upstairs window and shouted down at me, asking what I wanted. I felt foolish asking him whether Dad was there, but I did. He, of course, didn't know who I was, and couldn't hear me, so he said, "Hang on, I'll come down." It took him ages to do so, only for him to tell me the obvious: "No, I live here alone. What are you talking about?" I apologised and retreated to

Mum's car. All she did was kiss her teeth and utter a determined, "I will catch him!"

My parents' marriage was in casualty with a very poor prognosis, but they hadn't arrived at this point overnight. Dad had become less and less interested in his wife and family over the years and found his fun in other women, gambling and drinking. When he was at home, his controlling jealousy that my beautiful mother may find other suitors was eating him up, causing him to become increasingly vulgar and violent. I was more mortified than she was when he started throwing gross insults at her; referring to her as a "prostitute" and "whore," and in front of me, too.

On one very public occasion, my mother left the house to walk to the shops to buy a few cooking essentials for dinner, but as she reached the top of Kingsley Road, Dad opened the top bedroom window, called after her -- "Doreth!, Doreth!", and as she turned to look, he promptly started throwing her best clothes out into the street. Keeping her composure, Mum proceeded to the shops as originally intended. If Dad thought she was going to come running then he was sorely mistaken. She was beyond running after him and his grotesque behaviour. I abandoned my football game and scurried to rescue Mum's clothes from the dirty street, as my astounded friends wondered what the hell was happening at number 13.

Despite all of this, I sensed that my mother still loved him and hoped it was all an elongated blip, but the symptoms of a dying marriage kept coming.

I returned home from school one afternoon to find my mother crying. She told me that he'd hit her. It was extremely rare to see my mother cry, and in my emotionally charged response, I found the courage to confront Dad and tell him to "go away and leave us alone". He responded by slapping me so hard that his fingers left an indentation in my face. But I was beyond crying, and stared him down until he skulked away. On another horrendous occasion,

Dad threw a lit paraffin heater onto the bed in which my mother was resting. She would have been badly burned if she hadn't responded quickly. Worse, was the time my mother decided to stay the night in my bedroom. She suspected that Dad would come home well lubricated, and was fed up with his drunken tirades. It was about 2a.m. when he started pounding on my door, demanding that she get up and bring him his dinner. My mother became anxious but I just stopped breathing, involuntarily. In his alcohol-fuelled rage, Dad took an axe to my bedroom door, chopping his way in and lunging towards my mother, attempting to chop her up. I looked on in terror as my embattled parents tussled to win control of the lethal tool-come-weapon, staring into each other's eyes as they did so: I saw raw rage in my father's eyes and fear and disbelief in my mother's. It took a determined Aunt Vera, who rushed from her room downstairs to separate the two of them, but not before the axe had gashed the back of Mum's hand. My dad appeared to have lost his sanity and sunk to new depths. This realization seemed to dawn upon him as he froze and released the axe to Aunt Vera. As he withdrew from the room, his face painted a picture of regret and shame, but no apology passed his macho lips. Perhaps he was sober enough to know that no apology could compensate for what he'd done. That event would remain a vivid memory for me, and for my mother too, I'm sure.

As if that wasn't sign enough that this marriage was over, rock bottom came when Dad took a razor blade to his own face; emerging from the bathroom with his right and left cheeks resembling the aftermath of a not-so-wild cat attack. He then sneaked from the house and reported my mother to the police as his assailant. Uniformed officers came and summarily arrested my pleading mother, but she was only momentarily at Kilburn police station when closer scrutiny of his superficial wounds painted Dad a liar: his cuts were deemed far too neatly crafted to have been caused by Mum's elegant but potentially hazardous fingernails, as he'd falsely claimed. Mum was released and Dad was then himself arrested for wasting police time. Upon his release the same evening, he sheepishly returned home to my still seething mother, who promptly crowned his humiliation with a container full of her freshly produced urine. Dad's self-induced degradation was complete.

Ike and Tina Turner were having a house party compared to my parents. Dad hated Mum, and it was the kind of venomous hatred that could lead a man to behave as he was. As for my mother, she had given up trying to get her once beloved Skippy to love her the way she felt she deserved; the way he used to. I didn't understand what hatred meant until I saw it in my father's eyes. In one of my last memories of him at Kingsley Road, he was standing at the top of the stairs looking down towards the front door with defeat in his posture. His patent blood red eyes reflected his vengeful mood. Their marriage was deceased, but its funeral would have to wait for the inevitable green light from the divorce courts.

At court, Mum won the house and Dad was given his marching orders, heading out the door never to return. I recall him loading his personal belongings into his car and driving away without a word of goodbye. I was pleased to see him go, only because I hoped we could now have some peace at 13 Kingsley Road: no fights, no drinking, no arguments, no gambling, and no fear.

Well, I could hope.

18. OBEAH SPELLS AND EVIL HANDS

FOR AS LONG AS I CAN REMEMBER, my mother had a superstitious way of looking at the world; harbouring dark beliefs that came with her from Jamaica.

When she survived a horrendous car crash with a lorry near White City, Mum was hospitalised at St Mary's with a number of broken ribs and deep lacerations to her arms. Her car was written off but her injuries, thankfully, were not life-threatening. She wasted no time in blaming Dad for causing the accident, by using evil spirits, or, in her words, *"obeah"* (voodoo). "It's him, it's him cause it", she cried. I was in tears watching my mother shriek in pain whilst cursing Dad at the same time. He'd come to visit, but tried to stay out of sight by hanging around in the corridors; this only served to bolster the perception of him as a guilty man. I'm sure the accident was just that, even though there'd be no convincing my mother of that fact.

Once Mum was discharged from hospital, life became harder. Dad was now living with his sister and we were left broke – and there was no Child Support in those dark days. Life was suddenly very tough. One day I got home from school to find the electricity had been cut off because my increasingly stressed out mother couldn't afford to pay the bill. We spent the cold evening huddled around a paraffin heater and burned candles for light.

Most weekends I would borrow a friend's bike to seek out my dad in the hope that he would give me some money, to enable us to buy some basics. If I was lucky, I would come home with five pounds and immediately give it to Mum. Dad seemed pleased to see me, even if he never really said it.

I recall, with lingering shame, stealing a 10p coin from a table in the upper hallway of a neighbour's house. I used it to buy some bread. I was convinced the householder knew I had taken the coin and I expected to reap trouble for what I had done, but nothing came of it. Perhaps my shabby appearance made them feel sorry for me. I had taken it out of necessity and not criminal intent, but it was still wrong. Only days later, the same concerned neighbour was kind enough to offer me some food, but although my tummy very much wanted me to say yes, my too proud mouth politely declined.

My mother was descending deeper and deeper into depression, meanwhile, and the extended list of prescription tablets that were supposed to help appeared to have little to no effect. She was becoming increasingly convinced that dark spirits were trying to cause us harm.

I came home from school on a winter's night to find a collar-wearing black preacher subjecting the house to some kind of exorcism. In a semi-trance, he went from room to room before heading outside to the front garden, where he insisted that my brother, Leo, smash through some concrete that Dad had laid just before he left. Leo set about the task, at the end of which, the preacher reached into the dusty cavity and appeared to retrieve a dark brown, medicine-like bottle that had been buried there. It contained soil, a few pennies, and paper, upon which was written the names of my mother and my siblings, all spelt backwards. My name wasn't included, for some unknown reason. According to the now profusely sweaty preacher, the death-inducing voodoo bottle had been put there by my father. He further explained to my emotional Mum that the soil was from the grave of the assassin spirit charged with carrying out the deadly deeds, and the included money was its payment. It was all beyond terrifying to my young ears. 13 Kingsley Road was suddenly a lot darker than usual. When it came to bedtime, I tried to squeeze under instead of into it, in the belief that I might be safer there.

The result of my dad's alleged attempt at murder by obeah was that each member of my immediate family had to go to the preacher's house and part-take in a *protection* ceremony. After school the next day my mother whisked me off to his house somewhere in South London, where our ghostly enemies would be confronted and forced to quit.

When we got there, the large living room was jammed full of other black people, also seeking the removal of curses and spells cast by evil enemies. I tried to make myself invisible as the adults around me began praying increasingly louder; some going into *spirit* and speaking in tongues. As the minutes passed, the room worked itself into a frenzy of frantic body movements and random human utterances, which sounded as if they'd come from the dark subconscious of the room's fearful occupants. My mother joined them as I allowed my mind to phase me out and into somewhere far away. However, my temporary false escape was interrupted when I found myself being escorted upstairs by two older black men. I looked back for a moment and saw my mother nodding her head at me, as if to usher me on to whatever fate awaited me at the top of the stairs. As my gaze left her, she raised her hands to the ceiling and resumed speaking in tongues. She was either unaware of, or had sanctioned, what was ahead of me.

My body involuntarily tensed up as the strangers led me into the first floor bathroom. Closing the door behind us, the darker and slightly taller of the two, instructed me to remove my clothes, which I did, nervously, while keeping my fretful eyes to the dark vinyl covered flooring. With my school uniform now in a crumpled pile on the floor, I opted to retain my underwear, but the shorter of the two pointed to my white briefs and further instructed, "Take them off boy, and get into the bath. Quick, quick, boy!" My embarrassment must have been obvious, but I again did as I was told. These were adults, after all; evidently sanctioned to do whatever they were doing by the preacher man in a collar, and very likely, my mother too. Surely, they must be acting in my best interest?

The bath water, sprinkled with what looked like herbs and other vegetation, was barely tepid as I climbed in and crouched down in a futile attempt to salvage something of my teenage dignity. The two men, working in unison, immediately pulled me to my feet and began to pray while splashing me all over with the water. They had done this before. I'm not sure if my shivering was caused by the water or my fear. Their hands went everywhere: my head, torso, armpits, feet, buttocks, and my groin. For a moment, the peculiar duo ceased praying and chuckled when one of them made an incomprehensible comment about my genitals "...compared to the previous boy". If only I was brave enough to protest, but I was far, far too afraid. Instead, my brain went into a kind of limbo, or numbness, in order to deal with what was happening to me. I felt I had to allow it; that's what Mum expected me to do. After all, it was for my protection, wasn't it?

I recall being distracted by the water splashing off my skin and onto my grey uniform trousers, which was on the now sodden floor, straddled by my equally soaked white underwear. I allowed myself to escape on that odd but convenient visual as the men continued their ceremonial invasion of my now obsolete personal space. Yes, it was a useful distraction, albeit far too temporary. After a while, the two men hoisted me out of the bath, and with one on either side of me, lifted me up into the air. Turning me head-over-heels, backwards and then forwards, they only allowed my feet to momentarily touch on the wet floor before repeating their alleged demon-busting ritual. My shivering became increasingly pronounced as my salty tears of terror intermingled with the water on my face. With eyes bulging from their sockets, the two strangers were now praying at the top of their lungs, for my "protection and rescue from evil-doers, in the name of Jesus Christ!" Deep within me, I knew Jesus had nothing to do with this ceremony from hell.

As they set me back on my feet for the final time, I was promptly startled out of my bewildered wits by the taller one, who barked down at me, "Get dressed, boy!" Gathering my senses along with my soggy clothes, and without even daring to glance in his direction, I obeyed. Unwisely, I ignored the towel that the chuckling shorter man attempted to hand me, only to then find myself in a struggle to drag my wet clothes onto my dripping body. Although I tried to hurry in order to cover myself up, there was really little point in hiding my private parts now; the strangers had seen parts of me that I hadn't even seen myself. My repulsive body invaders, now with their previously invasive hands on their respective hips, appeared to savour a last glimpse before my pubescent genitals disappeared beneath my briefs.

On reflection, my self-appointed demon chasers could have done much more to me than they did, all "in the name of Jesus," and while Mum awaited my return downstairs. Tragically, future victims of such vile rituals, such as Victoria Climbie, would suffer a fate much worse than mine. At least I survived to tell my story.

Mum sang and prayed as she drove us back to Kingsley Road. Feeling numb and empty, my mind wrestled with what had just happened to me. Complete strangers had touched me in places that had previously been private and unseen by others. The ritual was supposed to have protected me from unseen demonic assailants, but nobody protected me from the protectors; in fact, I had been delivered to them by my own, well-intentioned, but terribly misguided, mother. In her post-Skippy tarnished mind, potential paedophiles were holy saints, but I wasn't sure there was a difference. Now wearing a crucifix under my shirt, which I was firmly instructed by the preacher not to remove "for any reason", I'd left South London feeling soiled rather than cleansed.

As we entered our gloomy house, I wondered what awful event might happen next. I had just been the victim of some kind of abuse, even though my young mind didn't know to refer to it as that; but looking back, that's exactly what it was. And I wasn't the only child victim earlier tonight; other boys and girls were subject to the same fate. It was another bad experience for me to be ashamed about, when in fact, the shame belonged to the black community, for believing in and perpetrating such practices.

It was wrong of my mother to have exposed me to her black magic way of thinking, but I knew she couldn't help herself;

this was her new 'normal', and by default, it had to become mine. There was no one I could speak to about it. If Child Line had existed back then, what would I have said? It would have been impossible to articulate my situation. There was nothing to do but just live with it.

Thereafter, I got used to coming home from school to find the Bible open on certain pages in my room, or to garlic cloves, secreted around my bedroom by my worried but well-meaning mother. When school friends started making comments about the "odd smell" in my room, I stopped inviting them home, but I never attempted to remove the garlic or the Bible. To do so would have caused my mother to become even more stressed, or even worse, make her think that I was working against her.

The battle of Jesus Christ versus the demons was very real, if only in my mother's mind. The so-called evil doers had succeeded in making her a prisoner of their fictitious spells, thus, robbing her of any post-Skippy freedom or happiness, and permanently undermining her relationship with reality. She was now Jesus' self-appointed crusader, and in the months and years ahead no demon would escape the sword of her tongue. Just a random creak of a floorboard would prompt a vigorous rebuke: "The blood of Jesus, demon! Get out my house and go back to the pits of hell where you belong!" My precious but damaged mother was destined to morph into something resembling a crumbling haunted house of her former self; the shattered windows of her lonely eyes reflecting a futile longing for a return to former good times that made life worth living. She was far too proud to admit it, but not even Jesus, in all his glory, could replace her Skippy, and neither could I. I was to be at a permanent loss as to how to rescue Mum from herself.

Despite Mum's conflicted feelings towards Dad, I still tried to see him, which made her accuse me of spying for him. That's how her mind worked. The truth was I wanted to see him. I guess the little money he gave me helped us to get by, and, despite everything, he was still my father.

19. GHOSTS AND DEMONS

GHOSTS WERE SUPPOSED TO BE THE STUFF of fiction novels by Stephen King and Clive Barker, however, a stay at 13 Kingsley Road would cause many of its residents and visitors to think again.

I was no more than six years old when I saw the first apparition at Kingsley Road; yes, there was to be more than one sighting. Mum would often sleep in my bedroom when Dad was working nights. When she left my bedroom to visit the bathroom, I had the foolish idea of trying to impress her by turning out my lights. I wouldn't normally put my head above the blankets once the lights were out, but for some reason I did so, emboldened by the knowledge that Mum would be coming back in a few moments.

I'm not sure what I expected to see, but as I stared into the pitch blackness, I became aware that I was not alone; something darker than the night was shifting about at the foot of my bed. I stopped breathing as my eyes tried to discern the semi humanoid-shape, now moving in a frantic manner and in my direction. I was frightened beyond my senses. Just as I opened my mouth to scream out for my mother to come and save me, the lights came on and I glimpsed what I thought was my mother's hand slip away from the switch and out of the door once again. She did not come in. I quickly scanned the room to see whether the terrifying apparition was still present, but all I could see was the rise and fall of the blankets as I attempted to catch my breath.

When Mum eventually entered the room, I told her that I was glad she had turned the light on, but she didn't seem to know what I was talking about. "What was it?" she asked. But I couldn't explain what I'd seen. All I knew was that whatever it was appeared to be after me. Mum could see that I was upset and before turning out the lights and joining me on her side of the bed, she undertook a ritual which I had seen her do many times before. It involved opening her Bible at Psalms 23 and assembling two pairs of shoes in certain one up, one down pattern, in front of the closed bedroom door. I would later learn that it was her way of keeping evil spirits from entering the room; a superstitious practice imported from her homeland. Of course, I was unsure what effect this would have on a spirit that was already *in* the room. Once in bed, Mum ordered me to sleep, and I was happy to try.

From that night on, the shadowy character would become a regular feature of sightings and nightmares throughout my youth.

In most dreams, the indiscernible character would chase me, but it would all be in terrifying slow motion and would leave me close to tears as the distance between us got ever shorter. In other dreams, it would be standing at the top of the stairs and, with its unseen power, would prevent my escape, by hauling me, again in slow motion, inexorably backwards, towards its dark, faceless presence.

13 Kingsley Road was dark and scary. It was a cold house, even in the summer months. Doors creaked and unexplained shadows and lights appeared and then disappeared, defying rational explanation. A number of relatives, who had the misfortune to stay, spoke of seeing spirits and ghosts in their room. One such visitor was Uncle Charley, my dad's half-brother. I heard him tell Dad about the ghosts he'd seen the previous night, sitting at the bottom of his bed. "It looked as though they were playing a card game," he said. My dad's only response was to grunt in acknowledgement, because he knew that his older brother would not joke about something like that. But my father's face told its own story: he disliked the idea that someone - something else - was sharing *his* house. Such talk frightened me even more, as it affirmed my fear about the house and the ghosts who shared it with us. Another reason for children to not listen in to adult conversations!

My head did not peep out from under the blankets at night time for many months, while I pondered bewildering questions: who/what was that creature that kept visiting my room, and who turned on the lights that first night, if it wasn't my mum?

Even while hiding I did not feel safe. When I was around nine, my brother Bunny was enjoying a pillow fight in the dark with some of his friends. As I cowered, peeking into the darkness from behind a chair of our bedroom and desperately trying to avoid being thumped, I saw a tall, white masculine figure gliding straight out of the far bedroom wall, above the bed. The ghostly form did not walk; he simply floated, at a funereal pace, towards the centre of the room. I was beside myself with terror and pleaded with Bunny to "please turn the light on". At first he must have thought I was fooling around, but as my pleading became more desperate, the pillow fight stopped and the lights went on. When they did, the pale figure simply evaporated. My brother and his friends looked at me in confusion as I quickly explained what I had just seen. Two days later, I overheard Bunny telling Mum, "He was right – it was a big white doppy (ghost) man - he came out of the wall. Can you come and pray in the room?" My mother obliged.

Bunny later told our parents that he had seen a "doppy man" (ghost) standing over my head with a metal bucket as I slept at the bottom of the bed. Mum knew he wasn't lying and told him to let me sleep at the head of the bed with Leo and him.

The ultimate ghostly experience came when I was about fifteen years old. Mum and Dad were now divorced and my siblings had all flown the nest, leaving Mum and I living alone at Kingsley Road. It was late Sunday evening and mum had not yet returned from church; she went twice every Sunday without fail. She was now a happy 'born again' Christian. Church, grocery shopping, and frequent visits to her doctor, were her only regular excursions from the house. On this particular evening, I had finished watching television and was making my way in the dark to my bedroom on the upper level. Then, in the dark, and heading towards me, was the same black apparition that I'd first seen as a young boy and in subsequent dreams. It seemed to be shuffling at speed towards me. When it reached where I was, I gathered my courage and bolted into my bedroom, switching on the light and slamming the door shut behind me in a desperate attempt to keep the faceless figure out. Years had passed since I'd last seen or dreamt of the specter, so its reappearance tonight was an almighty shock to me.

My back was still pinned to my bedroom door when I heard the reassuring sound of my mother coming into the house from church. But before I could leave my room to go and tell her what I'd just seen, I heard her blood curdling scream from downstairs: "Get out of my house, you demon, how dare you come into my house... Get out, get out!" With that, I took my courage in my hands as I ran out of my room and down the main flight of stairs to meet my uncharacteristically flustered Mum.

"What is it?" I asked, catching my breath.

She exclaimed, "Lord, have mercy on me! I just came into the house and was coming upstairs when I saw a black spirit coming down towards me." I was about to confirm the same sighting, but before I could speak, she raised her voice, as if speaking directly to our now invisible invader, "But I want the demon to know that this is *my* house and I'm not putting up with it! I am not sharing my house with evil: the blood of Jesus on you." She closed her eyes, raised her chin to the ceiling and began to recite the Lord's Prayer.

"I saw it too!" I interjected. My mother stopped praying. "What?!" she shouted back. I quickly explained what had happened in the minutes before she arrived home. For a moment, we said nothing, but just looked into each other's faces in perplexity about how to cope with the unwanted shadowy presence. My mother and I had separately witnessed something visible yet indiscernible and defying of reason or logic; something usually forbidden or undetectable to the human eye that had blatantly revealed itself to us, for whatever reason. God, I wish it hadn't.

Whilst we struggled to make sense of it, somehow we knew that it was evil and up to no good.

We ascended the stairs together, but our slow pace belied our fear. Mum started praying again, loudly, but in a faltering voice. She had been deeply shaken by the unfathomable presence that had confronted her in her own home. As for me, I was beyond petrified.

"Get out of my house, demon, and go back to the pits of hell where you belong", Mum bellowed. "May the blood of Jesus be upon you. Demon, get out!" she concluded. But would our uninvited visitor heed her plea? Only time would tell, but neither of us would forget this night and the reality that the incomprehensible can at any time make its presence felt.

I was quietly relieved that Mum had seen the figure too, because it confirmed that I hadn't imagined it. It wasn't in my head; the house had ghostly activity, and Mum was yet another witness to that fact. In addition to the characters already mentioned, I had also seen a white woman holding a baby, but only once, and again at the bottom of my bed. She just sat there, motionless, looking down at her baby. Only God could explain these sightings, because I couldn't.

My bedroom lights remained on for the next few nights, as I hoped they'd thwart my shadowy nemesis. When I eventually turned them out, I kept my eyes closed and my head buried deep under my covers.

Mum would later blame the haunting on my father's ill doings. She believed he was trying to kill her. I wasn't convinced, simply because I had seen that dark ghost years earlier, in happier times.

Our bathroom became Mum's prayer room. Every day she would go in there and pray herself hoarse; asking Jesus Christ to intervene by finding Skippy and turning his evil schemes back on him: "Meet him, Lord. Wherever he is, meet him! Counteract his wicked plan" she'd plead. She was looking to the Lord to extract revenge on her now ex childhood sweetheart. I was praying too, but my prayers were for her. *"Lord, please help my mother"*.

I was to have only one further experience with the dark spectre, which occurred one morning when I was in a semi-dream state. I became vividly aware that the same malevolent spirit was pinning me down in my bed. I couldn't see it but I sensed it. Eventually, I spat at it, and was able to struggle free. I felt my ghostly tormentor retreat. I told my mother about what had happened and she smiled, saying "Good. You have overcome it and it will never bother you again."

She was right. I never encountered it again.

The entire experience served to confirm for me that there were things in this world, and perhaps, beyond it, that I would never understand. But I guess if there could be a Holy Ghost, then it only follows that there could be other ones too. I'm no expert and I don't wish to be, but I know what I saw.

I was to be spared any further sightings or incidents involving the supernatural, until I moved into 14 Hampstead Hill Gardens some thirty plus years later. Thankfully, a significant incident there was witnessed at the time by a visitor, who was completely freaked by the *moving object*. I took it in my stride; I had been well trained by life, or should that be, the *afterlife*, at 13 Kingsley Road.

In the years ahead, demons unseen would increasingly dominate my mother's reality. Her obsession with them would come to fill the emptiness left by the absence of the man she truly loved.

20. FROM THE KNIFE TO LIFE

I WAS SIXTEEN and struggling with my sexuality. In my 'show' of denial, I continued dating girls and even enjoyed a terrific but embarrassing orgasmic experience with one, in my pants! My private sexual fantasies increasingly involved other males, but felt wrong, even dirty; I didn't understand that they reflected my intrinsic nature and couldn't be suppressed. My Christianity exacerbated my self-loathing, shame and guilt. God failed to answer my prayers; I didn't want to be gay – a sinful batty man, but I was. I resented my gayness as much as I feared the inevitable backlash from family and friends, if my forbidden secret became known. School life was miserable and home life was worse. Suicidal thoughts entered my head and progressively made some kind of imperfect sense. I consciously succumbed to them.

The day I decided to end my life felt different from other days. I went through it in *'goodbye mode'*, knowing that it would be my last. When I got home from school, Mum was busy sewing and chatting with Carol, Leo's then current dental assistant girlfriend. No one seemed to notice or care that I was home. I slipped into the kitchen, where Mum had a limited assortment of knives, mostly the small sharp kind that she used to peel fruit and vegetables. I picked a familiar one and headed up to my room.

Once there, I put on a favourite album: Experience Gloria Gaynor, side two. Gloria was usually successful in lifting my *'down'* moods, but as much as I loved her, nothing could numb my inner pain, at least not today. Sitting at the end of my bed, I could hear the usual pre-dinner activity emanating from beyond my door. My thoughts drifted from one bleak thing to another, but settled on the element of my life that made me want to quit living; my sexuality. Then, in my morbid daze, I picked up and looked quizzically at the knife's shiny blade; it was small yet mightily capable of any job that it was tasked to do. I wasn't distressed or tearful; just numb and empty. For an extended moment I wondered whether I could really do it, but with the handle in my left hand, I placed the blade against the inner wrist of my right, and with my eyes closed, I pressed it in. Looking down, I gasped somewhat as my weeping blood submerged its shine. I thought a*ll I need to do now is drag the blade down and cut my artery.* Just as I was summoning the courage to do it, my bedroom door flew open. Startled, I jumped to my feet and my would-be lethal weapon fell from my hand to the floor. An incensed Carol was standing there, pissed off about something: "Where is your brother?" she demanded of me. Hiding my wrist, I stammered my response: "I – I don't know." Kissing her teeth, Carol turned and exited as quickly as she had entered, not noticing what I'd been up to.

Nursing my wrist, I sat down and started sobbing. I would cry a river before the day was through with me. My scar would be as a permanent reminder of a dreadful place that I'd never wilfully revisit; a final place for too many of my gay brothers and sisters, offering only a solitary one-way exit; to the mortician's cold, cold table. Fear and internalized homophobia nearly killed me too, but I didn't want to die; I wanted to live. My life-changing low was a wake-up call to either accept my authenticity and sexuality or suffer the consequences. Self-love and honesty would be the way forward and my healing would begin today; both inside and out. My date with the mortuary would have to wait.

As overwhelming as it is when in the thick of it, we have to remember that depression is the consummate deceiver and suicide is never the answer to it. Never! With the right support, and there's lots out there, we can and do overcome it and the related shame. We were born for good reason: to live authentic lives, love, be happy, and enable a happier world. Just like bad weather, the clouds of depression always pass and the sun finds a way to shine through. We can help ourselves by letting go of people and other trappings (family, 'friends', jobs, religion, etc.) that make us feel shitty about ourselves, and embrace the things that bring us joy and celebrate who we really are. Whatever our current challenges might be, a brighter future lies ahead: trust it, believe it, and create it! We will survive and thrive!

21. I AM WHAT I AM AND IT'S RAINING MEN!

IT WAS 1979. I LEFT BRONDESBURY KILBURN with a bunch of high school qualifications and a special award of cash for 'promising pupil'. Beverley's son, Spencer, aged three, was my new best friend. I adored him and would collect him from nursery after school each day. He didn't think too much of 'I Will Survive', but went absolutely crazy for 'YMCA' and a song called 'Spacer' by Sheila B Devotion; he thought she was singing about him, and I encouraged it; it made me chuckle to see his face light up with the chorus.

Before leaving school, I confided in Francesca, my biology teacher, that I thought I might be gay. She had mentioned many times in class that gay people were "normal", and said the same thing about every teenager's favourite pastime, masturbation. I felt I could approach and trust her with my big secret. When I did, she offered to put me in touch with Richard, her occasional classroom assistant. Caucasian, thirty-something, thin, curly-haired, specs wearing, and often in sandals, he helped me and other pupils with our biology class work. I'd caught him peering at me from behind his specs from time to time, but didn't think too much of it. Handing me his number, she told me he was gay and that he would welcome hearing from me. I nervously agreed to call him but later chickened out of doing so.

Kingsley Road was now a peaceful place, well, apart from my disco music blaring out and my mother's praying. She was still praying the same prayer every day: praying for my father's demise. "Meet him, Lord, meet him! Wherever he is, meet him!" was the plea that she continually made to God during her daily bathroom prayer sessions. My poor depressed mother had gone from victorious, for winning the house from my dad in court, to feeling angry, embittered and lonely; lonely for my dad, even though pride prevented her from admitting it. Her blood pressure was getting worse, as was her type-two diabetes. My evangelist mum would go from room to room praying and trying to remove the evil spirits that she believed had invaded her world. She was sometimes joined by fellow female members from her church. The ladies would whip themselves into a spiritual frenzy, speaking in tongues and praying the house down. They'd always burst into my room and pray for me too, whether I liked it or not. The women would each hold me and pass me, one to the other, each time adding prayer on top of the last prayer. I just gave in to what they were doing and didn't complain; it was what they felt needed to be done. I loved my mother very much and knew that she loved me too. This was her way of protecting me.

I was now seventeen and had just stopped dating girls. Cynthia was the last. I was beginning to accept myself; I was gay, God help me! I was feeling just about brave enough to peep out from behind my closet door. I 'came out' to my cousin Doreene and she was frightened for me. "Oh my God, Vernal, what are you going to do? They'll kill you!" she warned. I didn't really have an answer, but I figured the only way was up from the depths to which I'd survived. I knew I had to live and love being myself, or die being someone I'm not.

My concerns about my sexuality were set aside for a night, and I went off to see another disco superstar in concert. This time it was Sylvester and his Two Tons O' Fun at the Hammersmith Odeon. Sylvester was the only black gay man I was aware of and I went to see his sell-out show alone. The flamboyant singer was larger than life and as camp as a Christmas tree, but proudly glorying in it. I was fascinated by him, in a scary way. At one point in his show, the star bent over while his bassist came up behind him and the two then simulated anal intercourse, using the guitar as an improvised ginormous penis. It was all quite shocking for my inexperienced teenage eyes. Sylvester caused me to sink further into my seat when he began playing with the breasts of his two smiling backing singers, Martha Wash and Izora Rhodes-Armstead, making reference to their "voices and titties" as he did so: "They don't need these dresses, y'all, cos these women can sang!" The two women would later branch out on their own as the Weather Girls and top charts around the world with their mega hit, It's Raining Men. Even later still, Martha would enjoy solo chart success.

To rapturous applause, Sylvester donned a glittering crown and proclaimed: "You can't be a queen without a crown, honey!" Then, announcing "Gloria Gaynor is the true Queen of Disco" – a bit of a dig, perhaps, at the rising star of her arch rival, Donna Summer – he went into a gospel-tinged rendition of Never Can Say Goodbye, which concluded his memorable set.

It had been a great show, and like Gloria's, the audience was mostly made up of gay men getting on down in the aisle. I felt right at home, even if I remained glued to my seat throughout in fear of attracting attention to my shy self. My dancing would be restricted to the privacy of my bedroom. Anyway, while Gloria and Donna tussled over ownership of the disco crown, I think Sylvester was now living proof that there was only one legitimate 'queen' of disco, himself!

Plucking up my courage, at last, I decided to give Richard, the classroom assistant, a ring. He greeted me warmly and instantly invited me over to his house share in Hampstead Village. By the time I pressed his doorbell, I was shaking in my sneakers and dripping sweat of anxiety at the prospect talking to a real gay man for the first time about what being gay means. When the door opened, someone other than Richard was standing there and I was then immediately pinned to the doorframe by an over-sized, over-enthusiastic Alsatian dog. This was not what I was expecting, at all! When the friendly beast realised there was something more exciting in its bowl than my being, it released my shoulders and retreated past the amused man at the door, who, before I could even say my name, called out for Richard. A bit slower than his four-legged house mate, a beaming Richard came running to welcome me in, and yes, he was in his sandals again.

I have no idea whether my biology teacher was 'in the know' about his true motives when she referred me to Richard for "support and advice", but I was expecting something along the lines of a caring counselling session. Richard, however, had darker intentions and wasn't at all interested in talking with me about my sexuality issues, or anything else. In the privacy of his upstairs bedroom, my inexperienced young flesh froze to the spot as the silent grinning older man removed my clothes and stepped out of his sandals and trousers. Now both naked, I said nothing even though I wanted to say something...like stop! He pushed me towards his single bed and was soon exploring my tense body with his hands and mouth. My mind went elsewhere as he put his hand over my mouth and proceeded to enjoy himself without any regard for me or the original purpose of my visit. My tortured childhood years taught me how to zone out and I did; I suddenly had something to be grateful to my siblings for. As he climaxed, I somehow manoeuvred myself off the bed and got dressed before he could stop shooting, but like a naughty school boy, I then waited with my head bowed for him to dismiss me with, "You can go now."

I left Richard's house feeling used and totally disgusted with myself. My first serious gay sex experience felt like a bad road accident. Richard was undoubtedly a predator, or worse, and my teacher had knowingly or unwittingly assisted him. I was angry and felt the only classroom one or both of them belonged in should be behind secured walls. I decided to put Richard out of my mind and ignored his subsequent attempts to contact me. I never saw my teacher again either.

Emboldened by twice feeling a kinship with other gay people, my next 'out' act was a huge leap forward, or that's what I was hoping. For some time I'd been purchasing *Black Echoes*, a weekly soul and disco music newspaper that featured a number of different charts, including the Billboard Disco Top 20. I kept a particularly keen eye on this chart to see which tracks were getting the most reaction on America's dance floors, and this would then inspire my weekly purchases at my local record shop, scarce pocket money allowing. The same newspaper also carried free personal ads, including a section for gay men and women. I'm not sure what made me do it, but I decided to place an ad myself, which read: *'Vincent, 17, black, gay, and considered good looking. Into Gloria Gaynor, Village People, Grace Jones, Sylvester and Donna Summer'.*

It took some considerable courage to place the ad, especially as there was a major risk involved. The newspaper did not offer box numbers to its free advertisers, so I had no option but to use my actual address: *13 Kingsley Road, Kilburn.*

It was stupid as well as risky to publish my home address in any advert, but especially a gay-related one. However, my teenage head thought the risks were worth the potential blissful outcome of meeting another gay guy...at last.

I held my breath to see what the response, if any, would be, but I didn't have to wait long at all! On its publication date, I went to the newsagent to pick up my copy of the paper, and on returning home, quickly turned to the personal ads to make sure mine was there, and it was!

Of course, in my single-mindedness, I neglected to consider the idea that someone I know may see the ad. To my total horror the doorbell rang, and my friend Marlon from number 19 was standing there: "Hey Vernal, have you got someone living in your house called Vincent? Look at this." He thrust the cutting of my ad towards my face but failed to notice that he was talking to my corpse. I had died on the spot.

Springing back to life, I had to think on my feet, fast!

"What? I can't believe this!" I said, affecting deep indignation. With that, I out-performed Daniel Day-Lewis and snatched the piece of paper out of Marlon's hand, while asserting: "I'm going to show this to my mum." I quickly shut the door in his face and ran up to my room in a panic. *"God help me!"* I mused to myself as I began to regret placing the ad. What on Earth had I unleashed? But God wasn't ready to help me just yet.

On the fifth morning of the ad's appearance, I heard my mother wail: "Lord, my house has turned into a post office!" A whole load of letters to someone called Vincent had been arriving all week. By the weekend I'd received sixty-four responses, and with the incident with Marlon in mind, I was both happy and anxious about it. But things were about to go from bad to worse.

The following week my unmistakably annoyed mother knocked on my bedroom door to tell me: "There is someone at MY front door to see YOU, *Vincent!!!*" I tried not to panic, but I did. *Who the hell can it be?* I thought as I nervously negotiated the stairs to the ground floor. I opened the door to see what some would call a stereo-typical *dirty old man* standing there, complete with off-white raincoat! Well into his sixties and as white as Caucasian could be, his oddly small smiling face was characterized by more lines than Paddington and Victoria stations combined. The short, somewhat twitchy-looking man kept his hands in his coat pockets and seemed to involuntarily shift about in his sparkling black polished shoes. Although he looked as though he'd made some effort to impress, I was only moments away from discovering that he was accompanied by motives dirtier than a sodden mudslide. In offering me his denture smile, he also offered his unwelcome opening line: "Hello, are you Vincent?" I was momentarily speechless, as I struggled to decide whether to deny or admit to being his target. The age of consent was still 21 for gay men, but this guy was at least three times over that threshold and obviously unconcerned about the potential legal consequences of pursuing someone my age. Perhaps he was a paedophile. Hell, he must be! For a moment I thought of Richard; other than liking young boys, they had curly hair in common too. Hmm, perhaps this was his dad.

In an attempt to stifle the audio of our interaction from my mother's justifiably inquisitive ears, I stepped forward, partially closing the door behind me. Whispering my timid response: "Yes. What do you want?"

"Well, hello there!" he proclaimed as if greeting a long lost friend. He didn't stop there, unfortunately: "I saw your advert in *Black Echoes* and thought I'd come to see you." Although my mouth said nothing, my distressed face should have spoken volumes: *go away*!!! But Vincent's unwanted visitor wasn't going anywhere, at least not until he'd shown off his special surprise: "Look, I've brought my sleeper van with me, if you want to come and have a chat with me in it."

What! The man's sordid intentions weren't even partially hidden. I was in a nightmare taking place in broad daylight. In his desperation for sex with a boy, he'd made his way to my address uninvited, and in his lustful delusion, or arrogance, he had the nerve to knock on my door and tell my mother that he'd come to see her underage teenage son; the deep in shit-trouble Vincent. What sort of messed up pervert must this man be to behave this way? And he's brought a mobile bedroom with him, too! I was beyond furious, but at the same shaking in my socks in fear about how to get myself out of the situation I had unwittingly created. If my mother didn't kill off 'Vincent' tonight, then I would happily do the job for her. Judging by her mood, if I was unsuccessful, Mum would nurse me back to health just so she could have the pleasure of killing me herself.

For a moment I just looked at him, wordlessly, taking in how his grey-brown curly hair framed his ghostly white face. But his smutty intentions is what should have been framed; by the bars of a prison cell. There was no way I was getting into his sleeper. I just wanted the ghastly apparition before me to go away.

"No, I don't want to do that" I asserted, finally. "Please, please go away!" My voice broke with emotion, or was it fear? However, in his quest to get his sweaty old hands on my young black flesh, he didn't quite hear me, or couldn't. Then, after looking me up and down as if he had X-ray eyes, he responded with: "Okay, but I'll wait in the sleeper for you for a few minutes. I'm parked just over there." He said, smiling and pointing to the grey vehicle concerned.

I said nothing else, but stepped back inside and shut the door on the sick fuckwit. Once within the safety of my personal space, I was gripped by the depressing possibility that he might be the first of many such uninvited creeps.

Oh God, why oh why did I place that damn ad!

Mum kissed her teeth at me for the next two hours, non-stop! I later discovered that she had opened one of the many letters addressed to the other me, Vincent, when I came across the empty envelope. My badly kept secret was out! But, perhaps to protect herself from the truth, Mum never confronted me about it or the strange man at the door. I never approached her, either. I wouldn't dare!

Despite what had happened, I decided that I'd got this far and could not now turn back. Surely it could only get better...surely!

There were a ton of respondents' letters to deal with, and some of them looked very promising indeed. I read each of them very carefully, especially the ones with photos. I decided I would write back to them all, even if I wasn't interested. It was the polite thing to do. However, the white guy who sent me a faceless picture with a black sex toy up his rectum found himself torn to shreds and in the bin, albeit with a little hesitation on my part. Although I was somewhat curious, and maybe even aroused, I feared the said picture would be found by my mother and I'd rather die an agonizing death of a thousand paper-cut slashes before allowing that to happen.

With a hazardous week behind me, and with somewhat tarnished confidence, I decided to go on a date with a Caucasian guy called Derek. Well, I thought I was going on a date. My unsuspecting sister Jan dropped me off at his address in Wembley after I told her I was visiting a former school friend. Derek, with his brown 'clone' tache that matched his fringe, was in his mid-forties but looked a lot older and fatter than his picture. He was mild mannered, at first, and I felt happy to be in the company of a real live gay man who wasn't Richard. But I wasn't in his ground-floor flat for ten minutes before his hand made its way to the front of my trousers. All my fantasies about a romantic first date hit the ground along with my pants, and we were soon having some kind of one-sided sex on his carpet. He was only after one thing, and he got it. I loathed every sweaty second of it.

At the agreed time, Jan returned and beeped her mini's horn to let me know she was waiting outside. Derek and I uttered an awkward goodbye, as I left and took my seat next to Jan. To my embarrassment, we weren't long into our journey when she asked me about the awful smell that had accompanied me into the car. I must have smelt of sex but made some excuse about it. Thankfully Jan didn't question me further, but her expression told me she was less than convinced. When I got back to Kingsley Road I couldn't get into the bath quickly enough; I was determined to rid my body of Derek's sweaty stench, along with the unhappy memory of what had happened on my first gay date. The memory would linger long after his smell was washed off my body and into the drain.

With the disappointment of meeting Derek (and Richard) behind me, my next date was with a twenty-two year old Irish guy called Raymond. He was very handsome, with a low-cut beard and an East London accent. I mentioned that I was a horror fan, so he took me to the Odeon Leicester Square to see a late night showing of *Alien,* which was the top box office hit at the time. Now this was the kind of date I was hoping for. He was a gentleman, too; so there were no advances in the dark of the cinema. I liked that. He dropped me home afterwards and I plucked up the courage to invite him in. It was a totally crazy thing to do on reflection, but I liked him enough to go with my heart rather than my fear, or so I told myself. In truth, I was pretty certain that Mum would be asleep by this late hour, but in upstaging even the scariest moments in Alien, she was standing right there when we walked in. For a moment I froze, not knowing what on Earth to say or do, but Raymond's warmth and charm completely disarmed her. Minutes later she was making him tea and chatting away with the biggest and warmest of smiles on her face. I was baffled and highly suspicious and struggled not to show it. Raymond was oblivious to my concern about my mother's uncharacteristically relaxed attitude and carried on making small talk with her. A nervously long twenty minutes or so later, Mum said a hearty good night, slipped from the room, and left Raymond and a bemused me sitting together on her favourite sofa. After a while, when he thought it was safe to do so, he leaned over and kissed my shy lips. It was brief, firm, tender, and oh so welcome. I really liked it, even if the bliss of the moment was cruelly interrupted by a freaky macabre vision in my head of Mum re-entering the room with her open Bible in one hand, a blood-thirsty machete in the other, and a homicidal look in her eye, which signalled the end of sinner son Vincent and his equally abhorrent lover to be. However, the thought was emphatically terminated by the presence of the smiling man sitting next to me. He wasn't my lover just yet, but if God answers prayers, then it wouldn't be long now. Raymond's beautiful kiss felt like it was my very first real kiss; man to man, heart to heart, and soul to soul. Our subsequent hot kisses were hotter and more passionate than the kisses before; they did all the talking as my mind forgot about my mother and my body began to levitate off the sofa and onto a new plane of *sexcitement*. I wonder if Raymond saw when my joyful heart leapt out of my chest to embrace his in a BIG THANK YOU for his having come into my life.

Oh God, so this is why I was born; to kiss and be held by this awesome man.

We spoke a lot by phone following our first date and I just couldn't stop myself from entertaining all sorts of fantasies about Raymond and me; *together-forever* kind of fantasies. Old love songs sounded fresh and full of so much more than just sweetly sung *lyrics*. Every kissing couple on my television screen was overridden by my vision of me kissing Raymond. He was my first thought in the morning and my last before drifting off to sleep at night. If I was lucky, I would find him waiting for me in my dreams.

Raymond, my Raymond, my Ray of light, be it day or night.

A couple of weeks later and I spent my very first night away from Kingsley Road as a burgeoning adult. Raymond invited me to dinner at the flat he shared with his mother, who was conveniently away. He picked me up after Mum had gone to bed, with the intention, he said, of me sampling his home cooking. So, with his scrumptious spicy tomato-coated pasta sitting in our happy stomachs, our keen kisses provided the dessert. Since our first meeting, my being inside of Raymond was my primary sexual fantasy. He kindly obliged. It was my first time, and I wanted the incredible experience to last beyond forever: my flesh and his as one magnificent manifestation of black and white perfection. If I had died after we'd climaxed together then I would have died a happy teenager, feeling that I'd lived a full and satisfying life. Mourners peering upon me at my funeral would be compelled to cease their weeping and wonder at the ecstatic expression on my face; the expression of a boy who became a man whilst inside his personal Ray of delight.

We repeatedly sought to exhaust our mutual sexual energy that night, and this appeared to happen when sleep got the better of Raymond, but I wasn't having it! He was stirred back to consciousness by me finding my way into him again, and he responded with his beautiful welcoming smile. My heaven was right here with him; inside of him.

The next morning, in a deliberate act of revenge, I was rudely awakened by Raymond's excessively loud singing. He was in the shower. Well, if I was into delivering drive-by punishment, then I would simply drive up and get Raymond to sing to my sorry enemies. He was no Johnny Mathis! I followed the sound and made him smile when he caught sight of naked me with my fingers in my ears and a feigned scowl on my face. His decision to splash water at me was the cue I needed to join him for a watery play-fight. As we slipped off each other's skin trying to get the better of each other, I delivered my verdict on his singing: "If you ever ruin Never Can Say Goodbye again, then I will do just that; say goodbye and dive out the nearest window to escape you!" Raymond laughed and accused me of "pure jealousy" and splashed me some more. Our mock wrestling soon gave way to sensual full-on body caresses. Looking me dead in the eye, my body reacted to his triple X sexualized whisper: "I bet all you want me to do now is drop this soap, right?" which he promptly did. Clearing the steamy water from my eyes, I was so hard I thought I would break. "Whoops" he teased, still looking at me, "I'm so damn clumsy in the mornings," He kissed me intensely, then turned his back and bent down to retrieve the bar; or so I thought. He was taking his time down there! I took the initiative and redirected the shower's jets before taking advantage of his predicament.

With our soapy sex play fresh in my mind, Raymond, who was now complaining about being late for work, dropped me off at Kingsley Road before my mother could even suspect that I hadn't spent the night in my bedroom. It worked like magic. Ray's magic.

Two nights later, Raymond, now my first ever boyfriend, took me to my first gay house party, somewhere in East London. I followed sheepishly behind him as we squeezed our way through the thrusting bodies in the partying living room. There was something approaching fifty guests – a good mix of black and white guys and absolutely no women. The music was my kind of music; soulful disco. It was strange to see two men dancing together, but I liked it. I liked it a lot. Raymond left me in a corner to find us something to drink. It was to be something soft for me and something a little stronger for him. I did my best not to look too obvious, but I was keen to check out the guys in the room. They were all sharply dressed, confident and happy men, but I must have been the youngest there. The black guys were especially well dressed and I noticed that quite a few had permed hair. My shy eyes would hit the floor every time they met someone else's. I was feeling right at home, and this had much to do with the realization that Sylvester and I were not the only black gay men in the world. We appeared to exist in significant numbers. Yes, black men were gay men too!

I was still awaiting Raymond's return when the most handsome black man tapped me on my shoulder and said, "Hey, cheer up, matey, it's not the end of the world. I'm Marvin. What's your name, cute guy?"

"I'm Vernal," I whispered, anxiously.

"Nice name - er, Vernon?"

"No, Vernal!" I said, raising my voice above the music.

"Oh, Verbal" he laughed. I laughed too, eventually. He was kidding with me and the penny had finally dropped.

"So what sort of name is that then?" his jovial nature was winning my approval. The smiling man with the angelic face was in his mid-to-late twenties and dressed to kill. I couldn't really make out much about what he was saying, because I was too busy wondering how one person could be so damn handsome.

"Are you with that white boy?" Marvin asked.

"You mean Raymond? Yes, I am."

"So is he your boyfriend or something?"

"I've just met him" I insisted.

"So can I give you my number then?"

My blush spoke for me. Marvin quickly wrote it down and slipped the piece of paper into my sweaty hand. "Call me. OK, Vinyl?" He chuckled and winked at me. I said I would.

Marvin left me and rejoined his giggling friends. One of them waved at me and mouthed "You are hot, baby boy!" My shy eyes turned to the floor in response. After a while I began wondering what had happened to Raymond. Finally, I spotted him making his way towards me holding our two drinks. Just as he placed my drink into my hand another black guy came up behind him and grabbed his backside in a brutal manner. I was surprised and disappointed, or perhaps just jealous. "Well it's been a little while since I last had fun with this,'" the muscle-bound guy said to Raymond, who didn't look at all embarrassed. I felt my teenage face give in to a sulk. The guy disappeared and Raymond noticed that I was less than sparkling. "Hey, what's the matter?" Before I could say anything, another black guy came up and did exactly the same thing. I was pissed off, not so much with jealousy, but embarrassment. I got the impression Raymond was well known for all the wrong reasons and I was going off him very quickly. I was learning the hard way that some gay guys were all about sex and that romance was rarely on the cards. I guess I was just a naive seventeen-year old, but I had my standards and I wasn't going to let them drop, at least not so soon! I'd had a childhood full of people treating me like crap and I didn't want any more of it.

In the middle of my sulk, Marvin came over again to ask me to dance. I agreed. Why not? I thought. Raymond was busy doing the same with someone else. That was my first ever slow dance with another guy, and an exceptionally beautiful dance it was too!

I was later introduced to another black man at that party and it turned out that he'd also responded to my advert in *Black Echoes.* He scolded me for failing to respond. It had been my intention to respond to every letter, I told him, but I hadn't managed to do that just yet. He was still pissed off.

Raymond? Well, it was good while it lasted; about a month, I think. I went back to my *Black Echoes* respondents and decided that there was another guy worth meeting; a very handsome young white man in his very early twenties, with straight blond hair and model looks. His name was Simon White. We immediately hit it off as friends and immediately became virtually inseparable. We had the same love of disco music and would spend hour upon hour enjoying the genre together at Kingsley Road or at the huge Trellick Tower apartment he shared with his much older partner. I soon guessed that theirs was an 'open relationship'. As well as disco, Simon adored 1950s rocker Little Richard; in fact, he was absolutely crazy about him. In between spinning our favourite tracks, we often got frisky with each other. It was fun; at least it was for me. I was exploring my sexuality and he was a great person to do it with.

A few weeks after our meeting, Simon introduced me to my first gay disco. It was called BANG! It was located on the Charing Cross Road in London's West End and held on Monday nights. From the moment I stepped into the vast club I was in awe; I could not believe my over-excited eyes. There were *hundreds* of gay men on the two levels dancing to the latest disco hits, played by DJ Gary London and DJ Norman. They even had sexy male dancers in tight shorts, busy strutting their funky stuff on raised platforms in front of the DJ stations. I'd never heard my favourite musical genre so loud: thunderous, pounding disco music, which impacted my chest plate with every beat from the super-sized loud speakers. I had died and gone to disco heaven. Everyone looked so happy, healthy, and free. There was absolutely no sign of the huge disease with a little name that only a few years later would bring unthinkable horror and destruction into our lives.

Simon went to the bustling bar to buy us drinks and I stood and watched the all-male crowd party to hits that I knew so well: 'Queen of Fools' by Jessica Williams, 'You Make Me Feel Mighty Real' by Sylvester, 'Bridge Over Troubled Water' by Linda Clifford, 'Heaven Must Have Sent You' by Bonnie Pointer, 'Your Love' by Lime, 'If You Could Read My Mind' by Viola Wills, 'Knock On Wood' by Amii Stewart... 'Never Can Say Goodbye' by Gloria, and 'Last Dance' by Donna. There was a gentle tap on my arm and I turned expecting to see Simon, but instead found a tall smiling dark-haired guy asking me to dance. The handsome man introduced himself as Peter, but I quickly explained that I wasn't alone. He was lovely about it and gave me his number anyway. It turned out his surname was Tatchell. Peter melted away into the crush on the heaving dance floor, and when Simon and I finished up our drinks, we did the same. By the time the thumping disco beat stopped, my clothes were soaked in sweat, my ears were ringing, and my nose was occupied by the strange smell of *poppers*. I didn't touch the stuff myself, but the drug was evidently popular among my fellow clubbers. I'd had a fantastic night, and there would be many more to come, thanks to Simon and Bang!

Peter would go on to become the official Labour Parliamentary Candidate for Bermondsey, and later, a world renowned human rights campaigner. Future catastrophic events in our community would bring us together again, and millions of others would join us in the fight of our lives.

I was now out of the closet, at least a little bit, and there was no going back now. However, for many years to come, I would be haunted by a feeling that my being gay was wrong, dirty and shameful. It was a feeling that had been drummed into me by the black community, the media and religion. My teenage years would become a distant memory before I would begin to genuinely believe that there was nothing wrong with people like me; gay people. For now, disco music and Bang! would be my refuge and making friends my new hobby. I was going to enjoy some sex too, and hope that love won't take too long to find me.

22. BLACK MEN LOVING BLACK MEN

I LEFT SCHOOL EARLIER IN THE YEAR with a bunch of passes at certificate/O level, scoring best in English, biology and history; pretty good, but not the stuff to win over any university - which was never discussed. My mother needed me to get a job as quickly as possible to help out with the household bills. Her finances were in a sorry state, so any job would do.

A helpful assistant at the local Job Centre put me on the phone with a perspective employer. The male voice told me that I sounded just right for his job, working in his antique furniture shop on West End Lane, West Hampstead. I wasn't entirely enthusiastic – what did I know about antiques? But I duly went home and changed into the only shirt and tie I owned and arrived five minutes early for my interview. On entering the shop front, a door chime alerted the owner. A middle-aged white man with knitted brow asked whether he could help. I smilingly told him my name and that I'd come for the interview. His reply completely beheaded me: "Oh no, I thought you were white" he laughed and continued: "My customers won't want to see a black person in here, no way. Sorry you wasted your time." I thanked him politely and walked out. I didn't know any better back then. When I got home I told Mum about my first job *interview* lasting about thirty seconds, but she had nothing to say, other than, "keep trying, you hear me?"

We both knew what had happened was wrong, but neither of us had any idea what, if anything, could be done about it. I had been the victim of blatant racism for the first time in my young life and it affected me deeply, but I had to pick my self-esteem up, dust myself off and get on with task in hand: finding a job.

My next interview was for the position of office junior with One Stop Records, a vinyl record wholesaler based in Harlesden, north London – CDs were still some years away. I was interviewed by a Caucasian Canadian man in his early forties who offered me the job on the spot. The salary was forty-five pounds a week and I would start the following Monday. Mum was very pleased and I was chuffed to have secured my first job. My remit wasn't anything exciting: I was to spend all my day filing and matching invoices with orders. The exciting part of the job was that I was surrounded by delicious vinyl records at wholesale price, and that, by itself, made the job worthwhile.

Raymond and I had very little communication following my observations at the party in East London, and even though I was still fond of him, I decided that I deserved better than what he had to offer. I wasn't willing to be his latest *black dick* on the block.

I found the courage to call Marvin and he sounded pleased to hear from me. I'd been thinking about him a lot since our meeting at my gay party debut. He was a much sought after hairdresser and we agreed to meet at his busy salon near Oxford Circus. Seeing him again confirmed both his beauty and his natural ability to make me laugh and forget my hang ups. It took some nerve on my part, but I invited him home where I introduced him to my unsuspecting mother as a friend from work. His being black, handsome and personable, won her confidence and she carried on sewing while chatting with him, indeed, they took on the air of family. I made my way to my bedroom and Marvin eventually followed. Once there, my nervous but eager lips yearned to mesh with his, but his older eyes and my younger ones met first and confirmed our intentions. We turned up Linda Clifford on the stereo – a song he requested called You Are, You Are – and propped up a chair against the door; serving more as a psychological barrier than a physical one against my mother, should she decide to enter unannounced. Her being only two rooms away didn't stop us from exploring each other's bodies which, in a matter of seconds, were free from any clothing. I caught my breath on seeing Marvin naked, taking in his luscious scent as I did so. My eyes marveled at what they were seeing; he was stunningly beautiful, all over. Kissing him felt different from previous kisses with white men; there was a profound emotional connection between us that seemed to flow from our blackness, and I found myself both riveted and empowered by it. If black men kissing one another was considered a shameful 'non-black' act by the wider black community, then my being inside of Marvin confronted them with the ultimate taboo which they long held religiously (!) sacred. The mere mention of what we were doing would be greeted with cries of "abomination" or even calls for our deaths. Yet, here we were; two passionate black men, one older and the other younger, making love that hate, ignorance, and adherence to outdated colonial-induced bigotry could never unmake. Our being black enhanced our closeness, and I could feel our hearts merge to celebrate our unison as natural and right; Marvin, me, and our bold black beautiful bliss. Once wouldn't be enough for us, we had to do it again, and we did. As we lay in each other's arms afterwards, I joked that if he ever got tired working as a hairdresser then he would easily find work as a fireman, complete with his own hose, or a chef, with his own giant rolling pin. Marvin put his hand over his mouth to mute his laughter, which caused me to laugh too. Then, faking Barry White's husky voice, he whispered in my ear: "I wanna be inside you too, babe", but my response was no joke at all. I was emphatic in letting him know that it was not going to happen; I wasn't ready to try that yet, if ever. Looking at his over-generous manhood, I was certain that no one in their right mind would dare take it, or should! He responded by saying that a man should bleed like a woman when he loses his virginity, adding that that's what happened to him on his first occasion. I retorted that any guy who was foolish enough to take a cock deserving of its own regional post code would surely be unable to walk for months afterwards. Marvin then sat straight up, and with a stern expression on his face said: "Get it right, V! It would be years, not months!" We both collapsed into each other laughing and holding each other close. Our mutual hysterics prompted us to cover each other's mouths to try and stop the sound of our foolery from carrying to my mother's ever-alert ears.

With my head on his chest, I glanced up at Marvin's adorable face and heard my besotted teenage heart say, *"This is love"*. His full-on caress again alerted my entire being to a bespoke, almost tribal connection that I sensed only existed between black men who love black men. Our straight counterparts were missing out on this prize. Homophobia had robbed them of the gift that comes with our unison as natural lovers and its inherent ability to disappear the tensions that make us unnatural foes. Even my teenage brain knew that it shouldn't be easier to reach for a gun and slay *a brother* than to embrace and love him, but our straight brothers are too afraid of their emotional vulnerability to drop their guns and embrace hearts.

Being intimate with Marvin was a revelation to all my senses. Even my novice heart knew that loving one another was our greatest asset and the natural grand prize in our evolutionary journey as black men. Marvin made me want to grasp and nurture that love. He single-handedly put the pride into my being black and gay and cemented it into place by being so exceptionally beautiful. I was very pleased to be with him, and deeply inspired, too, by his dignity and confidence in his sexuality. I began to feel my internalized shame begin to lose its grip. Thanks to Marvin, I now knew the reality of being black, gay and proud.

Within a matter of weeks, I'd gone from knowing no gay people to knowing a few. I was feeling much better about life; thanks to Marvin, but also, my ongoing friendship with Simon and our passionate love affair with disco music. I was to worry that my mother and her church sisters had frightened him off. We were busy playing records in my bedroom, as we often did, when the four larger than life black women burst into the room, praying, singing and speaking in tongues. Now, if Gloria Gaynor was afraid and petrified, then poor Simon was both horrified and terrified. Like a transfixed doomed deer, he found himself involuntarily rooted to the floorboards as the women drowned out our music with their impromptu trance-state gospel fest. I was acutely embarrassed, both for me and for him, but after a prayer or two, the stomping holy women departed and Simon quickly rediscovered his ability to move freely about. We both laughed it off, once we'd recovered from the shock of the experience, but I privately thanked heaven that we weren't up to any frisky business when the women came in; because while Gloria would survive, Simon and I would not have lived to spin another record.

Six months after joining One Stop Records, my employer went into receivership and I began working for a Christmas and party decorations company in Neasden called Chatsworth Press. That turned out to be a bad move. I spent my time being the office junior and an occasional extra pair of hands in the warehouse. My colleagues were mostly nice people, but there were a couple of them who were just nasty. To them good management meant shouting and being disrespectful. I hated the job and told my mother that I was never going back there. She was not at all pleased, but she knew something significant had led me to that decision.

I spent the next few months at a loss as to what I wanted to do with my so-called career. I really enjoyed theatre and dance at school, and thought it would be good to get into that field, so I took drama classes with a rather mouthy northern teacher based in Ladbroke Grove, named Richard. He was obviously gay too and thought I had real potential. He soon suggested that I audition for youth theatre, which I did. It was now the summer of 1981 and I took my nineteen-year-old self along to the Cockpit Youth Theatre near Paddington. As previously rehearsed with Richard, I read something from Shakespeare whilst stripping to my underwear. The bemused theatre director signed me up, perhaps out of sympathy. I was given a part in the summer production of *'Fires of Levana'*; a fictional post-nuclear apocalyptic musical, written especially for the youth theatre. I was over the moon! Even though I would not be paid, I saw the role as training for my future career in the theatre. Mum was happy because I was happy, even though money was still tight. I was on the dole and getting a little cash that way.

Rehearsals went well with the rest of the twenty-plus cast of budding actors and actresses, including Robbie Gee, who would later be cast for the big screen by Guy Ritchie, and Treva Etienne, who in future years would secure an on-going role in the popular TV series, *London's Burning*, and later become a significant star in America, too. He was extremely talented and a very nice personality too. My excitement was tinged with nerves as the first of only three performances was upon me. Dad, Simon and a few other friends and family members (not Mum, sadly) were in the audience – not that they'd be seeing much of me. I was more of a dancer than an actor, as my lines were very few indeed. My character chased the girls and danced to silly music. The climax of my role saw me dropping my pants and showing my ass to the audience as I chased a girl off the stage. I heard my dad laughing louder than anyone else at that point. Apparently during the interval he went around telling everyone "That's my son!" and that he was very proud. However, he would never say those kind words to me directly. The play went well and Time Out Magazine bothered to carry a picture of me with my dance partner, holding her above my head in a graceful pose.

My next audition was for the Old Vic Youth Theatre. I used the same piece that had got me a part in the previous show, and again, it worked. The production this time was much more lavish: Ibsen's *Peer Gynt*. I played a 'gentleman' in Morocco, as well as a demonic, gyrating troll, decked out in a grass skirt. I thoroughly enjoyed being part of the show, even if the audience, which this time included Jan, Leo and

Dad, fell asleep due to boredom during the one and only performance. At least they came, which was good of them.

That production over and I was rapidly heading towards my twentieth birthday with little direction and no money in my pocket. I decided to improve my chances for a future acting career and auditioned for Mountview Theatre School. Even though I was offered a place, I had to turn it down and go back to work because my mother needed the money. Eventually, mounting bills forced her to put 13 Kingsley Road on the market. It sold in a matter of weeks. Now, at last, she had some money and we could really move on with our lives – I hoped.

Brent Council offered us a two-bedroom council flat at 153 Melrose Avenue in Willesden Green. All my siblings had long since left home and were now all parents themselves living scattered around London. Beverley now had two children, Spencer and Mitchell; Jan had four sons of her own, including JJ, her eldest. The birth of Bunny's beautiful daughter, Nyisha, really changed him, and the same with Leo and the birth of Samantha, his gorgeous daughter. They became very pleasant people; so much so, that their treatment of me in our younger years was forgiven if not forgotten. Their roles as fathers meant they were no longer defined by their haemophilia; they were 'normal' fathers, first. I thoroughly enjoyed looking after my nephews and nieces, but especially Spencer, with whom I had a special bond. He was like the little brother I never had.

Mum soon made our new home into her new palace. The property was not self-contained, so we were effectively living with the ground-floor neighbours in one big family house. They were a very creepy white couple, whose children had been taken away by social workers. I had lived there only a couple of weeks before the female, who was always caked in dirt, started flirting with me. I was passing her in the passage way one day and she let her dressing gown fall open whilst looking expectantly at me. My skin started crawl as I passed her by. Her one-eyed husband was even worse, but thankfully, he didn't flirt with me. I kept my distance. My mother made it clear that they were not to come up to her part of the house without being invited and the couple mostly respected that, although they would sometimes break the rule when they smelt the aroma of her cooking.

The sound of arguing and stale smoke drifting upstairs was a constant irritation to my mum, but at least they weren't as bad as serial killer, Dennis Nilsen, who lived just a few doors away. It turned out that he'd murdered and dismembered fifteen young men in his homes in Melrose Avenue and also at Cranley Gardens in Muswell Hill. I watched from my bedroom window as the police erected a tarpaulin tent in his garden, to conceal their digging. Nilsen was eventually convicted of the killings and will spend the rest of his miserable life in prison.

Finally, Brent Council offered my mother a refurbished self-contained flat at 8 Harrowdene Close, Wembley, which she gratefully accepted. The flat at Harrowdene Close was much nicer, especially once my mother set about decorating it to her high standards. My bedroom was pretty ordinary, but it was very comfortable. It was great to enjoy some privacy again, for the first time since leaving Kingsley Road.

Oh, I'm missing someone. Huh, so much for black men loving their own kind. Linda Clifford is again playing on my stereo, and here I am with tears in my eyes. Oh Marvin, where are you? You're a runaway love.

My juvenile fantasy of a long-lasting relationship with Marvin was shattered when he told me that he loved his partner – one of London's very rare black policeman – and intended to make their relationship work. Our love affair was over before it could really begin. However, despite my pain, I was still very pleased to know him.

We didn't know it at the time, but the vicious hand of fate was already busy crafting a much more agonizing ending for us.

23. 'BORN AGAIN' - THANKS TO EXEGESIS!

IT WAS 1982. I WAS TWENTY-ONE YEARS OLD and my stage career had been all but abandoned through want of money. To keep my toe in the water, I had accepted an office-hours administration job at the Dominion Theatre on Tottenham Court Road. In the evenings I worked at the newly opened Barbican Arts Centre as an usher.

On the weekends, I continued attending acting classes. Selwyn, my new drama and voice teacher, told me that he sensed my potential and believed he had the answer to unlocking it: "Exegesis!" I had never heard the word. He explained that Exegesis was a self-actualization course to boost assertiveness and confidence. He suggested that I go along to a free introductory evening where all would be revealed. I had a lot of admiration for Selwyn and agreed to go along whilst secretly worrying about what the hell I was letting myself in for – with some justification, as it turned out.

The following week, I made my way to the Paddington hotel where the Exegesis introductory evening was being held. As I made my way in, I was met by a team of extremely glamorous men and women. They sign-posted me to the conference room. I took a seat amongst twenty-five or so other Exegesis-curious people. I gulped a glass of orange juice as a stunningly beautiful young woman at the front of the room introduced herself: "Good evening, everyone, my name is Kim. I am here to welcome you to the Exegesis and the greatest opportunity of your life." The only other name I heard that evening was that of Robert, the organisation's founder.

I'm not sure whether it was Kim's mentioning that the course had been utilized by top musicians or MPs, but forty-five minutes later I found myself signing up my broke-ass-self for the full weekend course, at the cost of a massive one hundred and fifty pounds. That was a lot of money for the low waged, like myself. I managed to persuade Mum that the course would help my career as an actor, so she gave me half of the money required and Dad stumped up the rest. That was one good thing about having separated parents; you could play them off against each other.

The following Friday evening I trudged through rain-sodden streets to the same hotel, and hopefully, if a little sceptically, took my place on the weekend course that would change my life for the better, forever – according to Selwyn and Kim. The ballroom was set out theatre style, with slightly dimmed lighting. My heart thumped along with those of the other seventy-nine participants in anticipation, as Kim took her seat at the front. She surveyed the roomful of misfits whose dysfunctional lives had brought them before her. Six attentive assistants sat three to a table, on either side of the room, and another two were posted at the doors at the back of the room. I pondered as I waited how they had got me to sit in the front row? I would more naturally be drawn to the rear of a room full of people, out of sight. I kept hearing Selwyn's voice say, "Give it all you've got, Vernal! You won't regret it." What was it that I was supposed to give my all to? And was I doing this for Selwyn, or for me? I was getting to grips with that thought, when a second realisation dawned upon me: I was the only black person in the room. Somehow this spelt danger to me. Although there was no rational reason to be afraid, that's how my mind worked, then.

Just as my mind was turning over all the reasons that I should make a dash for the door, Kim's superior tone pierced the air and the room fell silent. After a blunt greeting, came the house rules that we would have to abide by for the weekend. Sunday night seemed to be receding into the future like some vertigo-inducing Hitchcock camera shot. We were to get very few toilet and food breaks, and leaving the room outside of scheduled breaks was not permitted. Anyone who flouted the rules would not be allowed back into the room. My anxiety level crept up another notch.

With the house rules out of the way, Kim proceeded to single me out, before anyone else, to stand up and introduce myself to the room. I slowly rose to my feet and struggled to find something worthwhile to say. Annoyed, Kim barked at me to "speak up clearly, so everyone at the back can hear!" I did, but God only knows what it was that I actually said; my mouth moved and words came out. As I sat down again, I didn't even hear what those who followed me had to say, as I was too caught up the horror of being the first to speak.

I had been on stage before, though always hiding behind a role, so this kind of self-exposure was new to me; I was forced to be myself and it was scary. I was keen to see who was shaking at least as much as I was, and there were more than a few. With her shoulder-length blonde hair and sculpted black suit with matching high heels, Kim's air of supreme confidence filled the room. Each of us presented a superficial snapshot of who we really were; only sharing the good bits and hoping that Kim would be taken in by our rosy-hued portrayals of ourselves. But the lady was not to be fooled.

Under Kim's steely gaze and those of her inscrutable assistants, the room heard the participants' introductions in morgue-like silence. Things grew more bizarre as Kim rose from her 'throne' at the front of the room, and with a glass of water in hand, strode over to a plump, curly-haired white woman sitting in the rear row. She then emptied the entire content of the glass over her shocked victim. With the room now in stunned silence, the drenched woman politely asked Kim: "Why did you do that?"

"I felt like it," was Kim's cool response.

The woman sank back into her chair and Kim asked the person speaking to continue, which he did. From that moment on, whoever was speaking may have had the attention of most people in the room, but I kept an eye on Kim. The woman had got *my* attention, big time! She was awesome – and a bit scary with it.

What followed over the next three days was a series of intense workshops where we got honest and raw about the reality of our lives as they actually were, stripped of gloss. We then visualized the futures we each intended to *create*, and not merely wish for. The workshops were very intense, as we were encouraged at all times to remain 'present and in the now' and challenged to confront our deepest fears, which, I slowly came to discover, was mostly that of fear itself. "Fear was a state of mind – change it!"

We were shown the dangers of listening to the rational mind, or 'RAT' as Kim unlovingly dubbed it. "RAT", she explained, "is where your fear lives; fear of past happenings and dead events. It has nothing to do with now or the future, so don't allow it to steal your life away, as it has done to date. Stay present, that's where life is!" This was awesome stuff! I liked what I was hearing, and, somehow, I instinctively understood what was being taught. Something amazing was happening for me in that hotel conference room, and while much of it was uncomfortable, the intriguing character of the experience and sense of empowerment won out over my fear of what might come next. Anything short of death and I was up for it! Kim had me in the palm of her manicured hands and, though I was on edge, I had never felt so good. Yes, it was good to be uncomfortable.

We were re-learning our ways of thinking and communicating, and coming to understand the 'conditioning' impressed upon us by the significant others in our lives: parents, siblings, colleagues, and friends. My life, up until this point, had been a reflection of other people's wishes for me, rather than my own. In the Exegesis world, there were no accidents or acts of fate; everything was a product of direct intent. Life was about taking responsibility for my reality and living in the 'now' and not yesterday or tomorrow. I learned to take responsibility by saying 'I' instead of 'we' or 'they'. I was also taught the futility of "bullshitting" or lying through my life; the purity of "thinking and speaking from the gut", and the absolute power of crap-free, 'essence-based' communication was the way forward. One exercise in 'silent communication' had the participants staring into each other's eyes, softly, without the distraction of talk. This was one of the most powerful for me. I used to be far too shy to look anyone in the eye for more than a moment; but with Kim in the room, that irrational reticence, that literal aversion of my eyes from the truth before me melted away. Just like all fear, I discovered that my shyness was a pathetic frame of mind that I no longer had to hide behind. "Change your mind, change the outcome – take responsibility, in the now," commanded Kim. I heard her, loud and clear, and I liked it, a lot! Life was in the present moment, not in the past or future.

When rare toilet or food breaks took place, some participants seized the opportunity to disappear in haste, leaving behind their coats and belongings; fear of what they thought was going to happen next got the better of them; which meant they missed the point of previous exercises about not allowing our fear to steal our opportunities. In their cases, Mr or Ms RAT had won the day. But I wasn't going anywhere; I was so engrossed that wild elephants couldn't have dragged me from my seat. I had nothing to lose by staying. I felt myself changing and knew that it was a change for the better. I was feeling a buzz within my entire being that I had never experienced before. I was wide awake, receptive, alert, empowered, and capable of anything. At least that's how I felt, in my gut. I was the real me for the first time in my life, with all my internalized bullshit torn away. I liked the real me.

The final exercise had the remaining, or surviving, participants, close our eyes, only opening them when Kim asked us to. On the third repetition of the exercise, we opened our eyes to a room filled with happy, smiling former Exegesis graduates, at least one hundred and fifty of them – a gleaming Selwyn included. I found it quite overwhelming and very emotional. They greeted us with generous applause and loud cheers. After the emotional pummelling we had been through over the previous days, all we could do is look back at them in a happy daze. No, this hadn't been just another cathartic workshop; we had actually come to the end of an Exegesis, a shedding of our former selves by means of a very personal and fearless critical analysis of our lives. It was a life-enhancing process for me, unmatched in my experience. I truly felt free and *born again*.

The new graduates were warmly embraced by the former, like Selwyn, who had recommended Exegesis to me. After saying a heartfelt 'thank you' to Kim and Selwyn, I said my goodbyes to fellow participants and made to leave, only to have Kim intercept me at the back of the room. To my shock, the awesome lady was on her knees before me.

"I want you around me." she said.

I was surprised, but honoured by this unexpected invitation. "I'd like to be around you too", I replied. She asked me to call her office and arrange to come in to see her. We hugged again and I left; my mind whirring and my heart full.

A buzzing sensation continued to flow through me as I took my seat on the tube train home. Tears of joy swelled in my eyes and I sobbed openly, for all to see. It felt so good that I couldn't stop myself, nor did I want to. I was crying in gratitude for the sense of freedom I was feeling within my being; an unaccustomed freedom from the fear that had deprived me of happiness; freedom from limitations, self-imposed, or created by the wants and expectations of others; freedom, most of all, to be myself. I had been set free from the prison of my old ways of thinking and I was never going back. Great things were ahead of me and *I* was going to create them.

Arriving home, my mother greeted me at the door and I immediately embraced and kissed her. She stepped back from me with a look of disbelief mixed with fear on her face; because, of course, we did not show physical affection in our family. Well, that was her issue to deal with, not mine; I was no longer going to let myself be constrained by anyone else's hang-ups. I was genuinely pleased to see her and I was able to let it show.

Within days of my return, my mother had called my siblings and other relatives to tell them that she was 'living with a stranger' and that I was "no longer Ian". She was so wrong; as far as I was concerned I felt that I – the real me – was home for the first time. I was Vernal Walter Scott, no longer little vulnerable 'Ian'. I was intelligent, confident, articulate, fearless, and determined to live rather than survive my life; I was the complete opposite of the person I was before or pretended to be. I felt mighty real.

My mother became increasingly terrified of me. She kept watching me with an expression of deep suspicion, as if she feared that I might run off with her precious belongings. When I spoke with my new confidence, she would interrupt and counter: "That is not your voice; that is not Ian's voice!"

Mum went to church even more often, and I would hear her praying in her bedroom day and night for God to return me to the boy I was before. But God had no wish to revisit that tragedy upon me.

Once she came to understand that Exegesis was responsible for the dramatic change in me, she started screening my calls, often interrupting them by picking up the other receiver in her bedroom and telling whoever I was speaking with to "get off my line and don't call here again, you devil!" Phone calls from Kim, Selwyn or other Exegesis friends were abruptly curtailed in this way. When I saw Kim at a follow-up to the weekend session, she told me that she was fed up of dealing with my mother on the phone. "Do you know she threatened to sue me?" Kim laughed. Selwyn had had a similar experience.

The situation came to a head one night after I returned home from my shift as an usher at the Barbican. Like a scene from *Carrie*, the Sissy Spacek horror flick, Mum waited for me behind the banister at the top of the stairs. When I reached the landing, she leapt out and started pounding her open palm against my chest, shouting, "Demon, leave my son! Demon, leave my son!" When our eyes met, she realised that I was not impressed with her behaviour, at all, and she desisted. Retreating to her bedroom, she did her best to avoid me for the next week. This failed exorcism, though, caused her to pray even harder, the poor dear. She told everybody who would listen that I had joined the Exorcist instead of Exegesis. Her mistake made my head want to spin on my shoulders with laughter, just like the possessed character in the movie. That's how her mind heard the word.

I declined an offer to join Exegesis' business wing, a telephone sales operation. I spent a day at the premises at Kim's invitation, but was bored silly. I did participate in a couple of additional workshops lead by Robert, but it was becoming clear that I would need substantial funds to participate in other events, but my pockets were shallow at this time. There was, of course, no chance of winning my mother over to the idea of a further subsidy. Anyway, I was still electrified to my fingertips from the first event and didn't feel I needed my motivation topping up, at least not yet.

Being around anyone who had not done Exegesis became intolerable to me, because their mind shit was so obvious. Many long-standing associations bit the dust, including my friendship with Simon. Like a lot of other graduates, I was strongly encouraged to enlist friends and family to the course, but only one of mine did. Friends, such Simon, came to the introductory evenings, but did not sign up. Simon later told me that he had never come across such plastic and scary people and that he ran all the way home to get away from them. *Your loss,* I thought, and I meant it, too.

Meanwhile, controversy over Exegesis flared in the media. There were reports that participants were physically abused, humiliated, and forced to disclose sexual fantasies in front of other people. The media, of course, made no attempt to present the many positive voices that could have spoken in Exegesis' defence, if they had cared to find them.

For now, it was simply bash Exegesis time! I recall returning home from work one night to find the BBC's *Newsnight* programme reporting on 'Exegesis, the brainwashing cult'. Questions were raised in the House of Commons about the organisation and a short time later Exegesis ceased to exist.

I was not tethered to the burning cinders of Exegesis or its leadership, nor would I ever set eyes on Selwyn, Robert or Kim again. For all the media controversy and talk of cults and brainwashing, I remain grateful to Kim and Selwyn for the most demanding, liberating and exhilarating experience of my life up to that time. Exegesis was a gloriously life-transforming experience that put me in charge of my life; totally and completely. I hadn't forgotten the negative experiences of the past; it's just that I wasn't going to endlessly relive them anymore. The present is where I was and needed to be. Accepting what is, or changing it consciously and positively, was the cogent and stress-free way to be. I could let go of being mentally occupied by yesterday or tomorrow, or even the last or next moment; just let go and be in the now; simple, powerful and necessary. Discontentment and unhappiness thrive when we live outside of the now, the present.

I didn't want to merely exist; I wanted to live my life; honestly and forthrightly; loving myself for who I am and shaping my world as I desired it to be. Seeking the approval of others was no longer going to be a preoccupation of mine. I was going to be *un*reasonable, take risks and achieve the impossible. I was no longer a passenger in the car of life; I was in the driver's seat. Hello, Vernal Walter Scott! You're awake in the now.

24. LOVE TO LOVE YOU, MR SHAKESPEARE!

I HAD DATED GIRLS AT SCHOOL and thought that one or the other had been my first love, but then I met Graham, house manager of the Royal Shakespeare Company at the Barbican Centre. It was 1983. He was thirty-six, thirteen years my senior – white, tall, elegant, charming and very handsome. Graham had warm, inviting brown eyes and a cute, immaculately-trimmed beard, which matched his always well-groomed hair. He smiled a lot, and mostly wore a grey suit set off by pristine black shoes. He was passionate about all aspects of the arts, but in particular, theatre, opera, classical music, Barbra Streisand and Dionne Warwick. He had a particular passion for Jessye Norman. I only saw him from a distance, at first, but this didn't stop me from falling under his spell. I wasn't sure if he was gay, although looking back, his love for opera and Babs should have been major clues.

Nick, my supervisor, who was openly gay, eventually introduced me to Graham. I thought at the time that there was something more to Graham's smile than his words of welcome to the RSC team belied. What my heart heard was: *"Hello, love of my life, where on Earth have you been hiding?"*

Working evenings at the Barbican Theatre was great fun, especially when celebrities came in to see a show, as they frequently did; although the brightest star of them all, as far as my eyes were concerned, had to be Graham. The surprisingly tiny Queen Elizabeth II paid regular formal and informal visits, as did her son and heir, Prince Charles and his truly scintillating young wife and the most popular person in the universe, Princess Diana. We also saw other celebrities of lesser rank, included Jeremy Irons, Frank Finlay, Anne Diamond, Daley Thompson, and my favourite, newscaster Sir Trevor McDonald, who was very polite and kind. Once the curtain was up and the actors took to the stage, Graham would walk around and greet each of his ushers, taking a moment to ask us how we were. As the months passed, I noticed that Graham always lingered a little longer chatting with me – always just small talk, but those moments invariably made my night. I was totally in awe of him.

My ambition to get back on stage myself was dwindling, for I knew, in my heart, that I had lost my passion to be an actor. It was around this time that Gloria Gaynor, my disco idol, had a new hit with 'I Am What I Am', from the camp musical *La Cage au Folles*. The production of this record was very different from Gloria's earlier, heavy-orchestra-based dance hits, such as 'Never Can Say Goodbye' and 'How High the Moon'. Gloria's solid voice suited the fiercely independent lyric and the electronic sound of the accompanying music, and the British record-buying public agreed with me as the song entered the UK pop Top 20. Her latest anthem was number one on just about every dance chart, but it was especially popular in the gay clubs, for obvious reasons. The other great dance hit at this time was the fabulous Shannon with 'Let the Music Play'. I was lucky enough to get to see Shannon live on a whistle-stop promotional tour and was blown away by the power of her voice. But Gloria remained my number one diva of the dance floor.

Meanwhile, I was having a blast in my day job at the Dominion. There, I had the best seats in the house for soul music's top artists: Shalamar; Evelyn 'Champagne' King; Odyssey; my favourite gospel songstress, Tramaine Hawkins; Edwin Starr; the Jones Girls, Dionne Warwick, and of course, Gloria Gaynor, who enjoyed a number of sell-out shows there. During my lunch breaks, I would take my sandwiches and sit and eat in the front of the auditorium and watch these fantastic artists rehearse. I was very discreet and careful not to disturb them in any way. I did venture to the Royal Albert Hall one night to catch Diana Ross. The Dominion was a good size, but it was far too compact for the RnB/pop royalty that was Miss Ross. I mean, she needed space for her wardrobe, if nothing else. Entering through a door in the auditorium before making her way to the stage, the shimmering legendary lady put on a competent if not brilliant show, but I was very pleased to finally see her live. Nobody knew it at the time, but within a couple of years Diana's star would be over-shadowed due to the arrival on the music scene of a younger and more vocally adept version of herself: the phenomenal and unstoppable, Whitney Houston.

On Valentine's Day 1983, I could not ignore the strains of my favourite male vocalist of the time, rehearsing his signature tune, 'Never Too Much, Never Too Much, Never Too Much!' I made my way to the front row seats in the empty auditorium and took a seat with my McDonalds Fillet O'Fish, fries, and strawberry milkshake in hand. I had just about taken my first bite when the music suddenly stopped. There he was, looking straight down at me in his black dressing gown: Mr Luther Vandross himself.

"Er, hello," he said with a puzzled expression on his face, "Can I help you?"

I was intensely embarrassed. "No, er, I, erm..."

"Who are you?" He asked, with just a hint of annoyance.

"I'm Vernal..."

"Are you from the record company?" He quizzed.

"No, no," I said. "I'm Vernal Scott. I work here in the booking office... and I was having my lunch and I thought I would come and see..."

Mr Vandross began laughing at me with his backing singers, who were similarly attired in dressing gowns and casual wear – looking rather unglamorous with no make-up. "Ladies, this is the main man, Vernal. He's come to make sure our show is tight tonight, because I hear we're sold out." He looked at me as if asking for confirmation, and I nodded whilst rising to my feet to leave.

"Hey, it's okay, Vernal, you can stay, but next time, make sure you bring me some lunch too!"

I smiled at him and sank back into my seat, not knowing what else to do.

"Oh," Luther added, "let me introduce you to my singers."

Concerned that I was interrupting his rehearsal, I quickly shouted, "No, no, it's okay, no need to..."

By this time he was gleaming a white smile at me, and so were his singers. He was having fun with me. "This is Brenda, and this is Tawatha. Don't worry, Vernal, we'll be all dressed up for you tonight." With a playful frown he added, "Of course, I'm assuming you're coming to my show tonight and you've bought yourself a real live ticket..."

"Yes, oh yes," I responded quickly.

"Good! Pleased to meet you, Vernal!" With that his focus returned to his rehearsals: "Okay, one more time..."

I relaxed and chomped my way through my lunch, sitting as quietly as a mouse. With Luther's nods and smiles at me, I began to wonder if he was perhaps being a little too friendly. I felt as though he was singing just for me as he did a few lines from 'Forever, for Always, for Love', 'She Loves Me Back' and 'Bad Boy Having a Party'.

Finally, I waved goodbye and made my way to the box office, feeling very happy that I had just attended my very own private Luther Vandross concert. Later that evening, the great man put on an excellent show, at which every member of his eager audience received free Valentine's Day chocolates. I was amazed at the transformation of his singers, especially Brenda – the woman had gone from drab to fab. Mr Vandross was slicker than slick, but I did wonder whether his tight trousers were the best pick as they made the hefty soul superstar look as though he had knock-knees. Ah well, it didn't matter. I bought a souvenir t-shirt to mark the occasion, which had 'I saw Luther Vandross at the Dominion' printed across the chest, while happily reflecting that few fans had had as personal a glimpse of the man as I.

Gloria didn't rehearse, so I missed my chance to see her behind the scenes. She would turn up in her limo a few minutes before the show, do her thing, bringing the house down each time, and leave the building shortly thereafter.

Sometimes she would pause to meet a special group of fans: usually guys from Holland, with very strange names like Hans, Pim and Huub. I wasn't fortunate enough to be in the GG charmed circle, but I thoroughly enjoyed her shows; she had lost a lot of weight and could dance like never before. Edwin Starr was her opening act. He joked with the audience after messing up his words, saying, "I got my nose fixed and now my mouth don't work." The highlight of his show was when he invited members of the audience to join him on stage to sing his mega hit, 'War', and, after encouragement from a female member of the audience, he picked me. I left my sleepy nephew, Spencer, whom I had brought along to the concert, in the adjoining seat, and joined Edwin on the stage in front of the packed house. Edwin was brilliant and funny, and after a few chants as his impromptu backing singer, I returned to my seat and warmly applauded his act with the rest of the audience. Spencer slept through it all. Thankfully he didn't fall asleep when we accidentally met Quincy Jones a few weeks earlier at a fun fair at Hampstead Heath. Simon was with us and was the first to spot Quincy who was kind enough to give me his autograph, which I carelessly lost by the time I got home. I did seem to be living a star-crossed existence in those days.

After twelve months holding down two jobs, I applied for and secured a full-time job at the Barbican Centre booking office, with the help of a reference from Graham. It was time to bid the Dominion goodbye. Although I loved my brushes with stardom, I was keen to leave after a deputy manager took cash from my till and only admitted taking it after being challenged by another manager; who, thankfully, had checked my till with me before I left the theatre the previous evening. The guilty manager subsequently claimed that he had 'forgotten' that he had 'borrowed' money from my till this particular morning to buy some office supplies, and had fully intended to replace it. The truth is he was the first to suggest that I must have taken the cash. It was obviously time to leave.

So I went to work full time in the booking office at the Barbican by day, but retained my evening job as an usher at the theatre downstairs. The booking office managers were a brother-and-sister team. She was elegantly presented, with short brown hair. He had a flushed complexion that spoke of a love for the bottle, and wore a well-tailored suit. After a perfunctory induction, she introduced me to the twelve-strong box office team, saying: "Er, hello everybody, your attention please! Let me introduce you to Vernal. You may have seen him before, as he's been working as an usher in the theatre, but he's now joining us a daytime bookings clerk. He's also going to be the office runaround, our skivvy, so you can get him to make your coffee and run errands." I stood there with a lame smile on my face as she ended with a twinkly "Cute, isn't he?" In such belittling fashion, did she herald the start of my box office career; but it was nothing compared to what her brother was to dish out.

Her brother was gay, had a significant drink problem and was a racist. When he wasn't making lurid sexual gestures or going on about his obsession with Shirley Bassey and life-long friendship with the drag artiste Danny Larue, he was heaping abuse on people. "Black people should be made into tar and put onto roads," he told the office, with me, the sole black member of staff, in earshot. This remark elicited uncomfortable chuckles from the rest of the office staff. I gradually learned that the rest of the staff grudgingly tolerated his obnoxiousness out of fear of retribution from his sister and for their jobs.

The brother's incessant disparagement of black people in general, and me in particular, was accompanied, bafflingly, by unwanted sexual attention. He sat immediately behind me, out of sight of the other, mostly female, booking officers. On the rare occasion that he was quiet, usually after returning from a liquid lunch at the pub, I could feel his stare piercing the back of my neck. My hunch was confirmed, any time I had the unhappy occasion to seek his advice. He moved on from staring furtively at me, to physically brushing past me at any opportunity. Soon his hands were wandering, and they once found their way to my repulsed nipples. He seemed to feel that his sister's position of authority in the office gave him licence to behave as provocatively as he pleased; and although his sister knew what was happening, she did nothing to stop him. A couple of other managers, observed what was happening, and sometimes tried to distract him with made-up booking-related queries. However, everyone seemed fearful of upsetting the sister and brother's bizarre little fiefdom in the booking office, a situation which, I, in my post-Exegesis frame of mind, was not prepared to put up with for long.

Around this time, Tina Turner was riding high with her 'Private Dancer' comeback album and world tour. A colleague in the office decided to organise a staff outing to see the show at Wembley Arena, and I was more than keen to go. On learning of this, the brother said he knew the booking manager at Wembley, and unprompted by us, he had secured front row seats for our group. I was extremely excited, and went to thank him. He responded by saying: "I don't know why you want to go and see her anyway. She's not even black, but a kind of dirty colour." As usual with him, his oscillations between hostility and currying favour with me, left me agape. But I was relieved, at least, that he would not be joining us for the show. It was to be Shirley or nobody, for him.

The atmosphere was electric for the sell-out concert of the undisputed Queen of Rock. The legendary lady known for her hair, legs, rough voice and frantic dance moves, strutted her stuff only inches from us. In the course of the greatest live show on Earth, Tina performed 'Let's Stay Together', 'I Might Have Been Queen', 'I Can't Stand the Rain', the album's stunning title track, 'Private Dancer', and of course, the comeback hit single, 'What's Love Got To Do With It'. 'River Deep Mountain High' and 'Proud Mary' were in there too. Then came the point in the show when Tina, introduced her dancers and band members. When she was looking in our direction, I raised my hand and waved at her, and my heart leapt as the great lady enthusiastically waved back.

One of my colleagues shrieked: "Oh my God, Tina just waved at Vernal!" It was a little gesture that made a whole lot to me, I was thrilled, and we left feeling on top of the world. Tina could do no wrong – the ultimate entertainer.

Although Graham was no longer my manager, we still worked in the same building. Seeing him on an almost daily basis made my troubles in the booking office disappear, especially when I was greeted with a warm "Hello Vernal, are you well?" as he passed by my table in the staff restaurant. Then, one blessed lunchtime, he smiled and asked, "Can I join you, Vernal?"

"Yes," I replied, trying to hold my composure. He asked how things were going in the box office, but my Exegesis training momentarily abandoned me, as I lied and told him that I was enjoying it. I could hardly look him in the eye.

He began tucking into his salad, and asked, "What did you get up to on the weekend?"

My wits were slowly returning, as I cheekily responded, "I considered going to a bearded men's disco, but couldn't as I don't have a beard." Would he take the hint, I asked myself.

He laughed heartily and rubbed his beard. This was the first open indication between us about our sexuality. Our blissful small talk continued a moment or two longer when the canteen door opened and in walked the brother, whose stride faltered slightly when he saw Graham sitting with me; the brother, of course, regarded me as his property. The two men acknowledged each other, but not before the brother gave me a disapproving sneer before joining the cafeteria queue.

Then, to my complete surprise, Graham asked: "So, what are you doing next weekend?"

My Exegesis cool once again flew off like a rocketing pheasant. My mouth kind of opened up, but nothing came out. Was he asking me out?

He could see that I was slightly flustered, so he tried again: "Are you busy on Saturday night?"

"Er, no, I'm not working on Saturday," I finally responded, knowing as I did that any set plan would be binned without hesitation.

"Great!" said Graham enthusiastically. "Let's meet up and have a meal outside of this place."

"Sure, I'd like that," I said in semi-disbelief.

The brother, at this moment, with food tray in hand, appeared at the table, and asked if he could join us.

"Sure," said Graham politely.

He sat down, looked at Graham and, with a sleazy smirk on his face, said, "You'll be pleased to know that our boy has settled in well. Very promising..."

"Do you mean *Vernal*?" said Graham, deliberately.

I couldn't contain my grin. Finally, someone was standing up to him.

I made my excuses, binned my shepherd's pie and mash and made my way to the booking office. I of course floated back to the office; I didn't need legs or feet.

That Saturday, Graham and I went for a meal at Joe Allen's in Covent Garden. The date marked the beginning of many such outings. On a later date, as we sat together in prime seats at the Royal Opera House, taking in the lavish spectacle that is Strauss' Der Rosenkavalier, I kept peeping to my right at the beautiful bearded man who was sitting by my ecstatic side. Hang on, stop the performance! I need to pinch myself to make sure this isn't a cruel dream. Nope, he's here, and so am I. This isn't a dream, thank God! I did the same as we watched the Dance Theatre of Harlem's Swan Lake, and the same again through the various movie and on-going dinner dates. How I adored him: he could do no wrong in my eyes – and to my utter frustration, he didn't *try* to do wrong either! I kept my body cleaner than a new born baby's, and hadn't touched myself in a sexual way for weeks on end, in the hope that when my man juice was eventually spilt, it would be mixed with Graham's. It had better happen soon, or I was sure to explode in a gigantic cloud of white sticky stuff. I thought my dreams were about to come true the day he drove me back to his house in Hampstead. As we sat watching TV together, I tapped into my Exegesis gut-over-mind power and reached over and took his hand into mine, and just held it. He responded warmly, but that was it! Not once did he ever try to get into my pants, damn him! I knew that if we kissed he'd be hooked. My lips were built for kissing, and I was good at it too. I was totally smitten, but fear of rejection prevented me from initiating any other moves on the man I completely idolized. My blow-his-socks-off kiss would have to wait for another opportune moment. The evening we sat on the sofa in the home I shared with my mother, also failed to spur him to act, but that was perhaps very wise, given that she was only in the next room. With a multitude of lovely dates behind us, our lips had yet to meet, and the need to do so was driving me insane.

Other than Graham, music remained a constant passion for me. I decided to compile a cassette for him, featuring the finest soulful love songs from my now quite eclectic record collection. Roberta Flack and Donny Hathaway's The Closer I Get to You was an essential track, as was Esther Phillips' I Haven't Got Anything Better To Do, Scott Walker's Angel of Ashes, and You're My Man from the Sex O'Clock USA soundtrack – a movie I'd never seen. Aretha belted out I'm In Love, Dionne Warwick offered This Girl's In Love With You, and Gloria Gaynor hit the spot with Let's Make Love. To cork my message, just in case it wasn't entirely clear, Shirley Bassey crooned John Lennon's Something, and Jennifer Holliday delivered the knock-out blow with And I Am Telling You I'm Not Going, from Dreamgirls, the hit US stage musical. Now, even someone born without ears could hear that my musical creation was an explicit statement of love and seduction; even Stevie Wonder could see that. However, to my increasing disappointment, my elusive butterfly appeared to not get the message; perhaps he didn't want to. Still, every waking hour was consumed with thinking about him; fantasising about being intimate with him, even cooking his meals and darning his socks; that's before washing and ironing them, of course. I even permitted myself the outrageous fantasy of living with him, although that did feel rather far-fetched, or was it? I very much wanted to be deserving of Graham, and to this end, I would have climbed Everest if he'd asked me to, but just to impress him further, I'd conquer it twice, and offer to do it a third time while carrying him on my tired but happily determined shoulders. If I was lucky, the icy conditions would fasten us together, and we would return to ground zero as interracial Siamese twins. Oh, me and my besotted imagination.

Yes, I was feeling something much more powerful than Exegesis had managed to facilitate within me. Every time I saw my idol, an emotional earthquake wreaked havoc in the pit of my stomach. Exegesis hadn't prepared me for this, for love. I bored my confidante, cousin Doreene, senseless, with my stories about Graham and how wonderful he was to me. But as our dates became less frequent and eventually ceased altogether, it became obvious that he did not feel the same about me. I had to face the terrible truth; he was in love with someone else; an American guy who had just moved to the UK to join Graham, permanently. I was gutted to the point of distraction, but tried to console myself with little to no success. I was in love with Graham but he was only fond of me. I tried but failed to appreciate the value in that; fond was cute, but it wasn't love. I had little option but to accept the situation, move on and get over him, or at least try.

As I was leaving work one unfortunate night, I bumped into Graham and his newly arrived partner. I managed to smile through our mutual exchange of pleasantries before my corpse left the building and made its way home. Even a surprise encounter on the train with the legendary singer Madeline Bell couldn't revive my walking-dead mentality. Her autographed publicity photo provided evidence that our crossing of paths had indeed been real. I could remember her being extremely warm in telling me about her early career, including singing back-up vocals for some of pop music's biggest names along with fellow backing singer, Cissy Houston; who she recalled being "very pregnant" with daughter Whitney during a set they did together at Wembley. As a boy, I remembered Madeline sitting at the top of the UK charts as a member of Blue Mink, with their controversial mega hit, Melting Pot. I was of course much more into her later disco material, guesting with artists like Donna Summer, Cerrone, and the lesser known, Don Ray. I was especially keen on her tracks with a disco outfit called Space, but she seemed very keen to forget about them! Yes, I really did meet darling Madeline, but my heart only wanted to meet Graham. Everything was Graham.

Seeing him with his partner should have caused this miserable ostrich to lift his head out of the sand, but I couldn't let go, not just yet. After work one night, in a moment of madness, I asked a suspicious colleague to drop me off at Graham's house. His partner answered the door, and despite looking totally puzzled at my unexpected arrival on their doorstep, he welcomed me in. Graham was still out at work. His confused but very polite true love made uncomfortable small talk with me, but a short fifteen minutes later and I was out the door. I had come to my senses. A punishing reality had bitten, and bitten hard! I had no business being there and made my excuses and left. I felt I couldn't compete with Graham's choice; he was established with a great education and profession. I may have looked good at Graham's side, but my curly-haired Caucasian replacement looked the part too. It suddenly dawned upon me that I had simply been casual company for Graham while he waited for the arrival into the country of his true love. He had made his choice, and it wasn't me.

A few nights later, Graham phoned to cancel a planned date. My shattered heart knew whatever had happened between us was definitely over now, pending the word goodbye. He didn't ask me a thing about why I'd turned up at his house, which was fortunate, because I had no rational explanation to give; I just went with the feeling at the time and ended up going to his house, uninvited. It was patently the wrong thing to have done, but I couldn't undo it now, nor would I repeat it.

Strangely and unexpectedly, the happy couple invited me to dinner at their house, and even more bizarrely, perhaps, I accepted. I felt a need to hang on to something of the man my heart was convinced I'd been born to love, even if it was some sort of occasional friendship. The event was pleasant enough, but even a later Roberta Flack concert together at the Barbican Hall couldn't lift my mood. *Killing me softly*, indeed! As far as my heart was concerned, my Oscar-winning performance playing Mr Happy was a stunning box office flop. A subsequent threesome dinner at Joe Allen's, followed by what turned out to be the very final date cancellation by phone, was Graham's way of saying a long goodbye. I hurt like nothing I'd experienced before. In truth, and to his skill, the word goodbye wasn't actually used, but that was the tone and inevitable outcome. I guess it was kind of him to do it this way, because I would have surely crumbled to the floor if he had said goodbye to my face.

So, this is what real pain feels like; the pain of love lost. God, it hurt like hell... *Killing me softly*? No, there wasn't anything soft about this battering, especially as I was now sinking faster than the Titanic.

The emotion of the situation manifested itself in my inability to sleep. On one particularly restless night, I got out of bed, pulled on some trousers, a vest, some old training shoes, and walked out the door into the rainy night. I had no destination in mind; I just needed to get out. My tears followed me, as their saltiness mixed with the rain and found their way to my lips. In my emptiness, I felt dejected and somewhat mechanical. 1.06am became 2.15am as I continued to walk the near desolate streets of North London. Despite my now sodden white vest, to my tainted mind, the darkness offered some kind of camouflage, but I must have struck a disheveled ghostly sight to passing drivers as I continued on my hapless walk to destination nowhere. I wasn't ready to go home yet, so I just kept walking. The rain and my unyielding tears kept their own pace.

It was going to be a long walk if I was going to walk Graham out of my system; a very long walk indeed. Many years would pass before anyone would come close to making me feel as he did; helplessly in love.

Matters finally came to a head at the Barbican booking office when the brother manager grabbed my crotch. It was the final insult. All my pent up frustration with him came pouring out and I told him in no uncertain terms to keep his "fucking hands" to himself. I'd had enough of his nasty behaviour. It took Graham, who happened to be passing by, to calm me down. I later put in a formal complaint and the brother was subjected to disciplinary proceedings. He was forced to apologise, which he did, but at the same time, he sheepishly tried to explain that he "had fallen in love" with me "but had gone about it the wrong way". He was damn right about that!

My time at the Barbican had come to an end. I wanted out. No job was worth the price of my dignity, especially working with people I didn't respect. He could take his so-called love and shove it where Shirley Bassey wouldn't dare sing. Also, seeing Graham in passing, on an almost daily basis, was too much to deal with. I was convinced he felt the same; I think he sensed my pain. We both needed a final goodbye.

Looking back, despite the overwhelming pain involved, falling for Graham, my definite first love, somehow made it all worthwhile. He'd unwittingly taught me an important life lesson about love's awesome power and our inability to manipulate its authenticity for our own ends; he could not force himself to love someone he didn't, and I couldn't simply switch off the love I felt for him. I had been dancing to the rhythm of the deep love that had filled my soul, but when the music stopped, I had to accept the truth; I'd been dancing all alone. With my smile replaced by tears, it was as if my shattered heart had been encased in a 10 ton steel-enforced block of cement and cast to the bottom of my personal turbulent sea of unrequited love. The only thing visible from the choppy surface was the jaggedly engraved metallic tag: 'PROPERTY OF GRAHAM'.

In the years that would follow, potential partners would see that rusting tag and abandon their efforts to win me over, before they too got cast into the same cruel sea. Even my own determined efforts failed to rescue and heal my heart; the tears, the grief, my desperation to forget him; absolutely nothing worked. Not even my Exegesis-gifted rebirth could overcome this lost challenge.

Lesson One: love was its own boss, not me. It had its own wings and it used them to fly above and reign supreme over all my efforts to manipulate it into something less than it was. Wherever I went and whatever I did, my love for Graham followed like a second shadow that couldn't, no, that wouldn't, be discarded. My tears only ceased once I gave up the fight and conceded that love was much more powerful than me; it was in control and only further pain would come from my trying to resist or deny that truth. All I could do was hope that time and a future opportunity to love someone else might be kind enough to release me from my lonely prison on the hazardous seabed of broken hearts, just off the over-populated isle of crushed dreams.

Lesson Two: joy and pain are flip-sides to love's coin. Despite the risks, I'd be willing to flip that special coin again, because love is life's ultimate gift. A lesson learnt!

So, that's how things ended with my true first love, or did they?

25. THE PEOPLE'S GROUP

CULTURAL EXCHANGE

A new group has been set up in London to bring together gay and bisexual people of both sexes, different races and different interests. The People's Gay and Lesbian Group was conceived by black gay man Vernal Scott and plans talks and lectures, outings, discos and sport with the help of organisers for each interest. The group meets every Thursday at the London Lesbian & Gay Centre from 7.30.

Vernal Scott

THE SELF-AFFIRMING ENERGY UNLEASHED by Exegesis made my remaining at the Barbican Centre impossible. I *had* to be more than that; I could feel that buzz inside me. So I applied for a one-year, full-time arts management course at the London's City University business school. My desire to be an actor was gone, but I still wanted to be around the arts, in management, like Graham, who was kind enough to support my application by providing a reference. Receiving the acceptance letter for the course was an exciting event, which signalled a number of changes for me, including a decision to move away from my mother, and rent a room out on my own for the first time.

Kicking off in April 1985, the course put me on a series of placements, including the Barbican Centre (the concert hall rather than the theatre), Sadler's Wells, and the Royal Festival Hall, before culminating in a live music arts project called the Black Music Fair, organised in conjunction with my fellow arts management students. The course was extremely rewarding, and I had a thoroughly good time. My brief spell at the Royal Festival Hall was particularly memorable, because it gave me a glimpse of another favourite diva of mine: Miss Jean Carne, a black music legend. She was sensational. I had only attended one other concert there, and that was back in 1982, it was to see supreme jazz icon, Miss Ella Fitzgerald. I recall how an elderly and very fragile Ella had to be helped to and from the stage, yet her voice sounded as fresh and strong as the day she started singing. I was still very much a disco fan, but I became an immediate devotee of this great lady; although the immaculate Sarah Vaughan and her younger protégé, Nancy Wilson, remained my favourite singers of the Jazz genre.

The college course was great, but it still wasn't quite enough for me. I was able to thrive on very little sleep following Exegesis; I was buzzing and wide awake. Not even a full-time course could consume my energy, and halfway through, I began to think of what else I could do. In December 1985, the concept of the People's Group came to mind. I wanted to create a space where gay men, of different cultures and backgrounds, could get together to explore each other beneath the surface, in a non-threatening and non-sexual environment. The People's Group would provide me with an opportunity to share some of the confidence-building lessons learnt from Exegesis: – that's one thing that the majority of its graduates had in common; like Bible-wielding evangelists, we had to share our gift.

I approached the London Lesbian and Gay Centre in Farringdon and they agreed to let me have a large room on a Thursday evening. I then set about coming up with some relevant publicity and a press release, which I sent on to *Gay News* and other community publications. Some were enthused enough to carry a picture of me, suited and booted.

I had moved out a few weeks earlier to a room in a house-share in Victoria Road, near Wood Green. My landlord, the only other occupant, spent most of his time in Cambridge, so I often had the large Victorian house to myself, and I took good advantage by throwing a late-night party or two whenever the mood took me. Being away from my mother was good for me. She was now alone but still had Jesus and regular visits from my siblings and their children. She was also fully active in her church. Her evangelist role would find her singing in shopping centres such as Brent Cross or using a megaphone to beckon shoppers to Jesus on Harlesden High Street. I knew underneath it all, she was only missing one man, and it wasn't me; it was my dad, her beloved Skippy.

The freedom of my own place meant I could really enjoy myself, which included the odd one-night stand, and I mean odd! One such 'date' must have been on some kind of unnatural substance. He stripped off before picking me up and held me aloft above his head whilst facing my first-floor bedroom window. Scary or what?! I had met him through Tony Blackburn's daily radio show, which played sweet soul music in between offering a lonely hearts service. Once I had overcome my fear of him, the sex with this guy was great, and it was the first time that I tied someone up as part of a sexual act. That was, frankly, the only way I was going to sleep alone with this stranger on that night. I never had the courage to meet up with him again, though he asked to.

I was enjoying having my own space, but I regularly visited my mother for Sunday dinner. She always sent me home with a very welcome parcel of delicious food. That Christmas I joined Mum and my siblings and their kids for dinner and spent the night in my old bedroom. It was unchanged, but no longer felt like my personal space. I'd moved out and on.

I arrived at the London Lesbian & Gay Centre a little before half past six on Thursday, 17 January 1986, time for the first People's Group meeting. As I walked through snow-carpeted Farringdon, I wondered if anyone would bother to brave the freezing cold to attend. *Nobody knows who I am*, I thought – *why would they come? People want to party and have sex, not talk.* In the still-empty room, five minutes before the meeting was to commence, I dismissed all my competing negative thoughts by staying in the now. By quarter past seven, my positive focus was vindicated by the reality of over forty gay men and a handful of lesbians of all ages and races, sitting in front of me in the room. It was evident that I had touched a nerve with my 'Let's get below the surface' press release. A few of my personal friends were there too.

I gave everyone a warm and heartfelt welcome and explained who I was, why I had launched the group, and my aims and objectives. I was completely relaxed and in control, despite the fact that I had never previously had an audience of my own. I explained that the group would seek to challenge our perceptions of each other, and help us to understand who we really are as individuals and as a group. Over the weeks ahead, I told them, we would hear from guest speakers on a range of interesting topics.

With an average attendance of forty or more multi-racial gay men, the People's Group quickly became a thumping success. The handful of women who had initially attended gradually drifted away. It was a gay men's group, as had been my original intent. The racial mix was particularly satisfying, as the group attracted more ethnic diversity than the long-established Black Gay & Lesbian Group, which had been meeting at Gay's The Word bookshop in Russell Square for years. On occasion, the leaders of the Black Group would come along, but they were never impressed, because, as one of them told me, "there were far too many white people in the room". I had a lot of respect for their group, and that's why I consciously organised my meetings on Thursdays, to avoid any rivalry of Fridays. Both groups were relevant, in my view, and had a unique reason to exist. That said, my meetings were better attended, and had many more black participants, for whatever reason.

I took the People's Group through exercises to do with perception, expectation, trust, irrational fear, the power of staying present in the now, and the power of clear communication – 'say what you mean and mean what you say'. We also went on outings to the seaside, marched against apartheid in South Africa and Mrs Thatcher's nasty anti-gay clause 28 policy, and even put on something called the People's Group Lesbian and Gay Carnival, which attracted the attention of BBC television's *Ebony* programme. The subject of this particular broadcast was the black community's attitudes to gays. In my interview with the programme, I said, "It takes courage to discover and be yourself, rather than live up to the expectations and conditioning of Daddy or big brother." I didn't know it at the time, but my father had watched the broadcast and was appalled to find out that he had a gay son in this way. But the message was surely worse than the medium, as he didn't want a gay son at all! He sent me a message via a relative to either change my name or leave the country. I didn't bother responding. I was in the driving seat of my life now, and I didn't care whether I had his approval or not. He had his life and this was mine. I no longer carried the guilt and shame that nearly cost me my life. Any shame belonged to others, not me.

Six months into the life of the People's Group, I completed my arts management course and collected my certificate from Tony Banks MP at a little ceremony at County Hall. I was still on a high from my Exegesis experience, and felt capable of anything.

I was managing to hold the attention of the People's Group for three hours each week, but I was always looking for guest speakers. A couple years earlier, I had seen a gripping BBC TV documentary called 'Killer in the City', which was concerned with an emerging fatal illness that predominantly affected gay men. The illness was AIDS, and I decided that the group needed to have someone come and speak to us about it.

I lined up Anthony, a counsellor working with the Project for Advice, Counselling and Education (PACE), based at the Farringdon Centre. Anthony was Australian, tall, and strikingly handsome, with blond, curly hair. He was a volunteer for the newly established Terrence Higgins Trust (THT), and the then-developing London Lighthouse Project, which was working to turn an old, derelict school in west London into a safe, loving hospice, where people with AIDS could go to die.

Anthony delivered a riveting presentation on HIV/AIDS, explaining how it was transmitted, the discrimination that people affected by it were facing, and how they were being supported. Something profound happened to me during his talk, and by its conclusion, I knew that there was nothing more important for me to do with my life than to get involved. *Vernal Scott has got work to do,* I told myself. My purpose was clear: to make a positive and significant difference to combatting the challenges of HIV/AIDS.

One Thursday night, just a few weeks following Anthony's talk, I was in the busy cafe area of the London Lesbian and Gay Centre and found myself staring at a man who I thought I recognised but couldn't be quite sure. I made my way across so I could get a clearer view of the seated man. At once, I realised that it was Raymond, the guy whom I'd briefly dated after placing a personal ad in *Black Echoes* music paper when I was seventeen. I was now twenty-five, which made him about thirty. He was looking a lot older than his actual years.

I reached out and put my hand on his shoulder, and he turned to see who it was.

"Hello, Raymond," I started enthusiastically.

He looked at me with a confused expression on his face. After collecting his thoughts, he offered a polite but muted, "Oh, hello there."

I took the empty seat beside him. I was mindful of the fact that I hadn't seen him in five years or so, and continued to be struck by his aged, if well-presented appearance. It was great to see him. I often wondered what had happened to him. The last I'd heard he had moved to America – New York, I believed, so I really wasn't expecting to see him there that night.

Before I could even ask how he was, Raymond leaned forward and said in an accusatory tone, "I know what you're thinking!"

"Sorry, Raymond? I'm just really pleased to see…"

"You think I've got AIDS, don't you?" he interrupted, "I know everyone thinks that about me!"

"No, not at all! I'm so happy to see you; just surprised because I didn't expect to."

"Hey, thanks," he said, settling back into the grey plastic chair.

Relieved by the drop in tension, I asked whether he had come to attend the People's Group.

"Everyone thinks I've got AIDS," he said, ignoring my question. "Do you think I've got it? You do, don't you?"

Some people around turned to look, but Raymond didn't seem to be aware that his voice was carrying. "Do you think I've got it?" he continued, in agitated tones, "I won't be upset or anything. It's okay for you to say it."

I began to realise that Raymond was genuinely confused, paranoid even, and couldn't really hear anything other than what was going on in his mind. But I wasn't about to walk away from him; I had matured a bit since my sulking teenage years. I tried once again to connect: "You're looking good to me – very handsome, as always. Look, I run the People's Group upstairs on a Thursday night. It would be good if you came along."

"You know you can't catch it by just being close to someone, don't you?" he asked bleakly. Again, Raymond didn't hear me.

I had to accept that I wasn't going to get through. "Yes, I know," I said, and reached forward to grasp his hand. I looked him right in the eye and said: "It really wouldn't make a difference to me whether you had AIDS or not. I'm still your friend."

He seemed surprised and just gazed at me with his beautiful but fearful eyes. He was very afraid and I was very concerned for him.

As we chatted, or tried to, Anthony came by, rounding up the participants for a weekly support group he ran for gay men with AIDS. Upon hearing Anthony's call, Raymond rose, and as he did so, the awful truth became clear to me. Anthony came over to greet us both, and asked how we knew each other. I explained that Raymond was a dear old friend, and that we hadn't seen each other for a little while. A moment later, Raymond and I hugged and said our goodbyes. He promised to attend the People's Group at some point. I later sent him an invite to a house party that I was throwing the following week, and was over the moon when he turned up, looking smart, and mentally much more stable and coherent. Marvin, the handsome man from the East London party came too, and brought me a special gift; a Russian wedding ring, which I would wear religiously thereafter. Marvin wore the twin of the same ring. The rings symbolized the deep affection we still had for each other.

By the autumn of 1986, I sensed that my time leading the People's Group was drawing to a close. A small but vocal group of members wanted a more social agenda of parties and 'fun activities'. I felt strongly that the gay community already had a plethora of clubs, bars and parties, and that the group should remain as it was, with a mostly educational format.

In my view, there was room for a satellite group, for those who wanted to organise and enjoy parties. I had already established one called Positive Living. It had nothing to do with being HIV positive, so the name, in retrospect, was a bit of a coincidence: its agenda was simply to get gay men to break through any perceived barriers in their lives in a social setting. It took place on Saturday mornings, and had been very well received. However, my suggestion to form an entertainment-focused satellite was dismissed out of hand, and there was a determination to turn the main meeting into a social night. I had a bloodless coup on my hands, though one that was still pretty nasty towards me all the same. It was a good job I had a thick Exegesis-fortified hide.

The unkind comments and insults came thick and fast on one particular Thursday night. I knew then that I really had to go, even though many wanted me to stay. I hadn't been the perfect group leader and hadn't concerned myself with the formalities of 'forming and norming' groups. My Exegesis spirit told me it was simply time for me to exit, and so I did without complaint. A number of regular attendees who had been at the group from the start, also decided to exit at the same time, leaving it in the hands of those who sought a more lightweight agenda.

My last evening with the People's Group involved attending a party that its new leadership organised in the basement of the Lesbian and Gay Centre. I was having a good time dancing, when a black stripper suddenly appeared and started gyrating his way to the center of the floor and began removing his clothes. I was furious with what I saw as an attempt to trivialise what I felt had been valuable work for the group, and made my displeasure very clear. It really was time to go and leave them to it.

I headed to the cloakroom to collect my coat. Malcolm, a mutual friend of Raymond's and mine, came over and shouted above the blaring music: "Vernal, I don't know if you've heard yet, but Raymond died last night." We held each other as I sobbed on his shoulder. I shouldn't have been surprised, as I had seen how ill Raymond had become, but still, it was a shock to lose a friend. I didn't know it then, but Raymond's death marked the beginning of the AIDS crisis in my own life. I composed myself, grabbed my coat and left the People's Group forever with Raymond's passing on my mind. HIV and AIDS were going to be my focus now.

The new leaders of the People's Group almost immediately changed the name to Fusion, but internal conflicts and dwindling numbers persisted, and the once-successful group eventually disbanded.

26. HIV AND AIDS – MY PURPOSE!

Making a statement: (Sir) Nick Partridge (CEO, Terrence Higgins Trust), myself, Christopher Spence (Director, London Lighthouse), (two men living with AIDS,) Peter Tatchell, Jonathan Grimshaw (Director, Landmark).

IT WAS 1986, I WAS TWENTY-FIVE YEARS OLD, unemployed, and, following a row with my landlord at Victoria Road, back living with my mother at 8 Harrowdene Close, Wembley. With Raymond's passing fresh in my mind, AIDS was my new and only focus, and I was feeling extremely passionate about it, too! I had found my purpose in life, at least for now.

The first five cases of homosexual men with acquired PCP (pneumocystis pneumonia) had been reported in June 1981, via the Centres for Disease Control in California. Just a month later, a further twenty-six cases of gay men with Kaposi's sarcoma were reported in New York. A common factor, in all cases, was a significant weakening or impairment of the immune system, a condition later known universally as AIDS (Acquired Immune Deficiency Syndrome) and caused by HIV (Human Immune-deficiency Virus). It was soon ascertained that the virus was transmitted through unprotected penetrative sexual intercourse, blood transfusions or blood products, sharing of contaminated needles by drug users, and from mother to baby, in the womb or at birth. By the time of Raymond's death, there were over 10,000 AIDS cases in the United States, nearly 600 in Europe, and approximately 200 in the UK. The majority of cases were amongst gay men, just like Raymond, but there were a growing number of heterosexual cases too.

The world-wide picture was looking very grim, with some epidemiologists talking about the potential for AIDS to wipe out millions of people. There were also speculative assertions that the virus had originated in Africa, however, there was absolutely no evidence to support such dangerous speculation and I made it my business to challenge anyone who publicly made such statements. "Where's your evidence?" I'd demand. Representatives of the Terrence Higgins Trust and London Lighthouse contributed to such myths, and I understood why: they wanted to deflect the association of the virus with gay men, but it was irresponsible to speculate wildly, and to perpetuate a totally unproven conceptual link between HIV and Africa; which bore with it damaging implications and associations for black people. Of course I was outraged by it! By a wild speculative leap, yet another of the world's ills could be laid at the door of Africa. It was also totally unhelpful in solving the problem in hand: namely, how to prevent the further spread of the virus and to provide appropriate support to those already infected. Wherever it came from, the deadly virus was here, and we had to deal with the facts, not myths.

The sharing of contaminated needles amongst intravenous drug users, and in under-funded medical facilities in African countries, where the same needle was reused many times over, was turning out, along with penetrative sexual intercourse, to be the principal route of transmission amongst heterosexuals. Anal intercourse was the principal route of transmission amongst gay men. The facts were clear: this was largely a virus of equal opportunity that was predominantly transmitted through specific human activities, and not because people were either gay or heterosexual.

The facts didn't stop the screaming headlines of the homophobic press about 'the gay plague'. Suddenly, gay men were legitimate targets of hate crimes, and those even suspected of carrying the virus were losing their jobs, homes, families and friends, due to discrimination and misinformation. All over the country, there was panic about whether the virus could be caught from door handles, toilet seats, or plates and cups. The general public didn't understand that they couldn't 'catch' AIDS and that the condition could only develop once the virus (HIV) had already been acquired. The Thatcher Government's response, meanwhile, in the face of all-pervasive ignorance, was hopeless; like Ronald Reagan, our prime minister remained silent on the matter as hundreds and soon to be thousands of her fellow citizens became infected and died on her complacent watch.

It was predominantly young gay men, just like Raymond, who were coming down with AIDS in increasing numbers. AIDS was itself, a cruel acronym that failed to convey the gravity of its horrible symptoms and illnesses. The early flu-like symptoms often gave way to others that were severe to the point of debilitation, including chronic diarrhoea, catastrophic weight loss, headaches, loose teeth, shingles, skin lesions (Kaposi's), blindness, dementia, and even the loss of mobility altogether. Grown men were vomiting and shitting themselves privately and in public, as previously harmless bugs and parasites took hold of their bodies. This was compounded by social isolation, and fear of rejection by friends and family; many of whom were not just finding out that their loved one was dying from AIDS, but also learning of his sexuality for the first time. Overshadowing all this was the fear of a slow and agonising death, at what should be the prime of life. There was much condemnation from religious leaders who should have been there to help and support, but, according to many of them, AIDS was God's punishment against gays and our "lifestyles".

It was outrageous that gay men were simply being left to fight for their own lives. And yet, against all odds, the gay community demonstrated that it was capable of enormous goodwill, strength, and courage. We were not going to be defeated. We had come too far to allow this huge disease with a little name to destroy our lives, even if we privately feared that it just might succeed.

I applied to become a volunteer buddy at the London Lighthouse Project, under the supervision of Christopher Spence, its energetic and spiritually uplifting director, and was warmly accepted into the project. I had previously applied to the Terrence Higgins Trust, the premier organisation dealing with the growing AIDS crisis, but never heard back. A short time later I attended an AIDS conference hosted by the THT. From the floor I voiced my disappointment that I had not received a response to my volunteer application, in which I stressed the need to support and inform the black gay community. Tony Whitehead, the organisation's then chair, politely apologised and said he'd look into the matter, but I still heard nothing. I guess the Trust was too busy. I honestly don't believe they were deliberately neglecting black gay men, but I could see why some may have perceived it that way.

AIDS was affecting gay men of all races, but the service response was being organised by white gay men with white gay men in mind. There was nothing in their operational or service profile to make black gay men feel welcome. Joining London Lighthouse and the Terrence Higgins Trust in the line-up of self-help groups, were Body Positive, Body and Soul, Positively Women and the Landmark, which was based in south London. Frontliners, a satellite of the THT, was another such group, led entirely by gay men with AIDS; they gave an important voice to the actual life experiences of those directly affected by AIDS, and were quite rightly uncompromising in shouting about the discrimination they were experiencing. But they were also entirely composed of white men, and neither reflected nor represented the experiences and voices of black gay men with the disease. There was no effort on the part of funding bodies to ensure that recipient agencies addressed the cultural needs of black gays, which was a major failing.

I didn't allow myself to begin to see white gay men as my enemy; they were not. AIDS was the enemy, and I remain clear about that to this very day. But just because the majority of AIDS cases were amongst white gay men, this was no reason to neglect the needs of black gay men. White gays enjoyed having sex with black guys in their bedrooms and the saunas, but when our lives depended upon it, we were out of sight and out of mind. Not nice! I began to feel angry, in fact, I was furious. Black gay men and the wider black community were, to the extent they were acknowledged at all, an afterthought where the organised response to AIDS was concerned. This was eating away at me. Despite our obvious presence, somehow black people were invisible to the shapers of policies and services. I was especially angry that I was too small and insignificant to do anything about it. Or was I?

My frustration drove me to give up on the established organisations and set up the Black Communities AIDS Team (BCAT). I approached the black and gay community press and was heartened by the warmth of their response. *The Voice* newspaper was particularly interested and they soon made me the acceptable and regular face of the black gay community. In one of their articles, under a large photo of me sporting a Grace Jones-like flat top, they printed: 'Vernal Scott, a pioneer in changing attitudes towards gays'. In subsequent articles, I was thrilled when they stopped mentioning that I was gay, and instead, just quoted me talking about HIV/AIDS and the impact it was having on the UK black community.

> **AIDS: PUBLIC ENEMY**
>
> **COMING OUT FIGHTING**
>
> The black gay community-coping with AIDS and prejudice.
>
> Homosexuality has long been considered 'taboo' in the black community. Now however, with the posibility that even the most respectable families, in the most God-fearing of communities, could fall prey to AIDS, the time has come to do away with old-fashioned prejudices.
>
> "In the black community it takes a lot more courage than in the white community to admit that you are gay... It takes being willing to lose your friends...and family".

It was through such articles that I managed to get volunteers to help me provide support in the form of befriending and signposting on behalf of black people living with AIDS in London. BCAT did not have any money, but we did have committed black and Asian volunteers; amongst whom were Jeff, Aisha, and Mehboob, who all did a fantastic job. When the Landmark offered us some office space, Aisha and Mehboob became our first paid employees, though this arrangement was short-lived due to funding issues.

Then came an incident that confirmed what I had thought all along; that black gay men with AIDS needed to look to themselves for appropriate community services. Frontliners, a satellite organisation of the THT, produced a regular newsletter. The latest edition featured a review of an Eddie Murphy video. The unhappy author wrote: "This mutha-fucking nigger needs to learn some manners!" I couldn't believe what I was reading. The organisation had succeeded in being more offensive than their target dared to be: 1) they assumed only white gays would have been offended by Murphy's gay jokes; 2) they thought it acceptable to use overtly racist language; 3) they didn't consider or care about the impact such language would have on potential black service users and their willingness to use available services; and 4) they expected to get away with it. My fury wouldn't allow the latter to happen.

What Frontliners had written and published was totally unacceptable, and should have been patently so to whomever proofread the article. There was no defence at all for using such language, none! Here was a publicly-funded organisation that was responsible for providing support to people with AIDS, thinking that it was acceptable to use the word nigger as casually as if it were talking about the weather.

As well as making a series of irate phone calls, I made my feelings clear in uncompromising manner at a Terrence Higgins Trust Candlelit Vigil held in Covent Garden. I had been invited to speak to the candle-bearing crowd of a few hundred people. "Frankly," I said to applause, "Frontliners, the Terrence Higgins Trust and their funders should've known better." The black people present at the vigil were pleased that I'd said it, and so was I. I felt better for it. The Frontliners contingent, however, were furious. Michael, their director, turned his back and walked away from me in a huff. But I had no apology to make to him or anyone else. My point was simple: black people, with or without AIDS, did not need Frontliners or anyone else adding to our experience of discrimination. Tony Whitehead came over to apologise, and an apology was later printed in the same newsletter. The matter was closed but not forgotten.

Frontliners eventually lost momentum, but I don't think my speaking out had anything to do with it. Despite the distasteful incident, I was genuinely sorry to hear of the death of Michael, who was a true champion of people living with AIDS.

My growing profile in the black community wasn't without its problems, as I started being recognised in the street by the occasional stranger. One black guy came up to me in Virgin records in Oxford Street, and insisted in telling me that my sexuality was "nothing short of corruption by white people". At around the same time, a black fashion publication called *Root* carried a photo of me as part of an article in which they referred to black gays as 'odious and detestable'. I noticed that the publication carried a large amount of paid adverts by the Greater London Council, which was headed by Ken Livingstone, the man who would later become an MP, and later still, London's first elected mayor. The Greater London Council had an excellent reputation for challenging inequality throughout the city, so I called to make an urgent appointment to see Ken, which his office accepted.

A few days later I was shaking Ken's hand and taking a seat in his office at County Hall.

He was business-like, and to the point, and asked how he could help. I showed him the offending article and pointed out that his organisation was effectively funding homophobia by placing adverts in the *Root*. I wanted to know what he was going to do about it. He simply said, "Thank you for bringing this to my attention, Vernal. Leave it with me."

We shook hands again and I left. The meeting was over in less than ten minutes.

I trusted Ken and believed he would act in the interest of the gay community and decency. My confidence was promptly rewarded. In a matter of days I received a phone call from a worried journalist working for *Root*. He pleaded with me,

"Vernal, you're putting my job at risk. The article wasn't my fault. We can't get any advertising and may have to close."

My response was brief: "I have no sympathy for you, or your crappy publication. How dare you even bother to call me after referring to people like me as odious? Go and work somewhere else and remember not to repeat your mistake."

I shed no tears when *Root* magazine folded a very short time later; in fact I received the news with no little satisfaction. We might be gay, but we were not powerless punch bags.

Despite the on-going bigotry, our future as gay people was going to be bright and equal: because that's how we were going to create it and I intended to do my part. Onwards and upwards, brothers and sisters!

Oh foolish, foolish, foolish me. My optimism was destined to lie amongst the ruins of a most terrible war that AIDS had declared upon us. In the fight of our lives against catastrophic illness, fear, prejudice, and an unyielding stigma, the words I will survive were to take on a new, critical poignancy. But in all that there would be against us, we would not be abandoned by courage and love.

27. I'M COMING OUT!

CLARE RAYNER, THE UK'S BEST-LOVED AGONY AUNT, produced a helpful video for parents of gay children. Despite 'coming out' to myself years earlier and my subsequent activities related to HIV and AIDS, my family consistently failed to acknowledge my sexuality and I was beginning to feel like some kind of *dirty secret*. I decided to bring the matter to the fore, and in a very uncomfortable, and perhaps cowardly, attempt to detach myself from the potential fallout of directly coming out to my evangelical mother, I'd acquired a copy of the video. Quietly slipping it into the video player without making reference to its content, I joined Mum on an adjacent sofa to where she'd nestled in, in anticipation of some light afternoon televised entertainment.

Mum sipped at her tea as Clare's face appeared and began explaining what the video was about. With only seconds into the video, my now stationary but visibly disturbed mother began to make very audible grumbling noises. She was just warming up. A further minute into Clare's calm and very articulate introduction, Mum was showing signs of real distress. Plonking her white ceramic cup down onto the glass topped coffee table, she shifted about in her seat in a vain attempt at finding a position that would somehow facilitate her escape from Clare's unwelcome words. Another minute or so into what was clearly a grotesque horror flick, as far as Mum was concerned, she began throwing herself around the sofa in a state of complete grief. With teary eyes, Mum, with full-on Jamaican accent, demanded: "Why are you showing me this?!" However, other than an occasional glance at her from the corner of my eye, I did not reply, but kept staring ahead at the screen. She continued: "How could you do this to me?" I still said nothing, but if I had, then I would have made it clear that her emotional blackmail wasn't going to work on me today. This was the same emotional blackmail experienced by LGBT people in families around the world; a cruel, selfish, and destructive blackmail that kept our disapproving parents and siblings in homophobic bliss while we lived our inhibited lives in closeted misery. Mum went on: "You're not gay, you're just confused. I...I...I want to kick you!"

My baffled and increasingly angry mother could see confidence on my face, not fear or confusion, hence her desperate but unlikely threat to execute a physical assault against my person. To lessen the tension, I finally spoke up: "Mum, just watch the video. It will help you to understand..." She did not let me finish my sentence before side-swiping me with: "Understand what!?" Now, looking up at the ceiling and using her hands and fingers to make sure her intended listener could fully understand, Mum pleaded to the invisible heavens: "Lord, why this disgrace upon me? Lord, please help me: it's two girl children I have, not three! This isn't right, Lord!!"

In my poor mother's ignorant mind, my being gay also meant a change in my gender; I was now no longer a son, but a third daughter! My poor, poor Mum. In a moment of supreme confidence inspired by the lingering light of Exegesis in me, and with the patent insensitivity towards others that often accompanied it, I turned to my troubled mother and calmly asked: "Have you quite finished, dear?"

A look of incredulity consumed her face, and appeared to confirm that I was going to need the assistance of Harley Street surgeons to extract both her foot and slippers from my butt. Mum was not happy with me, but after a few pitiful insults about "dirty people and dirty lifestyles", she carried on weeping and wailing and my butt was spared. It seemed she was exaggerating her distress, as if trying to draw me into her drama, but I wasn't having any of it, and kept my composure intact.

Having had my lows as a suicidal teen due to well justified fears about how Mum and others might react to my sexuality, I was now wise enough to know that this drama had nothing to do with me or my sexuality; it was all hers and people who think like her. My sexuality was never the problem; homophobic and ignorant people are the problem, and I was putting the blame where it belongs; with the perpetrator.

My mature and very wise head didn't prevent Mum's insults from coming at me, thick and fast: "You're not G-A-Y!" She pronounced each letter separately, as if not wanting the actual word to pass her sanctified lips. "You're mad, M-A-D, you hear me, boy? Mad!" There was nothing holy about those unkind words.

Finally, after telling me that she had no intention of watching my "dirty video", she got to her feet and left the room in a huff, but not before warning me not to eat from her plates, use her cutlery, or sit on her chairs. Not only did my being gay mean that I'd shifted genders, in her ignorance, it also meant that I was a walking health risk: gay = AIDS. This was an increasingly common assumption throughout the UK and around the world; born out of prejudice as much as ignorance. I was angry but remained tight lipped and visibly unmoved.

Mum retreated to her bedroom and phoned my brother Bunny to tell him about his problem little brother. In a short while he arrived at the flat to add his protest to Mum's. He strode into the living room where I was still sitting, and without a word of hello, he abruptly shared his understanding of the situation: "I hear you've been talking to Mum about your nastiness."

"Oh, hi bro, how are you?" I said flippantly. I wasn't intimidated by him anymore, those days were long dead and buried.

Perhaps thrown by my unruffled reaction, he repeated himself, but a little louder: "Mum told me about your nastiness!" He then added his knockout blow: "You need to know that the greatest thing you could ever do is wake up in the morning and feel a woman's breasts against your chest."

Huh! Now I was ruffled by that odd pearl of redundant wisdom, and retorted with: "That may be your thing, brother, but it isn't mine." I added: "But you're right: sex with women is great, if you're straight!" I was as calm as I was clear, and I'm not sure if it was my accidental rhyme or its content, but my brother was not pleased. However, I wasn't finished with him yet. Feigning boredom whilst looking him in the eye: "Er, is there anything else you want to say, bro?!" He was speechless and somewhat thunderstruck.

In that moment, a long overdue comprehension dawned upon him: his little brother had grown up and was no longer going to be a victim of his bullying and intimidation. Between him and my mother, I'd had an afternoon of being Bible-bashed, cursed, insulted, threatened with physical violence, and then to top it all, told that my life (sexuality!) would be very different (straight!) if only I'd give in to the cure: a woman's breasts against my chest – in the morning; no, I mustn't forget the importance of the mornings, or the cure for my ailment won't work. Brother, please!

Kissing his teeth in disgust at me, Bunny turned and left the living room. I saw him whisper something inaudible to Mum on his way out the front door, and whatever it was caused her to start praying at the top of her lungs. Did he say something warm and kind about his kid brother, or tell her not to worry because I'd soon be wiped off the face of the Earth by the 'gay disease'? Either way, I wasn't about to ask.

I had indeed grown up. If anyone had a problem with my sexuality, then it was their issue, not mine; they could whisper, dance, scream, or shout all they liked. None of it would change what I couldn't: my birth sexuality and my decision to come out of the life-sapping closet.

Mum must have phoned my sister Beverley too; she later rang me to register her disapproval, although she was less confrontational about it than Bunny had been. I didn't hear anything from Leo or Jan about the matter, and didn't go seeking their views either.

I later learned that Mum had also called Dad, to tell him about their "problem" child. With the verbal iteration of his lashing belt of yester-year, he told her that no son of his could be gay, and if I was, then it had come from her side of the family. Thanks, Dad!

Things soon settled down, but I confess to teasing Mum on occasion, by deliberately walking around the flat with an exaggerated swinging of my hips. If she thought my sexuality meant she now had a third girl child, as she put it, then I intended to play the part. My deliberately camp behaviour prompted a relentless kissing of teeth and mumbling of prayers under her breath – that's when she wasn't shouting them out loud. As she prayed harder, I switched my hips harder; it was only fair to do so, in my silly over-confident mind. Actually, it was very inane of me; I know that now, but it made me chuckle at the time, under my breath, of course!

The dirty family secret was out, and damn the consequences! All I needed to do now was get dressed up as my mother, complete with her white Sunday-best flappy hat, and sashay down the aisle at her Pentecostal church on Leghorn Road. Now that would give her and her brethren something to pray and talk in tongues about! Well, I had to do something to exorcise their demonic homophobia... hmm, but perhaps not that. No, I had better park that idea.

A few months later, Dad and I crossed paths at my sister Jan's wedding reception. Occupying prime position at the top end of the hall, he skillfully constructed a Golden Virginia roll-up while simultaneously enthusing to the assembled guests about how proud he was of his wonderful daughter and her choice of husband. Mum insisted that I go and say hello to him. So, against my better judgment, I sauntered over and waded my way through with outstretched hand, expecting to shake his. But, instead of his hand, Dad stopped talking, carried on rolling his cigarette, smirked and then just glared at me with utter contempt written across his face. He then stood up from his perched position, turned his back in my face, and carried on talking to guests as if I wasn't there. His disapproval was as clear as my naked embarrassment. I was gutted.

Someone captured the miserable moment on camera, as I quickly exited to seek refuge outside.

I was furious with myself to the point of tears for affording him the opportunity to humiliate me in such a public way. My cousin Doreene came to find me and insisted that I go right back in there, and I did, even though I had nothing to prove. When we entered the hall, Dad approached Doreene and asked if she wanted a drink. She replied with "Yes, thanks, Uncle Skippy." I just looked at him with a vacant expression, which was how I was feeling. He then looked at my collar rather than my eyes and said, "You can come, if you want one too" and walked away towards the bar. Even though he couldn't even get himself to mention my name, Doreene and I knew his invitation was his macho way of saying sorry, and while I accepted his gesture, I would never forget the incident. In fact, some years would pass before I'd set eyes on my dad again.

The 'word of God' that Mum was receiving at her twice weekly Pentecostal church meetings was causing her to struggle with the reality of my now very public homosexuality; my work and sexuality had become a regular feature in the black press. I was still living with her at Harrowdene Close when she returned home from church one Sunday afternoon. She came directly into the living room, still wearing her coat. Looking at me wordlessly, at first, she suddenly burst into tears. Alarmed, I hastened over to ask what was wrong; thinking that she'd had a road accident or something. But her calamitous response was more painful than anything my mind could imagine:

"A church sister asked me if my son's name is Vernal Scott, and I lied and told her no, my son's name is Ian." Sobbing, Mum looked up to the ceiling in search of God's absent face, and continued: "I feel so ashamed. I denied knowing my own son, and I'm asking God to please forgive me".

Before I could absorb the enormity of what she said, Mum's tears turned to anger. She blasted: "Why is it *you* who must plaster yourself all over the newspapers with your dirty ways and those dirty people?" She wasn't finished: "How come nobody else is doing it, only you? You and that nasty disease! How come you're running *into* it when everyone else is running *away* from it?"

Standing there with my mouth agape, Mum's voice became background noise as my mind tried to decipher what was beginning to feel like a life-changing event. It was hard for me to hear; Mum needed her church more than she needed me and I had to be sacrificed, and based upon her own beliefs, she was willing to risk eternal hell's fire for having done so. She knew that a murderer would be more welcome in her church than a man whose only 'sin' is his homosexuality and his mother would be equally unwelcome.

I struggled to not think of Mum as some kind of Judas, but I'd be dishonest to say the similarity didn't cross my mind and, clearly, hers too. I was deeply hurt by what she'd done, but had to forgive her, and pray that she could one day forgive herself. Her tears were tears of shame, for herself as well as for me, but I also suspect they were tears of guilt.

Any guilt or shame, in my view, belonged to the church, not my mother. It was their intrinsic homophobia and wilful incessant ignorance about human sexuality that caused an otherwise good Christian to seek self-protection by lying. The fallout of telling the truth would have made Mum an immediate outcast, and that was too high a price to pay. The truth is that the (black) church would be transformed overnight if everyone involved was honest about having gay loved ones in their family. Heavens, the church would suddenly become a place of integrity. Lord, have mercy!

Not even the genius of Clare Rayner could salvage anything but agony from this dire situation. It was time for me to leave Harrowdene Close; staying would mean sacrificing my authenticity and dignity.

In all the courage that I knew Mum possessed in dealing with life's many challenges, the *gay challenge* proved to be one too many.

28. HOMELESS

MUM'S DENIAL OF ME AT CHURCH was the last straw, and my leaving home felt like the right thing to do, for both of us.

Monday morning could not come soon enough. Mum looked shocked when I knocked on her bedroom door with my falling-apart suitcase in my hand to tell her goodbye. She asked where I was going, and I said I had no idea, but that I felt we would both be happier if I left. She tried to contradict this and told me not to be so stupid, but I would not relent. Five minutes later I was out the door with just five pounds from my worried Mum in my pocket.

I made my way from Wembley and across North London to the homelessness unit at Haringey Council, which, I believed, had sympathetic equality policies for vulnerable people of various categories. Haringey was the borough in which I had previously lived as a student. I explained to the housing officer that I believed I was at risk of violence because of my sexuality, and my high-profile voluntary work on AIDS. Because of this, he accepted me as 'homeless', and told me I was eligible for housing. The officer then related the bad news: there was a long waiting list for housing, and that I could be on it for over a year. He explained that, in the meantime, they would put me in temporary accommodation, until a suitable apartment became available.

I waited in the reception area while the officer searched the temporary housing database to try to find me a temporary room somewhere in the borough. I was shortly dispatched to what I thought was going to be my new home, for now. However, when I arrived at the flea-bitten hotel on Seven Sisters Road in Finsbury Park, I felt very uneasy, to say the least. The elderly Greek proprietor led me through winding corridors to a room at the top of the stairs. Groups of men, mostly black, hung around on the landings. On opening the door to what was to be my home for the foreseeable future, my eyes beheld on a nursery-sized room that practically exhaled a reek of stale urine and cigarettes. The tiny garret window was dirty, and the carpet stained with the devil only knew what. I looked at the tatty single bed with the equally tatty bedspread and a sense of despair gripped my entire being. I turned to the elderly man and said, "Thank you very much, but I can't stay here."

Seconds later, and I was out the door and on my way back home to my mother's. She opened the door triumphantly, "Stupid boy!" she said, with mocking pleasure and some relief too; at least she knew where her youngest child was sleeping tonight. I smiled as I headed to my room, and my fresh sheets. *She must have been expecting me back,* I thought. It's those powerful prayers again!

However, I was not willing to be defeated, and the very next morning I took self and suitcase back to the homeless unit in Haringey. I told the officer from the day before about the dreadful state of the room at the bedsit he'd sent me to, and asked if they could send me somewhere decent. I stressed that I didn't care where it was, but it had to be clean. The very kind officer said there was a better place in Muswell Hill.

Walking into this Queen's Avenue hotel was like entering a different world. It was large, well kept, and my decent-sized double bedroom felt welcoming. I knew I could live there quite happily while I waited for a permanent home. I got used to the occasional spider or silverfish sharing my room, and to the noise of the many families and other individuals who shared the address. I was happy enough with a simple and reasonably clean room for the time being. My mother would be waiting a long time if she thought I was coming back tonight. There was no going back, not now.

I collected my unemployment benefit in Wood Green and scrimped enough to purchase a second-hand electric typewriter, which I used to write my thoughts and experiences on the UK HIV/AIDS challenge, especially the experience of the black community. I wanted to produce some kind of guide for local authorities, particularly community workers, so that they carry out their duties with confidence when the client is someone living with AIDS. I also continued to nurture my creation, the Black Communities AIDS Team, whilst volunteering as a buddy at London Lighthouse.

I would occasionally visit my mother during the day to eat some proper food, especially as I had no cooking facilities of my own. I'd raid her kitchen cupboards for biscuits and other non-perishables that I could munch on in my hungry moments in my temporary abode. I could tell that she didn't really mind and was quietly pleased that I was still alive. During one of my visits, she was busy preparing for a special church event, and was excited about the white dress she was making for the occasion, but she then slip the real reason for her happy state; she'd seen my father when she was driving in Harlesden, but had not stopped to say hello. I could tell that she was curious about what he was doing; it was now ten years since their divorce, and I knew that she missed him awfully, but her pride made it impossible for her to admit it. She never met another man who could replace her beloved Skippy; she didn't want anyone else but him, and Jesus Christ, of course.

Five months into my stay at Queens Avenue, and I was growing frustrated with the wait. The toilets were not being cleaned, and I was sharing my room with a growing number of bugs. I decided to go and see Bernie Grant, my local MP, who together with Paul Boateng and Diane Abbott, was one of the country's first African-Caribbean Members of Parliament. Bernie was truly wonderful and greeted me like I was his son. He said he would do everything he could to see that I was re-housed quickly, and he lived up to his word. The following week, I was given the keys to 33 Headcorn Road, just off White Hart Lane in Tottenham; my first home of my own. Thank you, dear Bernie!

The flat was carpeted and had no furnishings at all, but it had a front door and I had the sole key: it was *my* front door and *my* key! Like the other apartments in the low-rise block, it was designed for elderly and disabled people. It had a good-sized living room, with a cute little balcony that overlooked an ugly day care building opposite. The single bedroom was snug, but considering that I had no bed or bedroom furniture to put in it, it seemed spacious. The galley kitchen, off the living room, also seemed roomy, again, it had no appliances: no cooker, no fridge, no table, just empty cupboards. I had no money to buy anything, as my twenty-six pounds per week unemployment benefit did not stretch very far at all. Indeed, other than the clothes I had on my back, I owned one further pair of trousers and three shirts, all which had been purchased very cheaply from Wembley Market. My spare pair of trousers cost me three pounds, and they looked it, too! They were navy blue, with large grey stripes, and were extremely roomy in the seat, with turn-ups at the ankle. Between their eye-catching design, and my twenty-seven-inch waist, I pretty much disappeared when I wore them. I knew they looked terrible, but I was too poor to afford anything else.

I may not have had classy clothes, but at least I had a home, even if it was an empty one. I didn't bother heating the bedroom, because I didn't sleep in it. The room became a dump for newspaper clippings and other material concerned with HIV and AIDS. I slept on the lounge floor at night, falling asleep while listening to mellow tracks from my most treasured possessions: my old vinyl albums.

My dear mother decided to visit, and travelled by bus and tube to my flat. She was keen to show some concern for her youngest child's living conditions. She normally drove everywhere, but Tottenham was a little too far outside her accustomed circuit of Kilburn, Wembley, Harlesden and Willesden. She stepped into my flat wearing her beige raincoat, and a look of horror quickly invaded her face.

"Lord have mercy!" she wailed – the opening lines to the telling-off that she had, no doubt, been practising on the journey over. "You don't have anything here, not one drop of furniture! When are you going to get yourself a job?" She was just warming up.

Admittedly, I hadn't had paid work for about three years, not since leaving the Barbican Centre. I told her I was doing my very best, but she wasn't convinced. There was no denying that I was still stone-cold broke and needed money, but I was surviving, somehow.

Mum walked into my empty kitchen, and opened my cupboards to confirm her suspicions; they were completely empty apart from a lonely tin of kidney beans, which the previous occupant had left behind. "So what are you eating every day?" she demanded, incredulously.

"I get unemployment benefit and buy what I need from that. I also get housing benefit, and it pays my rent." I replied.

She looked at me in silent disbelief, as if to say, "You would rather live like *this*, instead of at home with me, and all the food you need?" I could tell that she wanted to cry for me, her youngest child. She continued to survey the empty wastes of my cupboards and countertops, when her eyes fixed on the only knife I owned, sitting on its spine, with the blade facing upwards. She looked me in the eye, and in a stern voice said, "Mark my words: someone will be leaving this place before too long." This was another of my mother's superstitions; she believed that a knife that falls on its spine meant that someone resident in the house would soon be departing. Of course, I was the only resident, but I didn't share her superstitions.

I tried to lighten the atmosphere by saying, "Yes, mum, it's you that will be leaving. You're only visiting, remember!"

But her prophetic countenance was unmoved. "You will not be living here for long, boy; that is for certain." With that, she flipped the knife onto its side, and walked out of the kitchen.

I tried to recall whether I had left the knife on its spine, as we had found it. I must have; I mean, who else could have? I lived alone, after all.

My mother began to bless the flat: praying in the kitchen, then in the bedroom, the bathroom, and then the living room. When she finished, she left, after giving me a much-appreciated ten-pound note. We didn't kiss or embrace, but I think we both wanted to. At least I did. I needed a hug.

That night, as I stretched out on my acquired carpet, I reflected upon my mother's visit and other things. By chance, my outstretched hand reached under the radiator, and I felt something strange. It was a film roll container, filled with one pound coins, which added up to six pounds in total. I immediately went out and bought myself some takeaway chicken and chips. I was going to eat well this week. The flat's presumably deceased previous occupant must have hidden the coins there. I silently thanked the kindly spirit, and slept a satisfying sleep.

The following week I received a letter from my mother, sharply criticising my choices in life. *"You've turned into a useless person"*, she wrote. But she signed the letter *Love, Mum*. I was hurt by her condemnatory tone, but I knew she meant well. I could understand that, from her perspective, I really had hit rock bottom since my glamorous days as a smartly-dressed usher and box office clerk. But despite my penniless state, and lack of even basic comforts, I had not a shred of doubt that my best years were ahead of me. Exegesis had not been a waste of money. Yes, the best was yet to come, but the worst would be in hot pursuit.

29. KNOCKING ON DOORS

1987 SAW THE BLACK GAY MEN'S CONFERENCE held in London, it was the UK's first such event. I was feeling very proud as an out black gay man and my attendance at that conference had a lot to do with it; it taught me that we have much to be proud of and that shame has no place in our lives. It was organised by Dirg and Savi, two employees of the much needed but short-lived Black Lesbian and Gay Centre.

I went to see my mother the following week, for a visit and some proper food. While I was waiting for the bus that would take me to the bottom of her road, I looked over at Brent Town Hall, and began to wonder what the council was doing about HIV and AIDS in the ethnic majority borough of some 275,000 people.

I decided to give the bus a miss, and instead, crossed the road to the Town Hall. At the reception, I asked for the race equality unit, which I knew was headed by Russell Profit, a highly respected advocate of minority rights. When I got to his office, I was told that he was too busy to see me and that I had to make an appointment. I said that was fine, and reached into my tatty Sainsbury's plastic shopping bag, which was serving as my briefcase, and retrieved a copy of the document I had been writing on UK black communities and AIDS. I handed it to the young black lady sitting at the reception desk, and asked that it be given to Russell. I told her it had my telephone number on it in case he wanted to reach me. I left the building, and continued on my way to Mum's.

The tremendous luxury of a landline phone arrived a couple of weeks earlier (the mobile phone had yet to be invented), and had been a gift from Christopher Spence, the kind director of London Lighthouse. He said he was frustrated in trying to reach me, and hoped my having a phone would help. It really was very kind of him, even if I was quite sure I couldn't afford to maintain it. As if the phone weren't enough, I also received another gift, this time from James, my American friend whom I'd met when I worked at the Barbican; I never let him forget that he took me to Wendy's for our first date. Not classy, but very funny. He was planning to visit the UK and asked to stay with me, and when I explained that I had no bed, he offered to buy one for me. Heaven!

It was the following day when my phone – my phone! – rang. The caller identified herself as Francesca, from Brent Council, and asked about my availability for a meeting with her director. She added that he had read, and was impressed with my document, and was hoping for an early meeting. I said I was available early the following week. Of course I was!

At 11am the following Tuesday, I found myself again climbing the steps of Brent Town Hall. I was met by Francesca at reception, and she guided me to the Committee Room where the meeting was to be held. My jaw almost hit the floor when the door opened, and I saw a gigantic wood-panelled room, and twenty or so expectant faces awaiting my arrival. I smiled anxiously, thinking to myself, *What the hell have I let myself in for?*

I was shown to a seat at the bottom of the table, and it became clear from the introductions that I was meeting with the great and the good of Brent Council. Chairing the meeting was Merle, the young black Labour leader of the council, flanked on either side by Charles, the chief executive, and David, the youthful black director of social services. Russell Profit, and other senior colleagues from different departments, took up the other places at the enormous table. I gulped when I realised that everyone had a photocopy of my document in hand, and for a moment, I was concerned about my grammatical errors and spelling mistakes, which I momentarily worried would be the only thing that they would want to talk to me about. But RAT was wrong, again!

The chairman thanked me for the document, and for coming to the meeting. She then asked what I thought the council should be doing to address AIDS in the borough. For the next twenty minutes, I explained how the virus was transmitted, the kind of care that those infected needed in the community, and the need for all staff to receive HIV/AIDS awareness training. I added that they needed to have a strategy and a plan that would deal with staff, clients and the wider community. I said I was happy to help in any way that I could. I said "I", because BCAT had now folded due to a lack of resources and I was on my own; although a sister branch of BCAT had set itself up in Leeds, and I understood it was well funded and doing fine.

I answered questions about the kind of training staff would need, and what to do about personnel who did not want to work with people affected by AIDS. I explained the need for the council to develop a specific set of policies, similar to its equality policies, that would seek to ensure people with AIDS did not experience discrimination in service provision, or as employees.

I heaved a sigh of relief as I left the room. I had sown a seed in the minds of the council's leaders about the gravity of the work that they, and all responsible local authorities, needed to undertake in order to meet the challenge of AIDS. I had a sense that I was in a position to offer them a service, but I wasn't entirely sure where to start to take the idea further. I certainly didn't see myself going around to London's thirty-two borough councils to give them similar advice, even though there was a desperate need to. I had no money and no organisation. There was no chance of my undertaking such a challenge. *And what about the rest of the country?* I asked myself. What indeed!

Some weeks later, Brent Council advertised a vacancy for the position of principal HIV/AIDS officer, to be based in the social services department. I worked hard at my application, and with the considerable advantage of references from Christopher Spence and Anthony Hillin from the Lighthouse and Gay Centre, respectively, I was shortlisted for interview.

The job interview came on a cold November morning. I did my best to hide the worn inseams of my brown polyester trousers by wearing my shirt over my waist rather than tucked in. I had nothing else to wear – I didn't dare wear the pinstriped Charlie Chaplin trousers again, after a group of children had laughed at me on Tottenham High Street a few weeks earlier. Upon my arrival at the interview venue, I discovered that I was one of twelve shortlisted candidates. Twelve! My competitors were all white gay men, some of whom I knew from the Terrence Higgins Trust or London Lighthouse.

The interview panel was comprised of six people, including the chair of social services. I felt pretty confident as I answered each question, but got stuck when asked how I would incorporate sexuality into my work, if successful. I found myself looking out of the window, before turning back to the panel and saying, "I will think about it, and seek to ensure that people, regardless of their sexuality, are included in my work." Half an hour later the interview was over, and I was on the bus back to Tottenham. I phoned my mum and asked her to pray for me to get the job, and I knew she would.

On the 16th of November 1987, I celebrated my twenty-sixth birthday. When the phone rang that morning, I thought it would be my mother calling to sing me 'Happy Birthday'. But instead, it was Brent Council, calling to offer me the job. Needless to say, I was elated and accepted straight away. We agreed that I would start on the 1st of December, which, coincidentally, would be the very first international World AIDS Day.

I was thrilled. I had no idea what I was going to do with nineteen thousand pounds a year, but I knew I would now be able to afford to eat properly, furnish my place without relying on charity and buy some decent pants without holes. My mother was the first person I called, then Christopher Spence and Anthony Hillin, to say an enormous thank you for their support. Then I called my good friend Lloyd, whom I'd known since my *Black Echoes* ad, and the party in east London. I was now back in the land of the employed, and I was ready!

On 1 December, I settled behind my desk. I acquired a lovely administrative assistant called Gerard, and shared my office with a lovely woman called Sally, who worked for the local health authority. My first meeting was with David Divine, the dashing director of social services, and my ultimate boss. He gave me a warm welcome, and offered me all the support I would need to get my job done. I later met with the chair and vice chair of social services, and later still, with Russell Profit, the Head of the Race Equality Unit, and his staff. A member of his staff was quick to warn me to keep a low profile in the local black community, as she felt I might come to harm if I were to be too open about being gay. I explained that I was there to write and promote HIV policy, not my sexuality.

My first wage packet came in before Christmas, and I went out and treated myself to some trousers, and shiny, hole-free shoes to match. In fact, I purchased quite a few clothes, and my kitchen cupboard was, for the first time, full of groceries. "Ah, that's better," my mother said when she next saw me. I could tell that she was proud of me, but was still very worried about my work, and whether it would mean harm would come to me.

I was off to a good start in my new job, or so I thought. But the local press had made quite an issue about my imminent arrival as 'AIDS boss', and made a particular point about my salary, which they seemed to think was excessively high. I did not concern myself with these stories, but worse was to come.

No sooner had I arrived, than I started to receive irate phone calls from black members of staff at the council, who were offended by a letter I had issued to all personnel explaining my work. I couldn't work out why black staff were so offended by the letter, until I managed to get a copy. The wording of the letter had been altered, and instead of explaining that *all staff* needed to be aware of HIV, it had been changed to read *particularly black staff*. The damaging implications were obvious, and I could see why offence was caused; the inference being black staff had more reason than others to be concerned with HIV and AIDS, and this was not the case.

My phone was ringing off the hook with outraged callers. My director was away, so I was forced to bring the matter of the doctored letter to the attention of the chair of social services; a formidable black woman who was known to take no prisoners. She looked at the letter in horror, and asked me to leave the matter with her, as she believed she knew who the culprit was. A few days later, the threatening phone calls ceased, and I received an apology from the race equality unit. It turned out that the entire incident had been a well-meaning error of judgment. I accepted the apology; it was time to get over it and get on with my job.

With the incident behind me, I visited as many staff groups as possible, explaining my work, and how we could all remain safe whilst working with people with AIDS. To my disappointment, one group of home care workers was having none of it, and decided to boycott the homes of people with AIDS. At the time, there were only a handful of cases of people with AIDS in the borough, and most of them were only getting in touch with public services as a last resort. But there was one client, a former policeman, who was in desperate need of home care, and whom no one was willing to visit. Thankfully, my request for volunteers from amongst the other home care workers was answered, and he was soon in receipt of services. The problem was being repeated up and down the country: people with AIDS were being refused services that everybody else could take for granted. And the shrill hysteria of the press didn't help one bit.

A few months into the job, and I was pictured with David Divine on the front pages of the local press. He had been dismissed, and like a lot of his staff, both black and white, I marched in support of his reinstatement. The protest did not sway the council, but I considered him to be an inspired leader and friend. I was personally very saddened to see him go but knew that he would go on to bigger and better things.

30. POLICE! UNDER HOMOPHOBIC ATTACK

MY FEET WERE NOW WELL UNDER MY DESK in my new job, but things were not going so well with my living arrangements. The trouble came from my immediate neighbour who lived directly opposite; a middle-aged Irish man who spent his time drinking and cursing at fellow residents. I was, naturally, wary of him, and kept my distance the best I could. Then, one night, matters came to a terrifying head.

I had returned home one evening from a candlelit AIDS vigil, the UK's first, organised by Peter Tatchell. Many hundreds of people attended; the crisis had grown, and so, too, had the ranks of people affected and concerned. It was well after midnight when I heard a tremendous pounding on my front door. I climbed out of bed and crept cautiously to the front door to peer out the peep hole. *Could there be a fire?* I thought. Against my better judgment, I opened the front door and in a split second, my neighbour's fist sailed through the opening toward my sleepy face, missing me by less than an inch. I struggled to close the door against the man's bulk as he tried to barge his way in. "You dirty AIDS carrier!" he snarled drunkenly at me, "I'm gonna fucking kill you... you stinking..."

Knowing that I was in great danger of being beaten to a pulp, my strength surged, and with one great heave, I managed to force the door shut. He continued pounding while I grabbed my phone to call the police. Two officers arrived in less than ten minutes and I did my best to explain what had transpired between my neighbour and me. By their reaction, I got the impression they were familiar with him. He was soon under arrest, but this did not prevent him from promising to "deal" with me upon his release. Before they left, the police advised that I speak to my housing department the following morning.

A sleepless night followed and I rang the housing department as soon as they opened. A concerned re-housing officer came to my address within two hours sporting three sets of keys for alternative properties they wanted me to take a look at. The officer explained that they will be evicting my neighbour, but because the process was likely to take many months, they needed to move me now, for my own protection. I didn't argue.

My mother's superstitious warning about the up turned-up knife blade came to mind; I was unexpectedly on the move...by pure coincidence, of course...of course! Hmm...

The first two properties were better than Headcorn Road, but I truly fell in love with the third; a gorgeous newly converted top-floor flat in a Victorian house at 25 Cornwall Road in Hornsey. I moved in within days. My homophobic attack had been a blessing in disguise; it transported me from run-down Tottenham to hip Hornsey. I was now just a short stroll from Finsbury Park, where I attended a one-off soul spectacular with Roy Ayers and Cheryl 'Got To Be Real' Lynn. Yes, this was a good place to be real.

After a few driving lessons under the guidance of Malcolm, my old friend from the People's Group, I quickly passed my test and purchased a used Peugeot 305, which was now sitting outside my new abode. I could now drive to and from work, and anywhere else, if I so pleased.

I later upgraded to a slick new convertible, which, unfortunately, brought me to the attention of the local police; who evidently believed that a young black man could only have obtained such a vehicle by criminal means. It got to the point where I got into my car expecting to be stopped. On one alarming occasion, I was pulled over on London's bustling Holloway Road by a van load of aggressive officers and instructed to "get out and stand on the pavement". I obeyed. Seven officers then simultaneously invaded my car interior, bonnet, and boot. I couldn't help but worry that they may be planting something incriminating, but ten minutes later I was on my way home, and yet another police stop was over. However, my plight did not end there.

Just a few days later, whilst at home, I answered a determined knock at my door only to find two police officers demanding to see evidence that I owned the car parked outside. I was calm on the exterior and completely livid on the inside. I didn't know my rights so I showed them my documents, but objected to the harassment I was experiencing. Moments later the unapologetic officers were gone, leaving me to stew in my continuing fury.

It was around this time that I was troubled by the first of infrequent premonition-like dreams and visions concerning me or people known to me. In the first life-like dream, I was being raped by an unidentifiable masked intruder. Rape was no fantasy of mine! I was so disturbed by it that I mentioned it to a colleague at work before driving to my mother and then on to a close friend to see if they could make sense of it. On my return home that night, I was shocked to discover my front door kicked in and that I was the victim of an attempted burglary. The very personal 'invasive' nature of my dream suddenly made awful sense; it had been a forewarning, of sorts. Sporadic similar dreams followed which would again alert me to imminent events over which I had no control. For example, I dreamt about a friend recovering from surgery and correctly told her the location on her body where it had taken place. More dramatically, I had a dream about someone else close to me, who appeared to be in the unlikely setting of a prison. The next day she phoned and I of course told her about it, but she said it made no sense. However, three months later she started a prison sentence which our friendship did not survive. I mention these dreams, not because I believe I possess supernatural abilities, I don't! They are rare. Frankly, dreaming up winning lottery numbers would be much more useful to me.

My police magnet was eventually stolen and later found burnt out. The thief did me a favour. It was time to refocus on my passion; my work. But no dream could prepare me for the unimaginable slaughter that my wide-awake eyes would witness in the months and years ahead. Indeed, my waking hours would become a living nightmare.

31. BRENT HIV CENTRE - MEETING THE CHALLENGE

MY JOB WAS GOING WELL, but like the rest of the country, there were an increasing number of local residents being diagnosed with AIDS – men, women and children. I was becoming overwhelmed, so I decided to put in a proposal to my management to expand my team. The Thatcher Government, meanwhile, began to accept that local authorities needed additional resources if they were going to be able to provide adequate services to local people with AIDS, as well as mount effective HIV prevention campaigns. The AIDS Support Grant was made available for local authorities to bid for and I set about the task. I was joined by a new assistant, a very capable young Irish gay guy called Angelo. He was open about his own HIV positive status, as was my deputy. The workload was suddenly more manageable.

The YOU AND ME KIDS CLUB

Support Group for Children affected by HIV and AIDS

"THE YOU AND ME KIDS CLUB" is about getting together and having fun! So come along and take part in –

ROLLER DISCO, SWIMMING, PICTURES, THEATRE, ADVENTURE HOLIDAYS, NATURE TRAILS, COMPUTER GAMES, CRAFT WORKSHOPS, PAINTING AND MUCH, MUCH MORE

WE WOULD LOVE FOR YOU TO JOIN US

My original job description was solely to develop HIV/AIDS policy, but there was now a need to develop specific services to meet the needs of people with HIV and AIDS. The idea to create the Brent HIV Centre came to mind. It would

be a non-residential community care center that would provide a range of services to men, women and children affected by AIDS and HIV: welfare rights, case work, staff training and some therapeutic services. It would also provide HIV prevention campaigns. My management were sold on the idea.

I met up with Michael, a very likeable official from Whitehall who was partly responsible for allocating AIDS-related funding to local authorities. He was extremely helpful and I later submitted a successful bid for additional funds to renovate Park House, the building that was to become the Brent HIV Centre. It was an unused office block on Manor Park Road in Harlesden. When the conversion was completed, the building had a lift to all floors, offices (including one for me), a therapy room, a large training and meeting room, a large lounge and a kids' crèche facility. The Centre housed twelve staff: case workers, welfare rights officers, HIV staff trainers and outreach workers. I wrote all the job descriptions and interviewed all the staff, apart from one; the post of outreach worker, which was filled by my sister, Beverley. At least four members of staff were HIV positive, which I believe helped to make the service more sensitive to users' needs. The team was very diverse overall and included a transgender male to female case work manager.

Once the Brent HIV Centre was operational, I found myself learning on the job much of the time; remember, my previous full-time job had been as a booking office clerk. The client load was approaching thirty: seventy per cent were gay men; twenty-five percent were heterosexual African women and men; four per cent were white heterosexual women and men; and one per cent were the children of adult clients. HIV was largely an equal opportunities virus, but not completely so. Education levels, self-esteem, and socio-economics, played a significant role in its incidence, though the virus itself did not discriminate on grounds of race, nationality, religion, class, marital status, gender or sexuality, age or physical ability. The Brent HIV Centre had a lot of work to do, but we were up for it.

I wanted to be sure the Centre offered help across the spectrum of people affected. In addition to the Kids' Club, the centre offered a series of support functions specific to particular client groups' needs, such as gay men with an HIV diagnosis, and their partners, and African clients. To combat the social isolation that accompanied HIV/AIDS, the Centre also served as a focus for social events, including cultural celebrations, for all individuals and families affected by the illness. One or two clients doggedly, but understandably, concerned themselves with medical issues around the causes of their disease and its treatment, including whether HIV was really the cause of AIDS. I instructed my staff to stay well clear of contentious debates and to refer any concerned client back to their health care provider.

The Brent HIV Centre had quickly become an essential cog in the wheel of HIV/AIDS services in north London. I was proud of what I had achieved with the Centre and was going at my work with great gusto. The service did not grow by itself; it grew because I wanted it to, and because of the efforts of everyone working there. I was willing to knock on any door, write letters and make calls to whomever, to make sure that my service users had every resource they needed.

I wasn't the perfect manager, not at all, but I was committed and passionate in performing my duties, and I would not stand for less in my staff. Our service users had to come first at all times and I made no apology for it. I had to sack two members of staff for work performance issues; a task that I did not enjoy and didn't make me popular. I was confronted by *Sack Vernal Scott* signs on a picket line at one point. The sacked member of my care team was hoping he could save himself by resorting to the aid of his trade union and Socialist Worker colleagues. I wasn't intimated and did not for a moment reconsider my decision. I would have been more impressed if he had shown half the commitment to working with our service users as he did in seeking to save his own skin. When his efforts to get himself reinstated failed, the sacked man and two of his friends who were still employed at the Centre, accused me of sexual harassment. The newly appointed Director of Social Services came to see me immediately and explained that he had no option but to take the allegation seriously. I was to be semi-suspended and be subjected to an investigation and hearing. I was promptly barred from being in the building at the same time as my accusers. I was livid and so was my Director, but I had little choice but to comply with the council's procedures. The ridiculous and baseless allegations included one that I had walked around the building naked. Another alleged that I had paraded around in tight trousers, with a visible erection in my pants. Of course, nobody bothered to ask the complainants why their eyes were fixed on my pants in the first place. The sacked man also claimed that I saw him on a tube train one night and had jumped on top of him, forcing his legs on my shoulders in a simulated sexual act. His colleague, another white gay man, corroborated the lie. Rampant Vernal! Altogether, these were the most contrived allegations in the history of the world, but I had no option but to answer them.

My fury cooled into determination. I had to clear my name. Thankfully, my deputy and other members of my team told the truth about how I behaved at work, but I still had to wait almost three months for the hearing to conclude. I argued that, given the gravity of the allegations, my accusers would surely have mentioned them at the time that the incidents had allegedly occurred, rather than to wait, not only until one of them had been sacked, but until a further four weeks had passed after his sacking. My representative and I tore the allegations, eight of them in all, apart, and showed up the pathetic inconsistencies. I got so angry that the chair had to call for a break so I could calm down. I was spitting nails. I bitterly resented what had happened to me, and most of all, resented being kept from my work.

I was relieved but not too surprised when the panel, which included an independent expert on gay sexuality, threw out the allegations and totally exonerated me of all charges.

The staff members concerned, both white gay men, felt that black men were good for fucking, but not for managing them. I had swiftly but politely rejected their advances in the past, and their subsequent baseless accusations were the stuff of hurt feelings. I would come across white gay men like them again and again over the years; bitter nasty people, but, thankfully, the majority of white gay men were nothing like that. Lesson: when you're a black manager, expect shit to come at you. When you're a black gay manager, expect even more shit to come at you.

On my first day back to normal working patterns, I climbed the stairs and poked my head around the door of the office which my remaining accuser shared with other team members. With the biggest, most generous fake smile I could muster, I said, "A very good morning to you. I hope you're well. We'll have a team meeting a little later."

He responded with a nervous, "Good morning, Vernal."

I felt empowered, in control, and ready to take the Centre forward again. That's why I was there, not all that sexualized BS. I had work to do.

My exaggerated smiles and insincere gestures of goodwill towards my thwarted accuser soon became unbearable for him and I yelped "good riddance!" on reading his resignation letter.

It was now time to get re-focused on the important work of the Centre. The challenge posed by HIV/AIDS wasn't getting any easier and I had a lot of catching up to do. The most recent statistics showed that Brent had the second highest infection rate in London and yet the Government was under-funding our service by £200,000 a year. One in 275 pregnant women in the borough was HIV positive, according to an anonymous survey. One of the most depressing facts was that whilst many gay men were doing their best to modify risky behaviours, the heterosexual community had largely resisted changing their sexual behaviour. Many heterosexuals, probably encouraged by misleading press coverage, seemed to think that they were immune to the virus because of their sexuality. They confused sexuality with sexual activity and it was important for the Brent HIV Centre to redress the situation.

AIDS was confronting society with issues that for centuries had been deeply disquieting taboos: death and dying, disfigurement, sex and sexuality. It was hardly surprising, therefore, that the instinctive response to the disease, particularly in the media, was hysterical and vindictive rather than open and supportive. A journalist had once refused to shake my hand, fearing that doing so might put him at risk. Fear of the unknown, though, can only account for some of the inhumane and unconscionable behaviour that manifested itself towards people diagnosed with HIV, and towards homosexuals in general. The atmosphere of oppression hanging over gay and bisexual men, deterred them from accessing HIV prevention education, owing to fear of rejection by family and friends, who were unaware of their true sexuality. Some gay men were unhappy to identify themselves as such and lived their lives in the closet; as if they were heterosexual while maintaining clandestine sexual relations with men. This presented an obvious risk to themselves and their female (and male) partners. Only the most courageous of people at this time were openly gay, and of those who were infected, only those with steel in their souls were willing to be open about their illness. The situation was even worse if you were a black person with AIDS. Many in the black community were unsympathetic and ignorant and were inclined to look for scapegoats. The black churches were particularly hostile, and blamed everything bad in the world on homosexuals. Ignorance and hasty condemnation ruled, whilst compassion was heartbreakingly lacking. Yes, I had work to do!

32. HE AIN'T HEAVY, HE'S MY BROTHER!

MY COLLEAGUES AND I at the Brent HIV Centre quickly established close relationships with all the local hospitals and clinics concerned with treating residents with HIV and AIDS. The Rodney Porter Ward, at St Mary's Hospital, was well known to us as a centre of excellence for in-patient care services for people with AIDS. I had been to the ward, on many occasions, to visit local residents.

I was in the middle of another busy day at the Centre, when I received a call from Carol, the patient intake manager at the Rodney Porter Ward. She was calling to tell me that she had a new Brent resident on the ward. She sounded a little strange.

"Vernal," she said, hesitantly, "he says he's your brother."

I sat up in my chair. "What?"

"He says his name is Earl Scott."

Bunny!' I leapt to my feet, knocking my coffee all over my keyboard. "Earl – we call him Bunny." I quickly explained. "Yes, he's my brother. What's happened to him?" For a moment I thought he may have had a road accident or something.

"He collapsed in the street outside his home and was brought to the hospital by ambulance."

"Collapsed? And he's on your ward?" I asked deliberately, a dawning sense of realization choking my words. "He's on Rodney Porter ward?"

"Sadly, yes," she replied softly.

I tried to remain composed, as I closed the conversation. "Thank you so much for calling. Please let him know that I'm on the way."

I hung up the phone, and drove the short journey to St Mary's Hospital in a haze of conflicting thoughts. *'Bunny, you've been keeping a dreadful secret...'*

On my arrival at Rodney Porter, a sympathetic Carol explained that Bunny had Pneumocystis pneumonia (PCP), which was the reason for his collapse. I knew what that meant: AIDS! My brother had AIDS.

"Do you think he understands what this means?" I asked, whilst absorbing the awful reality of what I'd just been told.

"He hasn't seen the counsellor yet. I'm not sure whether he knows he's HIV positive."

This angered me, but it was not uncommon. The human element, provision for the care of the emotional well-being of people with an HIV diagnosis, often lagged behind medical treatment. "Forget the counsellor," I said. "He's my brother. I'll speak to him."

She smiled and showed me to Bunny's room.

He was alone, lying on top of the sheets with his arms up, partially covering his eyes. He greeted me with an almost embarrassed, "Hi, thanks for coming," trying to force himself to smile.

"Hey, what happened to you?" I asked, pulling up a seat next to his bed.

"I don't even know. I was walking, and then I couldn't breathe. Man, I thought I was going to die."

I loosened up my tie as I prepared my thoughts. For a moment I wondered what to say; what to ask.

I said, "You know you have HIV, right?"

"Yes," he replied quietly. "They told me a few months ago. But I didn't want to believe it."

"And do you know what happened today, why you collapsed?"

He shook his head.

Instead of delivering a lengthy speech, I decided to just explain the facts: "You have PCP; it's an infection that people with AIDS get."

Bunny stared into my eyes without speaking, at first. I looked straight back at him, hoping that I would not have to repeat my words, because I didn't want to.

"People with *AIDS*?" he asked finally, raising his head off the pillow.

"Bunny, you have AIDS, brother. But it doesn't mean…"

He interrupted: *"AIDS?"*

"Yes," I said. "AIDS."

As I tried to find the words to say to ease the impact of the bullet I had just hit him with, I could see the tears well up in his eyes. I heard myself say, "Go ahead, brother, it's okay to cry. Cry as much as you need to today, but tomorrow you must fight."

Through his sobs, he asked, "Fight?"

"Yes, the more you know about this disease, the more you can do to fight it, so you can remain healthy for longer."

"I'm frightened and don't know what to do."

I was emphatic: "I'm here, and my team at the HIV Centre will help you. There are a lot of people who can help. You are not alone and never will be."

I left the hospital half an hour later, and headed home; I couldn't face returning to the office, not today, so I called my deputy and said that I'd see him tomorrow. I was deeply upset. I had framed Brent's policy and services on HIV to help people affected by the condition, but I never once imagined that my own brother might become a client. How could I have been blind to the danger? AIDS had come right to my mother's doorstep. Although Bunny and I had never been close, I was devastated for him. He had been through so much physical pain throughout his life, because of haemophilia, and now he had to deal with AIDS. *And what about his poor kids?* I thought.

My tears dried, and my temper rose. *The Government is to blame for this,* I thought. People with haemophilia control bleeding episodes with concentrated clotting factor, derived from large quantities of donated blood. It was well known that HIV had been passed on to some people, prior to the introduction of screening which was introduced in October 1985; in fact, this was a major route of the virus into the heterosexual population. There was a very good chance that my brother now had AIDS thanks to the Thatcher Government's lack of diligence for the quality of the blood supply. I was furious. Bunny's acute haemophilia meant he had long been dependent on blood products, and was therefore exposed to multiple opportunities to become infected with HIV.

Bunny and I had agreed upon who should know about his diagnosis, so when I got home I called my sister Beverley. She was, of course, extremely distressed about it. I told her that Bunny, understandably, wanted to remain in control of who else knew, but that I had managed to persuade him to let me tell our mother so that she could pray for him. 'Stop complaining, and start praying, and you will see how prayer will deliver you from any obstacle or problem,' is what she'd always say. Bunny liked that idea, as he too believed in the power of prayer.

I was beginning to find strength through prayer myself. Before the AIDS crisis hit, I would have described myself as an atheist, but dealing daily with all this pain of my own, and sharing that felt, in some cases, even more acutely by others, I began to find comfort on my knees, in prayer. I may have abandoned Jesus Christ, for a time, but He had not abandoned me. As prayer became increasingly important to me, I saw Jesus Christ as my higher source and saviour. God, once again, became real in my life; even though I knew I would never be welcome as a gay man in the vast majority of black churches. I also knew that some in the gay community would struggle with the combination of my sexuality and my Christianity, but the struggle was now theirs, not mine. I was feeling God's love, and condemnation of my sexuality came not from Him, but from men; sometimes men of ignorance and violence, who had the blood of gay people on their hands. It was crucial that confidence in my faith came from within, or I'd risk finding myself dependent on affirmation by others who may harbour 'issues' about my sexuality.

I went to see Mum after work the next day, to tell her about Bunny. To my surprise, she reacted as if she already knew. She looked back at me with hollow eyes that shed no tears. She then started to pray, and pray, and pray some more. I left her that evening, still on her knees in her living room, deep in prayer. If prayer could save my brother, then our mother was going to have a damn good try.

My next concern was for my other relatives with haemophilia: my brother Leo, and my 11-year old nephew, JJ. They had also been treated with blood clotting products. Oh God, had they been infected as well?

Thankfully Leo's test came back negative, but when JJ's results came back we were devastated to learn that he too was HIV positive. JJ was brave and confident and didn't let the diagnosis faze him, even when, at one point, his school separated him from other children in an ill-conceived HIV prevention measure to protect them from infection. This infuriated me, and Jan, his mother, even more so. She began to distance herself from me, as according to Beverley, our other sister, Jan blamed gays for contaminating the blood supply. She reportedly said: "If anyone in this family should get that virus, it's Ian." After a time, Jan stopped speaking to me altogether, but I called JJ often. He had a lot of love around him, from his three brothers, and his mother. I could live with her rejection; I had to.

Bunny recovered from his initial bout of PCP and returned to his home. He came into the HIV Centre on a few occasions, to see the care team, and the welfare rights officer, a very capable Caucasian woman. Bunny's health seemed substantially improved. He was taking AZT, the most effective treatment for AIDS patients then available, though its rate of success was a rather hit and miss affair. Bunny was interested in seeing whether herbs and alternative therapies might help. I was very pleased that he was being proactive about his health, and thought it a good sign.

There were lots of people who didn't believe that medication was the right intervention for treating HIV; indeed, there was a strong contingent of people who believed that HIV had nothing to do with the onset of AIDS, and that scientists and doctors were, at best, misguided, or at worst, in the pockets of the pharmaceutical industry. Some of my clients started very vocal arguments with me about it, but I would explain to them that my staff and I were there to provide community care services, and that we did not have a view on the science or politics of AIDS. Our role was uncomplicated and clear: to provide the best possible services to men, women and children living with HIV and AIDS.

Meanwhile, there were more agonising waits for test results for my family. Bunny had been involved in a long-term and deeply loving relationship with Anita, the mother of their wonderful young son. Upon learning of Bunny's diagnosis, Anita made the harrowing, but wise decision to have herself and their son tested for HIV. There was a strong chance that she was infected, but there were cases in which the virus had not been transmitted between sexual partners, even where unprotected intercourse occurred on a regular basis. I prayed about it.

Eventually, the results came back. Their son was in the clear, but Anita was HIV positive. The news was yet another devastating blow. For a while, I raged in my mind as to whether Anita had become infected owing to my brother's denial of his HIV status. It was well known that early recipients of blood products were at risk of contracting HIV; Bunny *must have known this*, I told myself. I was quietly furious with him, but eventually I had to accept that anger would not serve any useful purpose. It was all an enormous tragedy, and no person was to blame for HIV.

Bunny became a regular patient on the Rodney Porter ward, due to repeated infections. I tended to visit him during the day, so that our mother and immediate family could see him in the evenings, without having to listen to all the issues that I wanted to discuss with him. My mother would bring him Caribbean goodies from her kitchen, together with lots of fresh fruit. She would always end her hospital visits with a prayer, placing her hands on my brother's shoulder, as she asked God to deliver her son from this place. The other patients, mostly gay men, looked on in respectful good humour at the nightly ritual. Some of them tried to make light conversation, and my mother and Bunny would always smile along, even if they didn't look too comfortable doing it.

Though we didn't discuss it, Bunny was acutely aware that he was in a heterosexual minority on a ward where most patients were gay men at various stages of the progression of AIDS. Naturally, their significant visitors were often gay male partners, and friends. During one of my visits, I overheard a father talking to his son, two beds away from Bunny's:

"I didn't even know you were gay. Why didn't you tell me, Mark? And now you've got this *fucking disease...*" The emotional father put his face into his hands, and started sobbing.

His very ill son raised a pitifully thin hand to his dad's shoulder, and mouthed something that I couldn't hear.

I was able to discern his father's impassioned response: "I love you too, son, I love you so very much! Please...please forgive me."

Mark didn't survive long after that visit, but I knew his love for his dad had not died with him.

It was following one of her visits to Bunny's bedside that my mother called me at home one night. This was something she did reasonably often after visiting him, if I hadn't been present too. I was of course glad to be able to offer reassurance where I could, but I would stop short of saying anything that was beyond my experience or of a medical nature. He was my brother and she was my mother, and I wanted to be there for them both.

"I've just come from the hospital, but Bunny isn't getting any better." she declared.

"Don't worry, Mum," I said, trying to be helpful. "He's going to be out of the hospital before too long."

She then came out with what must have been on her mind all along: "I can't stand to see him in there with all *those* kinds of people!" She meant, of course, gay men.

I was beyond livid, and responded with: "Mum, how *dare* you! Let me tell you something, every person on that ward is someone's precious child. Do you think the pain being felt by their mothers is any less than yours? Listen, call me back when you're ready to apologise."

With that I hung up on her and felt no remorse for doing so. I was tired of the unrelenting homophobia in my own family, and this felt like the final straw.

There was much talk at this time by Christian groups and others, who enthusiastically claimed that AIDS was some kind of punishment from God for the way in which gays lived their lives. But I knew this to be offensive rubbish, and saw no need for gay people to apologise for the way God made them – us! If there was ever an equal opportunities virus then the scourge of HIV/AIDS was it, and people like my mother were repeatedly being forced to face that agonising truth, but not wanting to learn the lesson.

Immediately my phone rang again. It was my mother.

"I'm sorry," she said. "You're right. I'm so *upset* at the situation. Please see with me," she pleaded, using the Jamaican vernacular for "try to understand". "I am doing my best, too."

I said that I understood, but didn't want to hear her say anything like that again. Perhaps it was insensitive of me, but I told her that perhaps God had brought AIDS to her doorstep for a reason, and that that reason might be to teach her to set aside her prejudice about other people. But she wasn't listening anymore; she was crying. I told her that I accepted her apology, and would come to visit at the weekend.

I really did feel very sorry for her, but then again, I felt sorry for every parent in her position, including my sister, Jan. I knew my mother meant well, and that she was hurting beyond comprehension. Three members of her family were HIV positive, or had AIDS, but it offended every fibre of my being to allow prejudice against other, equally innocent victims of the disease-- gay men-- to go unchallenged. Still, beyond standing up to my mother like this, I felt there was little I could do. I felt powerless. Information and a sympathetic ear were all I could offer.

33. THAT'S WHAT FRIENDS ARE FOR

HIV AND AIDS WERE MOWING A DEVASTATING PATH through my friends. Some of them simply disappeared. Chris, an 'in the closet' African-American GI, was one of too many of them. I'd try to phone, but the number would then ring and ring or was already disconnected. Occasionally someone would call me to ask whether I'd heard that a mutual friend or acquaintance had passed away or was ill. My novelty *'black leather jacket'* phone book had lost its original humour and was gradually becoming an unintended book of remembrance for those lost.

One particularly sunny morning, I was driving to work in my red Ford convertible. Linda Clifford was singing at full power on the stereo, blasting all my negative thoughts from my head; despite the desperate woes around me, disco still offered a sanctuary. As I approached Manor Park Road, I thought I recognised a familiar figure walking along the street. It was Marvin, the hairdresser, the very first black gay man whom I'd met – and kissed – way back in 1979. We had stayed in sporadic touch over the years, mostly by phone.

I pulled over to the side of the road, jumped out, and called after him. But as we approached one another, I could tell that this was not the Marvin I'd seen just six months earlier. Marvin was always immaculately presented, from head to toe; he had to look perfect. But the man before me now was painfully thin, and his usually flawless brown skin was dry and peeling.

He greeted me with a warm but somewhat vacant expression. I did my best to appear upbeat, and made no comment on his appearance, other than to say that it was good to see him. It was. But he was obviously self-conscious about how he was looking, and, unprompted, he began to offer an explanation: "Hey, I went to do a hair show in Nigeria, and caught some nasty bug from the iced-water, it really wiped me out. Be careful if you ever go there!"

"Hey," I said, trying to keep the conversation light, "I see you're still wearing my ring."

He raised his finger and laughed weakly. "Yeah, of course!"

We both wore the twin Russian wedding rings he'd bought for us as a gift for my twenty-fourth birthday. He put one on the third finger of my left hand, and the other on that of his own, and we both wore them three years on. I loved that ring, almost as much as I loved and adored him. He was a very special man.

Marvin said he needed to get to the shops, so we hugged and headed our separate ways. I saw his frail frame in my rear-view mirror and wiped a sorry tear from my eye as I drove away. I knew what was really ailing him. I'd seen that emaciated state before, and it wasn't down to any water bug! Marvin was once the most handsome man I'd ever set eyes on, and the dramatic change in his appearance must have been extremely difficult for him to deal with; but he was still beautiful to me. I decided that I was going to stay in regular contact with him.

It seemed as though someone I knew was being diagnosed every other week, all gay men, many of whom I had known for years.

Another friend, Leon, and his younger partner, John, lived only a five-minute walk away from where I lived in Cornwall Road. Leon was a very flamboyant, larger-than-life, Jamaican-born gay man, who was utterly and unashamedly camp. He was also one of most warm and generous people I'd ever met. He was always the life and soul of any party, and he made his presence felt with his generous smile and provocatively sexual dance moves. John was in his very early twenties and of Nigerian descent. He had aspirations to be a fashion model, and certainly had the looks to make it, I thought.

One day I got home from work and found the two men sitting in front of my house. I was a little irritated, because I just wanted to hit the sofa and chill after a busy day, but I was polite and invited the couple up to my apartment. The fact that they were there uninvited should have triggered something in my mind, but perhaps I was too tired to twig.

John and Leon sat in separate chairs on opposite sides of the room, and after some stilted conversation and awkward glances between the pair, Leon finally urged John, "Just tell him!"

John insisted, "No, I can't. You tell him."

"What's going on?" I asked, wearily.

"Vernal," Leon blurted out, "John's got HIV, and he wants your advice."

This was very unwelcome news indeed. I'd had many conversations with friends who thought they might have HIV, or others who'd just got the test result and wanted a friendly ear. Offering an ear was the least I could do. But, despite all my experience, I often felt pathetically inadequate in such situations, which is how I was feeling now. Still, I was conscious that John and Leon needed to hear something from me that might, somehow, rescue them from the enormous ramifications of HIV. Even though I knew I possessed no such power, just looking at John's desperate eyes looking back into mine, made me wish I did.

My immediate reaction must have been a disappointment to them, because I found myself momentarily incoherent and fumbling for words, but I got there in the end.

"Hey, John," I said gently, "talk to me, my brother. It's okay..."

The terrified young man started to speak but was immediately overcome by tears. I paused to allow them to flow. Tears had their role; they articulated what words couldn't.

"I assume you've been tested?" I asked.

"Yes. I got the result this morning; this bloody morning!" His voice was breaking, but I sensed there was some fight in him, which was a good sign. He was going to need all the fight he can muster in the months ahead.

Having found my usual rhythm, I sought to offer comforting words: "It's a new beginning, my friend, the beginning of you taking the most precious care of yourself. Information is key."

I reached out my hand to comfort him, but John retreated into a foetal position on the sofa and carried on crying. *Cry today, but fight tomorrow, my friend* I thought. His child-like sobs, and my insufficient-sounding assurances, made me want to sob too. I couldn't possibly find the right words to offer John, because there were none.

Leon got up and went over to his young lover. Scooping him up into his arms, the two men rocked slightly to the rhythm of John's heaving frame. "You're going to be fine, just fine" Leon reassured him.

Leon peered at me over John's shoulders. The shattered look in his eyes confirmed that he was at least as frightened as his young partner. I got up and left them alone for a while. When I came back into the room, I gave them all the information and reassurance I could.

Blackliners, located in south London, had replaced BCAT, and was doing excellent work with its support services designed for black communities affected by HIV and AIDS. I recommended that they give it a try and they said they would. Half an hour or so later the two men left to make their way home. I was left feeling convinced that I hadn't been at all helpful, but I often felt that way. I knew all the right words, but I couldn't take away the God-awful diagnosis or the fear that came with it. The couple were right to be worried, of course they were.

I stayed in almost daily contact with Leon by phone, and went to see him about four weeks after he and John had dropped in to see me. On my way in I was alarmed to pass a doctor on his way out; his name was Andrew, and I knew him well from professional circles. We exchanged pleasantries, but his very presence told me things must be pretty bad behind Leon and John's front door. *So soon?* I conversed with myself.

As I entered the living room, an extremely ill-looking John looked over from an improvised daybed and greeted me: "I'm so pleased you've come, Vernal. I'm so sick. I feel like I'm dying."

"No, no, no. You are not!" I responded, in auto-pilot. But looking at John, I feared he might be right. He looked deathly unwell. So soon, I thought. I went over and gripped his hand in mine. He seemed weak and broken.

Leon, greeting me with an embrace, stressed: "Vernal, I'm telling you, he can't keep anything in. If it's not coming out of his mouth then it's coming out of his arse." Leon was drained. Taking a seat, he continued, "I can't keep up with the cleaning of sheets and towels. Oh, the vomit and shit! Oh God, it's too much, Vernal!"

Both men were at their wits end. I again felt inadequate by talking about how their local social services department could help with cleaning and other domestic tasks. Leon confirmed that they'd been in touch and that an assessment was due shortly. I told him I could help out with the cleaning in the meantime, but he said it was okay and that he could deal with it until social services kicked in. John, looking oblivious to our conversation, remained quiet and deep in thought. It must have been hard for him to hear how his illness was impacting on Leon. He didn't need guilt as well as AIDS, but he knew Leon loved him and was just letting off steam. We all needed to do that!

Breaking the silence that had invaded the room, I told them I knew Andrew, their doctor, and that they couldn't be in better hands, but John's hapless expression made me shut the hell up and take a seat myself. Who the hell was I fooling? The situation looked dire. When John wasn't staring at the ceiling, his eyes searched my face, as if waiting for me to say or do something that would make his nightmare go away.

An hour later I decided to make my way home. As I went to leave, John called after me with a voice I will not forget: "Vernal, please be honest. Am I going to die?"

"No," I said emphatically, dropping my briefcase and going back to grip his hand again. "No, John! Listen to me my friend, you will get through this. We're not going to let anything bad happen to you. I want you to have a *strong mind*. Tell yourself that you're going to be fine, and I'm sure you will be".

Within a matter of a few weeks young John was dead. AIDS had turned his once beautiful body into an unrecognizable torture zone of one debilitating symptom on top of too many others until he could take it no longer, and with a final farewell breath, his body simply stopped. I attended his funeral to support an emotionally battered but controlled Leon. Grieving family members and the couple's many friends were there in good numbers too. At various points the Catholic service was stunned into silence by loud, almost primeval howls of grief from John's inconsolable African mother. Piercing our hearts with its raw honesty, her wailing confirmed the horrible outcome of a battle lost, and a pain words could not begin to articulate. Her distraught face bellowed what her stricken mouth couldn't: *My precious John – my son, my child! I love you too much to let you go, today or ever!* The young Caucasian priest's impassioned homily was abruptly muted by our collective gasps when John's mother suddenly stood, lurched forward, and started grappling with her son's sealed coffin. Her streaming tears appeared to fall and create miniature puddles as she franticly tugged and jostled whilst begging and pleading with the casket's precious but stone silent occupant: "Johnny, please don't leave me. John! John!! John!!! Don't do it! You must not do it. Get up, Johnny, get up, please..." In her blinding imprisonment to grief she had become completely oblivious to our presence. Equally distraught relatives dashed from their seats and struggled to restrain and calm her. One lightly slapped her about the face, as if trying to return her to her senses, whilst another tried to get her back into her seat. Yet another, in an attempt to bring some kind of impossible relief to John's mother, used his hands as an improvised human fan over her face. The chaotic scene prompted audible sobbing on just about every pew in the North London church.

Steadying himself with an improvised prayer for "peace, comfort, and God's love upon us all", the somewhat flabbergasted priest regained both his composure and command of the service, before then resuming where he'd left off. John's mother was once again in her seat, and his delivery was also, again, flawless. As I wiped my own tears, my mind began to drift into some kind of surreal reality-come-fantasy. I started seeing a radiantly smiling John. He seemed so real and very much alive. With rejuvenated, robust arms lovingly thrown around his mother, he implored her to be happy for him, because he was now safely beyond any concept of pain, shame, or indignity. Most of all, he was free from the fear of what another tomorrow or symptom might bring; his final tomorrow had come, and with it, the gift of an infinite freedom that had no physical constraint. In his new state of 'being', there were no tomorrows; just an ever extant now. There was no fear, disease, stigma, loss, hate, prejudice, race, nationality, religion, or geographical country. The renewed John knows only peace, truth, and oneness with his birth universe, which, in joyous reacquainted love, had welcomed him home.

As the dreadful incessant wailing resumed in my ears, my visualization of John's smiling face was replaced by the reality of the grieving around me that my eyes and mind had, momentarily, successfully escaped. In the months and years ahead, I would reflect that only parents sharing his mother's experience were capable of duplicating that terrible sound; that patent, humbling wailing, and, of course, the pain would always be uniquely personal. The unfolding, relentless AIDS-induced slaughter would ensure that I would hear that sound again and again, in similar, recurring circumstances. Indeed, some thirty years later, by the time I'd come to write this book, there would be a staggering thirty-five million AIDS-induced deaths around the world, including twenty-two thousand in the United Kingdom; and the pain and heartbreaking funerals would have accompanied them all. In wading through what has become an immense sea of grief-stricken tears shed by those of us left behind, it would seem to me that the only happy people must be those whose final tomorrow had come and set free from the prison of a most horrific and merciless sickness. However, in the midst of our despair, I would become conscious of, and take great comfort from, a most illuminating and invaluable realization: that in all of its apparent destructive finality, death was incapable of destroying love.

Leon, nobly, took a back seat throughout the service; selflessly allowing John's mother to mourn and release her emotions, while his, as anticipated, and probably expected, remained hidden and unacknowledged. Poor Leon, he looked so lost and helpless. Courageously, he still managed an occasional smile, even if it was a cheerless, detached one. When I asked him how he was doing, his reply was typical: "I'm fine, V." He was being so very brave, and dignified with it. Yes, John's mother's pain was distinctly awful, but so was his.

I perused the pews of teary-eyed people before resettling my gaze once again on Leon at my side. When I did, I was immediately taken aback, causing me to do a *double-take*. For a split second, in the corner of my eye, I thought I'd caught sight of John; it seemed there was one more person who he wanted to hold – and kiss – goodbye. My action prompted Leon to ask whether I was OK. In response, I simply put my hand on his shoulder and mirrored his earlier answer, "I'm fine." My perceived 'sighting' would remain unshared.

Following John's funeral, Leon decided to answer nagging doubts about his own HIV status, and got tested. It came back positive. As always, I told him that I'd be there for him, and I was. I had no doubt that he'd be there for me too, if the tables were turned.

Marvin, meanwhile, took a turn for the worse. During a coffee moment at work, I made my weekly phone call to see how he was doing, but instead of hearing his welcoming tone, his cousin answered. She told me that Marvin had collapsed at home and been taken to the Central Middlesex Hospital. I was horrified and immediately made my way to the hospital. As I walked in the sunshine, I tried to tell myself I could be wrong, and that something other than HIV could be behind his rapid deterioration. *Gay men get everyday illnesses like everybody else, right?*

The Central Middlesex was no St Mary's, and did not have the best reputation for HIV/AIDS care; in fact it was pretty dire. I'd heard first-hand horror stories about AIDS patients being forced to get out of bed to pick up food trays from the floor, because ignorant, frightened, or prejudiced (homophobic!) nursing staff refused to get too close. Yes, even as we died, we were being robbed of our dignity and the common respect afforded to non-AIDS patients. Our almost certain demise was not punishment enough; we had to be subjected to deliberate inhumane derelictions of care, too. Such experiences were not uncommon across the country, and the culprits would rarely, if ever, be held accountable.

When I got to the ward, I asked the first nurse I saw where I could find Marvin. She began to tell me that I must have the wrong ward, but as we were speaking, I spotted him in a bed tucked away at the end of the open ward. I pointed Marvin out to her. "Oh, *him!*" she huffed, and without another word, she walked on past me. Not a good sign, I thought.

Marvin's eyes lit up on seeing me. "Hey, V!" He smiled. I noticed that he looked to see if my ring, matching his, was still in place, which, of course, it was.

"And what are you doing here, mister?" I said, bending down to embrace him. This seemed to agitate him.

"No, V, please don't do that, please!" His eyes darted around to see whether anyone had noticed the physical contact.

"Hey, what's wrong?" I asked.

He almost whispered his response: "The staff seems to have an attitude problem."

I knew what he meant straight away. He had picked up on their homophobia. I pulled up a chair, and instinctively went to hold his hand, but he pulled his away and said, "Hey, man, didn't you hear me?"

"Hey, I'm sorry." I realised that he was worried my actions might 'out' him, but that of course wasn't my intention; I just wanted to show I cared for him. "I hear you," I said, looking around at the mostly black nursing staff, who all appeared busy and paying us little or no attention.

He smiled at me. "Boy, you're still so handsome."

"Hey, you too! In that big bed all by yourself - I thought you were trying to hide all that stuff?," I said cheekily. He chuckled back at me. "I'm just saying... just saying!" he said sweetly. He kept smiling at me. He'd lost even more weight than when I last saw him. He couldn't afford to lose much more.

"So tell me, Marv, what's going on? What are you doing here?"

He explained: "I was at home doing some chores, and my legs just gave way beneath me. Man, I was on the floor and couldn't get up."

"So what are they saying is the problem?" I queried.

"They're carrying out tests for this and that. I don't really know what's going on to be honest, but they've already told me that I have some kind of chest infection".

My heart sank when I heard this, but I was determined to keep something of a smile on my face, for him, for my friend. *Not again, God, not again!*

"Hey" I said, "I'm happy to ask them the latest, if you'd like me to?"

Marvin responded positively, "Sure, go on then." he said, seemingly relaxed about my suggestion.

I quickly located the head nurse and asked if I could have a quick word. I explained that I was a friend of Marvin's, but also mentioned my professional role. She responded warmly, and took me into a side room. Before I could finish asking my question, the young black woman just came right out and told me, "Marvin has PCP and other complications..."

For a moment, my mind drifted, as I pictured my friend, then and now. The contrast made me want to fall to my knees. I didn't want to hear what she was saying, but I just did. Marvin didn't just have HIV, my dear friend had AIDS.

I told her that he didn't appear to be aware of his diagnosis. To my dismay, she told me that the staff counsellor was away, and so no one had spoken to Marvin as yet. *This sounds like a pattern,* I thought. As I had with my brother, I offered to speak with Marvin about his condition, and the nurse agreed, with some apparent relief. "Thank you", she said genuinely.

I took a deep breath and made my way back to Marvin's bed. As I approached, I could see that he was no longer alone. His elderly mother and two female cousins had arrived, and were busy making themselves comfortable. I had met them on earlier, happier occasions, and they greeted me warmly. I could also see he was greatly comforted by their presence. His mother and his cousins meant the world to him and I decided that I would make my excuses and leave them to each other's company.

I quickly explained: "Marv, I've had a word with the head nurse, and I'll come back to see you later today."

Marvin raised himself up on his elbows, saying, "Vernal, anything you have to say can be said in front of my family."

I tried to persuade him otherwise, but he was insistent. In line with his wishes, I told them all what I'd learned.

By the time I left his bedside, Marvin and his two cousins were in tears, trying to console each other in the aftermath of the bomb I had just dropped. His mother remained seated with a look of shattered disbelief on her face. She was too shell-shocked to move. All over the country, loving mothers, just like her, were hearing the same news about their gay sons; it was her unfortunate turn.

Marvin's reaction told me that he didn't know he had HIV, although he must have suspected, or so I told myself. I turned to look back and could see he was crying, with his hands over his face. His cousins were holding him. I was gutted for all of them, but especially for him.

I made my way back to my office, and attempted to bury my thoughts under the mountain of work that awaited me. There was so much to do; too much to do, and none of it would save my friends, Leon and Marvin.

I drove home with my car stereo at full volume in a vain effort to drown out my thoughts. As I ascended the stairs to my flat, I heard my phone ringing, and raced in to see who it was. It was one Marvin's cousins from the earlier hospital visit. The family lived up north, but was staying at Marvin's flat in Harlesden while he remained in hospital.

She was crying, softly: "Vernal, we've just come from the hospital - we didn't want to leave him there. We're worried and confused. I don't think we heard you right. Did you really say... did you say... did you say... Marvin has AIDS?"

I took a breath and tried, unsuccessfully, to explain myself without inflicting any additional damage: "Darling, I know it's difficult, but there's no easy way to say it or to hear it. Yes, he has AIDS, but that doesn't mean..."

She was no longer listening; she was sobbing. I respectfully held on until we could resume our conversation. I did my best to reassure her that the love Marvin's family was giving him was an important part of dealing with his condition, and a short while later, she thanked me warmly, and hung up. I looked down at the ring on my finger, and brought it to my lips.

I visited Marvin as often as I could during his stay at the Central Middlesex Hospital and kept the conversation light. I wasn't his doctor, I was his friend. Our mutual love of divas replaced any talk about his illness. Without question, we agreed that Aretha was the ultimate voice, but disagreed about who was next in line.

"Miki Howard's great, we agreed"

"Whitney Houston... maybe when she's older", said Marvin

"Ah, Stephanie Mills. Yes, Miss Mills!"

"Patti Labelle! Patti's my girl" insisted Marvin

"Anita Baker " Marvin suggested, with a grin on his face. I could tell he wasn't serious. "Not that I can understand what she's singing. " Marvin quickly qualified. "She sings like she's got marbles in her mouth." We both laughed. Eventually we agreed that it was a three-way tie between Cissy Houston, Chaka Khan and Stephanie Mills.

"Oh, but what about that girl?" Marvin quizzed.

"What girl?" I asked.

"That Dreamgirl woman?"

"Oh, you mean Jennifer?" I offered

"Yes, Miss Holliday! Now, that woman can bring down the roof with her voice!" I had to agree.

We then chatted about disco ladies. "I know Gloria is your one and only," he said. Yes, he knew me well.

"Of course, Gloria Gaynor is the Queen of Disco!"

"Well," he interjected, "I kinda lost interest after '(If You Want It) Do It Yourself'! I loved that tune; it reminds me of my time in New York. We went crazy to that tune. But my number one disco diva is Linda Clifford. Though, Loleatta Holloway is hot too."

"What about Sylvester?" I proposed.

"Man, that queen is too camp, but I like his Two Ton Girls..." Marvin retorted.

The two of us could talk forever about our mutual love of music. If only we could.

During another visit, the mood was very different. He told me he was in agony due to sores in "difficult-to-reach places".

I just thought he meant bed sores, and I told him to bring them to the attention of the nursing staff.

But he looked me in the eye and said, "No way, V! I can't ask *them*. These fucking things are killing me."

I was puzzled, and asked him if he wanted to show me.

He said, "Yeah. Close the curtains. Here's the ointment. Please, please, put some on for me." I took the tube in my hand expecting to apply some to his back or shoulders.

Despite all the AIDS symptoms I'd seen over the years, nothing prepared me for the sight I was about to behold. Marvin wrestled his pajama bottoms down to his knees, and

I quickly realised that the sores he wanted to show me were not on his back. He turned on his side, so that his now naked backside was towards me. I gasped in disbelief at the sight of his buttocks, including the crack; the entire area was skinless, bloodied raw flesh, which was inflamed and weeping. In my shock, I just stood there fixed to the spot with the unopened tube in my hand. What I was seeing was beyond my capabilities or anything in the tube. This needed professional intervention, and that wasn't me.

"Please V, please!" Marvin pleaded. But he couldn't see what I was seeing. I snapped out of my trance. "Marvin, I'm no doctor, but what you've got here requires more than the application of whatever is in this tube, mister, trust me. Please wait there, while I get a nurse."

He grumbled at first, but then agreed that I should do so, "quickly". I put the sheet lightly over him and asked the nearest nurse if she could please take a look at him. I stayed on the other side of the curtain as she went in and did whatever she had to do, but only after donning the correct protective clothing, of course. Five minutes later, she came out and said, "All done!" She drew back the curtains before walking away, and I was faced with a sulking Marvin.

"Listen, Marv, you couldn't see what I could see. You needed a professional person who knew what to do."

He said, "It's cool, V, I understand. I shouldn't have asked you to do it. I was too embarrassed to ask them. You did the right thing. It feels okay now."

A short while later, his mother and cousins arrived for a visit. I said my hellos and goodbyes, and made to exit. Before leaving, for unknown reason, I mentioned to his smiling mother, who was now seated by her son's bed, that Marvin had given me the ring on my finger. Her response was as clear as it was cutting: "Yes, and there are some things I don't want to know."

It was time for me to exit, and I did. I had tried to lighten the mood, but put my foot in it instead. Marvin had been occupied by his cousin's shopping bag and I don't believe saw the exchange between his mother and me. Oh, I felt like crap.

The image of Marvin's raw backside was set to haunt me into the future, but so was his mother's response regarding my cherished ring. That night I went to bed tearful and guilt-ridden. Marvin didn't deserve this living decomposition; no one did. God, *where are you*? I prayed.

Work the next day was as busy as usual, but I was unsettled and felt a need to go back to the hospital to see Marvin. When I got there, just after 2pm, I came across an empty bed. My heart left my body and crashed to the floor. *Oh God, no, no, no!* But just as I was thinking the worst, I heard his voice from some distance behind me saying "Hey, V!" I turned to see Marvin shuffling towards me using a walker; one careful step followed the next. The radiant smile on his face generated a similar happy smile on mine; I was so very, very pleased to see him.

Marvin was in a surprisingly upbeat mood. If he was aware of, and angry about, the ring incident then he wasn't showing it. "Hey, you're here again" he laughed, as he sat on his bed and wrestled his feet free of his slippers. "Don't you have other people to see, matey? Not that I'm complaining at all. I'm glad you're here". He added, still smiling at me.

I sat on the chair closet to him and said nothing; I just wore a smile. "You OK, V?" he asked me. "Yes, I'm mighty fine now that I'm seeing your happy face," I replied.

"Really?" he chuckled. "Well, whose face were you expecting to see, Gloria's?" We both laughed out loud, so much so that we attracted disapproving smirks from the nurse working a couple of beds away. Yes, it was really good to see Marvin this day, very good indeed, and we were going to damn well laugh if we wanted to. We'd earned it.

Leon's health, meanwhile, despite his very recent diagnosis, was showing a rapid decline. His weight loss was particularly striking, and, understandably, he was worried.

Strangely, perhaps, Marvin and Leon had known each other as acquaintances for many years, but lived in different parts of the city, and were completely unaware of the other's diagnosis. I didn't think it appropriate to share anyone's personal information without them asking me to do so. I kept that rule at work and in my private life.

I did my best to support Leon after his chronic AIDS symptoms resulted in his admission to Whittington Hospital. I did some of his personal laundry, bought him basics such as skin creams, fruit juice, and other requirements. Most visits found him in good spirits, and we spent the time chatting and laughing about his fond and not so fond memories of his too-brief time with John, the love of his life.

After work one night, I turned up at the hospital with a shopping bag of items that I promised to bring him. As I approached his bed, I could see that Leon had a female visitor, who had her back to me. He made frantic but subtle gestures at me, not to come any closer. I took the hint, and left the bag of shopping where he could keep an eye on it and made my exit. His visitor was his mother, who had flown in from Miami. Leon had told me that she might come, and he was worried because she was extremely homophobic. My future visits were choreographed to comply with Leon's wish that his mother and I never met.

Leon's mother's visit appeared to do him the world of good, and he soon returned home to his flat. While she was out one day, he called and asked me to come over. When I got there, I found him in solemn, *goodbye* mode. He insisted on giving me a few mementos, including a copy of the defamatory *Root* magazine article about me, which he had kept all those years, as well as a photo we'd taken with Gloria Gaynor, during my first 'speechless' meeting with her. We laughed as Leon recalled how we met Gloria when she opened a short-lived nightclub in Tottenham. After her performance, we stalked her on her way to her dressing room. When she twigged that she was being followed, she offered a generous, "Hello, there guys. What can I do for you?" Leon lied and told her it was his birthday, which prompted Gloria to reach into her Prada bag for two publicity pictures, which she signed; one for him, and one for me. Leon and Gloria chatted for a moment or two, but when it was my turn, uncharacteristically, words failed me; my mouth opened up and nothing came out. My one and only chance to meet the original Queen of Disco, and musical idol, had come and gone, or so I thought.

Leon and I had a lot to laugh about, as he skilfully skipped past the photos of John and other friends who had shared his diagnosis and were now gone. It was good to spend those quiet moments with Leon. They were to be our final moments together.

Leon died only a few weeks later; yet another wonderful gay man gone too soon. Following his death, I phoned his mother to offer my condolences, but was met with fury. "I know exactly who you are," she shouted. The conversation went downhill from there. She blamed me for his illness and his death, and ended the call with: "You're not welcome to call me, nor are you welcome at my son's funeral." With that, she slammed the phone down in my ear. Yes, it hurt to be the object of her rage; we had never met, but I had to respect her pain and her wishes. Many of our mutual friends told me to ignore her and go anyway, but I remembered Leon's unselfish example at John's funeral, and knew that it was right to follow it. Besides, he and I had already said our goodbyes. His funeral was for his mother and everyone else who had yet to do so.

All around me, in my private life and at work, the dreaded diagnosis and death toll were rising. Charles, Paul, John, Andrew, Richard, Rick, Colin, Nigel, Graeme, Tim, Margaret, Elizabeth, Karen, Patricia, Alan...Leon.

Occasionally in life we meet someone special who captures our heart and all our senses. Charles was such a person. He was a beautiful artistic gay man who appeared to be completely besotted with me. His generous smile in my direction quickly became generous embraces. Tragically, when our mutual feelings became obvious to us both, all the coward in me could do was run in the opposite direction; I was good at running away from people who wanted to love me; especially loveable, HIV-diagnosed people like Charles. I felt that I had to run away to protect myself from the inevitable trauma of loving then losing someone. It was easier for me to cope with my feelings about Charles, as I did his wonderful artwork, from a considered distance. I'm sure he was baffled by my behaviour, but I knew this didn't lessen how he felt about me. My decision was truly my loss, and I would learn, the hard way, that true love doesn't come around too often in life; love is too rare and precious a gift to allow it to slip through my hands, as if it were water from a tap. Yet, despite this knowledge, I was bound to repeat the same behaviour again and again; I was too afraid to love and lose. Being a one-man show was a safer option.

Perhaps one day I would allow myself the gift of sharing love with someone else, even if it may appear, for whatever reason, to be a time limited adventure. Life is about love and loving, and everything else is dust waiting to happen; I know that now. Sorry, Charles... if I could turn back time... You were braver than I.

Too many people were being lost – far, far too many; leaving behind devastated loved ones: mothers, fathers, grandparents, children, siblings, friends and lovers. There was too much loss and too much pain, and it was all compounded by the awful stigma of contagion, guilt, and shame. AIDS was the "dirty" disease; it didn't have the respectability of cancer or heart disease. Somehow, people with AIDS were themselves dirty, sub-human 'sinners' who were being punished by God and getting what they deserved. The media was unrelenting in their portrayal of AIDS as 'the gay disease'. HIV infected babies and people with haemophilia, were portrayed as its 'innocent victims'-- as if gay people were in some way responsible for their own plight. It was truly a terrible time to be gay, and even more so, to have HIV or AIDS.

AIDS had created a war zone in my life, in our lives! I was weary of the funerals and burying people, some of whom were younger than my twenty-eight year-old self. But even though I found myself exhausted at the close of each day, nothing could stop me from doing all I could the next day. There was nothing more important than to give myself to this challenge. This was my purpose and nothing was going to deflect me from it. I would pray each night: *"God, I need you to make me stronger. I need you to enable me to fight and win in this war with AIDS. I feel like I'm losing. Help me!"* The task of helping the sick and the abandoned was surely God's work, and I needed to be his heart, hands and feet.

By the time Marvin left hospital he'd lost the use of his legs and was confined to a wheelchair. His family took him back home up north, but we stayed in regular contact by phone. I put together a video tape of some of his favourite divas, which I knew he'd love. He phoned to say thanks when he received it and I could hear it playing in the background: Aretha, Patti Labelle, Miki Howard, Stephanie Mills, Chaka Khan. His delighted cousin told me, "Vernal, that's all he wants to watch. Thank you so much for sending it." Marvin was a fighter and I hoped he'd get through this, and yet I knew in my heart that he too would one day be gone.

The next morning I found myself gazing at my tired reflection in my bathroom mirror. I had deliberately avoided being tested for HIV, and I began to feel that it was perhaps time for me to face whatever the result would be. Like many gay men, the thought had crossed my mind many times over, although I didn't believe I'd had at-risk sex. But I also knew a lot of gay men with HIV and AIDS who felt the same, until the dreaded result confirmed that they must have. Only a test could confirm the truth, one way or the other. Every time I got a bad cold, or thought I'd spotted something unusual on my skin, I'd convince myself that I was HIV positive. But when I asked myself, *"Vernal, can you handle a positive result?"* The answer was a resounding "No!" I had work to do and my HIV test would have to wait for another time.

34. NEWS OF THE WORLD: 'SEX ON THE RATES!'

It was 1989 and I was determined and I was determined to put the Brent HIV Centre at the heart of the AIDS prevention campaign in London. The only way to stop AIDS, was to stop people from getting HIV in the first place. The Gay Men's Health Crisis in New York and the Minority AIDS Project in Los Angeles were doing amazing work with their explicit safer-sex campaigning in the United States. They were being effective in saving lives, and I wanted to do something similar.

I soon made contact with Phill Wilson, a very handsome L.A.-based black American gay man, who was openly living with HIV. Indeed, he had a very high profile in HIV campaigning across the States. I was delighted to learn that he was making a fact-finding trip to London, and had asked to meet with me. When he came to the office to meet me, I was stunned by his good looks, and he seemed equally taken with me, but he later told me that his surprised expression was because my accent over the phone had led him to assume that I was white. This was, of course, in the days before the internet, Facebook and webcams. We both laughed. I said that does happen sometimes.

I told Phill that I would like to bring him back to London, to talk to gay men about safer sex, and how to enjoy, rather than fear it. He said he'd love to, and in anticipation of the visit, posters were printed up and distributed to London's gay venues. The principal poster read: *Brent HIV Centre presents Phill Wilson's Eroticising Safer Sex Workshop*. The venue was to be the London Lesbian and Gay Centre, former home of the long defunct People's Group.

Phill gave me a long list of materials that he would need for the workshops. The list included dildos of different sizes, a blow-up sex doll, a harness, hundreds of condoms, and an equally generous supply of lubricating jelly. My deputy knew exactly where to go to buy the stuff, and he set about the task with great enthusiasm.

The day of the first workshop arrived, and Phill and I made our way together to the Lesbian and Gay Centre. I felt confident of a good turnout, but neither of us was prepared for what we saw: enormous lines of eager gay men of all races, ages and sizes, queuing up to get into his workshop, which, fortunately, had been booked in the large basement of the centre. "Wow!" said Phill on seeing the queues of people, and a fantastic giant poster we had commissioned, proclaiming the event. The poster – painted by Bill Wilcox, formerly of the People's Group, and now with Fusion – was to be the backdrop to Phill's presentation. I was thrilled with the turnout. The Brent HIV Centre had demonstrated that there was a real demand for this kind of work in London, and as a result, an organisation called Gay Men Fighting AIDS (GMFA) would later follow our lead.

Phill captivated the audience immediately, and delivered his workshop with his characteristic flawless professionalism. Workshop activities included teaching the guys how to 'negotiate safer sex' before they got into the bedroom or wherever else the mood took them; how to suck cock safely; to fuck safely, using lots of lube on a condom; and using role play and 'dirty' talk to make the experience more fun, if that turned them on. A highlight of the session was Phill Wilson demonstrating how to roll a condom onto a dildo using just his mouth. It earned him thunderous applause. Phill then got participants to role play at negotiating safer sex, as if they were strangers in a bar. It was all great fun, as well as being educational, and served to demystify the exact meaning of 'safer sex'.

When the local press produced a headline exclaiming, '*Sex on the Rates!*' My management at Brent Council summoned me to explain myself. A short while later, Mum phoned in a hysterical state. "What are you doing in the *News of the World*?" she screamed. The national press were onto the story. The London *Evening Standard* carried a lurid article about the event on page three, referring to me as "*Jamaican, Vernal Scott*". It was true that my parents were Jamaican, but at this point I had never been to the place.

Undeterred by the publicity, I saw to it that the Brent HIV Centre took our safer sex message to every community centre in Brent that would host us, including the notorious Stonebridge estate, offering workshops aimed at heterosexuals. I fronted the workshops, supported on a couple of occasions by Simon Watney, author of *Policing Desire* and prominent gay activist, as guest speaker. Most audiences were receptive, but not everyone was welcoming. One man shouted at me, "We don't need you coming here talking about HIV and AIDS, because we don't have no batty man living here." I politely explained that HIV did not discriminate, and that everyone needed to know how to stay well, while continuing to enjoy sex. At another session in my old neighbourhood of Tottenham, where I was the guest presenter, the reception was even more hostile towards me and my message about safer sex. Things got so nasty that I was forced to curtail my presentation to the predominantly black audience. I honestly felt that my personal safety was at risk. In their eyes, AIDS meant gay, and gay was not welcome! Homophobia was, ironically, rebounding on its espousers, its irrationality barring some segments of the heterosexual community from even listening in prudent self-interest, to messages for the benefit of their own health.

Not to be defeated, my safer sex campaign continued with the hiring of the Tricycle Theatre, in Kilburn, for what I titled *The Safer Sex Show*. All tickets would be free, and allotted on first-come, first-served basis. On hearing of the project, Brent's chief executive summoned me to his office, to seek assurances from me that there was not going to be any simulated sex in the show. I put his mind at rest.

Finally, with Simon, my friend from Kingsley Road days on the turntables, *The Safer Sex Show* went live and the capacity audience enjoyed a series of acts who all performed on a theme of safer sex. I'm not sure quite where the drag act who did Jennifer Holliday's 'And I'm Telling You I'm Not Going' fitted in, but it went down extremely well with the diverse audience. At one point, I took to the stage doing a little Michael Jackson moon walk, then cracked a few politically acceptable jokes, before blowing into a condom, to demonstrate that any guy who said he was too big for one was a liar.

God's Other Children: A London Memoir   293

A local journalist asked me to explain what my Centre was aiming to achieve with our work on safer sex. My response was clear:

"The Brent HIV Centre is taking safer sex out of its current context of illness, death and dying, and aims to put it where it needs to be; into a context of opportunity, satisfaction, health and fun. Safer sex information needs to be communicated in an attractive, exciting and creative way, in order for the public to be excited about it and actually use it; the latter being our goal. Our overall aim is to promote good health and save lives. In our society, where sex is either taboo or the subject of humour, the threat of HIV demands that we become more open and explicit about sex and that we cast aside our inhibitions about the subject. With increasing HIV statistics, it remains extremely important that the safer-sex message reaches as many sexually active people as possible."

In response, a local Conservative politician was later quoted saying that my work on safer sex was "disgusting". That comment alone cemented my belief that I was doing the right thing. The Conservatives were in government, but they were woeful leaders in dealing with the AIDS crisis and I would take no lessons from them about how best to meet the challenge we were facing: the greatest challenge of our time.

35. CALIFORNIA DREAMING

It was early 1991 and America was leading the fight on HIV and AIDS. Supported by my employer, Brent Council, I flew to Los Angeles to attend an AIDS Institute and Black Gay Leadership Conference, headed by Phill Wilson. The idea was that I'd bring back ideas that would help with local service development.

It was my first trip abroad and was I very excited to be on American soil. I was in awe of sunny Los Angeles, which seemed to exude its own air of excitement and possibility. Phill Wilson met me at my hotel, which doubled as the lavish venue for the conference. It was great to see his handsome smiling face again. He introduced me to his life partner, Chris Brownlie: both men were both open about living with HIV, in fact, Chris was living with AIDS. The city was in the process of building a hospice in his name, along the lines of London Lighthouse. The couple was known nationwide for their AIDS advocacy, and Phill was seen as a leading light on the challenges and solutions in the AIDS crisis. He was a huge inspiration to me.

The conference, attended by a couple of hundred delegates, ran for just under a week, ending with a gala party at which the guest speaker was Natalie Cole, the jazz singer and daughter of Nat King Cole. The entire week was full of inspirational talks and workshops, designed to inform, guide, and support delegates working in the HIV/AIDS field. Many of the speakers were themselves living with HIV or AIDS, and I found myself tremendously moved by their stories of resolute courage; not just to survive, but to live! These men and women were anything but 'victims'.

The conference was extremely useful and I quickly gathered useful ideas and a ton of information to help with my work back in London. I networked feverishly, making lots of new friends in the process; the novelty of my British accent proved to be a winning asset.

I was soon reintroduced to a living gay Christian legend: Carl Bean, now Bishop Bean. He'd had a ground-breaking Motown disco hit back in 1977 with 'I Was Born This Way'. It was one of my all-time favorite tracks. I remember that it took me a lot of courage to buy the record back then, even though the indifferent shop assistant failed to bat an eyelid. My immense anxiety in asking for the record turned out to be completely unnecessary, as anxiety often is.

Bishop Bean recalled meeting me in London a few years earlier, in the midst of a homophobic fist fight that had broken out at a Commonwealth Institute AIDS conference we were both attending. He was the main speaker and I was in the audience. A small but vocal contingent of black homophobes decided to invade and disrupt proceedings. One thing led to another and a fight broke out, but fortunately the homophobes came off worse, owing largely to a hefty black lesbian who would have none of it, and whom I shamelessly hid behind. Bishop Bean and I laughed at the memory and he kindly invited me to come to his church in downtown LA on Sunday. I promised to be there.

I was also introduced to Kevin; a lively young African American whom I would spend much of my time with for the remainder of my stay in LA. He was great company and we shared similar taste in music, as well as other *treats*. We had fun singing along to tunes on his car stereo, as he drove me around the safer parts of LA for some much appreciated whistle-stop sight-seeing. A track called Joy and Pain by Donna Allen was on repeat play as we sang our way down Sunset Boulevard.

With Marlon Riggs

Marlon Riggs, a gay film director, and Keith Boykin, an activist and broadcaster, were other notables whom I was honoured to meet during my stay. I was also very pleased to meet the suit-clad Randy Cochran; a popular black gay porn star, who delivered a riveting conference presentation about his life and work. The delighted attendees drooled their approval as he reminisced about his catalogue of best-selling triple X titles. I had seen a few of them myself, so it seemed rather strange to see Randy standing there with his clothes on. His presentation was intelligent and eloquent, but the packed room dissolved into laughter when he said his mother was one of his biggest fans. He didn't appear to be joking, either! Randy also revealed some insider industry secrets, such as porn directors bringing in other 'bottoms' or 'tops' to play the actual sex scene, and then applying some crafty editing to hide the switch. But he assured us that when we were watching him on the screen, we really were watching him, and "no one else!" he insisted. "Well, thank goodness for that!" someone shouted, as the room erupted again. The only person not laughing was Randy himself; he took his 'art' very seriously indeed; I guess being a porn performer in the era of HIV and AIDS had to be taken very seriously, whether a condom was used or not.

With Randy (L) and Phill (R)

My spell-casting accent worked on Randy too, but I blushed with embarrassment when he asked me for a date; I knew what *'date'* meant! His approach was respectful and warm, but I declined; mostly because my attention was taken elsewhere. There was some very nice eye-candy at the conference, and though Randy was truly lovely, my eyes were busy elsewhere. I jokingly told him: "I'd be far too embarrassed to be seen on the town with you." He took my subtle rejection in good humour, and we both laughed it off before he moved on to pursue other potential conquests. Randy was definitely *randy*!

Sunday came quickly. I showered and suited up to attend Bishop Bean's church. When I got there I was stunned at the huge number people – hundreds-- gathered outside. The smiling Bishop greeted everybody at the door with a generous hug, and I was keen to wait in line for mine.

As I took to a pew, I struggled to remember the last time I'd attended church for a non-funeral related service; just to give praise and thanks to God. In all honesty, the relentless onslaught of AIDS had rendered me a virtual atheist: our loving God appeared to have abandoned some of his children, at least the gay ones. The Bible was readily used to hammer our coffins shut, whilst His representatives, gleeful men of the cloth, celebrated our "sinful" and "self-inflicted" early demise. Even though I still found myself praying, I was feeling increasingly detached and angry with God. How could he preside over such pain, grief and loss? And more to the point, how could I continue to believe in him as a healer when those healing powers were nowhere to be seen?

Despite the conflict in my head, heart and soul, here I was in Bishop Bean's capacity-filled church. Within moments, the building was rocking to the sweetest gospel music my ears had ever heard. The congregation was predominantly black, as was the choir, but there were a good number of whites in there too. Gay people, transsexuals, and people with AIDS were also visibly present. *London had never seen anything like this,* I thought to myself, and it was perfect: a faithful reflection of the diversity of the City of Angels. After a couple of songs, Bishop Bean, now long departed from his disco days, took to his pulpit, and preached like he was preaching for his life. He may have done this every week, but it felt genuine and authentic. My hardened heart began to melt with his uplifting emphatic words: "God's love is for everybody!" His thunderous voice got through to me and my eyes welled up with tears. The Bishop had loudly proclaimed a truth that I'd never heard from the mouth of a black preacher before now. He continued: "God loves gays and people with AIDS too." I wiped a tear from my eye as he went on and took me by surprise: "There's a very special young man in the congregation today, and he's come all the way from London, England. His name is Vernal Scott, and he's doing great work over there caring for people with HIV and AIDS. Vernal, please stand so we can show our appreciation."

I stood on awkward legs and smiled through the tears flooding down my face. I mouthed a silent *"thank you"* to the Bishop, and to everyone else. I could only surmise that Phill had told him about my efforts back home. I was truly touched.

When I sat down, I tried to compose myself, but found I couldn't. I then just broke down, crying like never before. I was moved to the core of my soul by the message that I needed to hear: God loved me too. It was the first time that I had heard a (black!) preacher declare-- and a congregation affirm-- that my sexuality was no barrier to God's love, and that it was an evil lie that God hates gay people. My trip to LA was turning out to be trip back to God, thanks to Bishop Bean, whose words allowed me to accept in my mind what I had long felt in my heart. From this moment on I would open myself up to God, or so I thought. However, in the writing of the final chapter of this very book, concerning religion and homosexuality, I would be prompted to again re-evaluate my view and understanding of God, the Bible, and religion, and the outcome would signal profound and permanent change. For now, at least, I needed God and he appeared to need me.

At the end of the service, one of the choir members came to greet me. I was amazed to discover that it was David Nathan: a highly respected writer for *Blues and Soul* magazine. He had written the very first article that I had read about my idol, Gloria Gaynor, back in 1975. I was thrilled to meet him and we agreed to stay in touch. He was a white Londoner who had long since made America his home. I would later discover that we had a dear friend in common: Marvin! It was indeed a small world.

With an emotional morning behind me, my guardian angel, Kevin, decided I needed some light relief, so that night he took me to a tribute party for 'disco queen', Sylvester, who had died of AIDS in 1988. Bravely, for the time, Sylvester had been quite open about his illness towards the end of his life, and managed a smile for his fans, even when confined to a wheelchair. The salute to his memory starred Chaka Khan, decked out in a hideous leopard patterned outfit. I was mortified when Kevin shouted: "Get off, Chaka, you look a mess!" With all the noise going on, I'm sure she couldn't hear him, at least I hoped not. There were hundreds of gay men there, all sharing memories and celebrating the life of 'the fabulous Sylvester', a true disco superstar. I was thrilled to be part of it.

I took the opportunity of being in California to fly to San Francisco, Sylvester's adopted home town, and the first epicentre of the AIDS crisis. The virus had hit the city hard; too hard, and it was now a tarnished reflection of its former flamboyantly happy self. Every gay man seemed to either have AIDS, or had just buried someone who'd died from it. People were dropping fast and gay men, in particular, were in survival rather than living mode.

I accepted an invitation to attend a workshop on safer sex at the home of Reggie Williams; a prominent and charismatic black gay man living with AIDS whom I had met at the LA conference. Reggie's workshop was more like a party, with a good supply of drink and food. There was also an abundance of condoms, lubricating jelly, and sex toys everywhere I looked; all for the purpose, it turned out, of demonstrating the correct use of condoms, of course! I'm not sure if it was the drink or the subject matter, or a mixture of both, but lots of the men present got themselves a little excited, and that included me. As result, my first night in the city was truly fantastic, and for all the right reasons.

My whistle-stop visit to the wounded gay capital of the world gave me a welcome opportunity to meet up with Colin, a much cherished friend and fellow Londoner, who was also visiting. A very successful white gay man in his early forties, his handsome features and close-cut beard reminded me of darling Graham, my long lost love from my days at the Barbican. Colin and I last saw each other at a London Lighthouse social event, where he fit right in amongst the other white, middle class, well-to-do gay men living with the virus who frequented the project; the actual hospice facility was still under construction. HIV appeared to be a virus of equal opportunity, but one's pre and post infection socio-economic status made a difference, especially in the fight to stay healthy and survive. The gay men in Colin's group made up the majority of the client profile at Lighthouse; they were hit the hardest by the pandemic in our capital. I was often the only black face at support functions, but I always felt totally welcome.

The London Lighthouse, as intended by Christopher Spence, its impassioned creator, provided an essential refuge in the endless sea of AIDS-related fear, death and dying. Christopher behaved like a loving father towards everyone who was lucky enough to enter his West of the city sanctuary. He exuded love and kindness as naturally as water poured from a tap. I recall a cold November weekend of 1986 when he took a group of about fifteen of us away for a dormitory stay near Brighton. It was an opportunity to acknowledge our individual lives, and current, mostly health-related challenges, in a safe space and without the distraction of phones, doorbells, or anything else. Most of the men were at various stages of AIDS-related illness, and I felt like something of an intruder as I listened in to their intimate stories and life paths, which ultimately led them to the doors of the Lighthouse. When it was my turn to 'share', the lights inexplicably dimmed and Christopher briefly left the room and returned with a large cake, complete with 25 sparkling candles. It happened to be my birthday, and to my embarrassment, someone had told him. After a chorus or two of 'Happy Birthday' from the gathered men, I stood on unsteady feet to thank them for their kind surprise. Then Christopher, in his fatherly mode, put his arm around my shoulders and said: "Vernal, look at all the love on the faces in this room. It's love for you, Vernal! Let the love sink in, and enjoy it!" As I took a breath and scanned the faces smiling back at me, I started to well up and cry. I sat down and cried some more. These wonderful gay men, despite their Kaposi's and other life-threatening illnesses, took the time to secretly bake me a cake, just to let me know how much they appreciated my being around. I was touched to my very soul, and my audible sobbing was confirmation that I felt as they did. We were brothers, and I loved each of them dearly, and they loved me back. It was then that it dawned upon me: the Lighthouse was much more than an aspirational world class AIDS hospice; more than anything, it was about love; the same love that we were all feeling on my 25th birthday near the sea. I recall how we held onto each other's hands that night and sang from our hearts to music from Christopher's portable stereo. Dionne Warwick made us smile with That's What Friends Are For; Bette Midler made us huddle and cry with The Rose; and Whitney Houston, the world's new singing sensation, lifted our spirits with the Greatest Love of All. Tragically, many of the men who celebrated with me that night would not live to see the formal opening of the Lighthouse by Princess Margaret, or subsequent fund-raising lunches hosted there by Christopher and our angelic advocate, Princess Diana.

More important than their cash, well-off gay men like Colin were also highly educated, and they made it their business to educate themselves further about the virus and how best they might survive it. They knew information was the key to survival, for those already infected as well as those trying to avoid becoming so. Extra cash in your pocket meant you could afford to chase a potential cure instead of waiting for it to come to you. Colin was in that lucky group. He didn't have time for California dreaming: in the fight for his life, he'd determined that dreaming was for the poor and waiting was an occupation for the doomed. He was wide awake and dealing with the reality of his situation. He was fixated on finding *the cure* and had the cash to pursue and pay for it. But what would the elusive cure entail should he come across it? A diet, a pill, a mixture of both, an injection of some unofficial cocktail, herbs, weed, exercise, or neither of the above, or perhaps a bit of all of them? Hey, perhaps HIV wasn't the cause of AIDS after all, or perhaps it was. No, of course HIV is the cause...isn't it? It must be... hmm... yes... no... yes!

As complicated as life with HIV was for those infected, it was almost as complex wading through the maze of forceful theories about how to survive it. A good formal education could only help with that daunting task. That said, from my position in the challenge, one's prospect for survival appeared to be random luck: the educated and uneducated alike were experiencing similar outcomes; life and death for members of both groups. On one hand, education mattered, but on the other, it seemed to mean little when the result was the same unavoidable early pine coffin.

Some months earlier, back in London, Colin discovered that a past uninhibited sexual encounter had resulted in him contracting HIV. It was one night of care-free passion, which gifted him with the virus and its life-threatening consequences. This, of course, was no gift at all, but he didn't blame the other person; there was no point in doing that! Colin hadn't been raped; he'd been a happy and very willing participant, and like most (gay) sexual encounters at the time, condom use didn't cross his excited mind. Why should it? Back then the virus had yet to make it presence felt, but was now doing that with devastating outcomes.

As he drove us across the famous city bridge in his blue sports car for two, Colin explained that he'd come to San Francisco to take advantage of the many pioneering treatments that had not yet reached London. He repeated his determination to beat the virus, and I knew he meant it. I tried to sound supportive, and I was, but I worried that my fears for him might come through and undermine my attempt at reassurance. As I glanced over at him, I could see that Colin was fighting fit; he looked healthy and I could see the determination he spoke of in his eyes. If anyone could beat this disease it was Colin.

We spent a wonderful afternoon sight-seeing at his favourite city highlights before hugging a warm and somewhat intense goodbye. There was something unsaid in the air between us. As I walked away from him, I turned around and went back to hug him again. Our unexpected kiss was a reflection of something that we'd both been carrying for each other but had never acted on, until now. I truly cared for him and found him very attractive, but I wasn't sure whether anything beyond a friendship would, or should transpire between us. I was young and not the wisest person on Earth, but I knew friendships often outlasted love affairs, and there was much to value in that.

A day later, Colin and I spoke by phone and promised to meet up on his return to London. I wished him well and then flew back to LA to stay a few days longer with Chris and Phill. They had a great apartment, befitting their celebrity status. Chris took me to look at the building which would bear his name as a hospice for people with AIDS. His own condition was now quite advanced AIDS, but he was no victim; he made it clear on a few occasions that I was offering assistance inappropriately. For example, when we went to the launderette and I offered to fold his clothes, he got really pissed with me about it. But a moment later all was well again. I didn't take it personally. Chris had fought back many times against AIDS-induced illnesses that threatened his life. He didn't need me, or anyone else, making him feel like a victim.

I later went to spend some time with another interracial couple I'd met at the conference, Mark and Alex. Alex and I got unexpectedly close when his partner was away for a day. It was a one-off night of fun. When Mark came home in the morning, the two men exchanged knowing glances and smiles, and so did I. The couple enjoyed an 'open relationship' and I guess what happened fitted within that. It had been 'safer sex', of course, and we were both expert at that.

Unlike a lot of people at this time, or even now, I knew that it was perfectly possible to have great sex with someone with HIV, without putting myself at risk. On a previous occasion, back in London, I had reacted angrily when a guy waited until after we'd had sex to tell me he was HIV positive. I felt that he'd selfishly taken away my right to choose. But the truth was that I didn't know my own health status at that time, and I later accepted that my attitude had been hypocritical. I duly apologized to him and learned a lesson: staying HIV negative was my responsibility, no one else's. It was a fact that the majority of people with HIV probably did not know they had it, because they looked and felt well. Perhaps I was one of those. I hadn't been tested and wasn't in a hurry to be tested either. For now, at least, ignorance was my way of coping.

A very handsome Latino doctor called Saulo often visited my hosts. A very slim man, with jet-black hair and a cute handle-bar 'tache - he was stunning! "Everyone fancies him!" Alex and Mark chuckled, but they quelled my excitement by making it clear he was straight as an arrow, and "happily married, with kids".

Saulo and I got talking during one of his visits, and our friendly exchange led to an invitation to go to Disneyland with him and his two girls. On the day of the trip, I think I had a better time than his kids! Saulo was an attentive, loving dad, and his girls were in love with their daddy. The time I spent with the family reignited my own deeply burning desire to be a dad; I longed to be a father, but knew it was never going to happen.

A few nights later Saulo and his gorgeous African-American wife, Denise, invited me to dinner. Denise was a very successful doctor in her own right; brimming with energy, and possessing an admirable sense of purpose. Their home was beautiful beyond belief, complete with pool and a maid.

Over dinner they took it in turns to tell me about their experiences of London and how much they both loved the place. Denise made a comment about my accent and asked if it faded when I got tired. "No," I said, "I'm British, and my accent doesn't fade to black-American ghetto at night." We all laughed. There were odd moments when Denise would just look at me without speaking, as if she was trying to suss me out or something.

It was getting late when Saulo offered to drive me back to the apartment. I said goodbye to Denise and thanked her for a delightful evening. When we arrived at Alex and Mark's, Saulo surprised me by switching off the car, and asked if he could come in and have a quick word with me about "something very important". I was curious about what the hell it was that the delicious Dr Saulo wanted to talk to me about at this hour – it was now approaching midnight, and my hosts had gone to bed.

As we entered the living room, Saulo suddenly exploded into tears. For a moment I just stared at him, trying to fathom what on Earth was going on. He looked at me through his tears and struggled to speak. My natural reaction was to approach and put my arm about his shoulders, which is what I did.

"Vernal, I don't know how to deal with this," he stuttered.

I said nothing, because I still didn't know what was going on. He continued.

"I'm feeling... something is going on for me about you and it's got me torn up. I can't afford to deal with this shit. I can't fucking deal with this?"

Stumped, I asked him naïvely, "Is it something I said at dinner, or in the car? Saulo, whatever it is I'm very sorry." I thought back to the odd glances I had got from his wife at the dinner table, but that made no sense either.

Still crying, Saulo muttered: "No, no, it's nothing you've said. I just admire your freedom to be yourself. I feel trapped by my foolishness."

I looked up at the ceiling, trying to make sense of what he was saying. I was about to ask how I could help when he suddenly pressed his lips against mine. He was kissing me, desperately, and I was still trying to talk. I stopped talking and kissed him back. I shut out my thoughts as each kiss got deeper than the last. We forgot about my hosts as Saulo began to remove my clothes; our lips didn't part. I removed his clothes. A short while later he said he wanted me inside him and I happily obliged; I very much wanted to be inside him too.

Half an hour later and we were lying in each other's arms on the floor. I was silent and he was still sobbing, but now very softly, as we held each other tightly. For a while he looked at me as if I'd given him the key to his own freedom. Another half an hour and Saulo had gone, returning home to his wife and family. I fell asleep.

I was woken the next morning by the homely noises of Mark and Alex making breakfast in the galley kitchen, which was open plan to the room where I slept. I could tell that they were doing their best to not wake me. I raised myself up and greeted them with a "Good morning, guys". Mark immediately asked how dinner had gone last night. For a moment I hesitated but then decided to trust them with the truth about what had happened.

"Are you freaking kidding me?" said Alex. "You and Saulo did what?"

They both came over to the futon where I lay. I tried to explain that it "just happened!"

Mark shook his head in disbelief. "Dr Saulo? But he's not gay, Vernal! I've known him for years. He's not gay!!" "Well, he was gay last night" I replied, quite innocently, causing my hosts to laugh hysterically.

Alex just smiled and said, "Well, it just proves that we don't know him as well as we thought. Damn!"

Mark joked: "Vernal, we need to get you on that plane back to London before you cause any more havoc. We all laughed.

A couple of days before I left LA, Saulo phoned and he insisted that we meet up again. He'd been on my mind a lot too. We drove to a wonderful seafood restaurant in Malibu. My plate was heaped with food to the point that other patrons paused and laughed. The waitress put a large bib-like napkin under my chin and chuckled, "Eat up, honey!" It was very romantic, despite my looking like a glutton. Throughout the meal, Saulo looked at me as if I was going to be his dessert. He suggested we get a hotel room. He was a special guy, very much so, but I didn't like the idea of booking into a hotel just to deal with our passions and his new freedom. He said he understood. We later kissed goodbye; but goodbye was the last thing on his mind.

Saulo phoned me a few times after I returned to London, but we both knew we could do nothing with how we were feeling about each other.

I was surprised and disappointed when he called one night to say that he'd told his wife what had happened between us after dinner that night. I was very concerned for him. He said he wasn't sorry about telling her. "I can't live like this much longer. I really do love her, but I love you too, Vernal. I love you."

Things got worse when he told me that Denise had demanded my address. A lengthy letter duly arrived the following week. To say that Denise was angry would be an understatement. She was hurting badly. She blamed me for destroying her happy life, and said that she had lost whatever respect she had for me. *"I am completely devastated."* she ended. After reading the letter a couple of times, I contacted Saulo, at his office, and asked that he not contact me again. He was clearly upset, but said he would respect my decision.

I was young, but wise enough to know that we had no future together.

Saulo would eventually fade from my mind and heart; at least that's what I hoped. I decided to respond to Denise, letting her know that I was sorry for what had happened, but that I took no responsibility for the state of her marriage; that was between her and her husband. I wished them well, and I meant it. It was now time for me to put my focus back on my work.

My California dreaming was over. It felt good to be back home in London. My first international trip was one that I would never forget, for all sorts of reasons. I was feeling energized and inspired by what I'd learned, and was eager to apply my learning in my workplace. I wanted to do something big...very big.

God's Other Children: A London Memoir   311

36. REACH OUT AND TOUCH WITH SISTER WHITNEY

REACH OUT AND TOUCH

Sunday 15 September '91
REMOVING THE STIGMA

A gathering of all those who have been touched by HIV and AIDS in the company of friends, lovers, colleagues, celebrities and guest speakers. Your active participation will help to remove the stigma, and make this special event a powerful statement of remembrance, support and unity with the men, women and children who are living and have lived with HIV disease (includes AIDS).

J O I N   U S !
CARRY A FLOWER
IN REMEMBRANCE
SUPPORT & UNITY
Speakers' Corner, Marble Arch, London
GUEST SPEAKERS AND CELEBRITY PROGRAMME 5PM
ARRIVAL AT TRAFALGAR SQUARE APPROX 6.45PM
Final guest and celebrity programme and placing of flowers

UK HIV/AIDS VIGIL
AND PROCESSION WITH FLOWERS

Initiated and co-ordinated by Brent HIV Centre supported by Body Positive, London Lighthouse, Black HIV & AIDS Network, Terrence Higgins Trust, Positively Women, Panos Institute, National AIDS Trust, Standing Conference on Drug Abuse, Scottish AIDS Monitor, Names Project UK, AIDS Helpline (Northern Ireland), Welsh Voluntary AIDS Forum, Mainliners, Positive Irish Action on AIDS, Landmark, Food Chain, and Turning Point amongst others

MAKE THIS WORLD A BETTER PLACE

Whitney Houston and Vernal Scott: Embracing the HIV/AIDS challenge

I WAS VERY SAD to learn of the passing of Chris, Phill Wilson's partner. I sent some flowers and this dedication: "Farewell, Chris. Thank you for sharing your honesty, pain and joy with us. You have left a powerful statement that truly captures the essence of the quality and the courage that was Chris Brownlie. You will remain an inspiration for years to come."

Before his passing, Chris had written one of the most poignant statements about life with AIDS:

"It is courage, it is honour, it is integrity. It is bearing the unbearable, enduring the unendurable, and hoping in the face of hopelessness. It is the sweet pain of knowing that you are dying, and the overwhelming sadness for those who will kiss you into their dreams."

By 1991, Mrs Thatcher had been booted out by her own party, and I, for one, wasn't sad to see her go. She had been a very capable Prime Minister, but she lacked humanity for anyone who didn't look or sound like her, or whose lifestyle was 'different'. We needed a human being at the helm at this time of trauma and crisis, not someone who took pride in being referred to as 'the iron lady'. Norman Fowler, her by now former Secretary of State for Health, seemed more human during his tenure in the job, even if his stone cold 'AIDS - Don't Die of Ignorance' campaign failed to convey an ounce of empathy with the bereaved and dying. He disappointed many of us further when he voted in favour of Clause 28, the UK's infamous anti-gay legislation. Our horrible deaths were not enough; we were down and being kicked by our own government; the people who would have happily taken care of us, if only we had been heterosexual.

There were now between two and three million AIDS cases reported around the world. With my attention focused on the human experience behind the mounting, numbers, I began to feel a need to let the world know that the people concerned were not just statistics, but real men, women and children: our loved ones, friends, lovers, children, colleagues, and neighbours. Real people! My own client profile included teachers, a policeman, a scientist, authors, artists, lawyers, performers, business people, accountants, IT specialists, managers, caterers, students and health service staff. The youngest, born to an infected mother, was just eighteen months old, and the oldest was a gay man in his late fifties. They were of different nationalities and income brackets and possessed incalculable talent, skills, and accomplishments. Rejected by the ignorant and bigoted, these wonderful people languished in fear and undeserved shame.

I was finding it increasingly difficult to detach myself emotionally from the people to whom I was providing a service, and sometimes they became attached to me too. One such person was Margaret, who was a warm-hearted Nigerian mother who had come to London alone with the intention of finding suitable accommodation before sending for her four children back home. Perhaps it was because she was missing her children, but she referred to me as her "new son" and wouldn't stop thanking me for caring about her. Her shy smile was constant and her voice always soft, making her words just about discernible. One afternoon I offered to drop her off at her bedsit accommodation in Harlesden. As we drove, I listened intently as she found her voice and happily chatted about each of her "wonderful children"; the oldest was sixteen and the youngest just eight. Her husband died of AIDS two years back, so the children were currently being cared for by their maternal grandmother. When we arrived at the address, I reluctantly accepted Margaret's invitation to come inside, as she said there was something that she wanted to show me. The sad and dark infant-sized room served both as her bedroom and living space and the over-population of boxes, which I assumed contained her only worldly belongings didn't help. The petite woman reached up to one of the boxes and handed me a white envelope from on top. She asked me to open it, which I did, and found it was a lovely 'Thank You' card. I told her on previous occasions not to buy me or my team any cards or gifts, and repeated myself again, until the expression on her face made me shut the hell up. She had no one else to care for here in London, and all she wanted to do was show the kindness that was in her heart; a motherly kindness that she would show her own children, if they had been here. I took the card and gave her a big mother/son hug before leaving. In that hug, I sensed her fear about her own AIDS diagnosis as well as the intense loneliness she was feeling. As I drove away, a lonely tear fell from my eye onto the steering wheel, but it wasn't lonely for long.

Less than a month later and sweet Margaret was dead. Death came too ruthlessly quick to allow her the opportunity to say goodbye to her children, or me, her temporary but very privileged adopted son. Once again, my tears flowed for her and for them. For days after her passing I tortured myself about whether her last thank you card was a subtle hint to me that she knew she was on her way out, and was her way of saying a characteristically gentle goodbye.

I would sometimes sit at my desk and ask myself, who is the person that must live and die with AIDS in order to make this pitiless disease respectable? A credible answer evaded me. Anyway, I wouldn't wish AIDS on anyone, ever!

The annual Terrence Higgins Trust candlelit vigil was much needed, though it was largely perceived as a *gay* event - *'for them!'* Despite increasing mortality rates in all communities, the night-time event went mostly unreported in the mainstream media. In casting AIDS as a 'gay disease', the fact that every gay man had parents, siblings and other broken-hearted (mostly straight) loved ones grieving in the shadows of a hostile society, was overlooked. AIDS was the bigot's green light to publicly hate on gay people and get away with it. The relentless fever-pitched 'Gay Plague' headlines even included voices calling for our enforced quarantine. We weren't real people at all, or animals; we were just disposable waste. According to the press, "gay sinners" were afflicted by a "cesspool" disease of our own making. Their headlines turned a deliberate blind eye to the heterosexual 'Margarets' of the crisis, simply because they were an inconvenient interruption to the 'let's hate on gays' money-spinning bonanza.

A dignified death by the symptoms of old age was not to be our kind fate. Abandoned and alone in the fight of our lives, a hostile society, influenced by a vicious media, deemed us deserving of our suffering: our crippling fear; our unimaginable pain; our unyielding tears prompted by precious last goodbyes; our deaths. Our dashed hopes and dreams were destined to lie among the ashes in the cremation furnaces that would consume what AIDS had already destroyed; ashes that were once beautiful bodies; full of life, health and the optimism that made us believe the future was guaranteed. It was only yesterday that we were sweating up the dancefloor to I Feel Love and I Will Survive, and we had every reason to believe that we would do just that; survive and thrive. It was only yesterday that we cruised, kissed, and groped and each other, and gorged on the freedom of abundant sex; sex our way. It was only yesterday that the very idea of an early death was so ridiculously inconceivable, but our fleshless reflection in the bathroom mirror was confirmation that the good times had turned and a big disease with a little name was now playing Russian roulette with our lives. Swallowed up by clothes that no longer fit, it was now the survival of, not the fittest or most determined, but simply, it seemed, the luckiest. Like snow fall interrupting the sunniest of spring days, we were stunned by the cruelty of our physical disintegration and the terror-inducing reality of death's determined approach. AIDS had sabotaged our far too temporary rendezvous with happiness and the illusion of longevity of life that we assumed had been promised at birth. When our mothers delivered us into the world, their tears of joy and precious first kiss belied our pending fate and the fact that our eager infant eyes would mature only long enough to cry a tortured goodbye. AIDS would summon our mothers' tears again, but this time, to moisten the soil that would bury us.

We could rely on the sanctuary of the likes of London Lighthouse and St Mary's Hospital to facilitate our safe passing from a sadistically cold world, but they couldn't prevent our deaths from continuing to be vilified and splashed across the daily press as grotesque entertainment for the ignorant and the heartless, who ridiculed us in our plight as feeble and weak, but who would never, themselves, be capable of the extraordinary courage that it took to be a person living... and dying with AIDS. It was a bravery that camouflaged our deepest and darkest fears, but at the same time, demanded the retention of our dignity; AIDS could take our lives but it would not be allowed to take our pride. The shame didn't belong to those of us dying; but to those living, who were too indecent to feel any shame for their hateful utterances and failure to appreciate that we are all part of the same human family, and that at a different time and with a different disease, our fate could be theirs. If they could have desisted from gloating for just a moment, then they would have got some satisfaction from seeing the merciless terror that would occasionally slip from behind our mask of fearlessness. Consciously dying was petrifyingly scary, and despite the headlines to the contrary, we were only human. However, we will be long gone before we'd give our haters the pleasure of witnessing any tears of self-pity. We will die much wiser than them; wise in knowing that death is life's ultimate and inescapable act of equality, and that, in time, the ashes of those who hate us will blow in the wind, equal to ours. That is a promise that will not be broken.

Jesus Christ is said to have reached out to lepers, but in our struggle for life and dignity in dying, previously *good* Christians joined the tabloid chorus and condemned us as God's *other*, less than deserving, children. This religious perversion took on a contagion of its own, and meant that very few churches would provide a refuge to the reviled outcast children of their 'loving God'. The Bible was fervently used as a weapon to bash the already bloodied, until it too appeared to be stained blood red.

Little by little, though, the voices of those affected could no longer be ignored. The passing of Freddie Mercury, the lead singer of Queen, was marked by a first class celebration at Wembley. It was truly a magnificent event. Dionne Warwick had an American number one hit single with a supportive message directed to people with AIDS called 'That's What Friends Are For.' The song raised millions for AIDS charities and reaffirmed the status of its singer as a gay icon. Other stars were showing their support for people with AIDS too, including Madonna, Cher, Nancy Wilson, Patti Labelle, and Jennifer Holliday, amongst them. Newly 'Born again' Disco superstars, Gloria Gaynor and Donna Summer, whose early careers were greatly boosted by their gay fan base, were quieter. Gloria had been reported in a British newspaper as allegedly saying that she cried when a fan told her he was gay, and Donna's career suffered a calamitous collapse when she allegedly said AIDS was God's punishment. As a consequence neither lady was top of the list when it came to fund-raising concerts for people affected by AIDS. I later witnessed a televised press conference, where a tearful Donna vehemently denied making the remarks. Gloria made a similar statement, insisting: "Gay people are people too!" I was left with the impression that the repugnant creators of the Disco Sucks movement were still at work; attacking anything gay-friendly, black or female. Neither singer was homophobic was my conclusion, but the damage had been done.

The communities hardest hit by HIV and AIDS, such as gay men, transgender people, African heterosexuals, and injection drug users, faced additional levels of discrimination that was being exacerbated by HIV stigma; a reaction by the non-affected steeped in negative assumptions, prejudice, and discrimination. HIV stigma tarnished the identity, dignity, and self-esteem of its victims, causing fear, undeserved shame and guilt, and often becoming internalized by them. An HIV diagnosis meant dealing with the very real possibility of chronic illness and early death, but it also carried a particularly corrosive level of moral judgment by society; a judgment that is absent with other diagnosis. Cancer or diabetic patients don't usually feel guilt or shame, but this was somehow expected of people affected by HIV and AIDS. In the years ahead, HIV stigma wouldn't just influence how people feel about themselves, but it would also affect medication adherence and the willingness to access healthcare treatment services, which would be crucial to keeping HIV viral loads under control and maintaining the best possible health. The stigma would also prevent people from disclosing their status and accessing the social and emotional support that they need.

HRH, Princess Diana, was doing a fantastic job for our cause by meeting people with HIV and AIDS and making a point of shaking their hands without wearing gloves. She was a true gift to the anti-stigma effort, however, despite Diana and our candlelit vigils, the stigma loomed oppressively large; indeed, the stigma seemed more enduring than the virus itself. I felt strongly that it had to be removed if people with HIV and AIDS were ever going to be able to live and die with dignity. It was being perpetuated by prejudice and unjustified fear on the part of the wider public, and blame for this lie with the then government's instructive but empathy-lacking 'Don't Die of Ignorance Campaign, which showed zero compassion for those affected. The blame also lie with those who chose not to educate themselves about the reality of how the virus is transmitted or try and understand the very human experiences of those living with it. I was determined to stop the stigma and show the human face of the disease by putting on a national event that would enable people living with HIV and AIDS – men, women and children – to be seen and heard.

At my usual weekly staff meeting, I described the national event that I wanted to create. My team responded warmly and I asked them to share their ideas. I also asked if anyone could think of a name for the event. A number of good suggestions were put forward, but in an inspired moment a name came to me that spoke to my heart: '*Reach Out and Touch*.' There was unanimous approval. "That's it, that's it, that's it!" I said, gleefully.

We were going to need the support of some big celebrity names. Someone suggested Diana Ross because she sang the song of the same title, but there was little enthusiasm for her. Someone else suggested Madonna, but again, there was only a lukewarm response. The names kept flowing: Roberta Flack... Cher... Jennifer Holliday...Madonna, again! Then Martin, my community outreach colleague, mentioned Whitney Houston, but with a big smirk on his face, as if to say, '*Yeah, in our dreams!*' But that was the name that did it for me, without question! We couldn't do better than Whitney. "Whitney Houston is the one!" I announced to the room. They all tittered nervously, as if they expected me to laugh along, because surely I couldn't be serious. However, they soon realised that I was as serious as a heart attack.

"I'm going to get Whitney," I promised them. "I'll get on with that while you try to secure other celebrity endorsements and statements of support. Let's blitz them with requests and hopefully we'll get some support coming back."

I decided to pull together a team of people with relevant experience, to make the *Reach Out and Touch* in my mind a living reality.

From the outset I decided to invite representatives from key partner organisations, including the Terrence Higgins Trust, London Lighthouse, Body Positive and other leading charities. With little to no effort, they all agreed to offer their active support.

I contacted Peter Tatchell, who back in early 1987 had been responsible for organising the UK's first candlelit vigil. Peter was very keen on the idea, but immediately suggested that the participants carry flowers rather than candles, as it was to be a daytime event. This made perfect sense to me.

The event was now going to be titled *Reach Out and Touch HIV/AIDS Vigil*, tagged with *Procession with Flowers*, as a sub-heading.

In a matter of days I had assembled the planning team needed to deliver a well-organised and memorable event. The proposed plan was for the procession to assemble at Hyde Park and make its way to Trafalgar Square, where the flowers would be inserted into nets that would then be hoisted up, as if to make a giant wall of flowers. The remaining flowers would be laid out, like a vast carpet. There would be a stage for speeches and a gospel choir, both at Hyde Park and Trafalgar Square.

Once the content of the day was clear, I set about costing it. I would need twenty thousand pounds to make it happen. Tapping into my client-related money was out of the question; this had to be new money. Getting donations from wealthy celebrities seemed like the only answer. My outreach team, namely Martin, Beverley, Ashgar, and their active troupe of volunteers, wrote off to many of them. Most were sympathetic and offered endorsements, but none were willing to donate cash.

My sister Beverley suggested that I write to a leading male pop superstar, but I dismissed the idea at first, thinking that it too would be fruitless. However, after realizing that I had nothing to lose, I wrote to him and he completely knocked me out by giving me every penny I needed, and significantly more! I was amazed and deeply grateful. In a matter of days, the precious cheque had been biked to my office and was in my hands. I had been saved! I immediately responded to the enclosed private letter by sending him my heartfelt thanks but thought that I'd push my luck and ask for a copy of his then CD. To my delight, a copy landed on my desk the very next day, autographed in gold ink with a kiss. That very special angelic star was George Michael, and the CD was Listen Without Prejudice. He was still *in the closet* as a gay man at the time but trusted me. He was making wonderful hit music and could have kept his cash and secrets to himself, but we were on the same page regarding HIV and he wanted to put his money where his heart was. He would support future projects too, and I'd be eternally grateful. I love you, George!

George: A last Christmas in 2016 and true freedom would be his...

Martin, in his typical sarcastic style, reminded me: "Er, so how's Whitney doing today, Vernal?"

"*Oh yes, Whitney!*" I responded, thumping my desk in readiness to get on with that task. He laughed, but I didn't. It was time to get Whitney on board.

I had a large 3' x 5' poster of Whitney Houston on my living room wall at Cornwall Road. I also had a number of her recordings. Her latest CD, 'I'm Your Baby Tonight', featured one of my favourite tracks by the star, 'All the Man I Need'. The song was originally recorded by soulful disco diva, Linda Clifford, and later, by fellow disco stars, Sister Sledge of *We Are Family* fame. Whitney had applied her vocal magic to the already beautiful lyric and transformed the sweet ballad into yet another chart-topping Platinum seller, to add to the zillions she already had.

After a little bit of digging, in the days before the internet, I obtained a telephone number for Nippy Inc from Arista Records in New York; the number was conveniently printed on the label of my target's recordings. 'Nippy' was the name of Whitney's management company and was originally her childhood nickname.

I phoned the company and got through to an irritated receptionist who did her very best to get rid of me. She repeatedly asked me to explain who I was and why I was bothering her. Eventually, she had to accept that I wasn't going away:

"Okay, okay, hang on, Mr Scott. I'll put you through to someone who should be able to help you." I held my breath. There then followed a considerable pause, during which I feared I had been cut off. Then there was a click, and I heard a female voice say, "This is Donna Houston, may I help you?"

I gave the lady with the same surname as my superstar quarry a hearty greeting and swiftly explained my purpose in calling. The muted response confirmed that she was unimpressed. Growing impatient, this other Ms Houston asked patronisingly: "So, why on Earth would Whitney want to do an event like that?" Having got this far, I wasn't going to be put off. I again explained what the event was about, and why I felt Whitney's presence would have a positive impact on the participants, especially the children and young people. I pressed on, "And it would forever associate Whitney's name with one of the greatest challenges facing the human race today."

"Oh, okay. By the way, I'm Whitney's sister-in-law." Donna seemed a little less hostile now. She asked, "There will be children at this event?" I replied that there would indeed be children there. I added that I wasn't looking for Whitney to sing, but simply to speak about how she felt about the AIDS challenge.

"Hmm, I don't know Mr Scott. I certainly cannot promise anything. I tell you what, fax me the information and I'll talk to Whitney and see what she thinks." I said that her sympathetic consideration was all that I could ask and that I was grateful for it.

"Call me back this time next week and I'll have an answer for you, but don't build your hopes up because I don't think Whitney will want to participate. She may send an endorsement, at best."

The phone went down in my ear and that was that. My Exegesis-style optimism was flagging somewhat, but, nonetheless, I faxed the best and most beguiling letter of invitation I could muster to Whitney via Donna. That's all I could do.

The day's programme and logistics began to take shape. As well as arranging some supporting celebrities, I booked some HIV/AIDS activists to speak. I was particularly keen to ensure that we heard directly from men and women with AIDS on the day; Reach Out and Touch was about them. I went through my client lists and approached several people whom I thought would be happy to speak at the event. A good number of them agreed.

William 'Bill' Wilcox, a talented artist and former attendee of the People's Group was commissioned to paint a backdrop for the stage. On a recommendation we then found a company that would organise the staging, lighting and sound. Someone from Body Positive then helped us with our recruitment drive for volunteers; we needed a couple hundred of them for the day itself. The police were also consulted, and they agreed to provide a sufficient number of officers on the day, based upon our guesstimate of possible numbers.

A good gospel choir was essential as far as I was concerned, but I didn't want it to be a religious service. My sister, Beverley, recommended a choir that she felt would deliver the goods. The choirmaster was a very agreeable black man named Errol, who was eager to participate. I gave him a shortlist of the songs I wanted the choir to sing at the event: 'Reach Out and Touch (Somebody's Hand)', 'Lean on Me', and a ballad version of Sylvester's 'You Make Me Feel Mighty Real'. He said immediately that the Sylvester song wasn't acceptable, but he agreed that the other two were fine. I didn't argue and the choir was booked.

Wendy, a very keen Scottish designer, did an excellent job on the artwork for the *Reach Out and Touch* poster and newspaper copy. To my surprise, a member of the planning group from the Terrence Higgins Trust asked why there had to be black hands in the design. It was explained to him that HIV and AIDS were cross-cultural issues and the poster was intended to reflect that reality. Everyone else was happy with the design and we agreed to have buttons and badges produced using the same design.

Everything was falling into place, but what about Whitney?

The day arrived to phone Donna Houston back. She sounded like a changed person and her enthusiasm caught me off guard: "Hey, Vernal, how are you doing today?" In that very moment I knew that I'd secured Whitney Houston. I just knew it. Donna continued: "Whitney really loves the idea of *Reach Out and Touch* and would love to meet with you to discuss it further when she's next in London."

Reach Out and Touch was to coincide with Whitney's 'I'm Your Baby Tonight' UK Tour; specifically, her dates at Wembley Arena. Donna and I agreed Sunday 15th of

September 1991 as the date for Whitney's appearance at *Reach Out and Touch*. Result!!!

The smile on my face risked splitting it in two, but, of course, I kept my professional cool. Before saying goodbye, Donna told me that I would next hear from Robyn Crawford and/or Regina Brown, Whitney's personal assistant, and publicist, respectively. When I put the phone down I could not contain myself and let out a very audible "*Yes*!!!" God himself must have heard it. I had done it, so I thought!

Martin and Beverley went crazy when I called them to my office to tell them the news. Martin was especially amazed that I had managed to deliver on my word. "Whitney! Vernal's got Whitney!" he kept repeating, while fanning his flushed face. "No", I said, "We've got Whitney!"

They were both given strict instruction to not tell anyone else, not even other colleagues at the Centre. I had promised Donna that the singer's name would not appear in any pre-publicity because, as she explained, "Whitney did not want her crazy fans ruining the event". She added that Whitney wanted to attend the event, not as a superstar, but as a concerned individual, though she would speak. I wasn't entirely happy that I couldn't publicise her appearance, but I wasn't about to do anything that would ruin my chance of securing one of the biggest stars in the world for my event.

I was truly overjoyed, and over the moon and stars, too. Of course I told a few personal friends; I couldn't help myself. Some secret, huh! Wow, I've got Whitney!!!

A week later and I'd finally calmed myself down enough to read and approve the final draft of what would be the *Reach Out and Touch* event poster, which read:

'*Reach Out and Touch, UK HIV/AIDS Vigil and Procession with Flowers*; Sunday 15th September 91. Removing the stigma: A gathering of all those who have been touched by HIV and AIDS in the company of friends, lovers, colleagues, celebrities and guest speakers. Your active participation will help remove the stigma and make this special event a powerful statement of remembrance, support and unity with the men, women and children who are living and have lived with HIV disease (includes AIDS). Join us. Carry a flower in remembrance, support and unity. Speakers' Corner, Hyde Park – Guest and celebrity programme 5pm. Arrival at Trafalgar Square approx 6.45pm. Final guest and celebrity programme and placing of flowers'.

At the bottom of the poster, in small print, it read: Make this world a better place as well as:

'Initiated and co-ordinated by the Brent HIV Centre and supported by Body Positive, London Lighthouse, Black HIV/AIDS Network, Terrence Higgins Trust, Positively Women, Panos Institute, National AIDS Trust, Standing Conference on Drug Abuse, Scottish AIDS Monitor, Names Project UK, AIDS Helpline (Northern Ireland), Welsh Voluntary AIDS Forum, Mainliners, Positive Irish Action on AIDS, Landmark, Food Chain, and Turning Point, amongst others.'

I had recently been invited to lunch at London Lighthouse in the presence of HRH Diana, Princess of Wales. She was her usual stunning self as she stepped from her lavish car. She sent a letter of support, but we could not secure permission to use it on the poster. I had similar problem obtaining consent from the event's financial backer, so the final poster went to print without a mention of a single one of the event's most significant supporters.

Suddenly it was September. Whitney and her entourage were in town for her sell-out 'I'm Your Baby Tonight' stint at Wembley. As planned, I took a number of phone calls from Robyn Crawford, her personal assistant, and Regina Brown, her publicist. We arranged to meet together with Whitney a few days before Reach Out at the venue of the event, Hyde Park. I was told that Whitney was keen to meet me and I was keen to meet her, too! Pinch me, somebody!

On the agreed date I arrived at the Park Superintendent's office. The Superintendent welcomed Martin and me. He seemed happy enough with the arrangements we had submitted. Just then his phone rang and he announced the arrival of our VIP Party. *Wow, Whitney was here*! Martin started to fan himself with his hand.

We rose to our feet as two gorgeous black women entered the room, followed by a stern-looking white man. With pristine Colgate smiles, the women introduced themselves as Robyn Crawford and Regina Brown. The man was David Roberts, Whitney's principal bodyguard, who offered his hand curtly. *But where's Whitney?* I asked myself.

As we settled down, I sized up our company. Regina was pretty and petite, and took out a notebook. Robyn was clearly the boss; very tall, and wearing a smart trouser suit. Her physical presence was rather masculine, sitting with her feet flat on the ground and knees apart, but her manner was warm and confident. Robyn immediately looked me in the eye and declared, "Vernal, it's a real pleasure to meet you. We had you checked out and we know you're cool." I cocked my head, trying to work out what she meant, but abandoned this and instead outlined the rationale behind *Reach Out and Touch* and Whitney's critical role.

Robyn leaned toward me, saying: "Vernal, I tell you, I've been walking with Whitney for a long time, and rarely have I seen her as excited as she is about Reach Out and Touch". I said "Wow, thank you!" I added that it was a real pleasure to meet them and asked after Whitney. I was worried by her absence. Robyn explained: "Whitney wanted to come, but she's tired from the flight and needed to rest up before her show at Wembley tonight. She's really looking forward to meeting you on Sunday." Me too, I responded quickly, before moving on to discuss detailed arrangements about policing, crowd control and the hired truck-stage.

At this point, David Roberts, speaking with a definite British accent, interjected. He had looked less than happy throughout the meeting: "Are you trying to tell me this entire event is going to take place on the back of a truck? No way!" He was not at all impressed.

To my relief Robyn completely ignored him and asked me to continue, however, I wanted David on board too, and tried to reassure him that this wasn't a stadium concert, but a series of speeches and a few songs by a choir. A mobile stage was more than adequate for that purpose. David said nothing and I couldn't read whether I'd convinced him or not. "Ooh, a choir!" Regina exclaimed. I liked Regina, but I loved Robyn, she was wonderfully bewitching. The woman had 'it' in every department and I was drawn to her like a magnet.

As we concluded the meeting, Robyn warned, "By the way, Vernal, please don't 'big up' Whitney when you meet her. Treat her just like anybody else. She's a very down-to-earth person, nothing like all that stuff you see in the media."

'How on Earth am I going to treat Whitney Houston like an ordinary Jane Doe?' I asked myself. Hell, I would do my best.

"AIDS is very close to our hearts," Robyn confided, "Whitney wants to do her part."

My affinity with Robyn increased by the second; she was super cool, and we were on the same wavelength, perhaps in more ways than one.

I turned my attention back to David, who was patently uneasy. "Is that a British accent that I detect, David?" I asked, in the hope that this downer of a man would lighten up.

"Yes, I used to be a British policeman, many, many moons ago, but I've been working for Whitney for a few years now," he said, proudly. For a moment I thought I saw the suggestion of a smile behind his moustache, but I wasn't sure.

"Don't worry about David, Vernal," Regina chuckled sweetly. "He's never happy." David just shrugged.

Robyn piped up, "Will you be coming to the show at Wembley, Vernal? We hope so - we have four tickets for you for Friday, if that's OK?"

Martin answered for me. "Great, we'd love to!"

We parted with hugs for Robyn and Regina, and a handshake for a slightly more relaxed looking David. They soon left the park in a very ordinary people carrier. Martin and I returned to my car buzzing, as if with an electrical charge. Martin's face, always the barometer of his emotional state, was a glowing pink. "Robyn's a dyke, Vernal, Robyn's a dyke!" he burst out. That was his way of complimenting Robyn.

"Stop it!" I said, smiling at his child-like excitement.

"I swear that woman is as gay as picnic basket on Hampstead Heath!" He insisted, fanning himself. "Only Mike Tyson would sit like that... or a dyke".

"Stop it!" I insisted, trying unsuccessfully to conceal my amusement. "I think you mean she might be a Lesbian! We don't know that, and either way, I think she's pretty fantastic. Super cool." I enthused, and I meant it. Her sexuality was none of my business, and it wasn't Martin's, either.

"Come on, Vernal. We both know what she meant when she said she'd been *walking* with Whitney a long time." He continued. "Open your eyes: Robyn is Whitney's '*woman-friend!*'"

"If that's the case, then Whitney's got great taste. Now change the subject." I insisted. As I put my foot to the pedal, we looked at each other and in unison cried: "We've got Whitney!!!" To which Martin appended, "And she's one of us!"

As the event approached, my management back at the town hall wanted to know the identity of the 'secret major celebrity' that the press was guessing at. Some of the media speculated that it was Princess Diana – and I dearly wished that she could have joined us on the day, but Kensington Palace wrote to say she was unavailable. I put the town hall off the scent with a vague reply and they didn't press me further, thankfully.

Most of the press interest in Reach Out and Touch had been generated by Peter Tatchell, who took responsibility for that task. He was fantastic, especially given that he was having a bit of a rough time himself due to his 'outing' of hypocritical closet gays whom he believed had used their positions to attack other lesbians and gays. I fully supported him.

On the Friday, two days before Reach Out, Robyn called to say hello but not much else. She wanted to know how I was, and said that Whitney said hi, and was looking forward to meeting me. All very jolly, but I suspected something was wrong. We went over a few practical issues that I thought we had already covered at our meeting. She was double-checking, for her own purposes, I guessed.

Ten minutes later and my phone rang again. This time it was Regina: "Hi Vernal. How are you today, sweetheart?" Oh *God*, my heart started sinking. Something was up!

I prepared myself for the worst, even as I replied, "Fine, thank you. I just heard from Robyn a few minutes ago."

"I know," she said. Niceties dispensed with, she got to the point – perhaps the point that Robyn had wanted to make? "Have you heard any rumours about Whitney?" Regina asked.

I thought for a moment. I was honest and said, "Do you mean speculation about her being pregnant or about her sexuality?"

"Yes," Regina replied. "What do you think about all of that?"

"Regina, in all honesty, I don't consider Whitney's private life to be any of my business, or that of anyone associated with *Reach Out and Touch*."

Clearly, I'd given the right answer, judging by Regina's relieved tone. "That's exactly right, Vernal! It ain't nobody's business but hers! See you at the concert tonight, honey." And with that, she was gone.

In the next few minutes, I let my seldom-seen 'RAT' from before Exegesis get the better of me and decided to remove

Peter Tatchell as a speaker at the Hyde Park; just in case his presence was causing Whitney and her people to be anxious. I didn't feel at all good about it, but I called him and explained that I was worried about losing her. Peter's reaction was typically gracious, and he said he was fine about it. My decision still causes me regret to this day because Peter was, and is, a true personal hero of mine. He had worked tirelessly to make *Reach Out* the success I now expected it to be. I reassigned his speech to Trafalgar Square – after Whitney's planned departure.

That evening I took my seat at Wembley Arena. Martin and two other lucky members of my staff were there too. Martin and I both spotted Robyn at the same time; she was in the orchestra pit and appeared to be supervising some last minute issues in advance of Whitney taking to the stage. As she scanned the audience, I waved frantically to get her attention and she responded with a generous smile and formed the peace 'V' sign wither fingers.

Not too long later, Whitney, looking gorgeous, made a fabulous entrance. Her set included 'How Will I Know', 'I'm Your Baby Tonight', 'All the Man I Need' and 'Where Do Broken Hearts Go', and the totally awesome, I Wanna Dance With Somebody (Who Loves Me). Her mother, Cissy Houston, was there too, sadly, with a bandaged ankle. She joined her daughter on stage her gospel segment, where they performed together a medley called 'He/I Believe'. Whitney closed the segment with 'This Day'; kneeling on the stage when standing prevented her from delivering the precise note she was determined to reach – and she succeeded. It was very moving and a personal highlight for me. I was astounded by the depth and power of Whitney's voice. It was open, selfless and raw. 'My Name Is Not Susan' was the low point of the show for me – I just hated that song, but it wasn't as bad as the exaggerated kiss-a-thon between Bobby Brown and Whitney during her signature, 'Saving All My Love For You'. I ignored Martin's comments about "Poor Robyn", though that kiss was the least convincing performance of the evening. Who the hell invited him, I thought to myself.

Whitney was on great form. That amazing voice sounded almost as good as her mother's, but not quite! Cissy had dabbled in pop and disco in the past, indeed I owned a couple of her albums; namely, Think It Over and Step Aside For a Lady, which were very fine, mostly disco recordings. Cissy's roots were pure gospel, and her superstar daughter had been nurtured the same way, but Whitney had been 'constructed' by Clive Davis' Arista machine to please the pop market, and it worked, big time! Where Cissy's career faltered, Whitney's had soared to heights matched only by the likes of Diana Ross and Madonna. She was now the pop superstar that her aging and 'too black-sounding' mother could never be. I would struggle to name many white performers who could sing as well as Cissy, but, like many other fine black artists, she just could not break into a white-focused pop industry. Some would say it was racist. Impressive artists like Merry Clayton, Mavis Staples, and Gwen McCrae suffered a similar fate; theirs were voices that deserved to be at the top of the pop charts, but never were.

Whitney put on a good, if not brilliant show; very slick and professional. It was especially good to finally set my eyes on Whitney herself, live and in person!

Regina called me at home the next day, to ask how I was, and to get my thoughts on the show. I said I loved it, of course. She said that she'd never heard Whitney sing with such passion as she did during the gospel set, and I agreed.

I asked whether Whitney had received the package I'd sent to her hotel, which included a Reach Out and Touch T-shirt and badge, or "button", as Regina called it. Before we said goodbye, I asked that she give my love and thanks to Whitney and Robyn, and she said she would.

Sunday 15th of September arrived and it turned out to be a beautiful late summer's day. I donned a crisp white shirt and patterned tie, screwed up my courage, and took the tube to Hyde Park Corner; the rallying point for the event. I wondered whether anyone would even bother to turn up, but when I reached the entrance to the park my fears completely evaporated. There were so many many people! Among them were dotted *Reach Out and Touch* stewards, with their bright yellow jackets and badges.

Martin spotted me and rushed forward. "Vernal, we did it! Look at all these people!" It looked as if our expensive advert in the national press had paid off. We had advertised in Ireland, Scotland, Wales and England. We also advertised in 'community' press, including the gay press. Yes, we had done it, but the voice in my head still cast doubts: *"Are all these people really here for Reach Out, or just a sunny day in the park?"* I then noticed the flowers in every hand; it was confirmation that people in their hundreds or more were here for Reach Out and Touch; my big event, our event!

As we approached the mobile stage erected especially for the event, my excitement built; no nerves, just excitement. Bill Wilcox's hand-painted backdrop truly looked the part in the bright sunshine. The press enclosure at the front of the stage was filling with expectant photographers and eager journalists. I greeted Peter Tatchell, who had kindly agreed to stage manage the day. I also gave a warm greeting to my wider team and the choir master and his thirty-strong choir. Everybody was wearing a Reach Out t-shirt, badge and a smile. Nyisha, Bunny's gorgeous daughter, was there too. I couldn't persuade her dad to come, but I knew he was with us in spirit and that his daughter would tell him all about it later. This was going to be a great day. Everything was in place and everyone was doing what they were supposed to do. I was happy.

The crowd continued to swell; many hundreds were already standing in front of the stage, flowers in hand. People carrying flowers and banners streamed into the park from all directions. Coaches had brought people from Scotland, Wales, Ireland, and beyond. *Reach Out and Touch* had struck a nerve beyond the borough of Brent; it was a nerve that knew no national boundaries. This wasn't a small candlelit vigil held at night; it was an in-your-face, wake up and *see* people with HIV and AIDS and their supporters, daytime event! And I'm sure the participants were feeling what my team and I were feeling; a need to show that we cared by standing, openly, in the light of day, with those directly affected by this crisis. The idea had originated in my heart, and before my eyes, it was becoming an amazing reality. *Reach Out and Touch* might, or might not, make the world a better place for people living with HIV and AIDS, but it was a very public spectacle, bearing witness to personal battles with HIV and AIDS, to loved ones already lost to AIDS, and those they feared losing in the hours, days, weeks, months and years ahead. Perhaps, I reflected, we hadn't needed to mention Whitney in the publicity after all. The reverie suddenly broke. *"Whitney should be here by now,"* I heard myself say out loud.

The Brent HIV Centre had one mobile phone; a huge brick-like thing that was invented in the days before the elegant smartphones that would follow it in the years ahead. We had it with us in case of an emergency, and as I was thinking the worse, it rang. It was David Roberts, saying that they were working their way through heavy traffic but were well on their way. He estimated that they would be in the park within another ten to fifteen minutes. That's what I needed to hear; Whitney was on her way! It was my cue to get the choir master to kick off with our title song 'Reach Out and Touch Somebody's Hand', and the thirty-plus gospel choir did absolute justice to the lyric. It was the right song with the right choir at the right event. Emotions filled the faces of the people at the front of the stage, and among them, I could see many of our service users. I made a point of waving to them from the side of the stage.

Once the poignant song was over, I took to the stage to welcome the diverse and ever-increasing crowd. "Thank you for coming and welcome to Reach Out and Touch." I said:

"My name is Vernal Scott, the proud coordinator of today's event and manager of the Brent HIV Centre. You've come from Scotland, Wales and different parts of England. You've come from other European countries and beyond. Thank you. We are gay, we are heterosexual, we are bisexual. We are black, white, Asian and every other race. We are older and younger, mothers and fathers, sisters and brothers, lovers and friends. Whoever we are, wherever we live, and however we identify ourselves, we are united by HIV and AIDS, and we've come out of the dark and into the light today in remembrance, support and unity with our loved ones who have lived and are living with HIV and AIDS".

Peter Tatchell came over and whispered in my ear, "Ask them to hold their flowers in the air," which I did. I gasped a little at the sight of the sea of flowers which suddenly added immense colour to the sunny skyline. It was a wonderful, compelling sight. Peter gestured for the photographers to come onto the stage to get better pictures and what sounded to me like a million cameras then clicked away, all competing for the best shot that would grace tomorrow's newspapers.

I then invited our guest speakers to address the crowd. BBC broadcaster Bill Buckley spoke very eloquently about his commitment to the HIV/AIDS challenge, and why he wanted to show his support. The *London's Burning* actor, Treva Ettienne, spoke about the risks to heterosexuals. UK soul singer Ruby Turner and Carrol Thompson of Positively Women, spoke about the experience of women and children affected by HIV and AIDS. Jonathan Grimshaw, Manager of The Landmark Centre in South London, and another personal hero of mine, spoke about the experience of gay men living with HIV, as he was.

The speeches then paused for a heartfelt rendition of 'Lean on Me', the Bill Withers' classic. Many in the crowd were emotional and tearful at this point. Arms linked with arms, tearful eyes sought comforting shoulders, and lips kissed precious loved faces, and all the while holding their flowers in the air. It felt like a religious service, even though religion of the God kind was absent, by my own hand. In our crisis the religions of faith had mostly added to our pain and they were not welcome here today. Frankly, the evidence of what was before my eyes was confirmation that we knew how to love each other without people of faith showing us how. Indeed, we could show them a thing or two about love, and Sister Whitney was on her way to help us out.

We were still awaiting Whitney's arrival, so I asked the choir to sing our title tune again, while I left the stage to get an update from Martin. He told me that they were still five minutes away, so I asked the choir master to keep it up and the ever increasing crowd didn't seem to mind at all.

Just two minutes later and a blue people carrier pulled up to the rear of the stage. Whitney had arrived, finally!

David Roberts and his all-black team of burly security guards appeared out of nowhere and assembled themselves backstage. David greeted me, but Whitney was not stepping out of her vehicle until he was satisfied that he had his people in all the right places. With a nod from David, everything was set in motion.

With the choir singing their hearts out at the front of the stage, and the crowd holding their flowers high, Regina, Robyn, and Whitney emerged. Robyn and I exchanged a kiss, as did Regina and I.

Robyn then quickly introduced me to a shy but totally stunning Whitney, who greeted me with a warm "Hello, hello" and a kiss to each cheek. For a moment Whitney reminded me of a skinny teenage girl who was wearing make-up for the first time. She had a small rash of spots on her cheeks, but looked even lovelier, and a lot younger, than her publicity photos suggested. She also had a darkened front tooth, which never showed in her photos. But she was still gorgeous, and standing there smiling at me. I noticed she was wearing the event badge that I'd sent to her hotel, but she'd evidently decided against wearing the T-shirt.

I said, "Thank you so much for coming, it's very kind of you to give your time in this way."

With a smiling Robyn standing by her side, Whitney responded warmly: "Vernal, I wouldn't miss being here for the world. I really, really wanted to be here. Thank you for inviting me", her voice sounding as sincere as in her recordings. She actually blushed.

I shook off my star-struck daze, and quickly introduced Whitney and her inner circle to some of the people responsible for making the day happen. Then, the seemingly shy star, conscious of the audience, put her hand on my shoulder and said, "Okay, let's do it, Vernal!"

With that, Whitney, Robyn, Regina and I ascended the steps to the wings of the mobile stage. The choir was finishing up on another round of Lean On Me, as we waited. Robyn and Whitney linked arms and whispered to one another. They were clearly very close. I took the opportunity to thank Whitney for the tickets to her show.

"It was wonderful," I said, "And to see you singing with your mother... I've been a fan since my teens - her Think It Over album. Whitney laughed. 'Oh, you liked that!?'

"Yes", I said, "very much indeed" I added that I knew she sang in the backing vocals on that album, to which she chuckled, "Yes, but don't tell nobody!"

She then looked at me seriously. "Did you really like the show?"

"You're the best of the best. I especially loved your performance of 'This Day'."

She smiled at me, saying "thank you so much", and hugged Robyn, as if to take comfort from her, or perhaps to make something of a statement about their closeness. I began to see where the rumours about their alleged relationship had come from, but I thought they looked sweet together. *"Screw the rumours; live your life, girl!"*

As the choir wound up, Whitney unfolded some handwritten notes for her speech. I had offered to compose some words for her, but Regina told me "Whitney knew what she wanted to say" I was impressed, and said so.

Now was the moment for me to take the microphone. I could at last let my big secret out. I smiled at Bill Buckley and Ruby Turner, who were standing at the far end of the stage with Treva.

"Thank you again for coming to Reach Out and Touch, Europe's biggest rally and march in support of men, women and children who are living with and who have lived with HIV and AIDS. We also come to together in support of the people who love and care for them." I paced my address, making sure every word was clear. "We're in this battle for our lives together. Look around you, you are not alone."

"Our guest of honour could be anywhere in the world that she wants to be, but she has chosen to be here with you, with us, to put her name to this event and to this challenge: the fight for a cure and for human rights for people with AIDS. Please join me in giving a warm UK welcome to none other than our greatest love of all, Miss Whitney Houston!"

Whitney emerged to a thunderous uproar of applause from a crowd now numbering in the thousands. People were ecstatic at the unexpected appearance of the pop and soul diva. I backed away from the mic, but Whitney flung open her arms and folded me in them. I was in a full body hug with the one and only Whitney Elizabeth Houston, and she meant it. This was the hug of a lifetime. *Now this is Whitney Houston,* I thought to myself. The crowd continued to go wild as I joined Robyn at the side of the stage. Whitney waved enthusiastically to the hordes, calling out a hearty, "Hello, hello!" But the crowd wasn't ready to stop applauding her just yet. She was on our side. Yes!

(**Note**: Original video footage of Reach Out and Touch can be viewed at www.VernalScott.com or You Tube courtesy of Sky News ©). It can also be seen in the extensive 2015 ITV biopic, Whitney and Bobby: Addicted to Love. The latter includes an interview with Vernal Scott.)

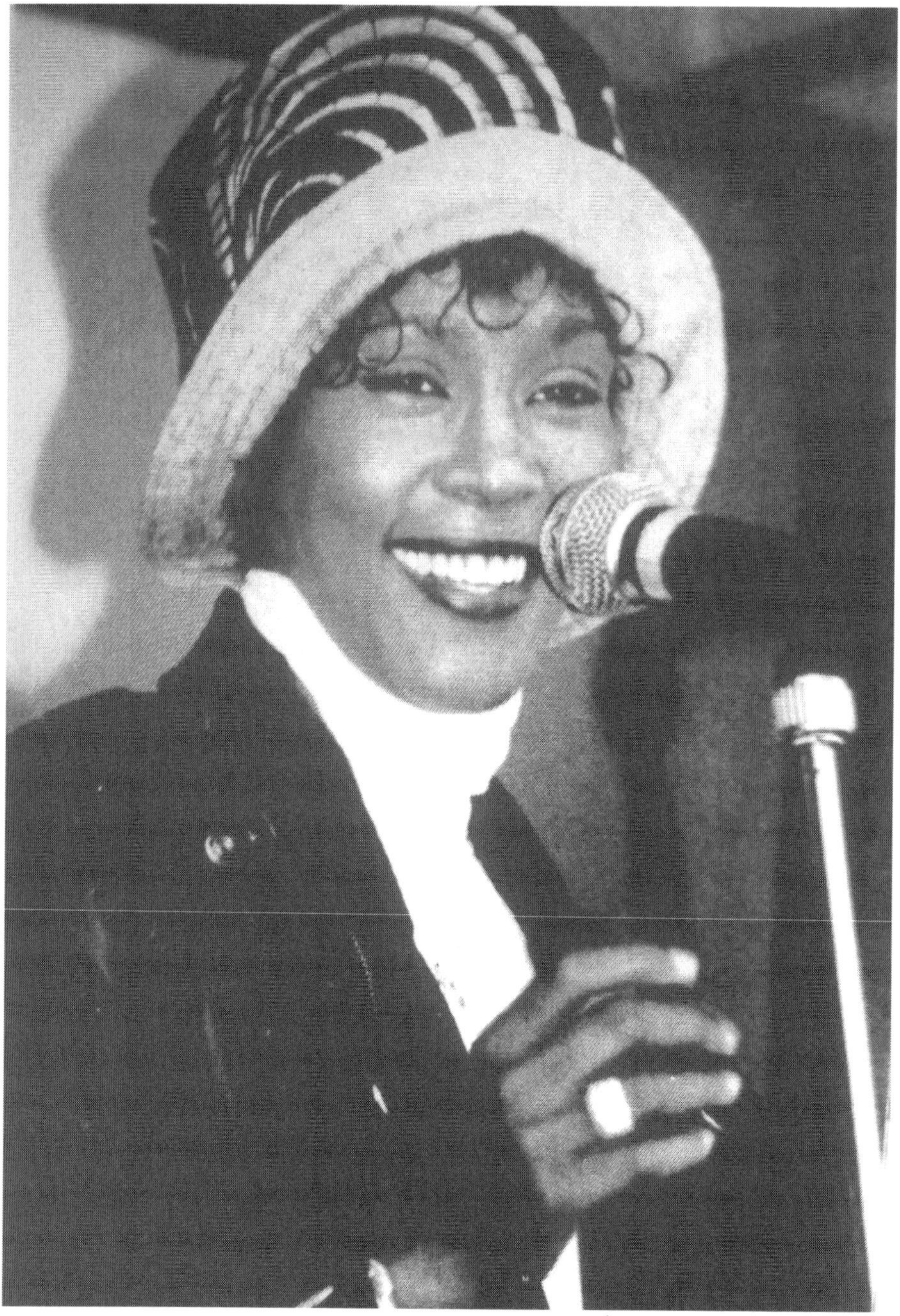

God's Other Children: A London Memoir   345

After a while the cheering subsided and Whitney was able to be heard. Speaking with great conviction, she said:

"Hello, hello, hello! God bless you all. It is great that you are all here today. I am honored to have been asked to open this event, the Reach Out and Touch Assembly and Procession with Flowers, focusing on those that have been touched by HIV/AIDS, to show support to the thousands of people who are living and the families who have courageously lived alongside their loved ones facing the realities of the disease. Yet, sadly, there is a stigma associated with those afflicted with AIDS. Even as we speak, it is sweeping away our children, our families, our loved ones!" Then, gesturing her remarks with thrusts of her pointed finger: "Our world must continue, through research, to work to find a *cure*."

The crowd erupted into a hurricane of cheering. There was no stopping them this time. *A cure* - that is what we were all hoping and praying for and Whitney tapped into that sentiment.

Our astute guest of honour realised that she had touched an important nerve. She looked elated as she retreated from the mic, waving frantically to the cheering mass before her. She then grabbed the mic again to close with a delightful: "I thank you. Thank you. God bless you and take care!"

I was as ecstatic as the crowd. Whitney's brief address had said it all, and she certainly hadn't needed me to write it for her, and no need for her to sing, either! To my knowledge, the event was her first public statement on HIV/AIDS and she had been the perfect choice.

As had been arranged with Robyn, I now expected Whitney to make a quick exit, to get back to her rehearsals. I gestured to the choir master to start a final round of Reach and Touch. That was the cue for Whitney and me to leave the stage. However, instead, Whitney approached the edge of the stage and then leapt four feet down to the platform below, where the choir was standing together with a large group of now goggle-eyed children. A couple of her bodyguards followed her. Whitney crouched down and flung her arms open. Beckoning the children, they all raced to embrace their pop idol and for a worrying moment she was completely submerged beneath a mass of over-excited little bodies. Frantic photographers added to the chaos and grappled with each other to capture the best shot. Whitney hugged and kissed the children and posed with them to the further delight of the photographers. I then returned to the mic and asked the crowd to lift their flowers to show their support of our purpose; the removal of HIV stigma. "It's all about love," I said, my voice choking with emotion. "That is what this is all about, nothing but love." It was pure magic.

Whitney beckons the children ...

Whitney organizes her instant family

The superstar had come to deliver love, but soon found herself buried under a ton of it. Sadly, she was rescued by her bodyguards; I say sadly, because future tragic events would prompt me to remember this poignant moment, and wish these angelic arms could shield Whitney once again; not from HIV or AIDS, but from herself. If only we could have foreseen her fate, we would have held onto our precious Whitney for longer than we did on that happy September day. If...

Whitney's bodyguards eventually hoisted her back onto the stage. She waved again to the crowd and then accepted a beautiful bouquet from Nyisha, Bunny's daughter, whom she hugged and kissed. I was sorry that Bunny wasn't in the crowd to see his daughter's special moment, but I hoped it might make that evening's TV news. Whitney hugged and kissed me goodbye, and I embraced Robyn and Regina too. Whitney handed me autographed CD covers from her first two albums; she'd signed them 'To Vernal, Love always, Whitney' – with a *smilie*. I was even happier now. Then, the anonymous people carrier whisked Whitney and her team out of the park. Loving hurricane Whitney had passed.

I took a moment to gather my thoughts while Peter Tatchell did the honours and wrapped up proceedings at Hyde Park. He skilfully directed the rally towards the route of procession to the laying of flowers in Trafalgar Square.

Up for air, Whitney regains her composure

God's Other Children: A London Memoir   351

My mega hug from the mega star

BBC London News asked to do a live TV interview, but I was too pressed for time. I did speak briefly with Tim Marshall of Sky News, but I was conscious of needing to keep a close eye on the event. Everything had gone pretty smoothly so far and I wanted to keep it that way.

I joined my cousin Doreene towards the front of the procession-- of more than five thousand people, according to the police – on a dignified, flowery procession to Trafalgar Square. The banner, at the front of the procession, read *Reach Out and Touch People Living with HIV& AIDS*. We were all proud to walk behind it. I took a moment to look behind us and saw an endless sea of flowers. It was a beautiful and very fitting statement of love.

It was dark by the time we reached Trafalgar Square. Peter brilliantly directed the laying of flowers and the square was soon transformed by a carpet of multi-coloured petals. Christopher Spence of London Lighthouse, author Simon Watney, and Peter all addressed the crowd, as did a representative from the World Health Organization. I then took to the mic to thank everyone, but as I began speaking, a young man leaped onto the platform and stood before me with his back to the crowd. He didn't say a word; he just stood there with tears streaming down his face. I didn't know what else to do, so I embraced him. The crowd seemed to sense what was happening and applauded. After a moment, the man climbed back down and disappeared into the mass of faces. That moment said it all for me; it needed no explanation.

Reach Out and Touch was at an end. My team rounded up buckets loaded with cash donations destined for AIDS charities. A few thousand pounds had been raised.

God's Other Children: A London Memoir   353

Only a short while later and I arrived back home at Cornwall Road and closed the door behind me. With the buckets of cash on the hallway floor, I imploded in tears. For the next ten minutes I just lay with my face in the hallway carpet, hollering my heart out. I was grief-stricken; for my family, and for all the thousands of people affected by HIV and AIDS who had turned out for today's event. I was glad that HIV had united so many of us in our fight for survival and dignity, but the price for this momentary show of harmony was far too high. There was nothing good about this disease, nothing! Our losses and pain were too much.

The enormous success of Reach Out and Touch hit me too. I was relieved that I had pulled off an event that had begun as just a thought in my head. I had done it and could now let go of the huge responsibility that had come with all the planning and managing involved, but there was more to my tears than that. I was all alone with my success and that hurt more than anything. I was alone and didn't want to be. I needed a hug or two…or three.

After a while I composed myself and sat down in my living room. There were many voicemails from friends who had seen *Reach Out and Touch* on television. I later took a call from lovely Robyn: "Hey, brother! How are you doing tonight? Whitney is so tired after her show tonight at Wembley, but she wanted me to call to let you know that she was thrilled with how everything went today. We consider you a brother. You can always call on her. We are your sisters".

I said I was so very grateful and asked Robyn to pass on my appreciation and love to Whitney. She added, "Vernal, Whitney wants you to know that you are always welcome to call her, you've got friends you'll never ever lose. Please remember that, brother."

I thanked her again, and said goodnight. I looked at the signed CD covers and I started crying all over again.

The next day the press was full of *Reach Out and Touch* stories. *The Independent* carried a picture of the flower-filled Trafalgar Square on their front page. Whitney's smile graced the inner pages of *The Sun*. Sky News and BBC's *Newsnight* carried footage from Trafalgar Square.

Reach Out and Touch said everything I was feeling about the HIV and AIDS challenge: the pain, the tragedy, the determination, and the joyful confidence of our inevitable triumph; we were in this to win. We had succeeded in taking AIDS out of the shadows and putting it and those affected in the light. *We will survive! We must survive!*

Some days later, once all the excitement about *Reach Out and Touch* had subsided, I returned to my office and reflected upon my meeting with Robyn and Whitney and especially the chemistry of love that was clearly there between the two women. I decided to put pen to paper and addressed my letter to Whitney, copied it separately to Robyn, the wind beneath her wings, as far as I could see. The first thing I said was thank you, and that she should never underestimate the considerable impact her appearance at the event made on all those present, myself included, but I then got the point. I said that her sexuality was nobody's business, and certainly not mine, but that I had a need to let her know that there was nothing to be ashamed of either...but I understood her position. I closed the rather lengthy letter with the words from the gospel song, This Day. The song that she sang on her knees at the concert: "Give us this day our daily bread..."

LGBT people know when we're among 'family' and Robyn and Whitney struck me as a lesbian couple, nothing less. My letter simply said this was mighty fine with me and should be with them, too. I never received a response to that letter but was pleased that I'd said it. Being LGBT should not be subject to shame and I wasn't going to collude with it.

Whitney was now working on her next project; her movie debut, The Bodyguard. I Will Always Love You, the first single from the soundtrack, would go on to become her greatest hit and I would forever associate the song with her appearance at Reach Out and Touch and her hand-written message on the CDs she signed for me.

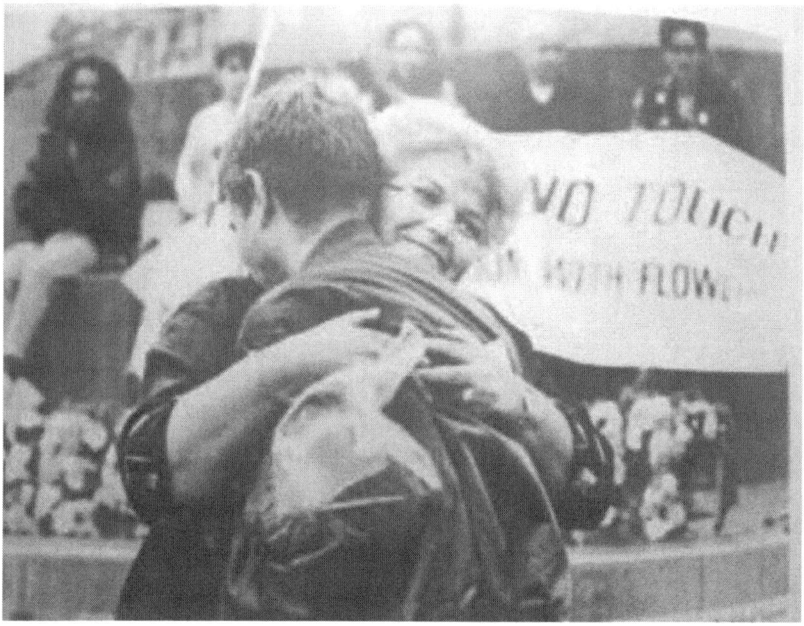

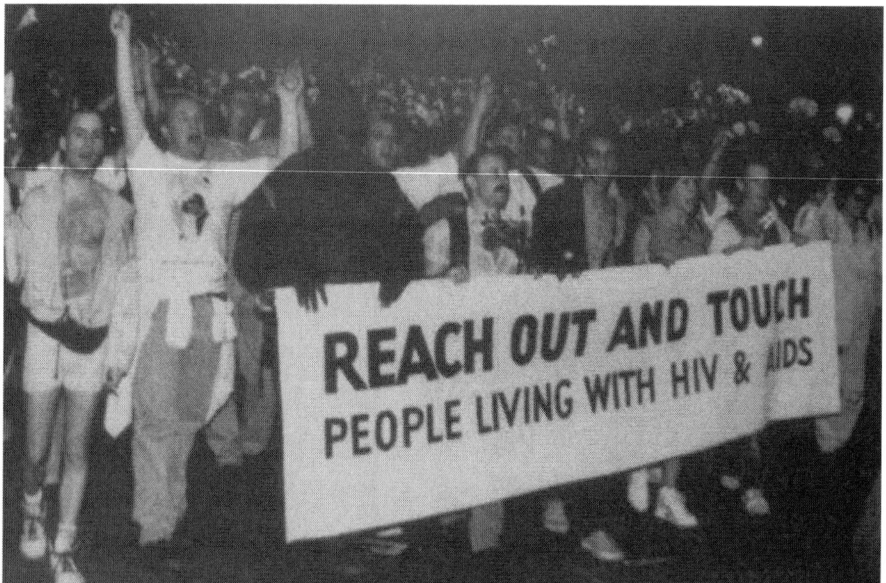
REACH OUT AND TOUCH
PEOPLE LIVING WITH HIV &

God's Other Children: A London Memoir 359

Simon Watney, Christopher Spence (London Lighthouse) and a representative from the World Health Organisation who flew in especially for Reach Out and Touch.

UK HIV & AIDS PROCESSION
WITH FLOWERS
REACH OUT AND TOUCH
PEOPLE LIVING WITH

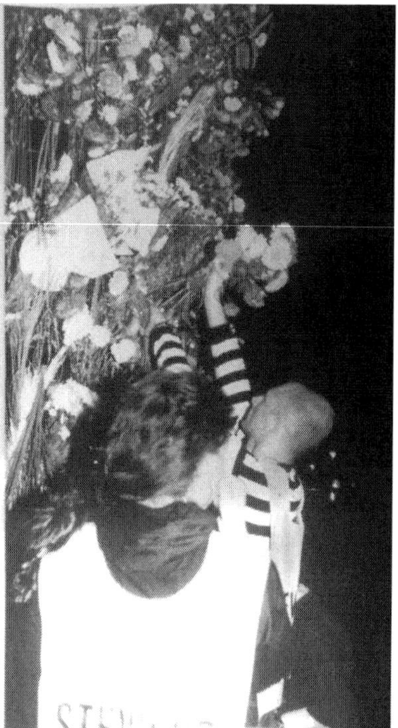

God's Other Children: A London Memoir   361

God's Other Children: A London Memoir   362

Reach Out and Touch wasn't a requirement of my job description, but of my heart. The men, women and children directly affected by HIV and AIDS should now know that they are loved and that our love for them cannot be erased by disease or death. I extend my heartfelt thanks to George Michael, Whitney, Robyn, and everyone who helped to make Reach Out and Touch a stunning success. Love is alive! Vx

God's Other Children: A London Memoir 364

37. SAYING GOODBYE TO LOVE

I WAS IN REGULAR CONTACT with Marvin by phone but could tell from his voice that he was becoming increasingly sick. During one call, he accidentally dropped the phone and had to call for his mother to retrieve it for him. He was weakening by the day. When his cousin called to tell me that he'd been admitted to hospital, the tone of her voice prompted me to immediately make the two hour journey by train to his family home city in the north of England. The city and weather matched my mood; grey and cold. The hospital felt the same, as I wondered its near-deserted corridors until a passing nurse showed me to Marvin's room. On entering, I was shaken by his skeletal appearance. It seemed that there was no torso under the bed covers; just his head, the white pillow it rested upon, and his twig-like arms at his absent sides. On seeing me, his delighted face lit up with his usual smile: "Vernal! You're here!" he enthused. His eyes quickly checked to see if I was still wearing the ring that he'd given me, which, of course, I was. "Well, who were you expecting, Aretha?" I replied in jest. Steadying myself, I went over to embrace Marvin and was careful to not cause further discomfort. It was so deeply special to hold him again, and as I did so I noticed his twin ring, dangling somewhat pathetically on his fleshless wedding finger; I then fully appreciated just how vitally important I had remained to him over the years. Our fond kiss and eager holding of hands confessed the *"I love you!"* secret that was long held safe by our hearts. Later, on my leaving, there was nothing left unsaid between us, and Marvin's beautiful but weary eyes confirmed that he too was now ready to leave.

AIDS claimed Marvin just a day later. I could not face seeing him being buried and decided against going to the funeral, but it was a decision that would haunt me. I should have been there for him, one last time.

Farewell, beautiful black man. Thank you for your love, which will forever live inside my heart. You are, you are... You're now a beautiful angel. Love, Vx

38. HEARTMENDERS - PRINCESS DIANA AND DIONNE

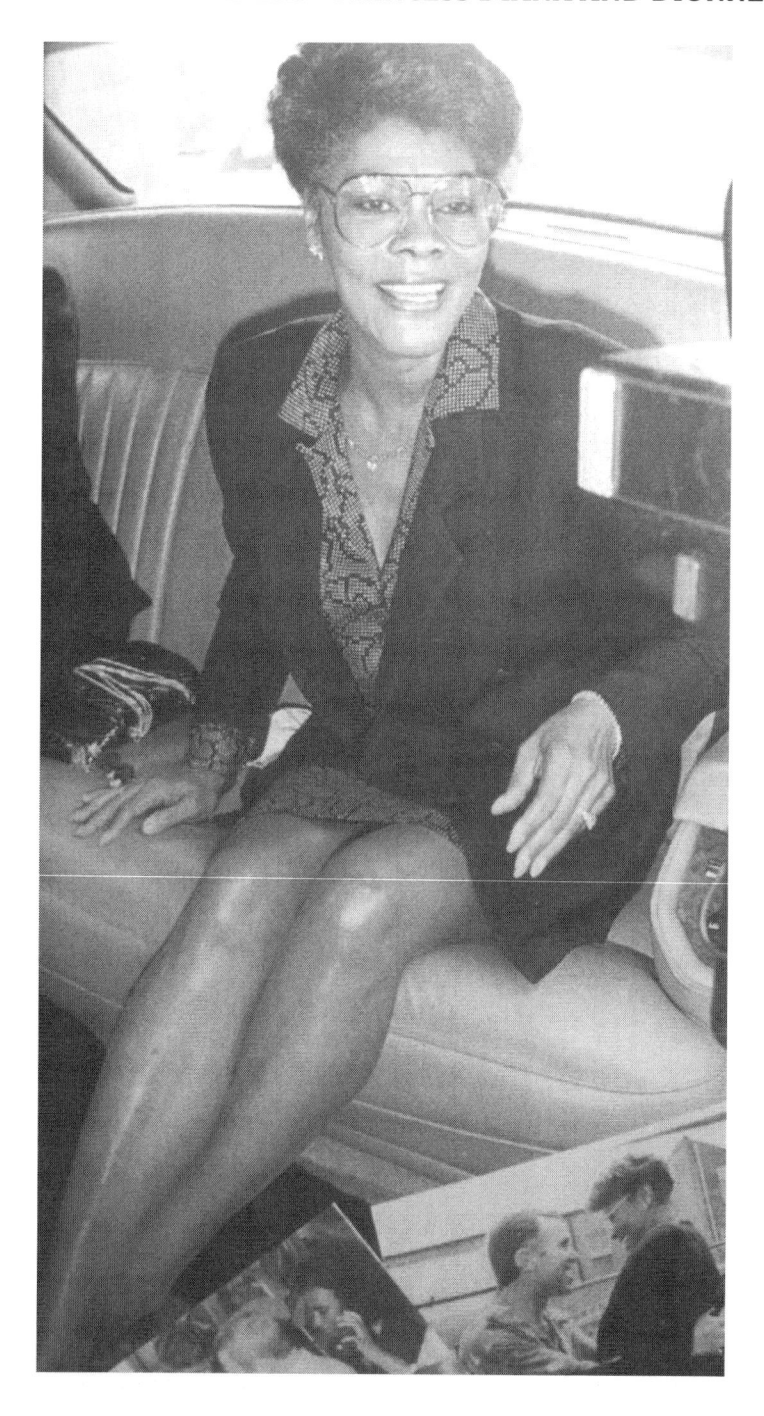

HRH DIANA, PRINCESS OF WALES, was doing an amazing job in working to lessen the stigma associated with HIV/AIDS. I was amongst the delegates at the Children and AIDS Conference, opened by the Princess, on the 22nd of April 1992. Looking her usual beautiful self, she said:

"Publicity about HIV seems to vary between sex and death horror stories at one extreme to complacency at the other. But behind this confused picture lies the reality of a growing world-wide affliction of untold private suffering. HIV does not make people dangerous to know, so you can shake their hands and give them a hug; heaven knows they need it! What's more, you can share their homes, their work places, their playground and their toys. We all need to be alert to the special needs of those for whom AIDS is the last straw in an already heavy burden of discrimination and misfortune. For our children's sake, we need to seize the opportunity to plan our response and organise our defences while we still have time."

Her speech was well received. God knows, we needed Princess Diana on our side in this challenge, especially as so many forces seemed to be against us. It was at this time that sober scientific estimations of the disease's ultimate toll began to be made. The World Health Organization estimated that there would be approximately ten million people with AIDS around the globe, by the year 2000; and that ten million children would be orphaned because of the disease by that time.

The Brent HIV Centre occupied the entire building in Manor Park Road in Harlesden known as Park House. We'd been in existence there for a while but had never had a formal launch. I wanted to put that right and spoke to service users and my management about the idea. They were happy to let me do my thing.

I contacted David Nathan in LA, the writer I met in Bishop Carl Bean's church, and told him that I needed a celebrity to formally launch the Brent HIV Centre. David's was known as the UK ambassador for soul music, and I knew that he was friends with Dionne Warwick, Whitney's cousin, the target of my approach. David was keen to help and it wasn't long before he called back to confirm that "Dionne would be thrilled to open the centre!" We agreed that 2nd June 1992 would be the big day. If Dionne was thrilled then I was ecstatic. She had done a tremendous job in highlighting the need to support people with AIDS. Her hit single, *That's What Friends Are For*, had raised millions for the cause.

Two days before our official opening and the Centre's service users and staff were buzzing in anticipation. To my surprise, my excited receptionist interrupted a meeting I was chairing to tell me that the great lady herself was on the phone for me. I assumed that Dionne knew a little about my work from David Nathan and perhaps Whitney, her cousin, who was now tearing up the charts with her *Bodyguard* debut movie soundtrack. It was a real privilege to chat with her and she sounded as cool as a cat. Ending our conversation, she enthusiastically purred, "Let me take down the address."

To my absolute horror, just a day before Dionne's official opening, I arrived bright and early to discover that the Centre had been burgled overnight. Not only had the thieves taken valuables from the building, but to make some twisted point, they'd defecated on the carpeted floors. I was furious and sickened. I wanted to murder the culprits, if only I could get my hands on them. I called my concerned director, who came straight away to inspect the damage. Fortunately, he also came armed with a pep talk: "Vernal, you and your team have put an enormous amount of work into this project and you shouldn't let yourself be defeated by this incident. The show must go on, you know that!" He was right. We were going to clean up and be ready for tomorrow's official opening. Everyone got to work on the task and by the end of the day it was difficult to spot any damage. The show would indeed go on.

Arriving at the Centre the following morning, I got a start when my disbelieving eyes saw my father get out of a car parked only a few feet from mine. He appeared equally shocked to see me but responded warmly when I said that it was good to see him. Then, impulsively, I invited him to the Centre for the opening with Dionne Warwick, later in the day and he agreed to come. I was so caught up in the moment that I took his arm and led him into the building. After a brief introduction to staff I gave him a quick pre-launch tour before saying goodbye. He promised he would go smarten himself up and return later.

A couple of hours on and everyone, service users and staff, were outside on the sunny pavement, excitedly awaiting the arrival of our delectable lady of song. Inside the building, her greatest hits CD was playing away on the stereo that the thieves had neglected to steal...'That's What Friends Are For' set the mood. Local MPs Paul Boateng and Ken Livingstone – formerly of the GLC and future first mayor of London – joined the entire senior management from Brent Town Hall out on the pavement with the rest of us. On my personal guest list were Graham, my 'Heartbreaker' from the Barbican Centre, who I knew had a soft spot for Dionne, Paul Thurlow, an ever-faithful friend, and photographer Robert Taylor, who was as supportive as any friend could be. With camera in hand, he had kindly agreed to take photos of the day.

Right on time, Dionne's slick golden Rolls Royce cruised into Manor Park Road. Her task was to cut a ribbon across the doorway and have the moment captured by the many press cameras outside. The dignitaries were lined up, including Brent Council's Conservative deputy leader, who was ready to greet Dionne before she cut the ribbon. A small crowd of onlookers gathered on the opposite side of the street to catch a glimpse of the legend as she stepped from her gleaming car. Robert clicked away, as I greeted Dionne and thanked her for coming. With that, I led her straight to the front door, bypassing all the dignitaries I had lined up so carefully earlier. With all the excitement and bustle of people, I had forgotten all about them. Whoops-- a classic 'Walk On By' moment! Anyway, it was too late to go back now; I wasn't keen to make myself look any more foolish than I already had. The dignitaries soon caught up with us, and mingled around as the photographers focused on Dionne chatting with centre clients – whom I wanted to make sure also received star billing.

Dionne pulled a cord to reveal a ceremonial plaque engraved with her name. She was then presented with one of only two *Reach Out and Touch Awards* - the other recipient being Tony Whitehead, chair of the Terrence Higgins Trust. We waited for a lull in the applause for Dionne to say a few words. She started to speak, but then, unexpectedly, paused. After a while she tried to speak again, but again stopped. Something was wrong.

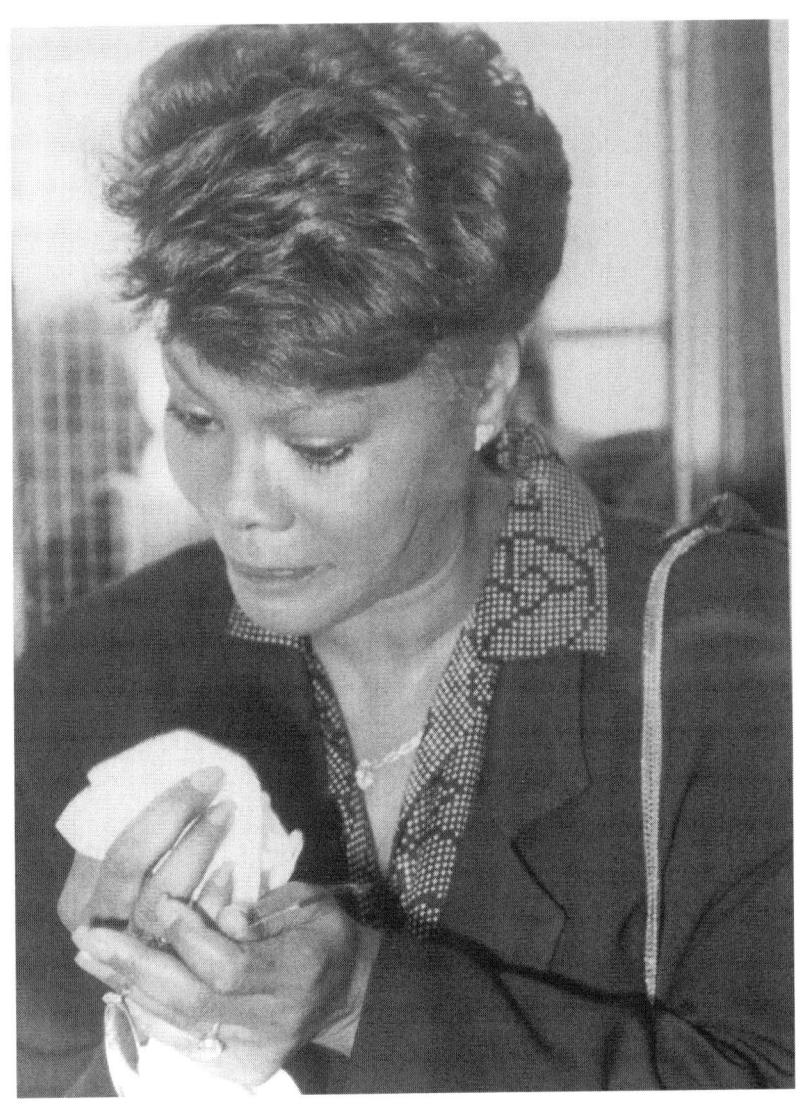

I of course thought she would recover her composure, but that did not happen. Dionne was completely overcome with grief and her emotional tears flowed for all to see. I asked the photographers to stop bustling around and show some sensitivity, but the distressed weeping diva of song provided them a perfect photo opportunity that they were not willing to sacrifice. Dionne's personal assistant didn't react at all, so, without thinking, I spontaneously went over to where she was standing and embraced her, and that's when the floodgates really opened. The legendary lady sobbed aloud in my arms, her body heaving with each emotional wail. It was immediately obvious to me that AIDS was very personal to her; a reminder, if one were needed, that the disease respected no boundaries of wealth or worldly success...Sylvester, Freddie Mercury, Rock Hudson. We were all in this tragic boat together.

Finally, Dionne managed to compose herself. Wiping her tears away, she took a deep breath, and gave a brief, but eloquent address. She then posed for a moment and then, with a generous smile, the now recovered diva of black popular music cut the rippling red ribbon, officially opening the Brent HIV Centre, at last.

Dionne cast a spell of happiness over the place that it had never known before. I introduced her to the MPs, Paul Boateng and Ken Livingstone. Paul Boateng, a fantastic supporter over the years, was as polished as ever. Ken appeared a little tired, but it was great to have him there. Dionne was gracious and was there to meet people with HIV and AIDS, not politicians, so she soon moved on. Before leaving, she kindly autographed my collection of her CDs, including 'Heartbreaker', my personal favourite. In a flash of sunlight, her glistening Rolls Royce whisked her away.

Graham left soon after, but we promised to meet for dinner in the near future. It was great to see him again. He looked as gorgeous as the day I had first set eyes on him at the Barbican Theatre.

My father had not shown up, but I decided not to contact him to ask why. I knew the reason: AIDS. He didn't want to be around it and did not want to be seen with his homosexual son. Well, he was welcome to his shame, which I certainly no longer shared. His cordial facade earlier in the day had been entirely false.

At home that evening I wrote a thank-you note to Dionne Warwick:

"Thank you for the unexpected phone call the day before your visit – after I got over the shock it really did help to sooth my anxiety. You shine a very special light which gracefully touches troubled lives around the globe, bringing with it cascading beams of hope and love. From our hearts, we love and thank you in return. Your friendships and leadership is much appreciated by all of us within the world's HIV/AIDS community. However, I am personally aware of the fact that taking leadership on HIV/AIDS can be a heart-wrenching journey, and there are moments when even the leader is in need of a shoulder upon which to cry. Dionne, please remember that's what friends are for, and here's a shoulder. The tears that you shed so openly at the Centre's launch touched my heart; they revealed your integrity, honesty and humanity, and an awareness within your own heart of the human cost of HIV disease and its devastating effect on the men, women and children whose lives it has touched. You are so clearly aware of the pain and suffering that lie behind the quarterly statistics and the fact that these represent our dear loved ones, who, in their thousands, have been lost to HIV. You are aware too of the millions of lives that must be saved and the need for continued research to find effective treatments and, hopefully, the elusive cure. Dionne, there was absolutely no need for a speech from you as your tears said it all. Thank you. You have committed yourself to this cause with a human touch that is like a breath of fresh air in the midst of all the ignorance, fear, prejudice and red tape. I am so extremely honoured to know that we share the same vision of the solution. It is due to exceptional human beings like you, Dionne, that hope survives and love lives!"

With two high profile events for the Centre behind me, my photographer friend, Robert, asked, "Where to now, Vernal? You've done it here."

I politely smiled and said, "There's still much to do here." But I knew he was right. I had achieved my goal.

Local MP's, Ken Livingstone and Paul Boateng

Dionne receives the first Reach Out and Touch award from long-term AIDS survivor and Brent resident, Paul Davis. Tony Whitehead, Chair of Terrence Higgins Trust, would be the only other recipient of the award.

Sadly, not too long after he presented Dionne with her award, Paul Davis lost his battle with AIDS. He was yet another beautiful gay man taken from us, but his wonderful sense of humour didn't die with him. He had left funeral instructions that we all have a drink on him, and that's exactly what we did; drinks were served on top of his dark pine coffin, which was stationed on a wooden stand in his living room. In a growing trend, the funerals of gay men were increasingly becoming bespoke works of art; designed to reflect the living spirit of the deceased, not their death. Paul, in line with his wishes, had gone out in style, but he ensured his spirit stayed with us, in more ways than one.

He was more than a client of the Brent HIV Centre; he was a man of immense courage and a friend. Despite his own situation, Paul often found the time to call to ask how I was coping. You have to be a special person to do that, and he was.

Thank you, Princess Diana. Thank you, Dionne. Thank you, Paul. You are powerful evidence that love is stronger than HIV and AIDS.

God's Other Children: A London Memoir   381

Vernal Scott (left) looks on as Dionne is moved to tears

Dionne weeps at Aids centre opening

SOUL superstar Dionne Warwick jetted into town to open Brent HIV Centre officially on Tuesday afternoon. She was greeted by a crowd thronging the Harlesden building.
  Dionne wept as she unveiled a plaque commemorating both the visit and those fighting HIV and Aids. She met local councillors and Labour MPs Ken Livingstone and Paul Boateng, before cutting a ribbon in front of a media scrum to open the Centre.

Presenting the singer with the first Reach Out and Touch award, Vernal Scott of the Centre said: "The men, women and children who make up our client group, and the staff and I, welcome the support of people such as Whitney Houston, Dionne visit is the icing on the cake.
  "The Brent HIV Centre strive to ensure that all services will serve our clients remain in graceful control their own lives."

MPs Ken Livingstone (left) and Paul Boateng

39. A CONVEYOR BELT OF DEATH AND DYING

A FEW WEEKS LATER, Graham and I followed through on our promise to meet up. We shared an intimate dinner at Le Mercury, a popular French restaurant on Upper Street, Islington. It was truly delightful to be with him again, and he was looking more delicious than anything on the meticulously crafted menu. Almost immediately, I realised that I still loved him very much, after so much time. He told me that his relationship was at an end, and that he would be keen to see me, if I was open to the idea. To say that I was completely taken aback by this unexpected development would be a crass understatement; I was truly stumped. I thought about it for a moment, and then, instead of dropping to one knee and sealing the deal, I heard my stupid mouth, rather than my pulsating heart, politely decline his offer. He was utterly graceful about it.

We completed our meal and hugged our goodbyes. I then sat in my car and cried. When I got home, I sat in the dark and cried some more. Was I mad? I had just turned down the man who had been my heart's obsession ever since I first met him ten years earlier; Graham, my dream man. I had secretly wished that the passing of time and success at my work would impress and inspire him to look at me as a potential partner, but now that he was finally making a definite move in the right direction, here I was turning him down. I didn't know why exactly, but I guessed my reaction was an act of self-protection; I had been badly hurt by the experience of my unrequited love of Graham, and a second round would have finished me off. This was the only rational explanation for my apparent madness. I didn't blame him for the experience; I was responsible for my own feelings, and love was its own boss; there was only my heart to blame. The decision, for the moment, at least, was made, and there was nothing to do but move on with my life. When I later overcame my fear and thought about approaching him again, a friend of his, who I'd stumbled across on-line, told me Graham was once again in a happy relationship. This helped me to rationalize my earlier decision as perhaps being the right one. I exhaled, and decided to leave him be; we were not meant to be.

Over the course of 1992 brother Bunny was in and out of hospital with various AIDS-related complications. During my visits I would place my hand into his and try to talk about happier times, but there were so very few of those together. We were now closer than ever; closer because of his AIDS, damn it! Despite its mission of determined destruction, AIDS had somehow healed our previously shattered kinship. I pleaded with Bunny to create a *life story* book for his children, by writing down his wishes for their future, but this caused him to cry, profusely. He said he didn't want to write it because he intended to be there for his kids in the future. My heart broke for him and I decided to not push the matter. Once again out of hospital, Bunny decided to host a New Year's party. All the family was there, including his treasured children. He had left hospital still suffering from a severe iteration of dermatitis, which caused large itchy lumps to form on his skin. I didn't hide my disapproval when he casually mentioned that he'd booked a flight to Jamaica. He said he wanted to try some special herbs which he believed grow there and might be effective in restoring his health. I told him in no uncertain terms that he should not make the trip because Jamaica did not have the necessary services should he fall ill whilst there. My plea, however, fell on deaf ears. Later, as I went to leave, we embraced at his front door and I again repeated my concern, but my determined smiling brother simply responded by telling me that he would phone me on his return to London.

Bunny was of course not the first person with AIDS to go on a hunt for treatment which he hoped would keep him alive. Colin, the handsome friend who I'd met up with when in San Francisco a couple of years earlier, ultimately returned to London without the elusive cure that he and millions of others had hoped to find. As organised in his dying as he was in his living, Colin, in an almost business-like manner, phoned and requested that I come to see him on the hospice unit at London Lighthouse. I was one of a privileged few who he wanted to say goodbye to in person. Arriving at the set time that he'd allocated to me – to us – I sought him out among the other *residents* sharing his prognosis. To my utter shame, Colin had to call out my name when I mistakenly walked past his bed: "Vernal, yes, it's me!" the familiar voice beamed, but it came from a face that I didn't at all recognize; it was distortedly swollen and miscoloured in foreign patches of dark blue, red and brown. Spiritually untouched but physically demolished, my dear friend looked as though he'd survived nine rounds with Mike Tyson but was cruelly pummelled for another nine, long after any fight in him had evaporated. It was as if AIDS had taken its revenge for his having had the audacity to try and beat it. I tried my best to feign indifference at his appearance, but I'm sure that I was unsuccessful. The tear that so obviously fell from my eye outed my feelings, especially so when it crashed to the floor. Our delicate, wordless embrace told my heart that my friend had been dealt a terrible final blow and that this would be our last embrace. Holding each other was the only communication needed now. A few nights later, dear Colin quietly slipped away and out of the body that was no longer capable or worthy of holding his magnificent spirit. A week after that, I attended his solemn but beautiful 'life celebration' service, which was also held at London Lighthouse. Perhaps *fitting* rather than beautiful; *beautiful* had left with Colin.

Farewell, my brave, wonderful friend. I am glad that you are free, but my heart breaks each time I remember your last smile, which you selflessly created just for me. Love always, Vx

I could understand why people were willing to try anything to stay alive, because we all knew the consequences of doing nothing. AZT, the only officially sanctioned treatment, was patchily effective, at best. It gave hope but rarely saved lives. Some even said it was the drug itself that was the real killer.

Bunny hadn't been gone long when I took a call at my office from my sister, Jan. Her tone alone told me that something was seriously wrong. She told me that Bunny had fallen ill in Jamaica and that we needed to get him back to London. I said I would see what I could do, not really knowing what the possibilities were. However, within a few minutes, my phone rang again. It was Jan, only this time she was crying. Bunny had died. I put the phone down and cried too. A surprised visitor to my centre caught me crying and I promptly fumbled my way through a messy apology, but reading me as she did, she kindly offered her shoulder, and I took it. God knows, I needed it. In the honesty of those heart shattering moments, I was forced to be human, not a manager.

Jan and I agreed to meet at our Mum's flat to break the news in person but found she was out. I used my key to get in and we waited silently in her living room to break news of her son's death. Eventually, we heard Mum's key turn in the door. As soon as she ascended the stairs, Jan rushed from the room and into her arms, shouting, "Bunny's dead." Mum, without saying a word, looked over Jan's shoulder and pinned me to the wall with a guilt-loaded expression which seemed to say, *"Why don't you have the answer to all of this misery?"* Still, without speaking or crying, Mum removed her coat and sat down on the nearest chair. Months of crying meant that she was now out of tears. Neither her tears nor prayers had saved her son from becoming AIDS' latest conquest. Its victory confirmed both Jesus' apparent non-intervention in saving my brother, but also the abandonment of Evangelist Sister Scott; abandoned like all the other mothers whose prayers went unanswered as their sons, gay and straight, lay dying at a time of their lives when they should have been striving. My beloved mother's face said it all: *Jesus, oh Jesus, where are you?*

Leo and Beverley soon joined us, but he was emotionally devastated. My two older brothers had relied on one another as boys back in Jamaica and especially so upon their arrival in the UK, so many years ago now. I had never seen Leo cry until tonight. Through his tears he pleaded for answers: "Why did he have to go all the way over there and die?" I didn't have an answer. I never did have the answer. I was just there feeling what everyone else was feeling; inadequate and empty.

Dad had returned home to Jamaica for good the previous year and it was decided that Bunny would be buried there. Mum and Jan flew over to ensure that my brother had the send-off he deserved. Later, according to what I was told, Dad reluctantly paid for the funeral after being 'shamed' into doing so by Jan. He, at first, showed little interest in contributing to the funeral of his own son.

As if losing Bunny wasn't enough, a few months later, Jan suffered the same catastrophic bereavement as our mother; her son JJ also died. AIDS took him too. I wasn't too surprised when Jan sent me a message through our cousin Doreene, saying that I was not welcome at the funeral. I decided to go anyway. Where I had respected the wishes of other grieving mothers, I felt no obligation to do so with my sister. For one thing, I had a close relationship with my nephew, independent of her. For another, I was a blood relative with a right to grieve. But most of all, what I could not leave unanswered was the insinuation, implicit in my exclusion, that gay people were responsible for AIDS, and therefore, for my nephew's death. It was a charge that I felt bound to repudiate by my presence.

Jan actually received me civilly and asked that I accompany her to the funeral home, which I was of course happy to do. Arriving after just a few minutes' walk from her home, JJ lay peacefully in his casket. Ice cold to touch, I noticed but did not comment on seepage from his neck onto the collar of his white shirt; I assumed that it was caused by his autopsy. JJ looked like he was sleeping; at peace and pain-free. It was all too sad, but mostly, I felt numb and that too familiar emptiness. Jan was putting on a courageous face, but I knew she was beside herself about the loss of her first child.

Mum and everyone else were at the church service, but Dad was nowhere to be seen. He would later make some glib excuse that it was not right to bury his own grandson, but if he was honest, he would admit that he was just frightened of AIDS. Jan deserved Dad's support on this day of all days, and it was quite unforgivable that he wasn't there for her.

As I took my seat at JJ's funeral service, I was suddenly aware that I was hearing that sound again; that uniquely terrible wailing that only a parent makes when dealing with the loss of their precious child. This time it was coming from Jan. That bleak sound had become so familiar to me; too familiar. I'd heard it at John's funeral and many others since, and now it was the turn of someone in my immediate family.

Other than seeing each other at future Christmas gatherings, Jan and I would not speak after JJ's funeral. She, as I understand it, continues to believe that gay people were responsible for contaminating the blood supply that ultimately claimed both Bunny's and JJ's lives. I was gay and "walk with the Devil", according to her, and she no longer considered me her brother.

Instead of showing compassion and understanding, JJ's passing was Jan's justification to perpetuate hate and prejudice. It was the same prejudice that, once his diagnosis became known, caused JJ to have to travel in a school bus separated from other children. She'd forgotten the hurt that such discrimination had caused, and was now a vocal champion of it. The pain she was feeling was of course dreadful, but it was no greater than that of John's mother. AIDS had claimed both their precious sons: one was gay and the other wasn't, but the pain felt by both mothers was undeniably the same. Blaming gay people for AIDS was unjust and only added to the hurt that we were all experiencing. There is never an excuse for prejudice, not even the loss of our loved ones. Jan, entombed in a very dark place in her heart and mind, had willingly embraced it, and I had not the inclination or patience to reason with her.

Tragically, AIDS hadn't yet finished with my family, as Anita, Bunny's partner, also succumb to the disease. Her death felt like the very last straw. My heart sank like an untethered anchor as I tried to grapple with what was happening to my family. It was if an uninvited guest called AIDS had taken a seat at our family table, and one by one, we were its meal.

The son Bunny and Anita had together, now orphaned, was going to be raised by Anita's family. He had been with Bunny in Jamaica and witnessed his father's gruelling death.

To say the situation was deeply depressing would be the understatement of a lifetime, but through all of this sickness and death, I knew two things: love was stronger than death and I...no, we, had to carry on.

I was interviewed by BBC's *Panorama* programme around this time. I spoke in general terms about AIDS in the black community and not once did I allude to the catastrophe that it had wreaked in my own family. Our tragedy was a private one. The programme showed footage of me greeting Dionne Warwick with a kiss and I was pleased that my experience and views were sought by the BBC. I looked confident and composed and had been the consummate professional on screen, but in truth, I was utterly torn up on the inside.

The AIDS conveyor belt of death and dying was going to continue churning out the bodies of friends and loved ones for some time to come. There was no cure in sight and I was burning out, but kept telling myself: *"Vernal Scott, you were not built to break."* In truth, I was extremely close to it.

40. TRIBUTE TO MY BROTHER

My next Annual Report (1992/93) carried my tribute to Earl, 'Bunny':

"It was your AIDS diagnosis that brought out the best in us as brothers. AIDS made the philosophical differences between us that had previously kept us apart seem totally insignificant; we both seized the awfulness of the situation as an opportunity to make up for lost time and to show how much we really did care for each other; me, wanting to care, and you, allowing me to do so. I don't know whose need was the greatest, mine or yours, but at last we were behaving as brothers should, all else aside, and for whatever time was left.

I am pleased that you reached out for me when thoughts of what could be ahead of you had become too overwhelming; I could see the fear in your face and hear it in your voice, though you never actually said that you were afraid. It seemed that suddenly all the horror stories we had read in the tabloids were threatening to become your personal reality. I do regret that some of my answers to your questions were not always what you so desperately needed to hear. But, in our hearts, we knew that comforting lies now would have to be answered later with the painful truth. However, in between the darkness and the light, we did our best to keep the emphasis on life and the living; the children, your recording studio, and of course the music that meant so much to you. As for death and dying, there would be enough time for that later.

Denial often tried to win the day. You would say: 'Why don't you come down to the studio and we can do some work together.' I would say: 'You really must get your will sorted out and the life plans for your kids.' You would cry.

I will never forget how devastated you were when you received a money order in the post for the medical error which had resulted in your becoming infected with HIV. What a lurid gesture this was, the final blow to your self-esteem and the house of denial that you had built around yourself; there was no hiding place; this was it! But was a few thousand pounds really supposed to sum up your life's worth? Did someone out there really think that this tragedy could be compensated for with cash? If so, my brother, you were severely short-changed. This was no compensation. A million pounds will not remove HIV, nor will it remove the guilt from those who could have prevented this tragedy from occurring.

New Year's Day '93 was very special as it found all the family together: eating, laughing and playing. We were in an optimistic groove about the future. It was all quite wonderful, but I'm sure that if we could have seen that the end was so near, we would have spent even more time together on that special day, and after. Less than a month later and you are gone; free from the fear, the denial, the stigma and the pain. Gone too is the endless hoping that tomorrow will not be the last. The final tomorrow has come. To most people you have become just another statistic, another not so rare any more heterosexual AIDS case. To your mother, she has lost a dear and irreplaceable son; to your children, they have lost a father whom they idolized, loved and protected; to your brothers and sisters, we have lost the cog in the wheel; and to your friends, a local hero is no more.

So I bid you farewell, my dear brother. I will always remember and admire you for the courage to smile through the heartbreak of your dashed dreams. And though we had both learned a long time ago that joy and pain were flip sides of the same coin, I do hope with all my heart that life's special moments were worth all the pain that you had to suffer at the end of the road. I wish you love and eternal peace, my brother. You really are free at last."

41. WE WILL SURVIVE

ACT-UP (LONDON) AT REACH OUT AND TOUCH

EVEN THOUGH WE HAD STARTED out with good intentions, by 1996, three years after Bunny's death, I came to realise that the Brent HIV Centre had become an excuse for Brent Council's wider workforce of four thousand staff to not have to work directly with residents living with HIV and AIDS. We had unwittingly colluded with the discrimination that I was fighting to stop. I decided to task myself with the difficulty of writing a report that would recommend the integration of Centre services into the generic supply of local social services provision. This would mean current and future service users would be served by all council staff, not just a handful. My report was quickly approved by senior colleagues and local politicians. Some service users disliked the idea, as did most of the staff, but the Brent HIV Centre as an entity was to be no more.

In fact, there was another much more important and compelling reason behind the decision to close the Centre; the stunning success of a new combination of antiretroviral drugs, which meant that people on it were suddenly truly living with HIV instead of dying because of it. This oh so welcome treatment would ultimately have the effect of combatting HIV to the point of making it virtually undetectable in the blood; so much so, that further down the road, those adhering religiously to the treatment, would be unlikely to transmit it to others, even, potentially, if not using a condom during penetrative intercourse. The new challenge, therefore, was to actively test and then treat 'at risk' people found to be HIV positive. Universal adherence to the treatment would mean, over time, a gradual overall reduction in new infections; in other words, treatment as prevention: test, treat, prevent! No, this wasn't the still elusive cure, and there were still possible serious health consequences for contracting HIV; but on the whole, people on the new treatment weren't just less likely to infect a sexual partner, they were also returning to an extended state of good health, and most amazingly of all, told to expect normal life spans. They were now more likely to die of symptoms of old age than HIV disease. Even pregnant women with HIV and on the new treatment could expect to deliver healthy virus-free babies. It was all so very hard for me to believe, but it was true; the grotesque reign of AIDS and its conveyor belt of death and dying that had claimed so many many precious lives had come to a long overdue end.

My initial excitement would later mutate to anger and then fury, as I began to appreciate that the same now successful grouping of drugs could have been with us years earlier, thus saving millions of lost lives, if only those in power at the start of the crisis (Reagan, Bush (Snr), and Thatcher etc.) had been willing to invest in research instead of bigotry. It took the unrelenting dogged determination and angry protests by ACT-UP (AIDS Coalition To Unleash Power) to force our complacent political leaders and profit-hungry scientific community to finally deliver effective, accessible and affordable drugs. With many hundreds of heroic 'nothing to lose' supporters shouting their poignant 'SILENCE = DEATH!' slogan, members of ACT-UP halted traffic and trains, chained themselves to buildings and lorries, climbed rooftops, invaded church services and business meetings, shouted down disengaged politicians, got themselves arrested, and even paraded the rain soaked body of a deceased colleague through the streets in his open coffin, in line with his last wishes. AIDS had claimed him too, but he wasn't willing to have his death hidden away; he wanted the visible reality of his lifeless body to get the attention of the disengaged public and those with power, and convey a message that had fallen on deaf ears when he was alive: *'This is what the outcome of life with AIDS looks like, in your face, and it's facilitated by your inaction'*. It was because of him and the other very brave men and women of ACT-UP led by, amongst others, an irrepressible former banker turned activist named Peter Staley and his equally determined friends in New York, that complacency was banished and successful treatments had at last been found. Thanks to ACT-UP, which sprouted branches in London and other major cities around the world, we could now go back to living instead of dying and once crucial stand-alone services, such as London Lighthouse and the Brent HIV Centre, could close our doors for a tearful final time with a sense of pride in knowing that we had done our part in rising to and meeting the greatest challenge of our lives.

Like wounded bloodied soldiers on their unexpected return from the savage front line of the cruellest of battles, the fight of our lives had left many of us feeling like distorted facsimiles of our former selves. Unlike so many of our dear lost friends and loved ones, the majority of us had somehow survived the catastrophe that had been AIDS and defied even our own predictions that we were all doomed. AIDS itself was the latest casualty, and we could all celebrate that! I, for one, had to now decide on what to do with my life, as I was suddenly surplus to requirements; the people who needed me for so long, no longer did. Exacerbating my new misery, I was forced to acknowledge that whilst AIDS had curtailed more invaluable lives than I wanted to count, it at the same time had given me a life and purpose that I had not known before its arrival. The modern plague had been an unexpected hellish gift tainted with blood and tears, and I would never be grateful for it. However, I could not deny that it had enabled me to realise what I was really made of; AIDS showed me that I was capable of being fucking amazing, and it had done the same for the men and women of ACT-UP, and others across our communities. We had suffered tremendous loses and our scars may never ever heal, but they'll serve as a reminder; not of our weakness, but our strength. We are stronger for our scars, and more determined than ever to survive into the future. Yes, we will survive and thrive! So fuck you, AIDS, fuck you!!!

In contrast to its grand opening, the Brent HIV Centre's closure was patently unceremonious. The removal of Dionne Warwick's plaque ignited within me conflicting feelings of agony and optimism. I would later take on a series of unfulfilling roles at Brent Council: Commissioning Manager; Contracts Manager; Organizational Development Manager. The latter role included an equalities remit, which I tried to enjoy, but my increasingly indifferent attitude was all the evidence needed to confirm that I had lost my direction. My passion and need to care for others had no outlet and this made me feel rudderless and lost out at sea. The death and dying that I had witnessed so much of was to forever replay in my head, and the related unceasing feeling of grief would, at random, prompt my tears. It was the same grief that in the middle of the night would feel as though it was snatching beats from my sleepless heart; a grief that was particularly dark and evasive of all of my strategizing to escape it. I could be in the middle of preparing a meal while listening to the radio and it would creep up and announce its presence if certain songs were played; songs that were once so very beautiful would, within a few moments, have me wiping away my tears: 'Memories, like the corners of my mind - the smiles we left behind...always something there to remind me ... keep smiling - that's what friends are for ...' These songs were now far too painful to be beautiful, but they serve as a lasting connection between absent friends and me. As lonely and grief-stricken as those moments were, I was not at all alone in feeling as I was; many of my former colleagues from the frontline of the battle were equally afflicted, but we knew that time was the only treatment for our ailment of piercing jagged glass memories and unrelenting survivor's trauma. It couldn't be survivor's guilt, could it? Well, if so, it's definitely misplaced…isn't it?

As an unconscious and futile distraction of more serious ones to come, I attempted to shield myself from my inner pain by buying a house in Luton, Bedfordshire, where my sister Beverly had been living for years. It was a magnificent old house called Hart Hill Crest. It had wood-panelled entrance hall, an office, dining hall, lounge with a working fireplace and tinted glass entrance. The house appears on the original map of Luton. In truth, I had bought a house which only served to compound my grief and loneliness.

The only other magnificent thing in my life was my middle bulge; comfort eating was becoming visibly uncomfortable and it was just a matter of time before people would shake my belly instead of my hand. I even became the office joker, but took the "have you seen behind you" comments about my increasing posterior in good humour. A colleague joked that I should expect to be boarded by passengers, if I made the mistake of standing too close to a bus stop wearing red. All very funny, but I knew that my weight gain was a symptom of the emptiness I was feeling inside. I was also very self-conscious about my ongoing hair loss, as I was looking more and more like my father every day, which I hated. So, I was gay, fat, balding, loveless, and forty was knocking on the door; I wasn't exactly hot property, in fact, I hadn't had a date in over two years, and there was little prospect of that changing unless my attitude changed. I couldn't do much about my hair, but being fat was something that I could control. A delightful colleague whom I often referred to as my wife gave me a copy of a Weight Watchers booklet and I took to the programme with much enthusiasm. I was determined to lose my belly and I lost nearly three inches off my waist in less than two months. I was thrilled to get back into my size thirty waist jeans and put my weight issues behind me.

After a couple of years away I began missing London. One day I was walking through Luton's Arndale shopping centre, when I had a sudden epiphany. "Vernal Scott," a voice inside me called, "this is your life, and it sucks!" RAT was right, on this occasion. I was bored with my life in Luton, and decided then and there to put my house on the market and move back to London. It sold fairly quickly and I put my furniture in storage and, as temporary measure, moved back in with my mother at 8 Harrowdene Close in Wembley. I searched for a new house locally, because I wanted to be close to her as well as my place of work. My old bedroom was exactly as I had left it so many years earlier and I quickly slotted back into life with Mum.

Mum was increasingly unwell with type-two diabetes but was really pleased to have me there for company. Despite her weekly churchgoing, she was very isolated. She still longed for her ex-husband, my father, but he had long since moved back to Jamaica. Apart from Jesus and an unhealthy obsession with her "demon neighbours" who lived below her flat, my mother's life was spent watching the God Channel and taking tablets to control her various ailments. She was also showing signs of mental confusion, but nothing so serious as to present a danger to her safety. It was a very sad picture indeed. The once resilient Doreth was being buried beneath a mountain of grief, loneliness, illness, and advancing old age.

I awoke one morning to my mother pounding on my bedroom door. "Get up! Princess Diana is dead!" I switched on the TV and struggled to take in the awful news. An hour later, I was in my car, having picked up a bunch of flowers, and on my way to Kensington Palace, Diana's home. I placed the bouquet in the gates where a small group of people had gathered. Some were crying. I had tremendous respect for Diana, and felt that she and her sons were the only royals worth my time. This was the least I could do to say a personal 'thank you and goodbye'. Her loss was crippling. It was as if the entire country, and perhaps the world, froze in shock. On the day of Diana's funeral, I went to watch the hearse carrying her coffin. It was a terrible early ending to the life of an amazing and beautiful woman who cared for people with AIDS at a time when everyone else would only spit at them. Diana, our 'Queen of Hearts,' would be sorely missed. Some weeks later, a friend and I drove to her home and burial ground at Althorp Park in Northamptonshire. It was some considerable drive, but she was well worth it. I felt a need to say another last goodbye and thank you to Lady Di; the woman who had reached out and touched with her bare hands and abundant love. We didn't know it then, but her son, Prince Harry, would later champion his mother's cause, and advocate for the normalization of HIV testing by undergoing his own HIV test on television. His older brother and future King, Prince William, would also show much of his mother's inclusive spirit by agreeing to an interview for a popular gay monthly. Yes, beloved Diana's spirit would live on in her children.

I eventually found a new home at number 20 Talbot Road, Wembley. The house had been subdivided into two flats, so I bought both and knocked them back into the gorgeous five-bedroom Victorian house that it had once been. It needed a tremendous amount of work and funds that I didn't have, but the work took several months and was well worth it in the end. When it was all finally finished, I moved in and rented out each of the four spare rooms to gay lodgers. This helped me to pay for the repairs and improvements.

Mum visited often, as I was living only a few minutes away from her. She was increasingly ill and struggling. I didn't really know how to help her, but I did my best, or so I told myself; but I don't know if we can ever do enough for our mothers. Filling her cupboards with groceries was the least I could do, and she very much appreciated it. Beverley visited her quite often too, but Leo and Jan, less so.

For some months, I dated a lovely guy named Spencer, whom I met at the Champion Pub in Notting Hill. The venue was a well-known haunt for black and interracial-loving gay men. We spent much of our spare time together, either at his flat in Notting Hill or at my house in Wembley. We started out as friends and soon became more than that. He was very special and I felt comfortable enough to introduce him to my mother and other people who were significant in my life. Sadly, despite seemingly *cementing* things on a trip away together to Naples, Florida, it didn't work out for us. I became depressed when we broke up. To be honest, I completely went to pieces. We later agreed to try again, but I then ended up calling the whole thing off, which in turn caused him to become despondent. Now, how messy is that? Well, it was about to get a whole lot worse when I found myself being physically attacked in a public setting by someone else he'd been seeing – another black guy. My assailant had earlier that day tried unsuccessfully to end his life by swallowing pills. The police were called, and to my surprise, they did a remarkable job in managing an exceedingly unpleasant situation. In the end, I decided that I'd rather be secure in my singledom than insecure in chaotic relationships. I was very used to being on my own, and here I was; alone again, naturally.

West Five in Ealing, West London, was a post-Spencer venue that I would spend the occasional evening in. It was very lively and full of too cute 'trolly dollies', or air stewards, to the rest of us. The various drag acts were popular with most customers, but listening to a night full of Kylie Minogue and here today gone tomorrow pop groups such as Steps, just wasn't my thing. With a feeling that there must be more to life than subjecting my senses to this soulless trite, I decided that being home alone was more appealing. On my last night there, a visiting photographer captured a picture which appeared in the following week's gay press. There I was, still wearing dear Marvin's ring (which Spencer wore for a very short time), and a smile, of sorts. But like the character in the lyrics of another famous song, if you look closely, you will see the tracks of my tears.

42. FACING THE FACTS: MY HIV TEST

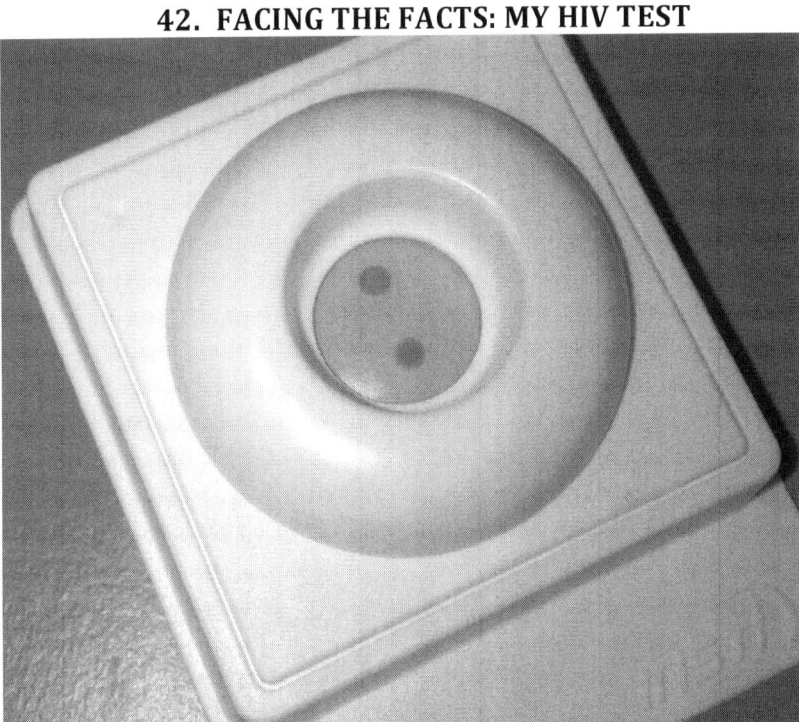

Modern HIV tests deliver results within five minutes; all very different from the nerve-bending long wait of yester-year. This picture shows that the patient tested positive for exposure to HIV - two blue dots. Non-exposure would display only one blue dot. I today strongly advocate regular HIV testing (three times a year) for all sexually active people, especially gay men.

ONE PARTICULARLY SCARY MORNING, I awoke to find myself unable to open my eyes properly, or coordinate my steps. I made my way to the bathroom holding onto the walls to get there. Something dramatic was happening to me and this was confirmed when my urine came out a frightening dark colour. I was afraid, truly afraid. I struggled back to my bed and a fever took hold of me. I stayed in bed for six days and sweated buckets.

When I finally reappeared at work, the whispers started straight away. Colleagues were thinking I had AIDS, and, the truth is, I was thinking the same thing. I had lost a significant amount of weight in ten days. On seeing me, one of my colleagues recoiled in shock and shouted "Jesus!" My waist was now 28 inches and only a belt with improvised additional holes kept my trousers up. As I looked at my reflection in the mirror, I knew that the time had come to get myself tested and to face what I'd been avoiding.

The Royal Free Hospital had an excellent reputation for its testing and treatment of HIV positive people; indeed I'd referred some there myself. I decided to go along, but these were the days before same-day results and I had no option but to wait a few days for my result. It felt like forever.

I popped in to see my mother, who started praying as soon as she set eyes on me. She was so disturbed by my appearance that she called my brother Leo, who promptly turned up on my doorstep, complete with his wife and kids, to find out what was wrong. I told him Mum had over-reacted and that I was simply dealing with the aftereffects of a bad tummy bug.

No one had to tell me the result. *I must be HIV positive* I told myself. What else could have caused the symptoms I was experiencing? I had been ill before, but I'd recovered quickly and pushed the issue to the back of my mind. It was different this time, very different indeed.

Morbid thoughts flooded my mind. How long might I survive? Who was I going to tell, or not tell? How would I deal with being a patient? I went to bed and woke up thinking about the same thing; my pending test result.

On the result day, I made my way by tube to the hospital in Hampstead, struggling to numb myself against my own thoughts as I went. Once there, they didn't keep me waiting too long, as the health advisor invited me to join him for my appointment. I took my seat in the leaflet-bound room, and before I could even think about my final funeral arrangements, he got straight to the point: "Your test result has come back and it's negative".

"Oh!" I said, obviously expecting the opposite.

I was on my way home less than ten minutes later, feeling both relief and confusion – but mostly relief. Of course I was! I did not have HIV and it was my intention to keep it that way; or at least, I was going to try.

In the months and years ahead, rapid, same-day testing was going to replace the long wait that I had to endure. Indeed, home-testing was on its way too, although that would be longer into the future.

HIV: If anyone knew the risks, the consequences, and the preventative measures needed, then that person was me. But sometimes our intention and the eventual outcome don't correlate.

43. I WANT TO BE A DADDY

I'VE ALWAYS WANTED KIDS. As a teenager I loved looking after my nephews and nieces, and hoped that I'd one day have children of my own. I believed that lesbian and gay people could be great parents and that the only barrier to this happening more widely was homophobia and prejudice. Social services departments across the UK and around the world are full to the brim with children born to heterosexual men and women, who, for one reason or another, failed to be responsible parents. Children need love and effective parenting; if this is in place then their parents' sexuality is immaterial.

I'd been approached by a number of lesbian women over the years, mostly couples, who asked if I was interested in fathering children through donor insemination. Two such attempts failed to yield pregnancies, which prompted me to consider adoption. I applied to a London social services department, after they placed an advert in the black community press seeking for prospective adoptive parents for a three-year old black boy who was at risk of HIV. This undoubtedly meant that he was born to an HIV-positive mother, but his HIV status was yet unknown. The advert caught my eye. I applied, and after a number of rigorous interviews at my home, I was accepted, but at the end of the process, the bubbly three-year old child was adopted by the woman who had been his foster mother since his birth. The experience sharpened my desire to have a child of my own.

Towards the end of 2001, I got a call from Titi, a black lesbian journalist of Jamaican parentage, who had become something of a friend. We met several years before when she interviewed me about the work of the Brent HIV Centre. We hadn't been in touch for about four years, so it was good to hear from her. I was glad to learn that she was in a happy partnership and raising her biological son, KC. I was a little surprised at this cosy domesticity, because the Titi I knew, a rather masculine, strictly trouser-wearing woman, didn't strike me as the maternal type.

On Titi's invitation, I visited her little family nest one afternoon in January 2002. Orla, her partner, turned out to be a heavy-set white Irish woman in her mid-thirties. She was pursued everywhere by KC, a bright-eyed and very cute mixed raced boy. Titi told him to say hello. The little chap then looked up at me and shouted, "Dad!" "No," Orla corrected him, "This is Vernal; he's come to see us". I got the impression that KC rarely saw men in his house, and that when he did, he hoped it would be his absent dad. I didn't know it at the time, but in that moment, KC *adopted* me as his Dad.

KC was keen to show me his toys. His boisterous, chatty personality demanded my attention: "Vernal, Vernal! Look at this," or, "Vernal, help me, Vernal! It's my jigsaw." The desire to be a Dad stirred in my heart, but this happened often when I was around children.

As I watched KC play, I told Titi and Orla that I had always wanted to be a dad. Titi offered to introduce me to some lesbian friends of theirs, who were looking for a dad who wanted involvement. But then, to my astonishment, and I think to Titi's too, Orla chimed up and asked whether I would consider having a baby with her. I was stunned and lost for words. I'd only just met her and we knew nothing about one another, aside from our brief exchange of pleasantries. I could have HIV or something else for all she knew.

Instead of running for the door, which is what most sensible people would have done, I remained where I was and began to contemplate the idea. Titi appeared just as perplexed. I got the impression that she hadn't been aware of Orla's desire to carry and deliver her own biological bundle of joy. She was acutely aware now!

Orla was still looking plaintively at me for an answer, when she incongruously turned her head and bellowed at her partner: "Titi, what did I tell you about putting your coffee cup on the arm of the sofa?!" Scarily reminiscent of the twisted lesbian lovers' scene from the Killing of Sister

George starring Beryl Reid and Susannah York, I practically jumped out of my chair. Titi, however, clearly used to such outbursts, responded with an apathetically meek, "I'm sorry Orla". KC didn't react at all-- a sign, I now realise, that he too was used to such outbursts between the two women. Less than two seconds later, Orla, evidently capable of displaying more multiple personalities than the possessed child character from The Exorcist, switched back to her more appealing *sweetness and light* persona and was once again looking at me searchingly; it was as if her volatile reaction to the trifle cup incident had never happened. That's bizarre, I thought. This would be an obvious sign to even the most pathetic of fools that something wasn't quite right with this woman, and probably, her partner too.

I broke the stony silence in the room by asking about KC's biological father. The two women looked at each other and nodded, as if to give each other permission to share a secret. Titi then explained that KC's father was Orla's brother. *I swallowed hard.* Orla continued. "My brother was happy to donate his sperm. He lives on the other side of the world with his wife and kids and has no involvement with our son". This disturbed me, but I tried to not show it. *So much for KC's need for a dad*, I thought. KC knew his biological father as his uncle, not his dad, Titi said. "And that's how it will stay," Orla affirmed. As I looked down at KC playing, I wondered what impact the two women's decision would have on him in the future. He had an 'uncle' that was really his biological father; half-siblings that he would know as cousins; and Orla, his father's sister was really KC's aunt. This could be very confusing for him, because like all children he needed the security of knowing who he really is and where he fits in; his true identity. And what if these two women split up in the future? Even the best of relationships can fall apart, and when they do, the children involved tend to suffer most. I knew all about that! The impact upon children of separated lesbian and gay couples will be even more of a challenge. Fingers crossed that won't happen.

KC, frustrated by the lack of attention being paid to him, climbed onto my lap and started pulling at my shirt collar. Calling my name, "Vernal, Vernal!" he reached up and touched my moustache and appeared fascinated by its coarse texture. This made me laugh. KC was winning me over, even if I had major reservations about one or both of his mums. *"You deserve a good dad"*, I thought, looking at him gazing back at me. Every interaction with him reminded me of the child I was missing in my life. I was instantly comfortable with him and him with me.

Not having a dad is tough for the child who needs one, and society feels the destructive effects of fatherless children every day. Single mothers do a great job on the whole, but to have your biological father 'reconstructed' into an 'uncle' may work for the adults in this particular scenario, but it could produce a very angry young man in later years. My father left home when I was a teenager, but despite his flaws, at least I'd known him and still had access, even if that access point was now staunchly homophobic Jamaica. This family was constructed around the needs of the mothers, rather than their child. *Amazing as it seems now, I still wasn't running out the door!*

Orla was looking for an answer from me, and I was getting close to giving her one, but first, I needed to make myself clear. I told them that I would only pursue parenting on the basis of full involvement. Orla immediately assured me that this is what they wanted too. "We're definitely looking for someone who wanted full, equal involvement; someone who could be Dad to KC, as well as the new baby".

This sounded great, but it was at odds with Titi's suprised reaction to Orla's revelation that she wanted a biological baby – her own baby! It all seemed too impulsive. Then there was Orla's outburst; the change of emotions like a light switching on and off, and Titi's uncharacteristically submissive response. Things weren't quite adding up, but Orla's earnest answer was the one that my desperate-to-be-a-dad ears wanted to hear. Anything less than full involvement would have been a non-starter. I looked at the women and I looked at KC and heard my mouth say:

"Yes, I will give it a go."

Orla's chest heaved and she burst into tears. She confessed that she had been plagued by jealousy about Titi's pregnancy with KC and very much wanted to have her own baby. Titi smiled but looked bemused with it. I was bemused too, by my own behaviour. I had come to visit her family, and forty-five minutes after walking in her door here I was becoming part of it. The world was used to instant coffee beverages, but here I was creating *instant family: just add Vernal's sperm!*

I was aware of the life-altering nature of the decision I had made, and of its suddenness, but, I foolishly reasoned, many heterosexuals bring children into the world without a thought, entirely by accident. KC deserved to have a dad, Orla and I both wanted a baby, so we would try. What was wrong with that? What this didn't take into account, though, was that many children are also born of stable and responsible relationships, where the partners have had a child after much thought. Now I was obviously not going to enter into a heterosexual relationship for the sake of having a child, as a forty-year old man of some (reputed) intelligence, I should have taken more care and gone a lot slower, in choosing and getting to know the mother of my child. If I was to supply the batter for the cake, I ought to have been more selective in choosing the baker.

Orla was more desperate than me to get the oven going. This was soon confirmed when she made mention of her body clock; she wanted to get baking, like yesterday!

KC returned to the floor to continue playing with his toys, completely oblivious to the adult decisions going on above his little head; decisions that would impact his life at as much as the adults in the room. Perhaps he was more sensible than I, with his two-year old self. Sure, he was; he was smarter than all of the adults in this Tottenham Town living room. KC was smart enough to play with his eyes wide open, while the adults were dumb enough to make life-altering commitments with their eyes wide-shut.

Orla, Titi and I discussed our mutual expectations in the days and weeks ahead. They repeatedly assured me that I would have full involvement, including legal Parental Responsibility. Apart from KC, my focus was on Orla; I wanted to be sure that we understood each other, and to this end, we left few subjects untouched. But she was thinking way ahead of me, including her outlandish idea about living in the same house one day and me being at the birth of the new baby, if we were lucky enough to conceive. I wasn't too keen on the living together idea, but the rest of it sounded good to me.

I decided to put any lingering doubts aside and allow myself to be trusting and excited. We didn't commit anything to writing; I was willing to trust what I was being told; surely Titi and Orla wouldn't do the *dirty* on me. In truth, the buck stopped with me and my decision to involve myself in the first place; I had to take responsibility, whatever the outcome of this venture would be. If I got covered in dirt I would have no one to blame but the man in the mirror. I was going to start with trust and optimism and work backwards, if need be.

For now, at least, everything seemed right enough, through my warped rose-tinted glasses. Frankly, even a return to slavery would look good through my blocked vision. I was particularly encouraged because Titi had been a friend for a little while, so whilst I didn't know Orla at all, knowing Titi gave me some reassurance that all will be well. Titi had been a guest at social events in my house and I considered her of good character, even if she wasn't a very close friend. I recall how we laughed together when we realised that her mother lived near my father in Jamaica. We talked about putting them in touch with each other at some point. No, there was no reason to doubt Titi, but Orla was an unknown.

A couple of weeks following our initial meeting, Orla started making loud noises about her ticking, thirty-six year old, body clock. She said she was keen for us to begin the insemination process as soon as possible. I agreed and said I'll get on with having another HIV test to reassure her, but to my surprise, she responded by insisting that a test wasn't necessary: "I trust you", she added. I was instantly very worried. I knew only utter desperation could cause her to be so impatient; her life and that of a new baby could be at risk if I was HIV positive and this was unknown to specialist health care staff. Surely, only a fool would have a baby with someone who was this recklessly and selfishly desperate: step forward, Mr Vernal Scott!

I decided to have another HIV test anyway, and the result was again negative; I didn't have HIV. Orla said she was pleased when I called to let her know. One of us had to try to be responsible, if that's what I could call my own actions. Passing HIV to a child for my own selfish reasons would be too much for me to live with. Orla, on the other hand, couldn't care less. She just wanted to be a biological mummy.

Surely, this was enough of a reason to come to my senses and run faster than Usain Bolt in the opposite direction, but my feet wouldn't let me. KC and the joyous idea of a new baby glued my feet to the spot.

In March 2002, Orla and I started trying to conceive; love didn't matter, consideration of the consequences didn't matter, common sense didn't matter, and of course, God didn't matter, either! I had turned a blind eye to Him in order to pursue my own objective; damn the consequences! Orla was an Atheist, so God didn't cross her mind in the first place. This was the 'Make a Baby Now!' project and I hoped and prayed that God would make it happen for us and forgive my blatant stupidity regarding the chosen process. I'd hopefully be able to forgive myself, should it all go wrong.

I was ready when an uncharacteristically timid-sounding Orla called to let me know "it's time"; time for do-it-yourself insemination. Yippee! Use of a clinic or intercourse was never considered by either of us; the latter would have been the one reason why I would have walked away. Anyway, I dropped everything and drove the forty or so minutes to Tottenham to play my role in the *new baby project*, taking with me an envelope of sexy male images; just in case my imagination failed me when it was time to *deliver*.

When I got there, Titi and Orla greeted me at the door with nervous hugs. I was nervous too. The couple waited downstairs as I made my way up to the bathroom to 'do my thing'. I peeped in on a contented sleeping KC on my way up. The women had perched a sterilized glass container on the windowsill; indeed the whole experience felt sterile and void of any *emotion*. The first thing I did was make sure I was totally private and the neighbours couldn't see in. The last thing I wanted was to have the police burst in and drag me into the streets with my trousers around my ankles because some nosey neighbour thought I was *flashing* at the window. Once I was certain of my solitude, I whipped out my manhood and tried to excite myself. As predicted, the unsexy environment thwarted any attempt to generate a sexy imagination on my part, or should that be my *private parts?* Indeed, it left me quite limp. Seeking to thrill myself in other people's bathrooms to meet a deadline dictated by a stranger's body clock wasn't an activity I was at all used to. I preferred a familiar environment, with a bed rather than a loo, to make me feel *sexy*. So, I had little option but to turn to my envelope of erotic goodies for inspiration, and thankfully, its content helped me to achieve what my imagination couldn't and I soon made the required deposit into the waiting container. It was all very mechanical, but *I delivered!*

A couple of minutes later and feeling like some kind of sexual deviant, I was saying goodbye to the two women at their front door; leaving them to put my baby-nectar to its intended use. As I left, our uncertain hugs and pecks to our respective cheeks confirmed the truth; we were essentially strangers and this was a *process*. We were friendly enough, but there was no real affection here. I guessed I could be grateful that I didn't have to participate in the actual act of inseminating Orla; that was Titi's job, thank goodness! Yes, that was a blessing.

Orla soon confirmed that our first attempt failed, but it marked the beginning of monthly attempts to get my ever-active sperm to meet her time-limited eggs.

The post-insemination phone calls and luncheon in a coffee shop somewhere in North London was sweet, but it couldn't rid the atmosphere of a sense of superficial *process*. Titi sipped her coffee and chain-smoked, while Orla continued to look at me from the other side of the table with desperate emotional eyes. When I got home I contemplated locking my precious testicles in my safe, just in case they turned up missing by the morning. *Desperate people do desperate things!*

The second attempt failed too, and it caused Orla to worry that I may give up on her. She blamed her excessive weight, but I said I wasn't going anywhere; we were both committed to trying for a while longer, at least. We gave each other further assurances by acknowledging how some people try for years without getting pregnant. We were going to keep trying, for now.

On a couple of later efforts, Titi was away at work during the tight window when Orla's eggs were hoping to meet my sperm, so Orla had to manage on her own. Titi preferred to be on hand, practically, as she was keen to remain an integral part of the insemination process.

It was strange, but I still felt a greater connection with Titi than I did with Orla; it may have been our history as friends, or our blackness and Jamaican heritage. Or maybe it had to do with something more obvious; that Orla and I, despite what we were doing, were complete strangers with nothing in common other than our homosexuality, our desire to become biological parents, and knowing Titi. In truth, neither woman had any affinity with me; they just wanted another child. Titi had warmed to the idea and I was the vehicle to their chosen destination.

I confided in a few friends and family members about my new 'family'. No one was ecstatic about it; of course not. They knew the whole thing sounded like insanity. One of my dear friends was almost hysterical as he warned me: "Do not trust an Irish woman, Vernal! She'll steal your shadow if she can, and I say that as an Irish man myself". I laughed it off, thinking *'Don't be silly'*.

I wasn't turning back now, but had to accept that my friends, my mother, and God, would not likely sanction what I was doing; it was madness, or at the very least, selfish foolery. Would I move a complete stranger into my house? Of course not! And yet, here I was trying to create a child with one.

My dear mother had an old Jamaican saying that she would recite quite often. In woeful voice, she'd issue her warning of bad times to come: "What's sweet to you today will be sour tomorrow!"

Future events would cause it to replay in my head like an old vinyl classic.

44. EVANGELIST SISTER SCOTT MEETS JESUS

IT WAS LATE MAY 2002 and Mum's health was rock bottom. Her middle name was May, but there was nothing of flourishing spring for her now, in fact, everything was more like a witheringly cold and decaying November. She had become my principal priority in the last eighteen months as her health took her from out-patient to in-patient care.

By June, Mum had been resident on the acute diabetes ward at Northwick Park Hospital for eight awful months. Getting to the hospital every night and being with my mother outweighed any obligation I felt towards Orla; as a result, she had to accept my apologies this month. My mother needed me more. Her doctor told me many times in the preceding months that she wasn't likely to return home again, but I always hoped and prayed she would.

As well as her physical health, Mum's mental health had been the cause of much attention well before her admittance to Northwick Park. She'd sometimes come to my office reception or the local police station to complain about her "evil neighbour downstairs". Things got so bad that I consulted with Leo and my two sisters and told them that we had to get her a mental health assessment before something serious happened to her or her neighbours. Mum was confused and delusional.

At my behest, a psychiatrist visited my mother at her home, and after a simple initial assessment, she decided to section my mother under the Mental Health Act, in order to conduct a more comprehensive assessment. The polite but assertive Asian doctor had originally offered my mother tablets that would help to "calm you down", but Mum sealed her own fate when she responded in menacing voice with: "You're going to swallow every one of those tablets yourself!"

The doctor took the potential threat in her professional stride, but she insisted that my mother voluntarily attend the mental hospital the next week or be forced to do so against her will. My mother was furious but kept herself under control. The doctor issued the admittance date and time, and exited, leaving my mother and me to deal with the uncertainty of what may lie ahead. The only current certainty was the guilt that I was feeling; an intense guilt that consumed my soul. I felt as though I had delivered a death blow to my own mother.

My mother started praying as I left to make my way to my office.

The fact that the doctor was Asian didn't help matters, because my mother had developed a totally irrational belief that they were particularly evil, especially her Asian neighbour in the apartment below hers. But my mother's aversion to Asian people wasn't limited to her neighbour. Some months earlier, I had accompanied her to an out-patient eye hospital appointment, to discuss possible cataract eye surgery to correct her cloudy vision. The unfortunate consultant, who happened to be Asian, sat stony-faced as my mother, without provocation, lashed out at him: "I am a Christian and I worship a living God. But you, you worship cow!" I apologized profusely on behalf my mother and told him she wasn't feeling herself, but she promptly told me to shut up and continued to assert why her religion was more superior than what she had assumed, because of his appearance, must be his. The startled man completed his examination and then showed us out of his consultation room without even a word of goodbye.

As we made our way back to my car, I tried to reason with Mum, and mentioned that her comments were unkind and should never be repeated. I went further, and said God might be Asian for all she knew. Well, if she could have seen me clearly enough I would have lost every tooth in my mouth. She was not impressed! I later told Aunt Edna, her sister, about my remark and we both ended up in a belly laugh about it. Indeed, the visualization made me laugh out loud for weeks. God had better conform to Mum's perception of him or there would be a serious rumble in the heavens upon their meeting. In all seriousness, her behaviour was purely a symptom of her diabetes. The only people she really despised were other blacks who were 'too black' for her liking.

Mum, wisely, agreed to go voluntarily to the mental health unit. Once there, she was detained and allocated a bed. When I visited later that morning, I took her cussing me out as my deserved punishment. She looked me in the eye and said a damning, "May God help you!" The embittered tone of her words penetrated my heart. I looked around and could see that she appeared to stand out when compared to the patients around her, whom, unlike my mother, were mostly visibly *disturbed*. *'My mother doesn't belong here'*, I told myself.

A moment later I heard her say "God must have sent me here to help these people". I agreed with her, as there was no point in doing otherwise. The truth is my mother had been there many times before, but on previous occasions it was to befriend and pray for patients in need of her Christian counselling. She was Evangelist Scott, after all; formerly of Harlesden's Jubilee Clock and her megaphone, shouting at passing sinner shoppers to "Get saved before the time of too late is here. The Lord is coming for His world!" Now, all of a sudden, she was a mental health patient herself. "God does indeed work in mysterious ways", I told her, and with that, a smile came to her face, and in turn to mine; my sweet mother, Doreth May Eubank Scott.

When she was told her church pastor had arrived to visit, my mother rushed to make herself look more presentable. She still cared about her appearance. She squeezed her painfully swollen feet into tight fitting shoes and straightened her dress, before making her way into the visitor's room. Once there, they greeted each other with the best smiles they could muster. She then went straight into telling him that I was to blame for her admittance to the unit, because I had become irritated by her repeated requests that I go on shopping errands to buy milk for her. The bemused elderly black man smiled at her without comment. I could tell he was deeply sorry for her predicament and could only get himself to say it was "an injustice," looking in my direction. Perhaps against my better judgment, I attempted to defend myself against mum's accusation about the milk, but she interrupted with, "You better shut up before I add cornflakes to it, too!" The pastor and my mother erupted into howling laughter at what they thought was her great sense of humour, at my expense. I didn't want to laugh, but I had to accept that it was rather funny...milk...cornflakes. My guilt-ridden face gave way to a wry smile, and then I was laughing too. We must have looked a picture, the three of us. *Oh, dear mother, I thought, you laugh all you want. God knows you've known enough tears.*

Mum needed help I couldn't give. In the preceding months I found myself in tears on many occasions as I watched my once formidable mother sink into diabetes-generated mental confusion. All the demons that she'd once fought so valiantly over the years, came to stay; but they were now only in her head. To her, every passing sound or random event was "the work of evil doers". She accused her neighbour in the flat below of being the principal source of all the evil that had beset her. Mum's mental demons caused her to threaten to take up her floorboards and inspect electrical sockets and appliances for signs of tampering or hidden microphones. She also became convinced that her car was being tampered with, and could smell that someone had been sleeping in it at night. As a result, she asked me to buy her a camcorder so she could try to catch the elusive culprit.

Thankfully, Mum's mental health assessment showed that her condition wasn't of sufficient gravity to cause her to remain in the unit, and her three-day stay came to a rapid end. I was more relieved than she was, I'm sure.

Leo went to collect her and drove her home to her flat. When I got there it was as if nothing had happened; she was singing and cooking as always. She really took comfort in her belief that God sent her there for a purpose, and all was forgiven in view of His greater plan. I only wish he'd do some work on my guilt.

Aunt Edna came to look after Mum for a while, but we had to accept that her diabetes was causing her left foot to rot before our eyes. Her reoccurring mental issues meant that she was readmitted to the mental health unit within three months of her return home; this time Beverley and Jan took her there themselves. I had nothing to do with it this time, as I was briefly away in Amsterdam.

Mum's gangrenous foot meant she was soon transferred from the mental health unit to Northwick Park Hospital, with its specialist diabetes treatment ward. The ward doctors determined amputation was the best course of action to take, but my mother was having none of it. On hearing their recommendation she started singing, only stopping briefly to tell them, firmly: "When the time comes to meet my saviour, I will meet Him as He created me – with two feet and two legs".

There was no changing her mind, and God knows I tried, as did her sister and other members of the family. Sepsis poisoning began to take a hold, and the doctors made us aware of the inevitable consequences. My mother ignored the concerns and fuss and just kept praying with her hands raised towards the ceiling above her bed.

Mum was now sixty-six years old, but white hair made her look older. She was also very frail. When she first arrived at Northwick Park in 2001, she was quick to impress staff with her singing talent and was able to walk unaided to and from her hospital bed using a walking frame, but only a few weeks later, she'd ceased singing and become bed-bound. I was present one night when she fell to the floor while using her walker for the last time. As I struggled to get her onto the bed, she looked at me as if to say, *'Why don't you just leave me where I am. I don't want to get up!'* She wanted to give up, but I wasn't having it. It took all of my strength to manoeuvre Mum back onto her hospital bed. Leaving my precious mother on the floor was not an option. As I wiped the sweat from my forehead and peered down at her, I wondered how on Earth I'd managed to move her off the floor, but as I looked more intently, I could see something other than pain on her face; it was a look of abandonment; not by me, but by Jesus. I then realised that my mother had stopped praying for some weeks now; her prayers receded as her illness progressed. Not even Jesus could heal my mother now and that reality was on her saddened face.

Her physical state was deathly poor, and her mind continued to play games on her. There were odd occasions when I would ask her about her day, and she would respond by saying something strange, such as "I took my baby to the nursery" or "I went shopping in Harlesden". No such event happened, of course, at least not in reality, but she was convinced of them. On another occasion she scolded me for "staying out all night" and for being absent when she checked my bedroom this morning: "Oh, so you think you're a man? Where were you this morning!?" she demanded to know.

It was truly heartbreaking to see my mother this way; my love couldn't relieve her pain or stop her demons. Perhaps

Dad could help, if only he was willing. My phone calls to him in Jamaica received a sympathetic ear, but he stopped short of offering to come visit his ex-wife. They had divorced over two decades earlier in a climate of mutual hatred, and he had long moved on. But Mum's hatred was temporary; she still expected him to come back to her, one day. She was stuck in the past, and her state of health was a reflection of her painful reality; he was never coming back and she no longer wanted to live with him. It had been twenty lonely years, and her prayers and Jesus Christ could no longer fill the gap left in her heart by her beloved Skippy's absence.

I couldn't bear to see my mother's life dwindle away, and as a last resort in December 2001, I jumped on a plane to Jamaica to see if I could persuade Dad to come to her rescue. It was my very first time in my parents' homeland. After booking into my hotel on Montego Bay's famous strip, I immediately went for a stroll to take in a few sights before Dad came to meet me at a previously agreed time. It was sizzling hot and everybody seemed to be wearing a smile. I must have stood out, because just about every street trader kept trying to get me to part with my cash. "Hey, British boy, come here, come here!" they shouted after me. Some of them were extremely hard to shake off and pursued me for a while before giving up.

Dad was waiting for me when I got back to my hotel. A security guard pointed me out as I approached, but he turned away, saying a very audible, "No man, that's not him". "Yes it is, Dad!" I shouted over at my startled father. I was much thinner when he saw me last, ten years or so earlier. "My God man, my son, is you this, Old Soldier?" We embraced awkwardly. I couldn't recall him embracing me before and it felt odd to do so now. He looked very well and younger than his seventy years. I last saw him on the day I dragged him around the Brent HIV Centre, in advance of Dionne's official launch. I didn't mention the fact that he failed to turn up as promised for the actual launch, there was little point; we had all moved on, Dionne too. My visit was about my mother, and I intended to raise the matter at an appropriate point.

I soon realized he wasn't alone, and was delighted to see that Aunt Vera and Lorna, her daughter, had come to see me too. Dad also brought along Fran, his now long-term partner since returning to Jamaica. She was very nice, but nothing on my mother, of course, but very nice all the same. She gave me a warm hug and said: "It's not my fault!" I just smiled. I was good to be amongst family. I was particularly happy to see my darling Aunt Vera again. She was as pretty and lovable as ever, and that patent curly perm was looking good too.

We made our way to the hotel's restaurant veranda and ordered a table load of food, on me. The sea views provided a welcome backdrop to city boy eyes as we ate and chatted the afternoon away, and it was soon time to get to the subject of my visit; my mother and the deathly situation she faced back home, in the UK. Dad said he was sorry to hear his ex-wife was so terribly unwell, before slipping into a reflective glaze, perhaps remembering their youth together. Aunt Vera started crying, her mind also full of memories of happier times concerning Doreth, her dearest cousin. Vera explained she stopped calling Mum after becoming exhausted by her relentless stories about the demon neighbour downstairs.

Sadly, lots of people began avoiding my mother for the same reason. If you called my mother you'd only hear one subject; the neighbour from hell downstairs. When once close people like Vera stopped calling, all my mother could do was talk to herself, when she wasn't busy praying. When I'd call, as I did almost daily, I'd only need to say "Hi Mum, how are you today?" and I'd be able to cook a full meal while my mother ranted away in the background about "the demon downstairs". I'd be patient with her most of the time, but when the rant became too much, I would make my excuses and end the call. The next day I'd call again, and she, as predicted, would simply repeat the saga all over again. Poor

Mum, she really couldn't help herself. I began to think she might benefit from being in the company of other people of her age and background. Brent social services carried out an assessment but she later declined their offer of a place at a local day centre. In the absence of Skippy, loneliness and Jesus Christ was her preferred company over a room full of strangers.

I got to the point and asked Dad if he would come to London, explaining that I believed his visit would do Mum good. But his fake sadness regarding Mum's predicament gave way to his true feelings. He stood up and walked a few steps from the table to lean on the seaward-facing wall. He then proceeded to lash out at my mother, blaming her for everything that had gone wrong in his life. I was livid, but my cousin Lorna pounced before I did, telling him, bluntly: "You were no angel, Uncle Skippy!" My suddenly sheepish father acknowledged this, with a meek: "I know that, darling, I know that". I just looked at him; my thoughts streaming back to the bad times at 13 Kingsley Road. He was still a very selfish and bitter man, now full of regrets about his own-goals and failing to take any responsibility. I was disappointed, but not surprised. My trip had been a waste of time.

Sensing Dad's uncomfortable state, Fran tried to ease the tension with her well-intended suggestion that the three women "leave the table and allow father and son a few private moments". I said "Thanks, but there's really no need for that".

I was now forty years old and no longer the suicidal teenager he'd left behind without even a word of goodbye. His leaving was, initially, a good thing for my mother and me, but she now needed him once again; she never stopped loving him. He was the only person who could possibly get her to want to live, but he didn't care. His rejection of my request was on his face before it came out of his mouth. He had truly moved on.

I declined to visit his self-built house in Clarendon and instead took a flight to Miami, where I chilled for a few days before flying back to Heathrow. I did have something representing Dad in my luggage, although it wasn't much. I had asked him, Aunt Vera and Lorna, to look into my camcorder and send Mum a message of encouragement. Dad managed to put on a good act, but I suspected this was more for me than his ex-wife. Vera and Lorna were both very genuine. I didn't ask Fran, for obvious reasons.

On my return to London, I dropped off my suitcase at home and made my way to the hospital, taking the video with me. She was pleased to see me, but not as pleased as she was about to be. Her eyes lit up like a little girl at Christmas on seeing her beloved Skippy and cousin Vera on the small screen. She waved heartily at them, saying: "Hello Skippy, hello Vera!" I hadn't seen my mother this happy for years. Her reaction to the video caused me to have to wipe a little tear from my eye before she could see it. The scene was oh so happy, and yet sad too. This was a close she could get to the man she loved; the same man who had now completely abandoned her to her fate with chronic diabetes. He was not coming back to save her from her possible death bed, but at least she now had something of him on video.

On subsequent visits, Mum's mind and eyes continued to play games with her. Her face again lit up when I walked into her room after work one evening. Her fading eyesight fooled her into thinking I was her beloved Skippy: "Oh, you've come" she said excitedly, raising herself up on her elbows. Her elated expression sank without trace when her eyes adjusted and she realized her mistake. It was yet another heartbreaking scene in the dwindling life of my dear mother.

She stopped asking to see the video when she realized the mystery woman who was accidentally captured was Fran; her replacement. In fact, she cussed and instructed me to "Turn off that dirty man". I did as I was told. She would never watch it again.

On good days, Mum thoroughly enjoyed visits from her church sisters, who turned her room into a rapturous church-like gospel fest; singing out loud and praising the Lord at the top of their voices. If singing could cure then my mother would be up and running after those sessions. On other occasions, friends of old would visit to keep her company, including Uncle Sonny, who offered to feed Mum when she didn't have the strength or coordination to feed herself. He was now very elderly and frail himself, but he was still the wonderful man whose joyous presence, so many years ago, made 13 Kingsley Road a better place.

On bad days, I'd find her confused and lying in her own faeces. This wasn't going to have a happy ending without the direct intervention of Jesus himself. She was mortally unwell, and the offending foot that had signalled the gravity of her illness had almost totally decomposed while still attached to her body. I was horrified to my core when the nurses removed the bandages and all I could see was a blackened, fleshless foot. The decomposition and sepsis was slowly contaminating her entire body. A caring doctor remarked that he was surprised she was still alive. "She's amazed all of us" he told me, as he rushed away to look after someone else.

I knew Mum's passing was going to happen at some point, but after so many months in that hospital bed, I had no idea when it would happen, and I dreaded the very thought of it with every fiber of my being. Yes, I wanted my mother to live, of course I did, but not in pain and without her dignity; my nightly prayers reflected this dichotomy.

I arrived one night and found Mum in a depressed mood, so I thought I'd lighten the atmosphere by telling her that I'd met someone I was hoping to have children with, but despite her ill health, she was alert enough to let me know she was totally unimpressed: "So when is the wedding?" demanded a pointedly patronizing Evangelist Sister Scott. I decided to drop the subject, in haste! *I should have known better* I told myself. She continued. "No wedding, no child.

Do you hear me, stupid boy!?" "Yes", I said, "I hear you, Mum!" Her put-down would have been significantly worse if she knew the person concerned was one half of a lesbian couple. In my forty year on this Earth, I never even heard her say the word. "One of dem", is as close as she'd get.

Regardless of Mum's opinion, and even my own tortured thinking on the matter, I'd already made up my mind to pursue fatherhood with Orla and Titi. I loved my mother dearly, but this was my 'stupid' decision, not hers; I was willing to take a chance and hope that everything would work out for the best.

I was momentarily deep in thought about my baby-making venture when Mum surprised me with: 'Mark my words, if it's the last thing you do you will have a child; a girl, I believe. I saw you and her in a dream'. My heart leapt. This was music to my wanna-be-dad ears; pounding disco music, actually!

Mum's ability to predict imminent or actual pregnancy was well known amongst family and friends, sometimes to the annoyance or nervous excitement of the women concerned. She had successfully made such announcements in respect of both my sisters, too, again with mixed reaction.

Pregnancy predictions aside, my mother, like most others, was tuned into her children on most issues affecting them. Unbeknownst to anyone other than my mother or father, I had been born with an extra piece of skin in my private region, and in my late teens I decided to have removed. It was of cosmetic concern to me; just in case some lucky guy found himself staring at it. Once the minor operation was arranged, I didn't tell a single soul about it, and yet my mother phoned the day before to say: "I know about your operation tomorrow". She even told me about the affected area – "I saw a towel over it" - and that the operation "was totally unnecessary". I was embarrassed and spooked, to say the least. I didn't bother trying to deny it, but ended the conversation as soon as I could. The operation went ahead as planned and the dissolving stitches disappeared over the promised period of time. I was happy, but would never forget Mum's apparent, and unwelcome, in my case, ability to foretell sensitive events in my life.

It was now the first week of June 2002, and Mum hadn't been well enough to leave her hospital room once in the preceding eight months. I had turned forty, and she had turned sixty-seven while occupying the same hospital bed. To celebrate her birthday, I bought her the best mango I could find. She barely acknowledged me before mercilessly ripping into her favourite fruit, only taking a breath to tell me "It could be sweeter!" I chuckled and sang happy birthday as I watched bliss replace the pain on her face; I imagined the sweet taste taking her back to Jamaica and happier times. Once done, she found reason to scold me, as she often did: "What are you still doing here so late. You must go home to your house when night-time come," she insisted. But I knew she appreciated my being with her. She'd often end with something more soothing, like: "I don't know what I'd do if I didn't have you". She even got into the habit of telling me she loved me. "You belong to me, you hear me, and I love you – you big head boy!" It was special. Although she had always written the word in birthday and Christmas cards, it was good to hear her actually say it to my face. "I love you too, Mum." I responded, and I meant it. I told her she "was the best Mum in the entire world and that I was lucky to have you too".

It was Wednesday 5th June, and like the night before, I was again by Mum's bedside. She was in a reflective mood tonight, talking about the highs and the lows of her life. She made a point of telling me to make good use of my fortieth birthday present from Gloria Gaynor; a beautiful white Bible, which the legendary singer had signed to me "with Love". I'd unpacked it in front of my delighted mother as she lay in her hospital bed. On seeing it, Mum raised her hand towards the ceiling and said, "Praise the Lord! That's the best present you could ever get".

There was nothing left unsaid between Mum and I now, well, almost. When I accidentally mentioned the previously forbidden subject of my sexuality, I was surprised by the warmth of her response: "People like you are born that way. You are God's other children". She spoke with considerable conviction, and although I didn't really understand what she meant by "other", I felt she meant that we, gay people, are part of the holy family, even if we only have 'second cousin' status. This was progress, as far as my mother was concerned, and a real 'wow' moment for me. It was an acknowledgement of a truth that would have made a huge difference if I'd heard it years earlier, but it was still good to hear it now. Yes, it was very good to hear it now.

As I sat looking across at her, I began to realise how very few happy memories we had together. There were no holidays to reminisce over, no restaurants, no cinema and no theatre outings either. In my tunnel vision in responding to HIV and AIDS, I had neglected my mother, and just about everything else that was important. My love life was another casualty. I did, however, find reason to smile when I recalled how comical she was one night many years earlier, in healthier times, as we sat in her flat watching the Millie Jackson Live at the Dominion video. Mum couldn't contain her feigned disgust at the soul music legend's outrageous adult performance. It was a far cry from the God Channel that would usually provide her TV viewing, but when I offered to turn it off, Mum, in her authentic Jamaican accent, barked, "No! Leave it on so I can see more of this slack woman!" This was "sinful" television, but Mum's wide eyes and raucous belly laughter told me she was thoroughly enjoying herself whilst hating on "dirty" Millie, even if the evangelist in her wouldn't allow such a confession. I remember how it made me laugh out loud just to see her laughing as she was. It was a rare jovial moment in her post-Skippy world. God knows I would struggle to find many other happy nuggets following his departure. It seemed that her true happiness left with him, and Jesus worked hard to offer some kind of substitute.

When I visited Mum on the following rainy Thursday evening, I had every reason to expect my visit to be the same as previous visits, but something was different; very different. Tonight she could not talk at all, her eyes were only partially open and her breathing was shallow. It was a complete contrast to the previous evening, when she told me, with compelling voice, to take care and that she loved me. Perhaps she knew the end was upon her. Hazel, one of the wonderful nurses who had cared for my mother over the months, came into the room, and, almost casually, said, "Oh, I'm sorry to tell you, but your mother's consultant said Mrs Scott isn't likely to make it to tomorrow. I'm so sorry." As I took in the words that I'd been dreading, Hazel asked if she should call my siblings, none of whom had visited all week. I nodded to say yes and she promptly left the room.

Apart from Beverley, I hadn't seen much of Jan or Leo during my mother's time in that hospital room. It was only the night before that she angrily demanded to know: "Where are my other children. It's just not good enough". It was just me and Mum, as usual.

I looked at my mother's listless face and I knew this was it; she had come to the end of her journey. It was time to say goodbye, on this horrible wet summer night. *"Oh my God, this really is it"*, I kept repeating to myself in something of a mini panic. I was alone with my mother in her last moments on Earth and I felt an awesome sense of responsibility to see her through the best I could.

Automatically, my experience of death and dying gained as a 'buddy' at London Lighthouse kicked in. I shut the door, removed my jacket, and climbed onto the bed to hold my mother close; as close as she probably had held me when we first met forty years earlier. She'd been the first person I'd seen on my arrival, and I was going to be the last person she'd see on her way out to meet Jesus, her Lord and savior. I asked Mum to blink twice if she could hear me, and she responded accordingly. Without thinking about it, I got up and started singing for her. I intended to give her the best church service ever, and I wasn't at all concerned about whether anyone else could hear me or not; I was singing for my beloved mother. I started with 'How Great Thou Art', then 'Take My Hand, Precious Lord', then 'Amazing Grace', closing with 'This Day'. These were of course chopped up edited versions, as I couldn't recall all the words to the songs; songs that she had sung throughout my life and hers. I'm sure she didn't mind if I messed them up a little.

Finally, I climbed back onto the bed and rested my cheek against hers, and for a while, that's how we remained; her heartbeat next to mine.

I sensed that we were in our very last moments together, and I reluctantly encouraged her to go:

"It's okay, Mum, you can go now. You look beautiful, and you can go as you are. God is waiting for you. He's up there...you can go now."

For a moment, Mum seemed disturbed. There was no way of ascertaining what was wrong, so I said I would tell everyone that she could not wait and that she loved them. But that wasn't it: there was something more. That's when I thought I saw her lips mouth the name "...Skippy...", but I couldn't be certain. Perhaps her last thoughts had taken her way back to the Jamaican mango trees of her happy childhood, and her Skippy, the sweetest bite of them all. Any bitterness caused by the events of the passing years didn't matter now.

"It's okay, Mum. Go to the light. Jesus is there waiting. One day Dad and I will follow you there. Go now darling, your parents and Bunny are waiting...they are in the light."

In those last very precious moments, it felt as though my mother and I were the only two people on the entire Earth. Her last breath nearly took mine with it. The most important person in my life had left the pain behind to be with Jesus; she had gone into the light. I held onto her for a moment longer before raising myself up to look at her. I noticed that her right eye remained slightly open, and for a moment I told myself that she was still here, perhaps still waiting for my father, her Skippy, to walk in the door. I then did something very strange. I got up off the bed, put my jacket on and walked out of the door. I made my way to the nurse's station and told Hazel that my mother was trying to sleep and she should call me if anything happened.

With that, I took the lift to the ground floor and headed out into the rainy night and to my car. I was crying, but I was also in autopilot. I drove to the Alperton branch of Sainsbury's, as if in some vain attempt to force some kind of normality back into my tragic day. *"Surely Mum was still alive",* I told myself. My haze continued as I wheeled my trolley through the aisles, picking up anything that caught my watery eye.

My mobile rang. It was David, my dear friend from Luton. He'd been calling me almost daily to ask after my mother. He could tell something was very wrong. I told him, "This is it, my friend, she won't last the night." In his usual reassuring tone, he told me not to worry and that everything was going to be fine.

My trolley was half full when a second call came through. It was Hazel from the hospital: "Mr Scott, please return to the hospital. I believe you know…" It was then that I broke down; right there in Sainsbury's. I left my trolley where it was, reconnected with David to say goodbye, and raced out to drive the ten minute journey back to Northwick Park hospital.

As I approached Mum's room, I saw a familiar sign on the door: *'Do not enter'*. I had seen that sign many times before when the staff had been changing my mother's incontinence pads or carrying out some 'personal' treatment. For a moment, as I sat outside the room staring at the door, I imagined that all was well behind it, and that my mother was waiting to see me. The minutes dragged on for what seemed like an eternity as my imagination ran riot.

"How could I have possibly thought Mum had died? How very stupid of me", I thought.

An everlasting twenty minutes or so later, the door opened and Hazel and other nursing colleagues emerged. She wiped a tear away and spoke with a broken, emotion-filled voice: "I am so very sorry, Mr Scott. You can go in now."

"What exactly are you sorry for?" I heard my inner voice of denial say. *"That you kept me waiting?"*

I walked into Mum's room without responding to Hazel, and there she was; lifeless and looking quite dishevelled. It appeared to me that the doctors had tried to resuscitate her, but their efforts couldn't revive the dead. It was true, my mother had died; indeed, she'd been lifeless when I left her earlier in my odd state of mind. Her spirit probably followed me out into the summer rain and into eternal freedom from her damaged body and her last abode; her hospital death room.

The painful truth was now undeniable. *"Oh my God, mum, you're no longer here, my darling"*, I said aloud to the eerily quiet room. The truth sunk in further as I looked down at my precious mother's now pain-free body. My mother hadn't looked this peaceful in years.

After a little while, I snapped back into my 'caring son' mode. I knew she would hate to not look her best, so I set about trying to make her look her usual, beautiful self. I straightened her head, which had become almost unnaturally positioned to the left, looking towards the now closed door. I closed her open mouth and patted down her hair, which had become totally white over the lonely years without my dad. It was as I touched her forehead that I felt the death-confirming coldness that started to seep in; it was a numb coldness that I'd felt before in similar circumstances. Yes, Mum really had gone; all of that living, loving, hoping, and praying, had led her to this lonely room and her final moment on this Earth. *"This wasn't the ending you deserved, darling"*, I heard myself say. But I had to accept that it was what it was; it was Doreth May Eubank Scott's ending, and it really didn't matter whether I thought it was fitting or not. I couldn't undo this stark reality, as much as my heart desperately wanted me to try.

I tried unsuccessfully to fully close her right eye, which had remained slightly open. In life my mother used to say that the dead are still looking for someone when an eye remains open post mortem. In her case, I felt confident that the person concerned would be none other than my father, her Skippy, the love and heartbreak of her life. I was deeply saddened that she had died waiting for him to come back into her life. Now, even in death, she was keeping an eye open for him.

Once I made Mum look her best, I went over to a vase which still contained the red roses that I'd purchased earlier in the week. I chose the best looking stems and strategically placed them around Mum's head on the white pillows. "There you go, Mum," I said. "You look fabulous, as always." I was no longer tearful. I accepted the reality of the situation. Crying couldn't change it. The lady of my life was now safe in the arms of Jesus. She was at peace and beautiful, once again.

I was sitting on the bed touching my mother's head in silent acceptance when my siblings began to arrive; first Beverley and then Leo and his wife. Jan arrived a little later. It was Thursday night and this was the first time any of them had seen our mother all week, and it was now too late. I was disappointed that they could not have prioritized seeing her before now, but there was no point in saying so, at least not tonight.

My mother was buried on the only blistering hot day of the month, the 17th of June 2002. The Hearse carrying her 'last supper' engraved coffin and generous flowers, paused outside her home at 8 Harrowdene Close in Wembley before driving to Harlesden High Street; a regular shopping site for my mother, and the place she would use her megaphone to try and lure passing shoppers to God with threats of "certain hell fire", if they failed to heed her words.

Her last church service took place at her regular place of worship, Leghorn Road Church. The service was attended by a couple of hundred people. As I looked out at the many sad faces, one stood out; it was my dad. Skippy had finally come to see his ex-wife. I heard my sister Beverley demand to know 'What are you doing here?' as he took his seat. Fran was in the country too, but she decided, wisely, to stay away from the service. Uncle Sonny and many other familiar faces surrounded him. Personally I had nothing to say to Dad, not today; this day was about and for my mother. For a moment the thought crossed my mind; p*erhaps his presence would cause her eye to finally close.*

Some of my work colleagues from Brent had come to the service, which was very kind of them. In fact, everyone at Brent Social Services had been very understanding towards me and my mother over the preceding months, for which I was very grateful. The flowers they sent were absolutely beautiful and really touched my heart. Friends and family from the decades were all there to pay their sincere respect; Miss Evelyn, Sister Warner, my mother's closest church sister - so many familiar faces. My mother would be proud of such a large turnout. Longtime friends of mine, including Lloyd, were there too. I also spotted Orla and Titi.

My cousin Maxine was kind enough to arrange the printing of the programme, and the choir sang the same songs I had when my mother was in her last moments, only this time they sounded as they should; heavenly, and with all the lyrics where they should be.

When I got to my feet and made my way to the platform over my mother's closed coffin, where I was supposed to share my memories and thoughts about my wonderful mother, I found that I physically could not get my over-emotional mouth to speak; I was overwhelmed. I paused and then tried again, but no sound came out. I decided to stop trying, as the tears rolled down my face. For a moment all I could do was stand there, looking out at the many faces looking back at me. My mother's Pastor tried to help by shouting "Courage, courage" at me, but it wasn't courage I was lacking, it was simply the ability to form words with my mouth. I looked down at the coffin below me and still couldn't speak. Realising that I wasn't going to be able to overcome my problem, Jan and Doreene came and stood either side of me, linking their arms through mine. It was comforting. After another minute or so, I found my voice and was able to finally give my personal tribute to my mother. I don't recall much about what I said, but I do remember saying that "my mother had been both my mother and my father". That's how I felt. I saw my father stand up and walk out at the back as I was speaking. I knew my mother had forgiven him and still loved him, but here he was, walking out on her again.

God bless you, my dear mother. You are now a wonderful angel.

We buried my mother at Alperton Cemetery on that beautiful sunny day, and on her wrist was a gold watch I'd purchased for her. I visited every day for the first two weeks until someone said to me, "Vernal, she isn't in there, you know? She's with you wherever you are." I knew this was true. I carried her with me now, and my heartbeat was hers.

On his return to Jamaica, my father, supported at a well-attended ceremony by Aunt Vera, erected a beautiful memorial stone in his ex-wife's memory. It was laid in May Pen, her birthplace: where she once picked mangoes with the boy who was to become her husband and life-long love. She could now truly rest in peace, and wait for him.

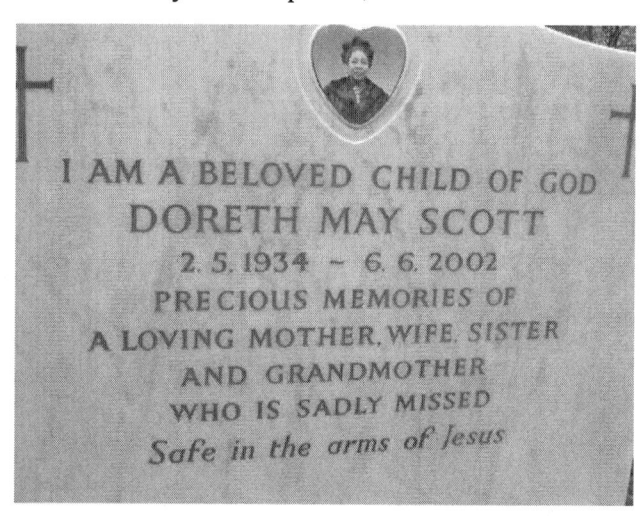

I AM A BELOVED CHILD OF GOD
DORETH MAY SCOTT
2. 5. 1934 ~ 6. 6. 2002
PRECIOUS MEMORIES OF
A LOVING MOTHER, WIFE, SISTER
AND GRANDMOTHER
WHO IS SADLY MISSED
Safe in the arms of Jesus

45. WHO'S THE DADDY?!

IT WAS NOVEMBER 2002, and my forty-first birthday was upon me. It had been five awful months since I buried my beloved mother, and I was missing her terribly. Her passing left a huge gaping hole in my world and made me realize that my life was empty of someone to love and love unconditionally. I still couldn't entirely grasp the fact that she was no longer here. I found some comfort from friends and family, and TV programmes by Jonathan Edwards, TD Jakes and Joel Osteen. Gospel music by Tramaine Hawkins and the soothing tones of Scott Walker and Barbra Streisand helped too. But nothing could quite rescue me from the grief I was feeling.

I needed some good news, and when it came, it did so in emphatic form. My phone rang and it was a deeply emotional Orla; the pregnancy test following our most recent effort was positive. She was pregnant! I was completely over the moon, and over the stars, too! That very morning I had been praying we would be successful. *"I'm going to be a Dad"* I heard myself say, again and again. Orla was too emotional to talk, so we agreed to chat again later.

I quickly broke all the rules and began telling close family and friends immediately. There was no stopping me. I had reason to smile again, thanks to God, and my mother too, of course!

The baby was due in the summer, and I was already looking forward to it. I was also looking forward to my new job: after sixteen years of service, the time had come to leave Brent. My work there was done; in fact it had been done for some time. I'd spent the last few years feeling rather lost and lacking in direction in my career. However, the racist murder of Stephen Lawrence in East London caused a chain reaction, mostly generated by his determined heartbroken parents, Neville and Doreen. A number of equality officer posts were popping up all over the place and someone suggested that I apply for Head of Equality at Islington Council. I applied and was successful. My remit was to manage a small team, ensure the council was meeting its obligations in respect of UK and European equality laws, and to promote equality throughout the four thousand strong workforce and wider community of Islington. The position was secondment for a year; I would then have to apply for the permanent job if it came up. Either way, it was time to leave Brent. I had previously applied for a job at the HIV Centre in Islington, and was offered that too, but I turned that one down because of a feeling that HIV specialist centres were increasingly a thing of the past, plus I was completely burnt out on the subject and its horrific consequences; the conveyor belt of so much death and dying had taken its toll on me in ways that would later become very apparent. For now, the feeling was that I had done my part and was proud of my achievements at Brent, but it was time to move on. My send-off was made rather special, when Paul Boateng, local MP and Treasury Minister in Tony Blair's government, made a surprise appearance to wish me well. He was very kind, and concluded his address with a heartfelt "Thank you", which he repeated three times in his native tongue. I was truly touched.

It was February 2003, and in advance of my last day at Brent, I decided, before starting my new job, that I would treat myself to a holiday to one of my favourite cities, San Francisco. I left my itinerary with Orla and Titi and jetted into the warm sunshine. It wasn't hot at that time of year, but anything was blistering when compared to London's icy February breezes.

Orla called me a few times to give me updates on the pregnancy and to let me know how KC was doing. I really appreciated that, especially as she had recently experienced a scare which caused her to fear losing the baby.

I had visited San Francisco a few times over the years, but it was now a city living in the aftermath of the AIDS catastrophe; which had decimated its once thriving gay community, including its local disco superstar, Sylvester. I was also shocked to see the hordes of homeless, mostly black people, living on the streets. It became virtually impossible to leave my hotel without being approached by people begging for money. *This was George W. Bush's America.* I caught up with Malcolm, my old friend from the People's Group, who had long made San Francisco his home. It was great to see him, but somehow the city had lost its appeal for me. I was happy to leave.

On returning to London, I was excited about my new job, but nowhere as much as my forthcoming fatherhood; I got butterflies every time I thought about it, and that was a lot. *Maybe I should pinch myself for the hundredth time.* I read books and jumped on the internet so that I could be fully informed about my developing baby. Orla and Titi invited me along to the first scan, and we all got excited at the little image on the screen and declined being told about its gender. But while we were waiting for copies of the pictures in the busy reception, Orla, seemingly unconcerned by the many people in close ear shot, announced: "I thought he was going to put his hand up my vagina". Titi looked at her and said an embarrassed, "Orla!" *Oh no!* I thought. Orla looked back at Titi with an expression of complete bewilderment; she'd done nothing wrong, in her view.

KC had a sleepover at my house a few months later. I was beginning to feel like a dad all of a sudden, and it felt good. But as great as things were with KC, I knew that Orla's brother was the great white elephant in the room; he was KC's biological father after all, and could assume his rightful role in KC's life at any time and leave me out in the cold. KC and the new baby were vulnerable to this, and so was I.

Orla was five months pregnant when I received an invitation to come over for a dinner and chat with her and Titi. KC wasn't interested on sitting his own chair; he had to sit on my lap, as always. He had become quite attached to me and both women could see this. At times he would refer to me as "Dad" and then try to correct himself..."Vernal!" Once the meal was over, I bathed KC, read him a story and put him to bed. It wasn't the first time that I'd done that.

When I returned to the living room, both women were sat together; they never touched or showed affection towards each other in front of me. Orla said they needed to have a chat with me about our mutual expectations and that I should take a seat. The smile was quickly wiped off my face as they explained that they'd had a change of mind about having a dad involved, and that they now saw me as some kind of 'uncle' who would see the children on special occasions, such as birthdays, Easter and at Christmas. I couldn't believe my mortified ears. I quickly asked whether it was something I'd said or done. Orla said no, "it's just that we've clarified the vision of our family, and a Dad isn't what we now want". I was lost for words, and so, apparently, was Titi, who allowed Orla to do most of the talking. Looking at Titi, I said, "You both knew from the outset that I wanted full involvement, and that's what you agreed would be the case. Now you've simply changed your minds?" A now irritated Orla said "Yes, Vernal, we've changed our minds. That's how it is!" I was gutted. "You're five months pregnant and I'm not in a position to change my mind. They looked at each other and smirked. I sensed that it was time to leave, and I did. Titi showed me out and as she did so, she said there was no need for me to collect KC from the nursery anymore.

The sweetness had just turned very sour indeed!

I drove home with tears in my eyes. My role as Dad had just been dismissed and the two women, one carrying my child, were totally unconcerned about how I felt about it or the impact it would have on KC and the new baby. I was beyond upset. I'd been completely duped and had no one else to blame but me. My rose-tinted glasses were now as clear as my pathetic stupidity.

I decided to refrain from making contact in the hope that this would help the situation. When Titi called to invite me to a 'murder mystery' dinner party they were hosting with friends, I thought my strategy may have worked. But when the event came around, Orla's used it to confirm her attitude towards me was still as negative as before. She was cold and hostile. I held my composure but called her the next day to try to reason with her. She abruptly told me that she did not want to discuss it. "I don't care if you're upset", she hissed. She then dismissed my call as if she'd answered the phone to someone who had misdialled.

The two women had moved the goal posts and there was nothing I could say or do about it.

The following Sunday we agreed to meet up in Palmers Green for a previously planned day out with KC. I again tried to reason with both women and told them I was feeling shut out, but Titi said "the matter wasn't up for discussion". Both women appeared arrogant and unconcerned. Orla was particularly cutting and nasty. Everything I said was met with comments such as "too traditional". She even said "Biology didn't matter - anybody could be 'dad' to the kids". KC could sense my unhappiness and came to sit on my lap. My spontaneous, reckless stupidity had come back to smack me bang in the face, and the damage wasn't being repaired anytime soon.

Moments later as we said a cold goodbye, KC clung to me and shouted: "I want to go with Vernal". Titi said, "Maybe another time". But KC wasn't having it, and started to cry and pull away from her, but he was no match for his much stronger mother. He looked back scores of times as they walked away from me. I felt so very sorry him, and for myself too. The sweet was suddenly grotesquely sour.

Titi was turning out to be the friend from hell. I had been used and was now being dumped.

It was the 10th of July, and Orla was eight months pregnant. Today was my dad's birthday. He and I had remained in touch since Mum's funeral last year; I tried to forgive him, for my mother if not myself. Before I could get my thoughts together to dial his number in Jamaica to wish him a happy day, my phone rang. It was Titi. We hadn't been in touch for about a month, as the nasty hostility had become too much to deal with. Her tone was more business-like rather than friendship, which was fine by me: "Vernal, just thought to call to let you know the baby arrived this morning, six weeks early". I jumped out of my chair with the shock of the unexpected news, and it took a moment to absorb it. Titi had no congratulations to offer, of course, neither did she volunteer to tell me the gender of my child, so I had to ask. She went silent, and I could hear her puffing away at a cigarette. Then, as if she were telling me the time of day, she puffed "It's a girl". "Great", I said. "And they're both OK?" I followed up. "Yeah, yeah, they're both fine", Titi grunted back. The stilted conversation was painfully awkward. Titi said "We didn't have time to shop, so if you're coming to the hospital you'll need to pop into Mothercare at Brent Cross and pick up some bits and pieces". Without waiting for me to agree, she began to reel off a list of essentials. When I thought that was it, she added, "Oh yes, Orla needs a feeding bra". I didn't even know that such a thing existed, but I agreed to get one anyway. I neglected to ask about the size but guessed it wouldn't be small. I put the phone down and tried to gather my thoughts. *"I'm a dad, my God, I'm a dad!"'* I repeated to myself. *I thanked God and my mother. The early arrival of my daughter on my dad's birthday wasn't at all lost on me.* But I had to do all of this shopping before I could see my child. *My daughter!* Of course, Titi was too busy calling people to do any of this herself; I was just another person on her list, it seemed. Of course I was.

Before jumping into my recently acquired FTO, I called Beverley, Doreene and Paul, to give them the great news. They were all happy for me, but they were also concerned; they were aware that relations had seriously soured between the mothers and me over the course of the pregnancy. Paul had been a real champion friend, and became my primary confidant.

The well trained staff at Mothercare came to my rescue as I struggled to make the right purchases. I eventually left the store with nappies, new-born baby clothes, presents for KC for him to give to the baby, and for the baby to give to him, and of course, a large feeding bra.

When I finally made it to the maternity unit at North Middlesex Hospital with my many bags and racing heart and mind, I saw Titi sitting in the maternity unit reception. She was with Orla's parents, who I'd met once before. They offered uneasy smiles as I approached to ask after Orla and the baby. Her parents had come from Cambridge and had already gone in to see their daughter and new grandchild, so it dawned upon me that I was not at the top of the list when Titi rang earlier. Titi answered without looking at me: "Fine to the first question and no to the second. You'll have to wait here as her parents want to go in again". Orla's happy mother said "Oh, the baby is so beautiful", before trying to catch her words. I felt as welcome as a piece of raw meat on a vegetarian's plate. Ignoring the woman's embarrassment, I asked Titi whether a decision had been made about the middle name. I had previously requested that a baby girl be given my mother's middle name: May. Titi replied that they were still thinking about it. Orla's parents and Titi then completely blanked me and carried on chatting as if weren't there. After a little while, and in exasperation, I stood up and approached the security guard at the door to the maternity ward. He was a tall black man with a heavy Nigerian accent. I said I was the father of a new born I was keen to see her, now! On hearing this, an irritated Titi came over and told the guard that I had to wait. The guard responded by telling her: "This is the father, he goes in now". "No he doesn't" said a now angry Titi. The guard ignored her instruction and ushered me and my bags through. *"Who's the Daddy, huh?"* I muttered under my breath, as I made my way in, leaving the guard to argue it out with a furious Titi.

A smiling nurse pointed out where I could find Orla, and in a short few steps I entered the room where a disappointed looking Orla lay under the covers of her six-bed room. She wasn't at all happy to see me. In an attempt to encourage a lighter atmosphere, I said "Hi Or" placing the bags down. Her bitter response followed: "Don't call me Or, my name is Orla, use it! And where's Titi?" She demanded. I ignored the question.

Her hostility was something I'd got used to, but I wasn't to be baited, not today.

"I guess that's my daughter over there!" I said, making my way over to the see-through plastic cot.

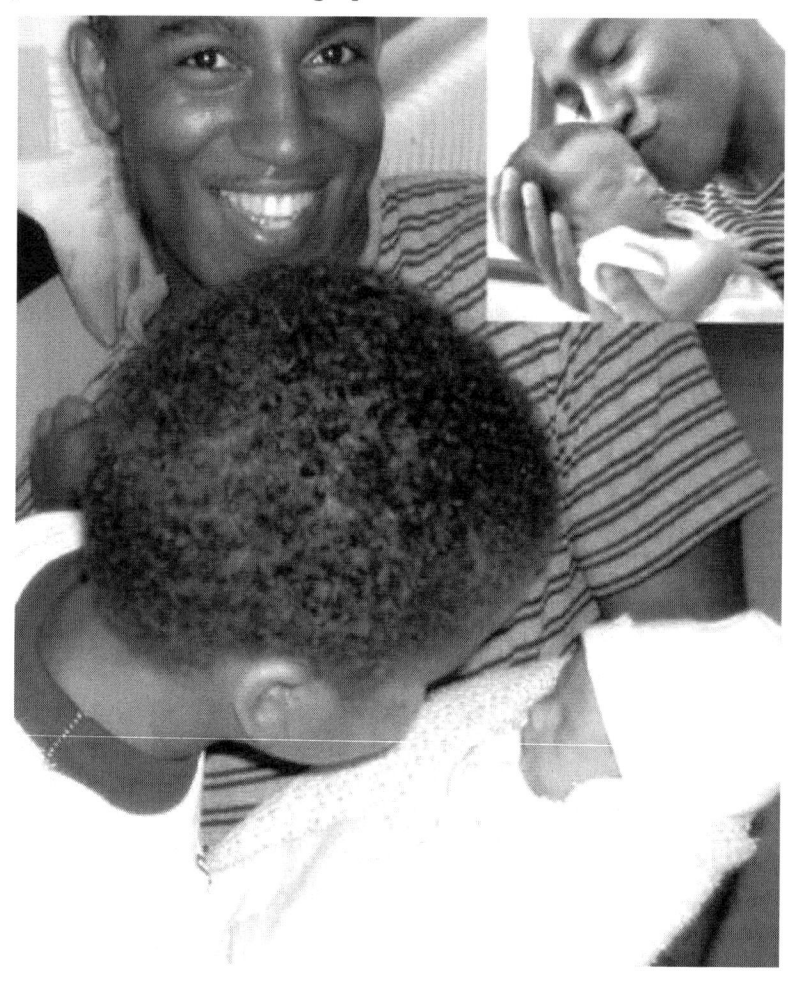

And there she was; I was peering down at the face of my daughter for the very first time; *my child.* To say she was beautiful would not do her justice; she was a little sleeping Goddess. For a moment I disappeared into my thoughts: *"Oh my goodness; this is my daughter!"* I was in love with my little angel and nothing else mattered for a while; not Titi, not Orla, nothing! Mum had gone, but I once again had a reason to love, unconditionally. I picked my daughter up, ignoring the demon gaze from Orla; I was now holding the most important human being in the world in my arms. My daughter!

As if overcome by a morsel of humanity, a less hostile Orla interrupted my dream state: "Her first name is going to be Roslyn, and we've agreed that her middle name will be May, after your mother."

"Oh, thanks" I said, and continued smiling down at my little angel, inspecting her cute fingers and toes. For a moment all the stress and turmoil of the last few months didn't matter. I wasn't going to let Titi or Orla spoil this moment. "Hey, lil' Miss May Scott", I whispered. *"This one's for you, Mum!"*

Titi came in with Orla's parents following closely behind. She too appeared less hostile. Orla looked relieved to see her. As I returned May to her cot, Titi asked if I would collect KC from the nursery and bring him to meet the new baby. I agreed and went on my way. I wanted to see my daughter, but I also wanted to see KC. Anyway, I needed some respite from the earlier tension.

I jumped into my car with my mind all fired up and shouted: *"Yes, May, I'm your daddy. Welcome, my sweet one. I will never leave you. Never!"* It was just a shame I didn't feel able to say those words in her presence. "Who's the Daddy?" I shouted to myself, as I drove off. "Me", came my emphatic reply.

As usual, KC was very excited on seeing me; it had been a while. He was even more so when we got back to the hospital and he set eyes on his new 'sister'. I held May as he and I posed for a few pictures, which another smiling nurse kindly snapped for me.

After a while, I decided to leave to call Dad and tell him that his birthday present was a new granddaughter. He was both surprised and thrilled; "Kiss her for me, please" he requested. As well as my dad, I of course called a zillion other people. I was happy to be a dad, despite the circumstances; I was going to do my best to make it work. I had to. It wasn't about me and my feelings anymore.

The next day could not come soon enough, and I made my way to the hospital as early as permissible. Titi wasn't there on my arrival to see Orla greet me with a deliberately contrived smile. Despite this, the atmosphere seemed a little happier than the previous day, and I spent my time just looking at May peeping back at me. I was in love with my cute girl. Orla and I barely exchanged a word for my hour visit. Just as I was about to exit, she brought me down off my cloud: "Oh Vernal, don't come tomorrow. There are other people who need to see the baby". I was not happy, but I did not respond. To further ruin my mood, she added "And please refrain from using that 'Dad' word around the children; they will know you as Vernal, not Dad. KC doesn't even know what a Dad is!" I left without saying goodbye; there was nothing *'good'* about this, apart from May and KC, of course. Orla didn't have a clue about what the children needed; it was all about her and Titi. Titi's strap-on, if she had one, may do wonders in the bedroom, but it didn't make her a dad. That was me.

I waited until I was in my car to vent, and I let rip.

In the hope that my absence would allow things to cool a little, I let two agonizing days pass before returning to the hospital to see my child. When I got there, I soon found that Orla's mood hadn't changed. She greeted me with: "Oh, it's you again".

I replied in kind: "Yes, the baby's Dad is here" I retorted, failing to appreciate that I was allowing myself to sink to her level.

"What did I say to you about that word?" She snapped back. I ignored her and went to look at my daughter who was fast asleep, content in her own little dream world. Seeing her made the aggravation worthwhile, it really did. I was her Daddy, whether Orla and Titi liked it or not, and I intended to be a Dad for life; not just birthdays and Christmas.

Orla and May went home to Tottenham within seven days; their departure was delayed because of an episode of premature baby jaundice, which the hospital successfully treated.

I deliberately let a couple of days pass before I went to visit. But as soon as I arrived, and we were on our way out again; to shop for 'baby things'. KC and I went in my car, and Orla, May, Titi and Titi's mother, who was visiting from Jamaica, made the trip to Monthercare in their car. I later picked up the bill for two boot loads of baby-related purchases, but not before I exaggerated a laugh when the cashier asked Orla when her baby was due; the new mother was not impressed. The baby was out of sight at the rear of the shop with Titi's mother playing Nanny. I really liked Titi's mother, so much so that she took my number. In a later phone call she told me "This isn't right, this isn't right at all!" She meant the way I was being treated. I thanked her for her concern and mentioned that my dad lived in Clarendon as well. I gave her his number and said goodbye.

I'd earlier set up a direct debit, paying two hundred pounds a month to the joint recipients, Orla and Titi – as per Orla's instruction. Neither woman protested about my money, of course they didn't! This unwelcome, "too traditional" Dad's cash was very welcome, even if the Dad wasn't.

I visited twice a week at first; Orla told me "this was more than enough". As before May's arrival, the pattern of my subsequent visits involved my collecting KC from nursery, then treating him to a couple of hours at a play centre, before making our way to his mothers' house. Once there I would spend a little while interacting with baby May before heading home myself. As young as she was, my daughter and I were already bonding, or at least I was firmly bonded with her.

Although I was treading on tip toes around them, Orla and Titi began to pick at everything I did, even things I didn't do. Orla insisted again and again that I was unreliable and I had let KC down. Her latest justification was that I had cancelled a visit due to a severe tummy upset. She did not want to accept that it was genuine. These baseless accusations were a precursor for what they really wanted to say; I was getting in the way of their 'family'.

In trying to secure my role in 'the family', I again brought up the subject of my missing Parental Rights. Orla's response was that I had to wait until she thought I had "earned" such rights, but it was obvious from her almost juvenile belittling attitude, that such a day would never come. Titi and Orla had the children and all the rights.

The option to go to family court crossed my mind, but I concluded this would only make matters worse. I didn't know what to do; this was not the vision of 'family' I had in mind, nor was it the one promised. I was no longer welcome, but I was being tolerated, for now.

In late August 2002, the mothers and I went to register the baby's birth, but even then Orla saw an opportunity to try to humiliate. "Are you happy with the surname, Vernal?" It was hyphenated, bearing both women's surnames. Scott was nowhere to be seen, apart from where the certificate identified me as the father. I signed where the clerk indicated with a feeling that my daughter had just been robbed of her true identity. The only consolation was that her middle name, May, was now official. *For you, Mum.*

Once outside the registry, I found it within me to suggest that we take some photos to mark the event, but while Titi willingly agreed, Orla refused, saying: "I don't want to stand anywhere near you; I don't know you well enough!" I couldn't help myself and retorted: "You knew me well enough to take my sperm, and to do so without insisting I had an HIV test". She had no answer, just an embarrassed smirk. In the end we posed with fake smiles, apart from the pictures I took alone with May.

In line with my on-going poor judgment, I suggested we find somewhere to eat. After we settled into our seats outside the coffee shop, I asked when they thought my family could meet KC and the baby. A red faced Orla hissed her response:

"Why should your family meet our children? You're just someone off the street as far as I'm concerned!" For a moment, I considered getting up and walking away; which was exactly what they wanted me to do. Instead, I kept a calm tone and asked the same question again, this time adding that I'd like it to happen on my 42nd birthday; 16th November 2003. After a series of glances and chuckles between themselves, the two women agreed. I got the impression they thought it would be a good giggle. Orla, characteristically, corked the moment with her next comment: "My baby is my gift to Titi. I would never willingly consent to you having legal Parental Responsibility, never! Do you get it?" I got up, kissed May's sleeping face in her pram, and went on my way.

When I got home I promptly deleted all the pictures we took, apart from those I took alone with May. The others were far too contrived to look at ever again with anything other than regret bordering on contempt.

I had been deceived by Titi and Orla, but more tragically, I had blatantly deceived myself. If the Olympics had a category for sporty fools then I would win it, and I deserved to; Vernal Scott, the world's greatest fool. I had discarded common sense in pursuit of fatherhood and the attainment of my personal bundle of joy. But sadly, or even predictably, the pretty bundle now had a foul odour, and it wasn't dirty nappies; it was the stench of two women who had decided to be as nasty and smelly as possible, hoping that I could stand it no longer. But I had no intention of walking away easily. After dealing with AIDS, and death and dying on a grand scale, I could deal with these two obnoxiously vile individuals, and if I couldn't, then I'd pray God would.

I loved KC and May unconditionally, but the circumstances couldn't be much worse than they were. There was no guarantee that Orla and Titi would be together for life, and whatever may happen with KC and his biological father in the future, I would always be May's father. I wasn't going anywhere.

My birthday rolled around quickly enough, and even though they were an hour late, Orla and Titi kept to the arrangement by bringing the children to my house at Talbot Road, Wembley. In the end, it was a pleasant day and I was happy that Leo and Beverley had finally met the children. My cousin Doreene, my good friend Paul, and former colleagues from Brent were also there. Another friend shot some video footage, which unbeknownst to me at the time, would come in very useful at a later date. I was kind or foolish enough to introduce Orla and Titi as the mothers in my new family, but the two women retreated into the garden.

Later that month I was invited to KC's birthday party at Orla and Titi's home. As a present, I bought him his first bicycle and he did his best to mow down as many of his guests as possible, apart from me, of course. I noticed that there were lots of 'family' photos around the place, but this Dad was nowhere to be seen.

When Christmas came, the mothers' told me that I was not welcome at their house, but said it was OK to bring my presents on Boxing Day. When I got there, Orla didn't waste any time in getting to her festive point: "Vernal, your visits are still too frequent". They hadn't seen me since KC's birthday, but there was worse to come. She added: "And we think you should now see the children for an hour, once a month, here at our house". I didn't react at first, but took a deep breath. I was finally being *disappeared*. One hour a month was offensive and unacceptable. KC and May would soon forget me.

"I'm not going to see the kids just twelve times a year!" I told Orla. She didn't bother to reply, but her smirk confirmed what we both knew; there was nothing I could do about it.

Weeks passed as the women cancelled date after date. Eventually, I was forced to write to them to complain that I hadn't been allowed to see May or KC in nearly nine weeks. I was ignored.

Matters came to a head when I was given a ten-minute notice by phone that the mothers' and children were on their way to Spain. Although this was for a holiday, I realised then that they could have easily been moving to New Zealand, and there'd be nothing I could say or do about it. It was time to act.

I knew I had no legal rights in respect of KC, he wasn't my biological child, but I did an internet search to find information on my rights regarding May. Orla had all the rights. If I was to have any at all, then they would have to be won in family court.

I decided to consult lawyers near my new home in Hampstead. Daniel, a Partner in the firm and their lead lawyer on family matters, agreed to accept my case, but he warned that he could offer no guarantees. I was willing to put my faith in him, and the man above.

The two women wrote to tell me about their "shock" on returning from Spain to find court papers waiting for them. But I had no apology to give; I was tired of having my nose rubbed in the dirt by them. Court was the only way forward for me, even if I was only awarded half an hour a year; I'd rather have that than continue to be toyed with by Orla and Titi. I was no longer willing to be their puppet. Court was unknown territory for me, but the women had given me no alternative.

We first went to family court in the spring of 2004, but due to the 'private' nature of such hearings, very little can be shared about the content. All parties attended, and after stating my case, I was immediately given 'contact' with both children. I was also awarded Parental Rights for my daughter. The two women were spitting nails. Titi was required to leave the court room when it came to matters specific to May, although she later successfully applied to be joined to future proceedings.

I was thrilled with the outcome of the hearing because it meant my daughter could not be removed from the UK without my consent for periods longer than a regular holiday. I had been awarded a pittance in contact time, but it was better than what I had been afforded by the two women. Five hours a fortnight was okay for now, but not forever. *What about sleep-overs and holidays?* There would have to be future hearings.

KC was thrilled on seeing me and it was great to be able to drive away with the children in the back of my car. One of the first things I did was take them to where my mother was buried, as a tribute to the great lady whom I continued to miss every single day. Whenever I imagined God was too busy to hear my prayers, I'd ask my mother to pass them on. *The visual made me smile.*

Contact continued until the mothers decided to withdraw KC without explanation. I decided against returning to court in the hope that his mothers' would change their minds without the court's intervention.

Eight months without KC had passed, and then one night, after I'd dropped off May to Titi at their house, I took a back road in order to avoid a traffic jam on my normal route home, and there, before my eyes, was Orla and KC. I immediately slammed on the brakes. On spotting my distinctive Mitsubishi FTO, KC shouted, "Dad, Dad, Dad" and tried frantically to pull away from Orla to get to me. She responded by dragging him by the arm in the opposite direction. I climbed out and shouted "I love you KC, I will always love you." He continued to shout and struggle: "I want to see my dad; I want to see my dad, please..." I watched as the distressed child was dragged out of sight. I drove away with a tear in my eye. I felt so sorry for him, but I was also pleased that he wanted to see me as much as I wanted to see him. Perhaps going back to court is the right way forward, but I then remembered; I wasn't his biological dad and had no rights.

By late summer 2005, the mothers also stopped me seeing May. Before this happened, I was instructed to stop coming to their house, and instead, had to collect and return May to Orla or Titi at a local sports centre. It was on one such drop-off that Orla pushed me in the chest, saying "Go on Vernal, go for it!" clearly wanting me to hit her back. But I was wise enough to not take the bait, as much as I wanted to. Instead, and with my good judgment back in play, I phoned the police. She then hurried away with May. The incident was witnessed by Paul, my friend of old, who just happened to be with me on this occasion. When the police arrived they were quick to tell me that my feet would not have touched the pavement on the way to the police station if I had retaliated. They then left me to go after her, and she ultimately received a formal caution. She had lost the plot.

Out of vengeance, the mothers' then insisted that I collect and return May at Tottenham police station; they were hoping that I'd be too embarrassed to comply, but they were wrong: Mount Everest would not have kept me away from my daughter.

When their tactics failed, the women decided to ignore the existing court order and unilaterally stop all contact, leaving me with no option but to return to court. At the same time, Orla approached the Child Support Agency (CSA), and I was soon paying four hundred and thirty pounds a month in maintenance. The CSA did not concern themselves with any 'special circumstances'; I had to pay or it would be docked from my pay.

Even worse, I was soon to learn that the family court system lacked any consistency, and that a heartbreaking eighteen months would pass before I'd see either child again.

In the intervening months, I was to play Russian roulette with my life as I sank to dangerous levels of depression, brought about by PAT – Post AIDS Trauma; a little acknowledged condition affecting people who were at the front of the battle. My on-going grief about bereavements in my family and amongst my friends, and now the loss of contact with the children, left me feeling as though I was about to break.

46. BROTHER LEO AND THE LORD'S PRAYER

IT WAS OCTOBER 2005 and Leo had been seriously unwell and resident at the Royal Free hospital for three months. He had a pseudo tumour - a complex blood clot in his lower abdomen, the size of a large orange. His doctors knew the clot needed to be removed or it would eventually kill him, but they were afraid to act because of the complexity of dealing with this type of tumour, which was further complicated by his underlying haemophilia - the original cause of the clot. He was now fifty-two, and had had a number health scares in recent years, including a near-death event which resulted in him needing a colonoscopy, but this was by far the most serious. I could see that he was very secretly afraid of what might befall him. I was aware that most people with haemophilia in 2005 did not make it beyond their mid-fifties, but was hopeful that my brother would be different. Unlike Bunny, our deceased brother, Leo was generally relatively healthy.

I lived across the road from the hospital, and was therefore able to visit him almost daily, often bringing my home-cooked rice and peas, topped with jerk chicken or roast lamb. He laughingly told me that his wife "can't cook black people's food" and that he appreciated my visits very much. As he cleaned off the plate, he said he didn't think it an accident that I lived so close. He also let slip that he often watched me as I walked past the hospital every morning on my way to Islington via Hampstead overground station. I suddenly felt very close to my big brother. It was during one of these happier visits that one of his female visitor's, who was obviously worried for him, held his hand and commented: "I don't look good wearing black, Leo!" In typical good humour, Leo responded: "Well, I don't look good in pine". We all cracked up, Leo laughing louder than the rest of us.

Before contact was stopped, I took May to see him in hospital. Like most people close to me, Leo was well aware of the battles I was having with the mothers, and he couldn't understand why they were so hostile. He encouraged me to "keep fighting" for my kids – plural!

Leo was increasingly pessimistic and depressed about his situation, and to be honest, so was I. His devoted wife was there every day and did her best to encourage him. The two children he had with her, and his daughter from a previous relationship, all visited, too.

One night when I was leaving his bedside, he looked particularly glum. I gripped his hand in mine and said goodnight and began to walk away when he called out for me to come back. He had something of an embarrassed look on his face: "I can't remember the words to The Lord's Prayer. Can you help me remember?" He asked. Perhaps he expected a different response, but I replied, "You don't have to worry about the words when you pray from your heart, my brother". I saw his face relax. I continued, "The Lord is my shepherd...the rest can come from your heart and God will hear you", I promised him. I meant what I'd said and he looked reassured. We said goodnight again.

Leo went into the operating theatre on a surprisingly warm day in late October. I went to see him beforehand and joked with him and his nurses about making sure they "strapped him down because he had wandering hands". He laughed and was in good spirits. I told him that I'd bring him some dumplings later, one of his favourite foods. I wished him well and I left for a long walk on Hampstead heath, and prayed for him as I went. The heath had become my sanctuary over recent years. It was a special place where my stress seemed to disappear into the trees.

Leo's operation went well, but as anticipated, he bled excessively both during and afterwards, so he was taken to intensive care to aid his recovery. By the time he went for surgery, he'd developed an infection which wasn't being treated effectively because doctors couldn't identify exactly what it was, and we didn't know it at the time, but it would play into the eventual outcome of his situation. Following surgery, Leo developed DIC (Disseminated Intravascular

Coagulation), which involves clotting in small blood vessels and additional random bleeding elsewhere.

Most of the family and his dedicated friends came to see him – Frank, Conrad, Ruben and Jeff, amongst them; these were life-long friends – no, 'brothers', since his arrival in the UK. Aunt Edna came down from Coventry, too. Leo was on a ventilator but looked peaceful and well. He was to be unconscious for some time, according to his doctor, who added that Leo could probably hear me and encouraged me to talk to him as normal, and I rose to the opportunity. Leo was addicted to fast cars and Formula One racing, so I spoke to him about that and told him he could come to watch it on my large plasma when he was better.

Leo's wife reluctantly left the hospital to freshen up and change her clothes, and I promised to stay until she got back. While I remained chatting to Leo, a nurse approached to explain that they needed to change his dressing and asked Aunt Edna and I to step into the corridor for a few minutes, which we did.

We stood in the corridor catching up on each other's news for what began to feel like a long time. The same nurse eventually emerged from the ward and hurried towards us. She asked that we come quickly as Leo has taken a sudden turn for the worse. On our re-entry to the ward, we were both shocked to discover that in the time we had been standing in the corridor, Leo had suffered a massive heart attack and resuscitation efforts had left him looking as though he'd gone ten rounds in the boxing ring and lost, leaving his eyes bulging from their sockets. I immediately left his bedside to phone his wife to get her to return to the hospital in hast. Sadly, Leo never regained consciousness, although his heart carried on beating until just before midnight, when it beat for the last time. His wife and both my sisters were with him. I decided to wait for the news across the road at my home. Emotionally, I couldn't be there, but I was with him in spirit. In truth, I felt Leo had left us at the time of his heart attack. I had said goodbye then.

His funeral took place just after my birthday and was well attended by his many friends and family members, including his three children. Some of my friends were there too. He was much loved, especially by his wife and close friends. His wife and Jan said a few emotional words before I did the same: "We will all remember his smile, that special smile", I said.

Leo was indeed a very special man, and it was a pleasure to say so before he was buried at Kilburn cemetery. I wanted him to be buried in the same cemetery as my mother, in Alperton, but for some unknown reason his wife felt differently. She also decided to omit acknowledgement of 'Brother' on his grave stone, but she did mention 'friends, dad, husband' etc. Although I remained in touch with his children, mostly via Facebook, his wife and I would not speak again.

The only picture we ever took together – Bunny (L) and Leo (R)

Rest in peace and love, my dear brother. Whenever I hear reggae music, I see you and our brother, Bunny, smiling back at me, and I hear these words: *"Turn up da bass!"*

47. BLACK BEAUTIFUL AND TRAUMATIZED

Venice Beach, California

It was January 2006 and I was still reeling from Leo's death and the reality that both my brothers were now deceased. The AIDS crisis had assaulted my tarnished senses with more death than anyone other than a mortician should ever have to deal with, and here was more of it. I was also increasingly down about my on-going fight to reconnect with the children. Yes, I was depressed, but I had no choice but to plod along and hope the darkening clouds would pass. I'd had pangs of depression before but had always found a way to recover, but this time felt different.

Work at Islington was going well enough, and despite missing the children, I was making a determined effort to enjoy life at 14 Hampstead Hill Gardens. In fact, I loved everything about Hampstead. My apartment was a huge one-bedroomed Victorian property, with an elegant living room boasting wide 18' floor-to-ceiling windows. The local area was lovely and salubrious and very different from my former home in Wembley. I would often see celebrities going about their normal off-camera lives; walking, jogging, shopping or eating out at a local restaurant. My next door neighbour was Lord Melvyn Bragg, the highly respected veteran presenter of the *Southbank Show*, who turned out to be a very pleasant man in person, even if I did find it odd to see him putting out his rubbish like the rest of us.

Going bald did not help my sinking self-esteem, as it felt akin to yet another bereavement. Although I had long accepted my hairline would suffer the same fate as my dad's, the reality was not attractive and I did everything I could to disguise it: I pulled it, gelled it, relaxed it, dyed it, and even read a couple of articles on how I might restore it. I looked pathetic. Even close friends commented on how "ridiculous" my head looked with patches of hair on it. A work colleague told it like only a black woman could: "Who do you think you're fooling with that rubbish on your head?!"

I had to accept that looking like an unfortunate black iteration of Arthur Scargill was both uncool and unsustainable. Thankfully, times had changed and this was no longer the Afro-sheen gleaming 1970s where every self-respecting black person had some incarnation of an afro on his or her head. This was the naughty *noughties*, and being black and bald was definitely in. Phew!

God's Other Children: A London Memoir 457

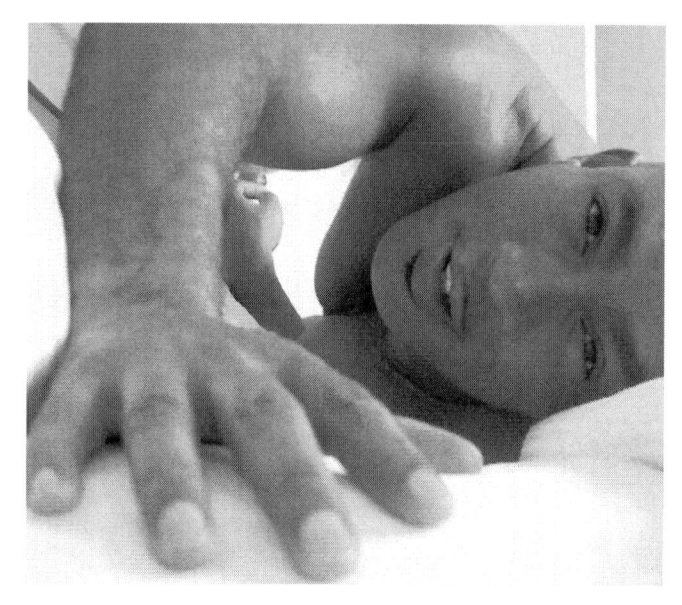

The first few days of complete shaved baldness were scary. I walked into Hampstead village feeling painfully self-conscious and feared I might be the perfect target for a sniper's bullet; as far as I was concerned all eyes were on my bald head. But my confidence was soon boosted when work colleagues and friends gave my new skinhead look an emphatic thumbs-up. "At last – very handsome!" said the same black colleague who had previously reduced me to rubble with her cutting comment about my former patchy hair line.

I was now feeling better about my appearance and yet my creeping depression haunted my days and nights. It caused me to drop three stone in weight, resulting in a need to have my suits altered so that I was wearing them and they weren't wearing me. I didn't appreciate how significant my weight loss had become until a colleague commented on it. I was thin, "too thin".

To improve my image further, I decided to join The Armoury gym on Pond Street, which was only a two-minute walk away from my doorstep. I was on a mission to transform myself from Venereal to Vernal; something I'd jokingly say about myself whenever I looked in the mirror and found I wasn't looking my very best. Weight-lifting had an immediate impact, and after a few months, I was looking better than ever. I was in my mid-forties, an often tragic confirmation of 'old age' for any gay man, but I now looked a fair few years younger than my actual age; there wasn't a wrinkle in sight and the increasingly popular botox had nothing to do with it, thanks to my parents' genes.

My excessive body hair had to go next. A friend once commented: "Vernal, you must be the missing link between ape and man." Black men were not usually as hairy as I was; certainly not my brothers or dad. I was caked in Caucasian-like body hair on my chest, forearms, shoulders, and back; I would have been a lot happier to have had that problem on my scalp! Even my mother made comments about my "monkey body hair" when it started sprouting in my mid-late teens. I was capable of growing a full beard in a matter of days.

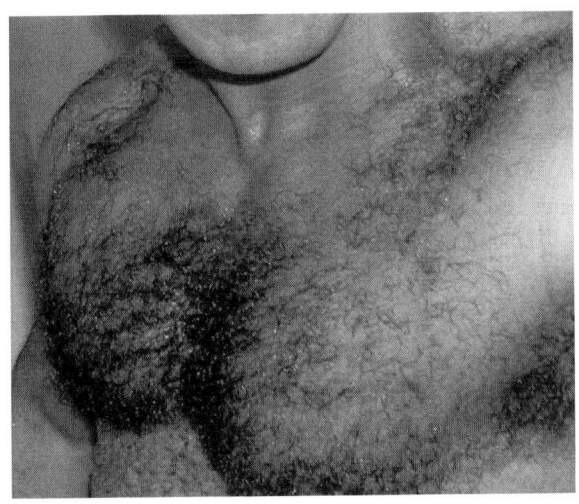

I took a shaver to my body with a vengeance, and the result was smoother, almost hairless, muscle. I liked it, almost as much as the guys who would later get to touch it. Finally, I looked in the mirror and saw an attractive, sexy, young-looking guy looking back at me. *Hello, Vernal!* With renewed confidence, it was time to push out of my loneliness and start dating again; it had been a while. I last dated a lovely German guy called Dirk. We saw each other for about twelve months, but my "issues" regarding my children got in the way – my way, not his. He was very patient, but the kids were my focus. Despite everything, he and I remained good friends.

I posted pictures of my new-look self on gay 'contact' websites such as Gaydar, Manhunt, and the sleazy but rampantly fun, Adam4Adam; I thought if I cast my net far and wide then I may just strike it lucky. My on-line age reflected my physical appearance rather than my birth certificate; I learned very quickly that such websites were all about looks, and nothing to do with substance; a gay man stating that he's forty plus may as well be ninety plus.

The requests for dates flooded in from guys of all ages, sizes, races and nationalities; like the hit song, it really was raining men. I even made it into the top five of Gaydar's Sex Factor competition, which made me chuckle. It wasn't to be taken seriously at all; it was just good fun. I was forty-seven years old and getting votes that even Barack Obama would envy, albeit for completely superficial reasons.

I didn't start out as a sex-by-appointment sort of guy at all; I was far too romantic - and inhibited - for that; inhibitions that may have inadvertently protected me from HIV and other sexually transmitted infections. Despite my sexy online image, I was a fairly sensitive person and cared about who I shared my body and bed with. I had a heart and soul that needed more than quick orgasms with complete strangers. *"I'm a human being, not an animal,"* I'd tell myself. Well, that's how I felt at first, but soon began to accept that there was much fun to be gained by relaxing my inhibitions and enjoying my body as an adult playground; enjoying sex for the sake of it... well, perhaps a latte, or even dinner, first.

I was well aware that my inhibitions about gay sex dated back to my homophobic Jamaican family roots, but my awareness didn't cure the problem. From boyhood through to my mid-thirties, I'd been haunted by a feeling that gay sex was "dirty" sex, and there were certain sexual activities that I simply couldn't allow myself to enjoy – at first! In my particularly low moments, I entertained thoughts about how much better life would be if only I were a 'normal' heterosexual man; into women and preferably married with lots of kids. But no, I was in love with the physicality, mentality, and equality, of sexual intimacy between myself and another man. I had to be true to that feeling – that need – and, of course, being gay was no longer a barrier to having kids, at least not for me. Plus, like most gay men, whilst I enjoyed women as friends, I had no desire to have sex with them, beyond the odd fantasy or two. Women tended to remind me of my mother, and I could not separate them from her physically. Strangely enough, any association between my father and the men I had sex with was non-existent, or simply did not bother me in the same way. My mother was too precious (and clean!) to associate with sex in any way, or that's the way my mind dealt with it. I fancied men, and that's the way God had made me. I was born this way, and shame was no longer going to be part of my thinking. It wasn't easy trying to exorcise my demons, but eventually they became less problematic and I could override them while enjoying the reality of the actual sexual experience. Yes, sex was a gift, not a curse.

Chemistry was important, and decent looks too, of course. If chemistry was lacking then sex wasn't going to happen and some dates never got beyond a coffee because this key ingredient was missing. Age wasn't usually a barrier, but I wasn't at all into teenagers; confidence and a mature head are always sexy, as is facial hair and shaved heads. Body piercing and tattoos were OK, but not a particular thrill. I wasn't at all interested in getting naked with anyone who couldn't be bothered to stay in reasonable shape. They didn't have to be a gym addict in any way, but I simply wasn't willing to shag through excess fat to get to an orgasm. I felt the same about guys who were out of their heads on alcohol or drugs. I never touched the stuff personally, as staying in control of *events* was important to me. My drink of choice was water, Pepsi Max, or an orange and lemonade mix. Forget beer. On a good night I might indulge in light 'ladies' alcohol like a Malibu and orange, rum and coke, or Southern Comfort mixed with Pepsi. That's as strong as my drinking ever got. Smokers might stand a chance if they were sexy enough, but to me the smell and taste was like garlic to Dracula. I therefore deliberately screened them out, unless they got me particularly excited.

My bedside cabinet heaved with freebie condoms and lube, which I regularly topped up courtesy of the well-stocked dispenser in the King William pub on Hampstead High Street. I invested in a good selection of gay DVDs too, which satisfied the urge most lonesome nights. My favourite studios were Raging Stallion, Titan Media and Hot House.

I was in my forties and enjoying the best sex of my life. Now, let me see, there was Jonathan, the two Johns... Adam, Jens, Darren, Francois, a few Pauls and Steves...Andrew, Grant, trucker Curtis, and Kostas 'the screamer', who, to my annoyance, and probably my neighbours' too, did just that! Oh yes, and spaced-out Rob, whose addiction to pills prompted me to ask: "Hey, do you want me to fuck or nurse you?" He laughed, but I didn't. Then there was ex-Etonian and Oxbridge graduate, Milo. The handsome tweed-wearing, early twenty-something hit on me on a gay cruising website with pictures of himself peering at me from behind black-framed thick-lensed spectacles. His approach was refreshing among the deluge of cock and arse pictures that would often be sent my way on such sites. Even though he was below my usual age bar, after a few exchanges expressing our mutual interest, we fixed a date over coffee near my home, off Hampstead High Street. In person, cute Milo smiled a lot and blushed even more. His shyness prevented him from saying much of a word, at first, however, over the passing hours he found his voice and an irrepressible confidence that I suspected was always there. It turned out that B*lack* was his *thing;* he didn't find his own shade at all sexually appealing, and on those simple criteria I guess I fitted the bill. We later made our way back to my flat where we chatted over more coffee and got a little closer, but avoided the bedroom. I wasn't in a hurry and neither was he. On a later date I bought him dinner, and on yet another, he returned the gesture following a leisurely stroll on Hampstead Heath, where he told me about his life; his Jewish and Greek roots, his wealthy father and little sister, even about the woman who cleans his house and does an excellent job on his shoes. Altogether we had a handful of dates spread over months rather than weeks. Boring Milo was not! He was always interesting and engaging, if somewhat self-absorbed; 'Milo' was his favourite topic, but he did express strong views on many issues, mostly political. Our politics were very different, passionately so, but we found enough in common to not be at each other's throats. To his immense credit, he was one of the early voices that encouraged me to write this very book, and being the well-connected media-savvy guy that he is, he even offered to introduce me to potential publishers. Tragically, once we did make it to my bedroom, my excitement was quickly killed off by his incessant need to engage with on-line chat via his phone, even when on his knees. Get the visual! It was my first ever threesome where the *third character* was an app called Twitter, or was it Facebook? I can belly laugh about it now, but it was all very off-putting for me at the time. Still, Milo had waited weeks for this moment, as did I, and he expected me to *perform,* but that was not going to happen! When he grumbled his disdain about my limp reaction to his naked ready-for-it butt, I simply said, "It looks like my dick has got better taste than my eyes." Within minutes he was gone, taking his dented ego with him, but not before sitting at my desk and rearranging the home screen on my desktop, as he said it looked an eyesore. I guess that was his odd way of dealing with rejection.

Surprisingly perhaps, Milo, some months later, got in touch again and we decided to meet up over lunch at an east of London Italian restaurant. I did the eating and he did the drinking and most of the talking. Now tweed-less and wrapped in a large multi-coloured scarf better suited to Caitlyn Jenner, white wine-sipping Milo struck me as very *different* now; flashing his lashes at me, he was being camp and provocative. I didn't know it then, but it was a foretaste of the Milo that the public would later meet via the media. For a moment, I wondered if he was under the influence of something other than alcohol but distracted myself by telling him how very impressed I was with the Michael Jackson tribute 'dance-in' that he'd organised months back at Liverpool Street Station following the singer's untimely death. In contrast, Milo was sniggering and in silly mode. Among his lighter but uncharacteristically disjointed utterances, and as if having read my mind, he told me that I was the camp one, but then went straight into wanting to know when I was going to do something useful with my life, adding that he could see me as a rare black Conservative

MP. I just kept eating my pasta and checking my watch. When it was over I picked up the bill and we hugged and lightly kissed our goodbye. Other than a later exchange of a few texts and on-line messages we made no plans to meet again.

Since the days of our fleeting moments together, Milo went on to create a mega presence for himself in the UK and American media as a kind of *camp Dylann Roof;* armed with a lethal shotgun of a mouth primed to effect merciless damage upon his already down and wounded prey; long-marginalized minorities. Arch Trump supporter and the new venomously verbal *darling* of the Alt-Right, Milo finds his name in the same heinous company as the KKK, White Nationalists/Supremacists, and other far-right iterations, but he'd carved out a peculiar niche for himself as their *acceptable-for-now* gay poster boy. His so-called Dangerous Faggot tour of USA college campuses draw capacity all-white audiences and require security personnel to protect him and them from invading black and feminist protestors, among others, who object to Milo's unrelenting attacks upon them and the beliefs that they have long held dear. Whilst occasionally and most oddly appearing to giggle to himself without obvious cause, perhaps due to the effects of too much lip gloss mixed with alcohol or an unseen comical voice in his ear, Milo wins standing ovations for his utter condemnation of the Black Lives Matter movement and his forthright support of Christian whites, whom he claims are the real victims in Obama's America. Having stoked the worst of their fears and unjustified phobias, Milo gives them permission to hate in public the same people that they have long hated in private. Feigning to be as petrified as his audience, he accuses minorities of invading America's vulnerable borders, importing terror and crime, living off free handouts, and wallowing in dishonest self-pity instead of trying to better themselves, like the good folk who've come to see him do. The posh potty-mouthed Brit idol goes on to refer to Donald Trump as "Daddy", and to others he detests, such as Hillary Clinton, Barack Obama, and the late beloved Princess Diana as "fucking cunts" and "sluts". He is equally nasty about any whiff of political correctness, the Left, identity politics, "fat ugly lesbians", scary Muslims invading the UK and USA, and even fellow gays. Undeterred by invading or secreted protestors trying in vain to shout him down, Milo almost weeps in his self-loathing about his homosexuality and disappointment in the ineffectiveness of electric shock anti-gay conversion therapy. Then, after attacking notable black American leaders such as Jesse Jackson and Al Sharpton, Milo seeks to pre-empt and undermine the inevitable accusations of racism with a statement in the form of a question most commonly heard after an all-night gay sex party than at an Alt-Right gathering of the white upwardly Christian faithful. He asks: "Do you know how many black cocks I've had in my mouth?" Relishing the gasps and embarrassed laughter from his audience, he is then heard insisting: "See, I'm no racist!" while licking his lips and appearing scarily oblivious to the fact that he has just confirmed his accusers' point. Sniggering Milo knows that his audience is either too daft or naive to grasp that they are an integral part of what I suspect is his sexual foreplay and the seedier *baiting* motive behind his behaviour. Publicly insulting blacks and then later privately spreading his legs for them almost guarantees Milo the joyous sexual punishment that he's hoping for; being impaled again and again onto the angry dark penis that his superior white flesh is only too eager to *accommodate.*

Disinterested to the point of boredom by the historical struggles of the LGBTQ community, Milo dismisses the idea that he wouldn't have a platform at all if it hadn't been for the earlier visibility and sacrifices of the Peter Tatchells of the left that had gone before him. Indeed, he behaves as though he would spit in the face of the Peter Tatchells if he ever happened across them. Milo has developed a particular disliking for anyone who dares to express themselves with feelings rather than considered thought, and praises facts over unwitting or ill-informed statements. Yet, despite this, he refers to himself as a Catholic; a Church that is known to protect child molesters and is steeped in myth, delusion, and much worse. But like a predator Catholic priest with his sordid eyes fixed on his next underage target, contradictory controversy is what gets Milo an audience. As a consequence of his own mouth, you don't have to look too far online to find people who either enthusiastically love or vehemently hate him. However, it is my view that some of his haters should go crawl under the nearest stone. These are the same people who fail to challenge racism in the gay community or elsewhere and yet find the time to challenge what I would call Milo's apparent *artificial intelligence* and immaturity. That's him summed up; a handsome educated jester with a vast vocabulary, self-loathing issues, and non-existent connection with underprivileged human beings, unless it's a connection via a black penis, of course; even though there's zero emotional involvement with the black owner feeding it to him. But at least he's honest about being a nasty talking sewer, while many of his haters and fans are no better in private. Those self-serving hypocrites can kiss my black ass, and hopefully do a better job of it than Milo did. I certainly do not hate him, not at all. Indeed, I find it all rather sad; there is a part of me which remains fond of that besotted shy young guy that I met years earlier in sunny Hampstead. Milo's new ego has killed him off, or so it seems. I do occasionally see glimpses of the uncorrupted Milo that I once knew, for example, when he appears to talk with sincere heart about the need to build quality schools in poorer communities, but I have no explanation for the hideous media whore of infamy that he has created himself into today, although I'd guess significant cash has something to do with it. I strongly suspect that without the noisy adoration by those warped enough to share his politics, the new Milo would simply crumble. Any prolonged solitude would compel him to face the daunting truth about why he, as a Jewish gay man, so despises the man in the mirror that he must target and disparage other minorities to try and make himself feel superior to his own inescapable truth. Milo, there you go, a bit of *deep* Michael Jackson for you to ponder in your mirror. If loss of attention doesn't sink him, then the boomerang-effect of his own unchecked mouth will undoubtedly do the job for him in time.

Twitter's decision to ban Milo confirmed his status as somewhere below acceptable, however contrived his feigned *indifference* appeared to be. There are reports that the ban was the result of online racism allegedly perpetrated by Milo or his fans against a black Hollywood actress. There are many thousands of objectionable people online, but Milo struck Twitter as too low for them. The goodness in him has been sabotaged by the ugliest of incessantly narcissistic *Trumpty Dumpty* egos, and I fear that Milo's mirror isn't cracked, but the man in it might soon be. Alas, I will for some time contemplate the loss of his potential as an enabler rather than disparager of marginalized peoples, but also, the realization that in the hating of his own sexuality he must also hate the men who he has sex with; men like me. Looking back, I find it somewhat amusing how Milo once oddly envisaged me as a potential black Conservative MP, but in an underhand Alt-Right rogue twist, beat me to prominence as a self-acknowledged Black cock-serving VIP. Crafty! Dignity matters and aware black brothers will increasingly opt to store our valuable *tools* elsewhere than in the Milos of the gay world.

Fast forward. Some years after our last meeting, a spitting Milo, now newly seething from a much publicised lost book deal worth many thousands of dollars, and humiliated by having been publicly dumped by the Conservative Right due to filmed interviews in which he appeared to condone paedophilia, wrote demanding a prompt apology of me for my disclosure about our past liaisons. Whilst acknowledging that we had indeed known each other, he was characteristically belittling about it. He promised that if I failed to respond he would not relent until my reputation was destroyed and I was left homeless and begging for his mercy. Frankly, his tone had me anticipating the line where he'd drag me out into the fields to make a bloody example of me in front of the other black cotton-picking bedroom fodder. Fortunately for me this is a different century to those past, where innocent black people were whipped, hung from trees, and had no option but to submit their dignity to pitiless white owners. Milo further suggested that I was seeking to profit from his fame; but whilst fame without respect might appeal to him, it does nothing for me. Still, he should take considerable satisfaction from the fact that I was subject to much online ridicule and bemusement following my disclosure. My reputation was indeed knocked, but my dignity was saved by the fact that I was simply honest about what took place between us, as accounted for in this very chapter. I did not dignify his treats with a response. Alas, in a change of tone, I would later hear from him again. This time to invite me to a signing party in Florida for his now self-published book.

Rewind! I remained busy in my humping Hampstead home. Most guys just wanted to get shagged, while others were into more creative sex, such as role playing, picture taking or video fun. Some wanted me to spit while others wanted a slap or two...or three. It was actually very good sex, even if it wasn't entirely my scene. A nice meal or hot latte in advance of unhurried sexual exploration was much more in line with my personal comfort zone; although I must admit, the occasional creative sexual adventure did surprise me with new unexpected highs. Again, chemistry was everything, but there'd be no mind busting actual chemicals or next day regrets for this wannabe stud.

Taking a break from my bedroom romps, I was for this Friday night nestled with Winston in a corner at Kudos, a bustling West End gay bar. He was a dear but seldom seen friend of a couple of decades. "Fuck 'em and dump 'em", he shouted in my ear, determined to be heard above the loud music. Drawing heavily on his cigarette, he insisted, "Never love them, V! Just fuck 'em!" Winston was among my black gay friends who felt that they'd been badly treated by white lovers. A guy called Alan, whom I'd never met, broke his heart over an eternity ago, but listening to Winston, the memory was as fresh as today's rain. He tore into his lost love with a razor-edged tongue: "V, I bet he was fucking some other nigga. Man, I knew something was wrong when he stopped returning my calls. No, my nine inches wasn't enough for him; the slut wanted three more, the cheating fucker!" Winston was convinced that his relationship ended because he was black and uneducated. I'd become acutely aware during my coming out years of racist sexual stereotyping within the gay community. Black guys were meant to be party animals on the dance floor, sex machines in the bedroom, but a serious embarrassment when engaged in worldly conversations at dinner parties. Our assumed lack of intelligence meant we were not considered the stuff of serious relationships, however, we mitigated this terrible flaw with our legendary scarily huge (but totally irresistible!) cocks, which we were expected to use with merciless savagery to torment (thrill!) our hapless (very willing!) victims, who were foolish (keen!) enough to let us into their bedrooms and between their sorry (happy!) legs. Our bed-busting orgasms would mark the end of our usefulness, at least until the next orgasm was required. Our supposed super intelligent white counterparts, on the other hand... well, let's just say, were not able to compete with us below the waist, or that was the fantasy; which reinforced the assumption that black guys were meant to be on top, and white guys, well, firmly on the bottom, if only in the bedroom! In reality, sexual roles, just like intellect or penis size, isn't dictated by skin colour; we were all individual men, with our personal desires, attributes, and flaws. In all honesty, the whole 'size thing' was of no interest to me: it's not what we've got, but how we use whatever we've got. Some black guys were happy to fulfil sexual fantasies of the Alans and Milos out there, whilst others, to escape sexual racism, would strictly date their own kind. Yes, we are good at sex, but we're even better at loving. I'd heard quite enough of him by the time Winston, tarnished by one or two beverages too many, asserted that "God hates white men so much that he couldn't be bothered to colour them in, the worthless shits!" Yes, it was time to rescue my senses and say goodnight to my embittered friend! We hugged our farewell and I descended the steps into Tottenham Court Road tube to head home to my lust nest, but didn't get too far before Winston called down after me with slurred but embarrassing clarity: "Remember V, if he's white, fuck him and dump him, before he dumps you, bro!" Having caught the closing doors and taken my seat on the semi-full Northern line carriage, for a brief moment I pondered whether Winston's anger had more to do with his HIV diagnosis than Alan, his now long-deceased ex-lover, but the jolting train snapped me out of it. I was just pleased he was still around, even if I suspected that he secretly yearned to be where Alan is. Gone!

Back home and my on-going dates took on a familiar ritual. I'd usually meet them at Hampstead or Belsize Park tube station and then stop at a local eatery for a quick salad or coffee. If I liked him, then we might go for a stroll on the heath before heading back to my place. If I didn't fancy him then I'd make my excuses and call it a day. Occasionally I would see someone again, and on even rarer occasions, someone would become a regular intimate friend. Sometimes I found myself having two dates in the same day; laughable numbers by some people's standards, I know, but this was new territory for me.

Some dates were great fun while others were mediocre and, occasionally, disastrous. I like camp guys but don't usually date them. I recall meeting up with a ginger-headed guy who swung his hips with more gusto than Tina Turner in her 'What's Love Got to Do with It' music video. I tried to keep ahead of him so people wouldn't know we were together, but he managed to keep up with me. I even contemplated breaking into a sprint but thought that would be a little too obvious. We ended up going for drinks at the Garden pub on Southend Green, at which point I made it clear that I wasn't up for anything more. He left in a huff and later sent me a text cursing me out for wasting his time and that he'd come all the way from South London "and hadn't even got any sex out of it". I didn't reply. Lesson: pictures can be deceiving, especially on 'contact' websites! His pictures had him decked out in army gear and looking like the ultimate macho man, but in person, he turned out to be all costume and no ammunition! Ah well, I guess the joke was on naive me.

I wasn't everybody's cup of tea either. One guy looked at me with such horror that I was convinced he would report me to the police for assaulting his senses. Other dates faded after just a latte or two, again, because the other guy didn't fancy me. I would take such occasions on the chin and say, "That's life, V, and there's probably a blessing behind it. Bye!" Admittedly, there weren't too many rejections to dent my shallow *Casanova Brown* ego.

I would occasionally find myself feeling emotionally vulnerable because someone had impressed my heart as well as my genitals. A cuddly former gym instructor was such a guy. Our simultaneous gushing climax felt like a memorable beginning, not a sagging end. Our subsequent conversation was great too, but we never met twice and he'd never know how I felt. This remained a pattern for me; never really telling special guys how I felt about them, thus giving the impression that sex was all I desired. Love would have been nice, too! My loss, I guess, but that's what it was for me on the whole; recreational sex, like a hot sweaty cardio down at the gym. This was the fun way to stay in shape, or so I would jest to myself. I got rid of my deodorant and now smell like a real man, but which man – ha ha! But hey, what goes up must come down. Really down!

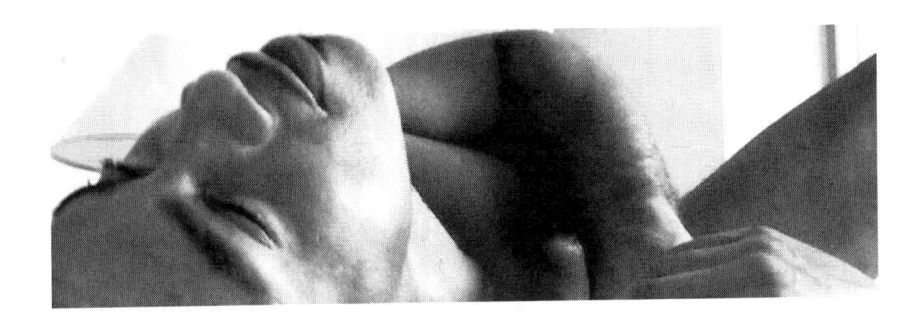

Greet Grope Goodbye

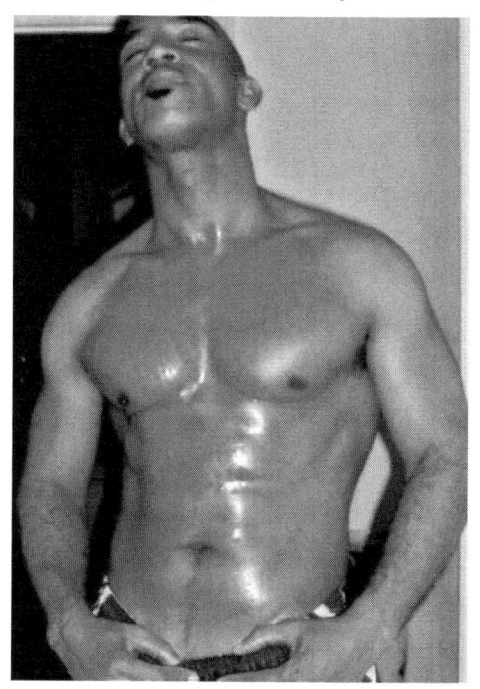

I said hi, he said bonjour

My skinny latte had an extra-shot, his tea had an extra sweetener

I kissed him once, he kissed me twice

He groped mine, I groped his

I stripped him, he stripped me

He sucked, I licked

I rolled on a condom, he added the lube

I entered, he moaned

He came first, I came second

We smiled, we kissed

He said merci. I said thanks

He said au revoir, I said goodbye

Next!

I appeared to be having fun, but my outwardly *'all is well'* appearance was seriously holed below my superficial surface by a creeping emptiness, which rendered me feeling lower than a snake's belly.

'Barebacking' involves penetrative intercourse without the relative safety of a condom. Given my considerable history in dealing directly with HIV, I knew all about safer sex and the potential perils of ignoring it. However, barebacking was now a symptom of my struggle; I left the condoms in my cabinet and began to play sexual Russian roulette with my life. I told myself *'If anyone should know better, I should!* The first time it happened it was unplanned and quite spontaneous. Once it was over, I immediately left the bedroom and fell to my knees in a sobbing mess in my hallway; I was distraught. I swore it wouldn't happen again; the lust demon got the better of me and the guy I was with. No doubt he could hear me and my self-recrimination on the other side of the bedroom door and perhaps thought I was crying because I had knowingly transmitted HIV. Either way, we said our goodbyes and never met again.

I was to bareback twice more with two different guys. One of them wrote to me online afterwards, asking: "Can we do it again?" I declined the offer; it had been a mistake... a repeated mistake.

Now into my fourth year at Islington town hall, it had been great for the first three years, but I now loathed it and it began to show. I was sleeping about four hours a night, if I was lucky and was almost zombie-like state during office hours. Survival mode was my night-time norm.

I was sitting in front of my office computer one morning and couple of minutes passed before my brain worked out how to operate it. This wasn't a new piece of equipment, and yet I was mentally blocked about pressing a simple button. A short while later, a member of my staff caught me crying, at which point I went for an extended walk. The tears just kept coming. If that wasn't enough of a warning signal, later that evening I found myself gripped by a chronic pain in the abdomen. NHS Direct advised that I either call an ambulance or make my way to the Royal Free hospital, which was a short walk away. When I got there I was soon being wheeled on a trolley through the emergency department with ECG pads attached to my chest. They thought I might be having a heart attack. Five hours later, following blood tests and a chest X-ray, the concerned doctor decided to keep me in overnight "for observation", but the pain had eased and I decided to go home, to his disquiet. I just didn't want to be there; I'd had enough of damn hospitals. When I got home, I stripped and crawled into bed, and, for a change, fell asleep within seconds.

Back at work, and a colleague invited me to spend Christmas with him, and I gratefully accepted. He and I had become close and we were spending a fair amount of time together. In the end I had about two hours sleep over the two days I was away. I headed home on Boxing Day in the hope that a return to my own bed would help. It didn't. Something dark and scary was happening to me; I was in some kind of meltdown or burn out. Days later, and I started coming down with all kinds of illnesses: sore throats, neck to waistline rashes, shingles, coughs, bed-drenching night sweats, headaches and diarrhoea, resulting in even more weight loss. My immune system was putting up a fight for some ghastly reason. My GP, with everything else exhausted, suggested another HIV test. My symptoms had convinced me of the inevitable outcome, but to my surprise and relief, it came back negative. The final conclusion was that I was stressed out and running on empty; this was the cause of my symptoms. I didn't know stress could be so physically taxing until now.

On reflection, it made perfect sense. I had started to burn out before I joined Islington and before my ill-fated venture into parenthood. Since 1987, I had dealt with the relentless death dying and bereavement of lovers, friends, clients and family, and I never understood that it had damaged me so very deeply. I was suffering from some kind of post-AIDS trauma that had caused me to shun or sabotage loving relationships, allow drift rather than to plan my life and career, feel pessimistic, take wrong decisions when the right one was staring me in the face, and take risks with my life by engaging in unsafe sex. My senseless decision to have a child with a stranger was a further symptom of my inner damage. I needed to heal and begin to be strong for myself, or my life would continue to be a roller coaster of self-inflicted disasters, or worse. As damaged as I was, I still appreciated life, plus I had two kids I wasn't about to give up on; I had to get well, for me and for them.

Barebacking and random baby-making was out, and my faith and prayer became my rock and my healer. As before, when I couldn't carry myself, Jesus Christ was my strength.

The barebacking issue came up again a little later, but this time for very different reasons. I was in Soho and decided to go into one of the many shops selling gay DVDs. The guy behind the counter was screening a 'view before you buy' bareback DVD and I wasted no time in making my feelings known:

"You're promoting disease and death with that stuff," I told him, bluntly.

He responded calmly but firmly: "Listen matey, you don't have to buy it, and nor does anyone else, but I'm telling you, this stuff outsells everything else, twenty times over." He laughed at my shocked expression, and mockingly asked, "Well, don't you believe in freedom of choice then?"

I responded just as calmly. "Sale number's doesn't make it right. These productions are seeking to glamorise dangerously unhealthy sex and we shouldn't buy into it."

He then let rip, to my embarrassment: "Well don't fucking buy it, and don't bloody criticise anyone else who does – it's their choice not yours! At least if they enjoy bareback as a video fantasy then they may not actually do it in reality! Have you considered that?"

As I stood there, trying to recover from his outburst, I had to admit that I hadn't really considered that point. Finally, I came back with: "Listen, perhaps this stuff does save some lives." A winning smirk came across his face. I continued: "Of course people watch all kinds of fantasy material involving death and violence, but Hollywood doesn't play with real guns and bullets; the same can't be said of barebacking." His smirk disappeared and frustration set in, but I wasn't finished. "For all we know you're watching people becoming infected with HIV right before your eyes: some sexy video, matey!"

I stopped to breathe, but the man's expression told me that he'd heard enough. He was making a living from these DVDs and resented having me interfere with his sales. He was right, I didn't have to buy such DVDs, and he also had a point with his video fantasy versus reality argument. I guess it didn't matter who won, but I had made my point, in a small way; we shouldn't be promoting unsafe sex. If I had my own way, the production of such videos would be banned in the UK.

As I walked away from his shop in the Saturday afternoon drizzle, the horror of our recent history came back to me; a history where death was often the inevitable outcome of condom-free sexual intercourse, but the AIDS war years was bow behind us; time, effective treatments and our survival rates had moved on. It was all very different from twenty years earlier, when Princess Diana and Whitney Houston demanded that a cure be found. An HIV diagnosis and the success of treatments meant that it was a totally manageable disease, and I was very grateful for that. Still, my post-AIDS trauma was still a living reality; feelings and memories that I just cannot move on from; that conveyor belt of death, dying and funerals. AIDS may have been curtailed but its effects were alive and kicking the crap out of me.

While we await a definitive scientific cure, we must rely on our own behaviour to protect ourselves, our partners, and future generations from contracting HIV. We must be willing to say: *I take personal responsibility for ensuring that I do not pass on or receive HIV during sex.*

I don't envy the work of organisations like the Terrence Higgins Trust, GMFA, or Positively UK, because they've got a maddeningly difficult job on their hands. Every time they promote the success of treatments, they simultaneously undermine their own HIV prevention message. I mean, why should anyone care about getting infected when they believe a pill will rescue them from the consequences?

As I conclude this chapter, overall rates of new infections are on a definite rise in the UK. 6,364 new cases were reported in 2011, compared to 2,938 in 1998, and reported infections among gay men are at an all-time high. *Oh Lord, did my gay brothers all die in vain?* It would appear that the success of HIV treatments since 1996 has caused mostly young gay men to ignore the risks and leave their condoms unused in the bedroom drawer. Disco dazed old-timers like me bore them to tears with our annual World AIDS Day tales about the AIDS war years; when getting HIV meant an almost certain early death. Today's handsome gym-toned young men cannot relate to the catastrophe of which I speak; they're much more interested in Lady Gaga, Miley Cyrus, Beyoncé, and the X-Factor than HIV; which they've rightly deduced will not necessarily kill them, even if it's an irreversible diagnosis. They have no idea about the awaiting reality of a life-long imprisonment of pills, clinics, side effects, and of course, the on-going stigma. Once infected, they will suddenly notice the biting, to-the-point, adverts on 'contact' websites by their horny sex-seeking peers, who proudly state: "I'm disease-free, and you must be, too!" Most of all, they will have to absorb the fact that a failure to take their daily pill will likely result in the prompt or slow demise of the beautiful person in the bathroom mirror, and signal the onset of a horrific AIDS-related death; the death that annoying older fools like me tried to warn them about. Yes, cutie, there is a significant price to pay for anyone with a *'fuck now – think about it later'* attitude. I have a genuine worry that if we ever get hit with the likes of the considerably more transmissible Ebola virus, then it could make the impact of AIDS on us look like it was a happy house party. And, to my annoyance, Gaga and Cyrus played on...

Working with charities I would later go on to test the public for exposure to **HIV**. The results now take less than five minutes. Get tested!

As for me, I'm happy to declare my body a forever safer sex zone. Yes, orgasms are great, but I don't intend to get an irreversible (and preventable!) diagnosis for one. I... no, we, have the power to be the cure we are seeking. In practical terms, it means regular HIV testing and making safer sex sexy and obligatory again. HIV is just one of many sexually transmitted infections out there, and that's why condom use makes perfect sense. We can spice up the sex, perhaps with a little *role play*, but let's all submit to the mighty power of the simple condom, and tell him: *No condom, no party in the rear, baby*! And if he says you're a bore then show him the door! Don't be persuaded by arguments about whether the HIV viral load is or isn't detectable in your/his blood tests: wear a condom if you're going to fuck and leave any possible regrets for others to contemplate. If condoms don't work for you, or even if they do, ask your sexual health advisor or GP about Pre-exposure Prophylaxis (PrEP). You, PrEP and condoms = the best combination.

Once again, the sexually active among us should make HIV testing an integral part of our sex lives; get it regularly - test, treat (to) prevent! It only takes five minutes and could mean the difference between a normal life-span and an early death. As well as using our little rubber friends and PrEP, we must also learn about risks caused by alcohol and drugs (or 'chemsex'), which can severely undermine our well-being. A bit of discipline and a lot of self-love helps too; love which starts on the inside of the person in the mirror.

Lastly, HIV stigma inhibits those 'at risk' from coming forward for testing and treatment, and ultimately, impacts us all. The stigma is not caused by people living with HIV; it is solely caused by those of us who remain ignorant about HIV facts. If we learn the facts then we'll stop the blight of stigma. HIV (and other STi's) is the enemy, not people living with it: they are not a walking virus dispenser; they are real, holistic people. Let's spread the facts, not the ignorance!

48. HIGH COURT SHOWDOWN: A FIGHT FOR JUSTICE

THE FAMILY COURT system was proving to be a tediously slow and expensive dinosaur. Deep pockets and considerable patience were essential requirements just to interact with it. Simply applying to the court cost nearly two hundred pounds, and that's before the involvement of lawyers. There were forms to fill, photocopying to be done, and respondents' who must be 'served' with a summons within the given deadlines. If you're lucky, you might get a hearing within three months, but applicants can expect to have to wait much longer if their case is potentially complex and needing more than a half hour of court time.

When your hearing date arrives, you can expect to be ushered in and treated like a case number rather than a father with emotions and feelings, who is desperately missing his children. You'll emerge quicker than expected, too, feeling as though you've just been through the legal equivalent of McDonalds; served according to a prescribed menu that has been dotted with tasteless bespoke trimmings to fool you into thinking that you'd been heard and justice had been achieved. Your teary eyes and broken heart will tell you the truth: you were just another unfortunate father in the UK family court system of over sixty-five thousand cases and justice has eluded you. You are now expected to be grateful for whatever measly morsels of 'contact' your court order has afforded you. Your server, the sitting judge of the day, may have been courteous and polite, or tore into you like a bully in the school playground, depending on his or her mood or temperament. An unhappy judge could result in an unhappy experience; so smile, speak when spoken to, and try to be invisibly present, even if it's impossible to do. Their unambiguous irritation at your audacity in bothering them with your pathetic pleas for reasonable contact with your children will leave your confidence in tatters on the court room floor. Adding to your disadvantage, Family courts operate 'in private', so judges, knowing that their treatment of you can never be reported by law, can treat you as they bloody well wish; so Daddy, you'd better be on your best behaviour if you want to get on their good side and leave court with more than huge legal bills in your hands, and an order giving you just enough time with your kids to plough through a real McDonalds burger. No, no, no, silly, there's not enough time for fries! Oh yes, before I forget, don't cry in court; do that outside, and definitely don't say you love your children, unless asked. You've discovered, the hard way, that the building you are in is all about 'bigging-up' the mother of your children. It matters not that she's hateful and implacably hostile, to the detriment of you and the children. She's automatically perceived as 'the victim', and you're the perpetrator. Yes, it's all your fault, Daddy! So, please remember who you are: you've served your purpose and the only thing to do now is avoid the fate of a used serviette by being cast into the trash can of your children's memories. You are going to have to be patient, strategic and remain optimistic, despite the many obstacles before you. The passing of time and the love of your children will have to be your greatest strategic tools.

Oh, the injustice of justice in the UK family court system.

I had good reason to be pessimistic. There were two mothers in my case and they were united in asking the court to restrict my contact with the children to posted letters, cards and presents, for the next four years. To my astonishment and immense disappointment, the court agreed to give consideration to this vile plea. Six different judges heard my application to date and concluded that the issues involved were outside their experience and expertise. Yes, being a father was bread and butter stuff, but my being a gay one was too much gooey butter for consumption in the lower court.

In February 2007, with my fate with the children in the balance, I climbed the steps of the High Court – the Royal Courts of Justice, for what was supposed to be the final knock-out hearing; the last opportunity to reconnect with one or both children. I hadn't seen either of them since September 2005 and missed them terribly. Against legal advice, I decided to apply for contact with KC as well as May.

As I passed through security and entered the breathtaking hall, I reflected upon the fact that my daughter had only been a few months old when I first approached the family court for help, and she was now three and a half years old. So much time had been lost fighting for what most parents took for granted; quality time with their children. I worried that she may have forgotten me, and that I may not see her or KC in the foreseeable future, if ever.

Both women were present with their legal team and I was now snuggled down with mine. Orla and Titi were seeking an order that would render me a phantom Dad forever; never to be seen, but occasionally heard from in writing. I had originally come to court seeking an immediate resumption in contact and increased contact time. The women were in breach of the original court for having stopped contact without leave to do so. Despite this, however, the tables had somehow turned in their favour, and instead of focusing on their unreasonable behaviour, I was being required to prove I was worthy of being part of the children's lives. This was a mammoth task after eighteen months of zero contact with them. I was now facing the real possibility of losing physical contact forever.

As per my original application, I was seeking an immediate resumption of contact with both children, or at least with my biological child, May. My quest wasn't cheap; I had now spent in excess of thirty thousand pounds on legal bills to get to this hazardous point. In addition, I was compelled to pay monthly maintenance of four hundred and thirty pounds via the CSA (Child Support Agency), thanks to Orla's application to them. She was determined to get her revenge, and this was one way of doing so. Even if the judgment went against me, I'd still be required to pay up, or the money would be docked from my salary at source. This would continue until May reached eighteen years of age or I stopped working. It was galling to say the least, but I had no option but to pay. The CSA didn't concern themselves with court orders or the complexities of lesbian and gay families; as long as your name was on the birth certificate then you had to pay. I of course had no equivalent of the CSA to top up my persecuted wallet. Despite having similar legal bills to mine, but with my monthly bounty to rely on, both women resigned from their respective jobs, citing stress caused by my on-going legal action as the reason. The fact that we were only in court because of their unreasonable behaviour was an inconvenient fact they were hoping no one would notice. They couldn't complain of violence, harassment, stalking, or written or verbal abuse on my part; only that I'd taken them to court. They of course didn't complain either, about the burden upon them of spending my money on a monthly basis, the not so poor dears! Now let's see; they had two cars, a new American fridge-freezer – plumbed in, of course, holidays to Jamaica, Spain and France, and cash left over to buy alcohol and cigarettes. These were all stress-related purchases, of course - not! They'd made good use of my semen and were now celebrating with my money. Galling, indeed!

Over two full days, the High Court heard arguments for both sides. The women's case consisted of pathetic inconsistencies and desperate lies. In a move straight from the gutter they were used to, they cited my teenage suicide attempt as a reason why the court should not allow me direct contact with the children; implying mental instability on my part. They were beyond desperate to get me out of their lives, once and for all. Through their fake sobs and onion-induced tears, they pleaded with the judge to only allow me indirect contact with May, and none at all with KC. If I didn't know them personally, then even I would have been swayed by their sewer-polished performances. As an escape, for a brief moment, I pictured myself halting proceedings by jumping to my feet and pleading with the judge to rescue the terrified tears being forced to run down their vile detestable faces, but as much as I enjoyed the mental distraction, the reality of my predicament made me snap out of it.

Their QC was clearly optimistic, especially when a so-called independent 'expert witness', who I had to pay for, swiftly followed by a representative from Cafcass (Children and Family Court Advisory and Support Service), took to the stand and agreed the children should have no direct contact with me for the period requested. Their professional words had sealed my hell-bound fate. According to these experts, the mothers were too distressed by my taking them to court, and this could eventually impact upon the children. Note, they didn't say the children were distressed by my actions, but by the mothers', and yet their considered, expert conclusion, was to dump rotten Dad. I felt sick with outrage.

Up until this point, I'd had a number of meetings with Cafcass officers, and found them to be condescending, offensively ignorant, and totally biased towards the mothers. They allowed themselves to be bullied and intimidated by them. I'm sure there must be good Cafcass officers out there, but I hadn't met a single one with any respect for dads or understanding of a child's right to have quality time with their father. One officer even put in writing that he could see no need for a father in a family such as this, and I was duly gutted and angered by his crass comment. My complaint against the officer concerned was upheld, but the damage was already done – in writing! Another officer from yet another child-related agency, said she could not understand why I wanted contact in the first place, and that I should be happy if I secured four hours a fortnight. It all painted a very sad picture of family court and its intrinsic inability to value the role, feelings and experience of fathers. That said, I'm sure there are bad parents out there, mothers and fathers, but I'm not one of those!

My faith in God was intact, but my optimism, given all that was against me, was dead and buried. I needed a miracle if I was to see my daughter again and yet another one, if I was to see KC.

As if things weren't bad enough, KC's biological father came out of the woodwork and added his voice to the mothers', insisting that I not be allowed back into his son's life. The same son he'd abandoned as a sperm. This was a man who lived on the other side of the world whom I'd never seen or spoken to. The same man who paid zero child support, while I paid through the nose.

My barrister was worried and said it would strengthen my chances in respect of May if I dropped my application regarding KC. There was nothing to think about; my heart and integrity wouldn't let me do it; I was the only Dad KC knew, and I wasn't about to drop him for the sake of winning some tarnished victory in court. I was fighting for both children, whatever the final outcome. If KC one day decided against having me in his life, then I would accept that, and fully support him developing a relationship with his biological father, if that's what he wanted. But, for now, I was it; his Dad.

My barrister further remarked: "Vernal, fathers usually have one mother to deal with, but you've got two on your hands." Her down-cast face said it all. Any lasting optimism on my part had just been buried and cemented over.

When I took to the stand, I was honest, articulate, and unruffled by the confrontational style of their barrister. I kept hearing Mum's voice telling me: *"Have faith. Let Jesus be your lawyer, and let God be the judge."*

Yes, the odds were stacked against me, but at least I was morally in the right, or so I told myself.

Deep down I knew I was going to be yet another broken-hearted father, set to leave court with his relationship with his children reduced to nothing more than a memory. I believed emphatically in God, but, at this time, I had to admit my faith in seeing some kind of justice was non-existent. I was discovering the hard way that campaigning groups like Families Need Fathers and Fathers4Justice existed for good reason. Eighteen months without being able to see either child was an injustice all by itself. I hadn't committed any crime, yet this had been my fate, our fate!

During a much needed lunch break on the second and final day of the hearing, my barrister could only remark: "Vernal, we've done our best". I detected her sense of defeat, but knew she was right. I also knew she was trying to prepare me for the inevitable judgment against me.

We had indeed done our best, and unlike the other side, we had been honest and acted with integrity. I could not in any way fault my barrister; she really did fight my corner. The judge didn't see or hear from the children directly, and therefore he had to rely on what Cafcass, the expert, and the mothers' had to say. I accepted my fate.

Praying like my mother may help; from my heart and soul and directly to God. It was my last resort, but perhaps it should have been my first. It was too late to pray now.

When we returned to the court room, the judge said he'd heard all the relevant information needed to make a decision. He also mentioned that he found the time to watch a DVD I had put together to try give him visuals regarding the quality of my relationship with the children before contact was stopped. He must have watched it privately because it wasn't played in court. The DVD included footage from the birthday event at my house in Wembley, when the mothers' were first introduced to my family and friends. It also included pictures and video footage of me and the kids in parks, on the heath, at home etc. At one point, I could be seen happily changing my daughter's nappy, while she playfully grabbed onto my face as I told her, "I love my baby!"

My video footage, of course, could never compete with the voices lined up against me. No judge would go against his own experts, I knew that much.

To my disappointment, the judge decided to reserve the issuing of his judgment until the following week. He thanked the respective legal teams and exited, leaving both sides in legal limbo. I looked over and could see by their faces that Orla and Titi anticipated victory. I'd be optimistic too if I had been on their side of the court room. Instead, I left court with my heart ripped out of my chest. My fight for justice was over and I was now awaiting formal sentence. I had started this fight expecting to win, and I was now facing certain defeat.

I returned home to phone calls from the friends who had been my rock throughout the entire saga. They'd all been incredibly supportive. Beverley, my sister, too. Jan was no longer part of the picture, due to her feelings about my sexuality.

I didn't know it until later that evening, but I had also returned home to my darkest night since the passing of my mother. I was in deep, deep trouble. A cloud of depression descended upon me and I felt I wouldn't make it through the night. At two or so in the morning, I reached for the phone to call a counselling service. It was available free to all employees of Islington. I wasn't suicidal, but was desperate to talk to someone; someone who would say all the right things to get me through the night. The man who answered the phone was fantastic and immediately made me feel that I was right to call. In addition to his support over the phone, he made an appointment for me to see one of their satellite counsellors in the morning. She was conveniently based at the Royal Free, just around the corner. I agreed to see her at the specified time. Vernal 'Titanic' Scott needed urgent help. I could try to sleep now. Try...

The next day when I met Riva, the appointed counsellor, I told her that her name was rather familiar to me. She echoed my words. We soon traced our histories back to the HIV war years of the '80s and '90s. She knew of me from my work at the Brent HIV Centre, but there was a further surprise. It turned out she was also the counsellor who offered support to Leo's wife following his death in this very hospital. It was indeed a small world.

By the time we parted company, Riva had managed to lift my spirits a fair bit and I decided to head to work at Islington, as we both thought the distraction would help until the court judgment came through.

A mind-numbingly slow week later, my office phone rang. It was Daniel, my lawyer, calling to let me know the judgment had just been issued and that I should brace myself:

"Vernal, are you sitting down? If not, I suggest you do so now."

My heart leapt in my chest and seemed to stop beating altogether. This was it! "Yes, I'm seated" I confirmed anxiously. "Tell me, Daniel."

"You did it, Vernal! The judge has granted you immediate access to May and to KC too."

I could have dropped the phone. I was completely overwhelmed by his unexpected words. Emotion took over and tears filled my eyes. I tried to speak but couldn't physically do so. I tried again, but my emotions tied my tongue to the roof of my mouth. I was just short of sobbing at my desk when I heard Daniel say he understood and that I should call him back when I was able to. I hung up and put my hands to my face, in a vain attempt to try and compose myself before my staff and the open plan office could see the state I was in. My tears were not to be quelled; I had no option but to let them flow.

I eventually got myself together enough to go and share the news with a couple of colleagues who had been rooting for me. They were as surprised at the outcome as I was. A short while later, I left the town hall with my mobile in hand, thanking God and my angel mother all the way. I called Daniel back and asked him to repeat himself, which he did, with an emotional but empowered voice.

"May... and KC too?" I interrupted.

"Yes, both children, Vernal" came the emphatic reply. I became emotional once again.

"When do I see them? I need to see them!" I interrupted again.

Daniel said he'd already put a copy of "the extensive judgment" in the post and expected me to receive it in the morning. He also confirmed that he too was shocked by the outcome and added that the judge wanted all parties in court the following week to hear his judgment in person. I told Daniel nothing on this Earth could keep me away from that date with justice.

God hadn't abandoned me…and I sensed my mother's hand too!

Daniel and I spoke for a while longer before saying an emotional goodbye. I thanked him, with all my heart. I then went for a short walk, praying as I went, to give thanks to God again. It felt like a major miracle had just happened, and swept away all the odds that had come against me. I felt relieved, blessed and protected.

Thank you God – oh, I'm sorry if Mum nagged you too much…thank you, thank you, thank you!!!

The monster mothers had failed, spectacularly. They had thrown everything bar the kitchen sink at me, and were supported in their efforts by cowardly court appointed officers. Truth and integrity had won the day. My opponents could now cancel their planned celebratory party and organise an exorcism of their demons instead.

Thank you, Jesus! My faith was renewed and glowing brightly within me. God had been carrying me the last few years because I certainly had not been carrying myself.

The two women failed to show up in court the following week, as they were apparently too upset to attend. As a goodwill gesture, I decided to send them a personally created 'KISS MY ENTIRE ASS' get well card, but thought I'd gain weight first, so there would be more of my backside for them to kiss. Yes, I was a Christian, but I was also very human.

I would of course never send such a card, but I thoroughly enjoyed the thought of doing so. I had a right to let off steam, and that was my way of doing it. I sincerely hoped they were feeling as shitty as they made me feel for the many months that I was forced to live without seeing the children. Yes, I was only human, even if they didn't appear to be.

I'll rely on my prayers henceforth; they're very effective. I need to pray like my mother did, from my soul, not my mouth.

I smiled as the judge read through his judgment. He confirmed that I would see both children in a couple weeks at an unsupervised child contact centre. It was only going to be a couple of hours a fortnight on a Saturday at first, and then progress to four hours, which would allow me to take the children home for the duration of the contact period.

Of course I wasn't going to settle for that, but it was a most compelling start, given how dire things were looking for me only a week earlier. I left the court on cloud nine and a half.

I sent my barrister some quality wine and chocolates, and treated Daniel to lunch at Carluccio's on Hampstead High Street; it was my heartfelt *thank you*, in person.

As the appointed day of my first contact with the children in now nineteen months drew closer, I went along to the selected contact centre in advance to have a look around. It turned out to be a substantial church building, in extensive, well-tended grounds. I was very impressed. Staffed by Christian volunteers, they really made me feel welcome and comfortable. They were truly wonderful people.

On the actual day, I arrived early, signed in and went to the hall where fathers waited for their kids to arrive. I was a bag of nerves. *What if they don't want to see me? What if they burst into tears and run away? What if I say or do the wrong thing? Maybe I should have brought some presents. Maybe I should sit down or maybe I should stand up.* I was driving myself crazy, until I heard myself say, *"Just be yourself, Vernal – Daddy!"*

I nodded at some of the other dads, but kept myself largely to myself as my big wait commenced. Occasionally, a volunteer would come into the hall to smile and put us all at ease. After about ten minutes, the lead volunteer, a delightfully pleasant older woman called Shirley, came to tell me that the children had arrived and she was going to bring them in to see me shortly. I braced myself as the children of the other six or so dads arrived in the hall... but where were mine? Hmm...

A few more seconds passed, and I looked towards the doorway again, and there they were; KC and May, smiling nervously at me. All my prior over-thinking went out the window, and I spontaneously dropped to my knees with my arms extended towards them. May appeared to hesitate for a moment and briefly looked back, as if to see if Titi and Orla might still be in reception. But in a flash, both kids hurtled towards me, knocking me completely backwards with the force of their body weight. They had grown! They shouted "Hello Daddy, hello Daddy" over and over, as I fought to get to my feet. It was music to my ears: pounding disco music! I was thrilled to the point where all I could mutter was, "Hey kiddies, hey kiddies..."

My precious reconnection with KC and May surpassed my most optimistic of fantasies. A minute later, it was if there had never been a separation at all. There was no doubt that they had missed me too, and the three of us embraced for what seemed like an eternity as other dads looked on. One of them looked as emotional as me. Perhaps he was hoping his kids would arrive and have the same reaction as mine.

May's Caucasian-like brown/blond hair had grown considerably longer, and she was very chatty and touchy-feely. KC, now seven, was his usual boisterous self, trying to get all my attention, as always. It was truly wonderful. At one point he stepped back and said, "I know you're not really my dad, but I want you to be my dad", before grabbing onto me once again. We eventually ventured out into the grounds and chased each other and some abandoned tennis balls before settling onto a bench and into the bag full of goodies I had prepared for us; ketchup-laden sausage sandwiches, cakes, and Pepsi Max. It was over all too soon, as we hugged and kissed our goodbyes, but I left the contact centre with a huge smile on my face and in my heart.

The fortnightly contact continued as ordered over the following months, and I eventually took the children home to Hampstead Hill Gardens, where Beverley and I put on a party for May's fourth birthday. Daniel and many other friends joined us. We had a lot to celebrate.

My relationship with May felt very natural; father-daughter. However, things were different with KC; the chemistry in our relationship had yet to recover from our forced separation at the hands of his two mothers. I feared that our bond had been irreparably broken. Our fortnightly *contact* was just a *fun day out* for him, and that was OK, as long as he was happy; but I detected his insecurity and anger. He was feeling vulnerable. This was being compounded by Titi's constant reminders to him that "Vernal is not your Dad!" And she was right, I wasn't; but this didn't stop him wanting me to be. I loved him and would remain committed for as long as he needed me, or until Orla's brother did the right thing and stepped up to the plate. KC didn't choose to be fatherless, and obviously didn't want to be.

A few months later, the embittered mothers decided to sabotage my happiness by again withdrawing May from contact, forcing me to return to court. In fact, they would continue to give me reason to return to court for months and years to come.

I started to feel completely stressed out and something had to give. In a matter of a few weeks I was no longer working at Islington. It felt fantastic to be out of there, even if the exit itself had been rather messy, including media reports of a pay-off. Jeremy Corbyn, the very principled Islington MP whose commitment to human rights brought him to my Reach Out and Touch event years earlier, was very kind and put his concern and appreciation in writing. His support meant a lot to me at a time when I was feeling low and somewhat friendless. Officially, I took redundancy and a good reference with it. The other plus was that I was no longer going to be paying Child Support – for as long as I was out of fulltime work. Orla and Titi could get back to work because I intended to take a break... a long break!

I flew to Sydney and had a ball... or two! I quickly settled into a very nice rental suite at Hyde Park Corner, just off Sydney's bustling Oxford Street. All I wanted to do now was rest and recharge my drained batteries - for the first time since joining local government back in 1987. Terry, a close American friend living in New York and working at the plush Hyatt, arranged to have a massive chocolate cheesecake delivered, just to say he was thinking of me. This was typical of him and the invaluable rock of a friend that he'd become since our chance meeting years earlier. Yes, the web offered creeps, but it also offered great new friends.

I hoped the holiday would re-energize and enable me to keep up the fight regarding the kids. It was unacceptable for the mothers to ignore court orders, and I was going to hold them to account. They failed to realise that I won more time with the children every time we went back to court, and I was very happy with that trend. On each occasion, the sitting judge ordered that contact be resumed and extended, despite the mothers' threat to go to prison before they would allow it. Judges were not impressed with such irresponsible threats.

Back in London after my too brief love affair with gorgeous Sydney, and I was now representing myself in all matters legal; no more expensive lawyers! I had become as good as any QC, or that's what I told myself. No, I didn't need to be a QC, I just needed to be myself; a committed Dad with excellent verbal skills. Verbal Vernal, ha ha!

Even though well intentioned judges had promised to reserve the case to themselves, we would inevitably find ourselves in front of yet another new Judge. This was sometimes to my disadvantage, as the mothers relentlessly tried to reverse the gains I'd made.

I decided to work as a consultant for a while and give local government a break. It was a challenge, but an enjoyable one. I found myself travelling and seeing parts of the UK that I'd only ever heard about, including Wales and Scotland. I travelled abroad a bit too, but only in a private capacity: USA, Jamaica, France, Canada, Spain, Denmark, the Netherlands, and of course, Australia. I never visited Wales or Scotland until I became a consultant. Freedom!

By 2011, contact was still fortnightly but had increased to ten hours, but this only happened after presenting my case before no less than fourteen different judges. I was determined if nothing else. Working in my favour were the children themselves, who voted with their feet by never failing to show up for time with their Dad. It felt great, but I wanted holidays and sleep-overs too. Those victories, if they were to happen, lie ahead.

One day I was at home opening the morning's post and happily reminiscing about the brilliant bass-heavy Grace Jones Roundhouse concert from the night before. The former disco icon appeared as unhinged as ever but put on an exquisite show, which was still ringing in my ears. One of the letters was from Orla, announcing that she and Titi had split up and are now living at separate addresses. I was unsurprised that the two demon women had split, but for a moment, my devilish mind wondered which of their respective multiple personalities had caused the rupture. The letter explained that the children were now being shuttled between the two mothers' homes on an alternate weekly basis. I was to later find out that the women had actually split nine months before Orla's letter, and that they'd told the children to keep it a secret from me; which explained the unusual whispering between the children and them not wanting to leave me at the end of our time together. My daughter had got into the habit of *needing* to use the loo at the last minute, causing us to be late for the drop off. I was furious that the children had been burdened with such a secret and decided to return to court, immediately. This time I was seeking more hours, sleepovers and holidays, which thus far had not been granted. KC was now twelve and May was eight, and they had not had an overnight stay with me since KC was a toddler.

Yet another Judge heard my case, but unfortunately for me, she was totally unsympathetic. She chastised me for returning to court and said she would order yet another report before making any decisions. I made my unhappiness clear, but the Judge admonished me and told me my behaviour would not be tolerated. I left court feeling very deflated. The two women, who were barely talking to each other, were delighted. We were ordered to return to court in the New Year - 2012.

There was no doubt about it; fathers get a raw deal in family court, unless they are lucky with the sitting judge of the day. All I was seeking, from my very first application in 2004, was quality time with the children, including holidays and regular sleepovers. But no, the whole world had to stop to allow for yet another report by Cafcass or similar organisation. I was very unhappy, but my faith remained intact. I was going to be optimistic, and pray on it; pray like my mother.

49. A MILESTONE OF JOY AND PAIN

It was Wednesday 16th November 2011, my fiftieth birthday! I decided to put all outstanding legal matters aside and celebrate my bi-centenary with a whopping big party. I hired the entire ground floor of the Green Carnation in London's Soho, complete with its fully equipped DJ booth and private bar. The day started well, with a personal video tribute to me from the survivor supreme herself, Gloria Gaynor. I was truly moved that the original Queen of Disco would take the time to do that for me, and I was quick to show it off on Facebook, where many very kind messages awaited me. It was a great start to a special day, but I was suddenly mindful of the special people who would not celebrate with me tonight: my beloved mother, brothers Bunny and Leo, nephew JJ, Anita, and too many friends stolen by AIDS: Marvin, Raymond, Colin, Leon, John, Trevor, Paul, Alex, Greame, Michael, Philip, Margret, Karen, Lois,

Nigel, Charles... Chris, Winston, Rick... Too, too many, but I knew that they would be with me in spirit.

Former Brent HIV Centre (Park House) was converted into flats in 2015

I arrived at the venue in good time, and by 6pm the hot and tasty Caribbean food I'd ordered had arrived in copious amounts; I was keen to feed my anticipated hundred or so guests, who would mostly be coming directly from work on this chilly November night. The venue was kind enough to provide me with my very own dishy Brazilian barman for the night. It was his job to make sure my guests were well lubricated throughout the evening.

Of course, great party music – disco! – was crucial to the success of my special night. Simon, my old friend from my coming out teenage years at Kingsley Road, and Ralph Tee, of Expansion Records, were my very capable DJs. We shared the same taste in dance and soul music, so I knew my guests and I would be happy. Kicking off with Gloria's Never Can Say Goodbye and Cheryl Lynn's Got To Be Real, early arrivals were already bopping away.

By 8pm the Green Carnation was turning red hot, and I was having a ball. It was fantastic to see so many friendly faces, which was much more valuable to me than the endless gifts and cards that were bestowed upon me. I felt very loved and appreciated.

My guests included friends from all aspects of my life; Brondesbury and Kilburn High School, my early coming out years, the People's Group, Brent HIV Centre, Islington, Marshall ACM – a company I was working with after leaving Islington, and Daniel, my fantastic lawyer in my fight to reconnect with the kids. Some family was there too, although Beverley didn't make it, and I had no expectation of seeing Jan, who remained estranged, thanks to her unrelenting homophobia. Bunny's children were there, as well as my dear cousin, Doreene, who read out a lengthy tribute from my dad in Jamaica. That was an emotional moment for me, causing me to wipe a tear from my eye. I remember thinking that it would have been very special if he could have said those loving words to me himself, but despite his eighty-plus years, he was still far too macho to do that. I had been regularly sending him money since my mother's death, and even though I couldn't erase the bad memories, he was still my dad. The kids, KC and May, were not there, but this party was for adults.

Daniel said some very kind words about my winning in court. My dearest friends, photographer Robert Taylor, Paul Thurlow and Dave Loweirnely, all delivered their own personal tributes too. It was all very lovely. I then said a few heartfelt words of gratitude, blew out my candles, and put a knife to my enormous rainbow-iced Caribbean, rum-filled birthday cake. Simon and Ralph cranked up the volume with Gloria's I Am What I Am, and the crowd started to bop again. I was very happy tonight.

The evening's major surprise for me was the arrival of Dirk, my ex-boyfriend, who secretly flew in from Germany for the evening. It was so good to set eyes on him again and it made my evening complete. He was now very much married to someone else, but I was thrilled that he wanted to get on a plane to make my birthday extra special.

God's Other Children: A London Memoir   503

God's Other Children: A London Memoir   504

I returned home in the early hours of the morning in a taxi filled with champagne, presents and cards. I was alone on my special night but was happy and feeling very blessed. I'd had a night to remember and nothing could wipe the smile from my face, not even deep sleep.

Vernal was awake again, and my old Exegesis spirit was back with a purpose. I was living in a one-bedroom flat, but thought if I got more space for myself and the children, I'd be working in line with the outcome I wanted to see delivered. I was especially keen to offer the kids their very own bedrooms. So on 8th of December 2011 I moved into a four-bedroom detached house in plush Emerson Park in Hornchurch, Essex. The kids loved it, even though they could not stay overnight. Despite this, I went ahead and purchased wardrobes and beds for their respective rooms. I had no time to fully unpack, because the next day I had to jump on a flight to see Gloria Gaynor in Utrech. She was the headliner in a sell-out live 'Champagne Christmas' concert that was being recorded for TV broadcast.

After the show, a group of her loyal Euro fans and I were invited to her hotel suite for a catch up, even though it was nearly one in the morning. I'd last seen Gloria in June in New York, following a fantastic show she did with Village People as her opening act. They'd originally toured with Gloria back in 1979. The macho men of disco put on a great show and still sported three original members, although Glen Hughes, the world's favourite 'Leatherman', had died of cancer some years ago. I was thrilled to finally see Gloria on her home soil; the city where disco was born. She was on top form, too.

After the show the Godmother of Disco was buzzing and chatting as ever. I thanked her for the beautiful video birthday tribute, and she kindly said I didn't look my age, which I jokingly agreed with. She sang happy birthday to Hans, her ex fan club President who was with us, and then spoke about her faith leading her to new projects. She also said something witty about staying up late with a room full of gay people. We laughed, posed for pictures, chatted some more, laughed some more, and then

kissed and hugged each other goodbye. Half an hour later, I was tucked up in my own hotel bed, not too far from hers.

Back home from Utrech, I set about completing my unpacking. I wandered between the empty bedrooms in my new home – our new home. I wanted it to be the kids' home as much as mine, but would they ever sleep here, I asked myself. The answer was "Pray on it".

God's Other Children: A London Memoir 508

God's Other Children: A London Memoir   509

That's Gloria's cute handbag, not mine!

50. GOODBYE SISTER WHITNEY, HELLO KIDS!

IT WAS 12TH JANUARY 2012, and the country was already looking forward to the London Olympics to be held in the summer. As had often been the case over the past eight years, I was reluctantly getting into a suit to attend family court. I was particularly lethargic today because, at the mothers' request, my case had been reserved to a Judge who appeared to take a personal dislike to me. The mothers were again seeking to turn the tables and asking the court to have my time with the children reduced, not only in hours, but from fortnightly to every three weeks. The Judge agreed to consider their request and ordered Cafcass to produce another report to aid her decision-making. Given my history with Cafcass, I was expecting the worse. It looked like my unwillingness to settle for fortnightly contact with no sleep-overs or holidays was about to backfire on me. I was just seeking what the mothers' already enjoyed, but the Judge wanted a report first. I was tired of this struggle; this on-going battle for equality. The Equality Act 2010 was important legislation, but it had a missing 'characteristic' in my view: equality for fathers.

Instead of calling the court to cry sick, as I was very tempted to do, I caught my train from Romford and headed to Holborn, the location for my latest effort for improved quality time with the children.

My High Court victory back in 2007 was significant, but it simply marked a new beginning of my legal fight. Orla and Titi, despite their splitting up, were still putting on a united front in court, but I wasn't up for the fight today. I just did not have the energy.

When I arrived in court I heard myself say, *"God, I need a miracle here today, I really do."* I signed in and made my way to the applicant's waiting room. I could see the *other side* had already arrived, and were sitting together in the respondent's room. Half an hour passed and we hadn't yet been called for what was supposed to be the first hearing of the day before the judge concerned. Then an hour passed. It didn't make sense. I went to find out what was happening but the clerk asked me to be patient. More minutes slipped by. We were then informed that our judge was delayed on another case and they were seeking an alternative. This was an unexpected development, indeed it was a first in my now extensive experience of fourteen different judges and many more appearances in family court.

Some two hours later than originally scheduled, we finally took to our respective places in front of the replacement judge; who just happened to be the very first non-white judge that I'd come across in my now eight-year legal saga. And, perhaps by coincidence (huh!), this judge did what all the others had patently failed to do; he took the case and shook it by the shoulders, and after close inspection of the facts, he immediately ordered that the children sleep over with me, and that this should start the following month. Titi was again spitting nails, but this time it was from every orifice on her miserable being. I had to pinch myself in order to contain my glee. Orla appeared to accept what she was hearing without much of a flutter. The good judge also ordered that we come back before him in March, after the sleepover, and made his intention to order regular sleep overs and holidays clear. He dismissed the need for further reports and involvement by Cafcass and reserved the case to himself. I couldn't be happier.

I thought back to my mood earlier in the day; just as I was about to give up and accept less than the children and I deserved, a miracle came along that enabled me to achieve this breakthrough. It really did feel like an amazing miracle, and I couldn't thank God and the good judge enough; I had waited eight gruelling years and spent nearly forty thousand pounds to be afforded that which most Dad's take for granted; quality time with their children. I also thanked my mother, who I visualized having a word in God's ear.

Orla and Titi once again left court with disappointment on their faces. I was all smiles, of course, and wasted no time in sending texts and making calls to concerned friends with the unexpected good news. Lesson: expect miracles.

Saturday 11th February, just a week away from the kids' first sleep over, and I began to worry that I may mess up and they would ask to be returned to their mothers in the middle of the night. A moment later I was completely relaxed about the whole thing; I was going to be myself and have confidence that this would be enough.

That night I turned up my super stereo in my living room and sang my heart out. I started with George Benson and Nancy Wilson, but soon all I wanted to play was Whitney. I sang along to 'Exhale', 'All the Man That I Need', 'For the Love of You' and 'My Love Is Your Love'. Sister Whitney was still struggling to overcome her well-publicized drug addictions but had recently released a new hit CD, 'I Look to You'. Despite some terrible 'come back' concert disasters in which her previously flawless voice completely failed her resulting in attendees walking out in disgust, her more loyal fans, myself included, were optimistic that Whitney really was on her way back to the top; step by step, one day at a time. She even had a new movie in the works called Sparkle. I'd written to her in 2011, the 20th anniversary of Reach Out and Touch. I wanted to wish her well and thank her again for the lasting memory of an amazing event. I was especially keen to catch up with Robyn Crawford, but she was nowhere to be found on-line. The two women had parted company some years back when it became clear that the Whitney and Bobby 'show' was here to stay. The most unlikely marriage in show business became a tabloid laughing stock, with drunken outbursts, court appearances, and too many cancelled public engagements. Bobby's spitting in Whitney's face was yet another symptom of a marriage that was doomed, so I was not at all surprised when she filed for divorce, winning custody of their daughter in the process.

The next morning I switched on the television to catch the headlines on Sky News, which I did every morning. The volume was muted, so I quickly adjusted it to make sense of why they were showing images of Whitney. In a matter of a few terrible seconds, the subdued presenter announced the death of the beloved superstar. I was beyond horrified. It felt like the death of Princess Diana all over again, but somehow, much more personal. Incomprehensively, aged just forty-eight, Whitney had been found unconscious in a bath in the luxury Beverly Hills hotel. *How on Earth could this happen?* I was struggling to take it in. It seemed as though she took all her gifts and threw them over a cliff in a long drawn out act of semi-detached suicide. Robyn Crawford, her true love, was the one gift that she should never have parted with; life went downhill from there, and in her desperation to drown out her pain, Sister Whitney only succeeded in drowning herself. My heart was telling me that Robyn could have saved her, if only Whitney would have picked up the phone and called her instead of her unobtainable church pastor, as it later transpired she did before getting into the bath. She also called and spoke briefly to Dionne Warwick. The Los Angeles County Coroner later ruled that her death was "accidental", citing the "effects of atherosclerotic heart disease and cocaine use" as contributing factors. Forensic examination further deduced that a drugs-high desensitized Whitney experienced acute shock when she stepped into the excessively hot bath water, causing her to pass out. Faced down and helplessly unconscious, she then drowned in just twelve inches of water. On discovering her submerged and unresponsive, the star's traumatized staff did their best to save her. On her knees looking into the death room from the hotel corridor, Whitney's make-up artist screamed hysterically at the top of her lungs as a bodyguard, having dragged Whitney from the bath, pounded on the singer's chest in what would prove to be a vain attempt at reviving her. Pat Houston, Whitney's sister-in-law and business manager, on seeing the futility of the situation, intervened with a simple yet devastatingly final: "Let her go. Just let her go." She then asked a concerned fellow hotel guest who had come to investigate the commotion to "please call 911". Also alerted by the commotion was Whitney's devoted teenage daughter, who went into emotional meltdown on learning of the death of her mother. She had to be sedated before being taken away by ambulance. In the unfolding chaos, Whitney's equally upset brother, who was also present, phoned their mother, Cissy Houston, to break the terrible news. Fumbling for words, he was only able to repeat his sister's name: "Mom... Whitney...Nippy... Whitney..." Incoherent and stuttering, he could not get his mouth to complete the sentence that he knew would inflict irreversible heartbreak upon his mother. Confused to the point of frustration by her son's inexplicable disjointed utterances, a perceptive and now fearful Cissy was forced to ask the unthinkable but unavoidable question: "Is she dead?" His mumbled confirmation prompted the harrowing reaction that he was dreading. It started with his mother dropping the phone, followed by her shrieks of catastrophic devastation down the phone line from her New Jersey home. The world had lost a superstar, but Cissy had lost her child and only daughter.

Under the same blaze of flashing cameras that she was accustomed to in her curtailed life, Whitney's cold body was later unceremoniously removed from the hotel, covered by common white sheets. Her autopsy revealed that in the relatively short time since our meeting in 1991, her subsequent drugs-affected life at the top had taken a ravaging toll. As well as liver damage and corrosive heart disease, her hair was found to be covered by a wig described as "tight-fitting", breast augmentation (implant) surgery was evident, and excessive cocaine use caused her teeth to fall out and be substituted with dentures. Not quite as beautiful as she once was, Whitney Elizabeth Houston, one of the greatest amongst the greatest of singers, our greatest love of all, and the woman who had stood with me and reached out and touched people with HIV and AIDS with love and compassion, was gone, and with her, a voice and presence that had reached out and touched the world.

Denied privacy even in her death, an invasive camera would somehow find the deceased diva of song in the L.A. funeral home tasked with preparing her for burial. A secreted picture of Whitney in an open casket would eventually make its way to the internet. In full make-up and dazzling gown, topped with immaculate hair and complementary jewellery, she looked as though she was taking a welcome nap before getting up to take to the stage. That stolen image would mark the final sighting of the fallen superstar before lowered flags and applauding crowds would serenade her on her final journey to the New Jersey cemetery where she would be laid to rest next to her father. Death had not erased her appeal.

My earlier musical tribute evening suddenly began to make some kind of imperfect sense. It was like one of those odd, almost telepathic moments when you think of someone and then they suddenly call you or appear at your front door, forcing you to say, 'Hey, I was just thinking of you!' I had been celebrating Whitney the night before her death and I now knew why.

With Whitney's music playing in the background, I took calls from equally shocked friends until late morning. The lyrics of I Look to You, her last hit, were particularly poignant: *"I'm lost without a cause, after giving it my all..."*

The pop superstar, like her peer, Michael Jackson, had become the latest world-wide reminder about the perils of drug abuse. She had touched millions with her beautiful angelic voice and unforgettable smile, and yet, no one was able to reach and free her from the chains of her lethal addictions; addictions which had their roots, in my view, in her denial of her authenticity as a bisexual or lesbian woman. Whitney had denied her inner truth to accommodate the wishes and expectations of religious bigots. It was an avoidable gut-wrenchingly tragic end to a uniquely gifted life.

I thought about those who had been close to her: her daughter, mother – Cissy, Dionne Warwick, and, of course, Robyn Crawford, her public 'assistant' and very personal friend. *Yes, what about Sister Robyn?* She loved Whitney like nobody else did and I hope she would now share that love with the world, as she came close to doing when we met years ago. However, a suspected 'gagging' clause or plain principle would prevent that from happening, for now.

I logged onto Facebook and replaced my profile picture with one featuring Whitney and me, which I normally displayed on World AIDS Day – with the *red ribbon* imposed above it. It was my way of saying thank you, and acknowledging that our paths had crossed.

By coincidence, Peter Tatchell was in my diary for a catch-up the following Wednesday. By the time of our dinner on Old Compton Street, I was already aware that the press was quoting him saying he'd "met Whitney Houston and Robyn Crawford at the Reach Out and Touch AIDS vigil organised by Vernal Scott". He was also quoted as saying "Whitney was happiest when she was in a lesbian relationship" and that her life went downhill when she was forced to adopt a straight lifestyle. He may have been right, but did it really matter now? Well, actually, it did matter. As I said to

Whitney (and Robyn) in my letter to her after we met, her sexuality was nothing to be ashamed of.

Over dinner I explained to Peter that Whitney's and Robyn's sexuality or relationship status wasn't what needed attention now that she's gone; it was the homophobia and related mechanisms that would cause someone, be it Whitney or anyone else, to have to remain in the closet about their sexuality. He agreed. I held a great deal of respect for Peter, and his remarks about Whitney hadn't changed that. He remained a friend and personal hero.

Friday arrived! With Whitney's premature passing still fresh in my mind, it was time to pay full attention to my overnight house guests who I was on my way to collect. By the time I got there, I was certain the children would not be handed over, and that Titi and Orla would try to sabotage the stay over. The agreed time of 3pm passed and there was no sign of the children. I was concerned. No sooner had visuals of yet another return to court crossed my mind, I spotted the children and Titi heading towards my parked car. Moments later, the two excited children were in the back and we were on our way. The first subject on their lips was "We're spending the night with Daddy!" followed by, "Dad, did you hear about your friend, Whitney Houston? She died." A short while later we stopped off at a shopping centre to buy some overnight pyjamas and the like. It would have been too much for the bitter mothers to supply them, of course.

As our first night together drew in, I wondered what I would do come bedtime if the kids got uncomfortable and asked to be taken back to either of their mothers' respective homes. But I needn't have worried. By 9pm I had the children bathed, in their night clothes, and we were happily sitting together on the sofa drinking hot chocolate and watching TV. It was bliss. At one point I went into the kitchen, looked up to heaven and said a big thank you to Jesus – and my mother, of course, because I was sure she had a hand in this wonderful development. Hey, don't mess with my mum!

I was emotional as I put May to bed. I got on my knees beside her and told my eight-year old daughter her very first bedtime story read by her Daddy. The story was one I knew by heart; about a man who had a beautiful little girl whom he loved very much, but he had to fight through lots of dangerous obstacles to get to see her and to let her know just how much he loved her.

Yes, it was our story, greatly curtailed and simplified. May smiled up at me because she knew who the star of this story was. She jumped up on her knees and gave me the most enormous hug ever. That special moment made my years of fighting for it worthwhile. I told her that I was the happiest Dad in the entire world and wished her a happy sleep before turning out the light. I then went into KC's room and gave him a huge hug too. I think we all went to sleep with a smile on our faces that night. I know I did.

The following day, as the children watched a movie, I tuned into CNN on my laptop to watch Sister Whitney's funeral. Presided over by Dionne Warwick and laced with musical tributes by the likes of Stevie Wonder and Alicia Keys, it was a truly wonderful, gospel-tinged send-off. I turned the volume down when Clive Davis spoke – the A&R man who discovered Whitney. I thought he was a nasty rattlesnake for going ahead with the Grammys party while her body was still warm in the hotel room above his head where she died hours earlier. Kevin Costner's tribute was the highlight for me, and the heartbreaking low was the image of a devastated Cissy Houston, following behind her daughter's lavish coffin while the speaker system played her greatest hit, I Will Always Love You. The song had been her first single following her appearance at Reach Out and Touch.

The missing tribute, of course, was Robyn's.

If I had been there and able to speak, I would have said:

"Goodbye, Sister Whitney. Thank you for reaching out and touching at a crucial moment in time when we needed you. We stood together and demanded that they find a cure for HIV/AIDS. Now that your show has finally ended and the audience has gone home, you can rest in peace in the knowledge that you made a positive difference where it mattered most; in our hearts. Exhale, dear sister, exhale."

As I looked across the room at my children watching TV, I wondered what the future would hold for them. I wished them long happy lives, full of love and free from fear, pain, loneliness, and tragic endings like Whitney's and Princess Diana's. I know that their lives are their own, and they will be the drivers towards their own respective destinies. But one thing was certain; I will be there for them, every step of the way.

When we returned to court in March, the good judge was true to his word, and ordered that children stay over with me whenever there is a school holiday e.g. Easter, Christmas, Half-Term etc. He also ordered that the children spend ten consecutive nights with me during the summer school holidays, and he permitted me to take the children abroad, if I so decided. I was elated. My case was the same as it had always been; the only difference was that a (non-Caucasian) judge with a healthy view about (black) dads had finally heard it. It shouldn't have made a difference but it did. There was no cogent reason why the very first judge back in 2004 couldn't have reached the same judgment.

Once the hearing was over, Orla approached me to say that she was no longer interested in court battles and wanted us to move on. Experience had taught me the hard way that she and honesty did not live on the same planet. Titi, on the other hand, made no such gesture; she was too bitter and hateful, but at least she was being honest, at last. I'd be more than an Olympic gold-winning fool to trust either woman ever again.

Love and healing is a song by Sister Whitney. It will take some considerable time to adjust to her physical absence, even though her music will undoubtedly play on. I was disappointed though not at all surprised to see Cissy, her mother, state to Oprah in January 2013 that she would never have approved of Whitney being lesbian and that she disliked Robyn Crawford, her *rumoured* 'girlfriend'. Well, like the title of her own disco hit, she might want to think it over! Her anti-gay stance caused me to remember the frantic concern by Whitney's *'Nippy'* people that I might 'out' her at my event. In fact, she was effectively outed by their own 'hush-hush' campaign and Robyn's (unashamed!) hard-to-hide love and affection. In Robyn I met someone who loved Whitney way above and beyond her public role as the singer's assistant; she presented herself as Whitney's equal – her partner – not a subordinate employee, and was undoubtedly the wind beneath Whitney's golden wings. I recall the pride in her posture, face and voice, when she told me: "Vernal, I've been walking with Whitney for a long time!" Whitney's subsequent divergence from her authentic self ultimately robbed her of her voice, life, and one true love. The singer's troubles took hold after Robyn left the scene and the world then watched in horror as drug abuse took a hold. Without Robyn by her side, Whitney's previously unassailable shining star sank below any point of rescue.

I am angry with Cissy and the Bible-bashing black community for allowing their ignorance and projected inner-shame about naturally occurring homosexuality to cause so much damage. Their corrosive religious intolerance damaged Whitney way before drugs ever did. Her addictions, just like her cavernously hollow 'Jesus loves me' rhetoric towards the end, were symptoms of internalized-homophobic pain planted by them. Robyn's only crime was that she was a woman, and for this reason alone, she had to go; even though her love was, evidently, good for Whitney. Hey, let's have the love of invisible Jesus; the fractious love of chaotic Bobby; or the strict conditional love of the black church; anything but the nurturing and protective love of lesbian Robyn. How pathetically cruel, sad and mad is that? We must now all live with the irreversible consequences. That said and meant, Whitney cannot be totally absolved of responsibility. She had options and chose badly. Very badly!

In closing this chapter, I am compelled to ask this poignant question; precious Whitney, where do broken hearts go? You paid a terrible price to appease bigotry, but we will always love you. Your sudden departure from our lives wasn't right, but it's okay, now. Thankfully, for one moment in time, you really did dance with somebody who loves you...Robyn. In the future, whenever love needs a song the world will continue to look to you, Whitney Elizabeth Houston. Your star will forever shine.

Love and gratitude, Vx

Postscript: Some months after Whitney's passing, published photos taken outside her funeral church service would reveal a solitary but familiar face among the weeping throngs. It was undoubtedly Robyn Crawford.

Unfathomably, to the world's further dismay, thirty-five months after her mother's death, Bobbi Kristina, Whitney's daughter and only child, was also found unresponsive in a water-filled bath. The sole beneficiary of her mother's multi-million dollar estate, she would remain in a medically induced coma for several months until her own death in July 2015, aged just 22. Like her mother, the official autopsy report cites the cause as 'intoxication and drowning'. The Houston tragedy was complete.

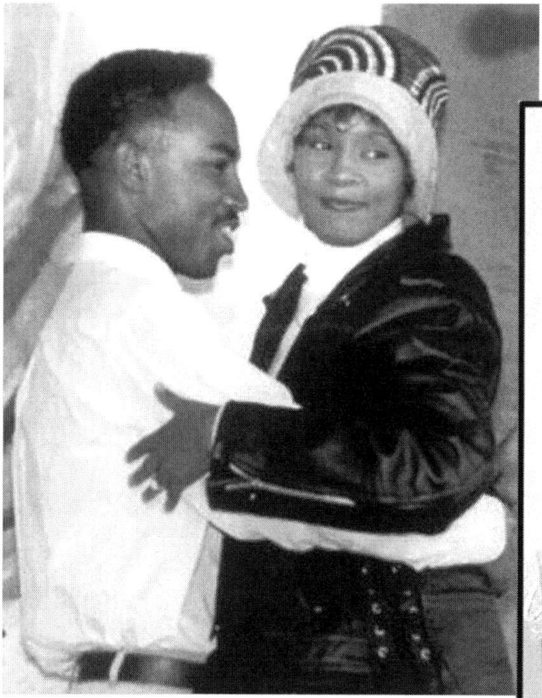

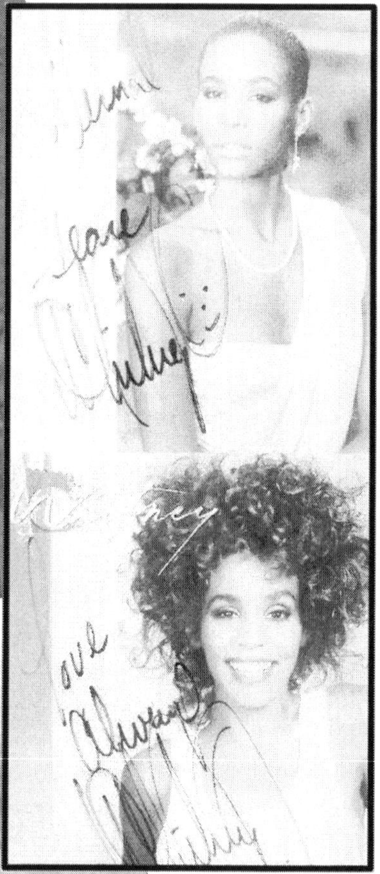

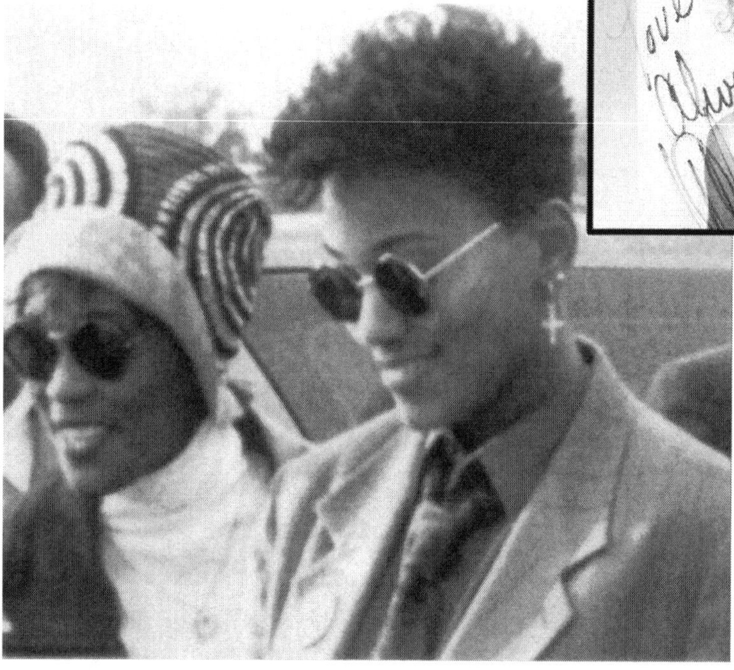

51. CANCER SCARE!

THE HOUSE IN AYLOFF'S WALK, Hornchurch, was quiet and provided the perfect context to put finger to keyboard and write this book. I was still absorbing Whitney's death when an ice cold shudder hit my spine on learning of the passing to lung cancer of Donna Summer, Gloria Gaynor's principal counterpart during the disco era. She was only sixty-three. By coincidence, just a few months earlier, I had gone to considerable effort to track down CDs that were missing from my Donna collection: Cat's Without Claws, The Wanderer, Bad Girls Deluxe, and her beautiful Christmas CD. I found them all on one website or the other, although Cats was a gift from Glen, a new Facebook friend. Her passing caused me to want to rediscover her music, and it, together with music by a number of other artists, provided a backdrop to my typing of this book. During my rummage for Donna tunes, I discovered I had a spare copy of her deleted Quincy Jones produced CD. I had originally purchased it for four pounds, but an EBay buyer was happy to take it off my hands for a handsome sixty pounds. Cancer had claimed too many of our stars over the years, and two or three people in my own life, too. R.I.P. Donna.

It was now summer and everyone's focus was on the London 2012 Olympics. KC and May were insanely excited about it, especially Jamaica's Usain Bolt, and they would make each other laugh by mimicking his famous pose.

I was taking a shower when I looked down and noticed a painless black lesion that appeared overnight under the nail on my left great toe. I was thought it curious and odd, but decided to ignore it until a friend suggested I go and get it checked out. My GP immediately referred me to a dermatologist, who then referred me to the Broomfield hospital, which had a specialist cancer unit. The suspicion was that I may have a rare skin cancer known as a subungual melanoma; the same cancer that had killed Bob Marley. On examining the lesion, the surgeon booked me in for an immediate biopsy, to take place two days later. I squirmed at the thought when he confirmed it would involve removing my nail to get to the lesion.

When I got home, I confided in a few close friends and tried to fight off a sense of pessimism about my predicament. I heard myself say *'I've come all this way in life just to die of cancer'*. I even saw visions of myself in my own coffin; all very depressing. I prayed about it. Then, very strangely, the phone rang and it was my dad calling from Jamaica for the first time ever, to say I was on his mind and wanting to know if all was well. I said it was – *I lied*. I was very worried indeed, but I told myself that only the biopsy would tell me the truth; I wanted to deal with reality and not fear.

Two days later, and instead of what I thought was to be a minor operation in a consultation room, I found myself robed and being wheeled into a full operating theatre, complete with two surgeons and a team of three assistants. Reality check! The principal surgeon was very chatty and did his best to get me to relax. He succeeded. He advised that I not look as he numbed my toe with a series of stinging injections. After a short while I couldn't feel my toe at all.

The entire biopsy took approximately forty minutes and I only looked down when it was over, and it wasn't at all a pleasant sight. Thankfully, instead of removing the entire nail, the surgeon only removed half, including the suspect lesion. Two hours later and I was back at home with a heavily bandaged toe. I now had to wait for the result, which I was warned may take a week or more. Over the intervening days, I distracted myself by thinking positive thoughts about myself and my future, and, of course, I prayed for a cancer-free result. *'God, I know you've still got work for me to do and you're not done with me yet'.*

The following Saturday, when the children saw my bandaged toe, I made up an elaborate story about tripping over as I chased an armed mugger down Oxford Street. They laughed but remained curious about what had really happened to my toe. I skilfully deflected the issue and changed the subject to school. Both children were doing well and were always happy to boast about being top of class in one subject or another. I was very proud of them. KC, even though the school had mounting concerns about his volatility and 'anger issues', was a master at maths and reading, and May loved reading and writing. The young author was even trying her hand at writing short stories; her latest effort being 'Annabel the Detective'. Very impressive! The children were a good distraction for me and I wasn't going to worry them with my cancer scare. Our usual activities would find us at the cinema, a park, bowling, meeting up with friends, ice skating, or even baking cakes; the latter activity was down to May and I alone, as we had the same taste in cakes. OK, it was an addiction. KC was happy to leave us to it, as long as he could watch a favourite TV programme or enjoy his Playstation 3. No, no need to worry their little heads with my health issue.

A miserable week passed before I finally heard from the hospital. The principal surgeon himself called to let me know my result was in and I was in the clear. I was elated and stopped listening after the word "clear" came down the phone. That's all I needed to hear. I said thank you and put the phone down and thanked God on my grateful knees.

I had to attend the hospital to have my dressing changed on two occasions, but I did the task myself after that. No more cancer scare, no more hospitals. Back to living!

My sincere best wishes to anyone dealing with the consequences of cancer.

The experience reaffirmed the reality that time and life were precious and I should use them wisely.

52. I'VE GOT WORK TO DO!

WE WERE COMING TO THE END of 2012 and I was feeling rested and upbeat. I was particularly pleased to be nearing completion of my book – the one you're reading. The next step was to find a publisher, or get really modern, and self-publish. I was already making notes for my next book called, Nine Ways to Kill Dad. The kids helped me with the title, and it's a humorous, back-slapping manuscript. If it never makes it to publication, then, perhaps, it wasn't fiction after all, and the kids have done away with me and buried me under the patio; my final tragedy.

I needed to get back to greater productivity in general and thought I'd explore some of the various interest groups on Facebook. I was particularly interested in a London AIDS Memorial project, as well as the opportunity to work with various HIV and sexual health charities.

Peter Tatchell, the UK's most high profile human rights activist, got in touch to ask whether I'd be interested in becoming a Trustee of his Foundation. We discussed a number of matters of concern, including Commonwealth nations, religion and sport, and how homophobia affects them all. These issues relate very strongly to those mentioned in the prologue to this book, so I was definitely interested in knowing more.

The year was ending on a mixed note. On the upside, the children had enjoyed a number of happy sleep-overs with me, including five consecutive nights in the summer, and as ordered by court, this will increase to ten next year. Not too surprisingly, Orla and Titi have separated. Their venomous toxicity ultimately poisoned their own relationship and both women are now living with new female partners and mostly communicate with each other via email or mediated services. The children and I remain in the middle of their spats, but I do my best to offer some kind of stability via the fortnightly contact and occasional sleep-overs.

Orla, perhaps influenced by her new partner, has been more civil towards me of late, but all trust between us had been destroyed by her hateful behaviour over the years, which is impossible to forget. My focus is the children, and that's where it will stay. Titi remains as hostile as ever, but that doesn't bother me one bit.

Despite the upheaval caused by the mothers' split, May is doing very well at school, but KC, who is also very talented, increasingly displays aggressive behaviour at school, and towards Orla, his non-biological mother, in particular; a sign that he'd been damaged by her and Titi's warped vision of family; a family designed primarily with the needs of the two women in mind rather than the children. Things got so bad that he was excluded from school, and following a disturbing outburst between him and Orla, she resorted to threatening him with the police. Turned out onto the streets, a dejected KC had to make his way on foot to Titi's house. The incident prompted an immediate change in his living arrangements, which until now, like May's, had been split equally between the addresses of the two women. Orla soon declared KC's living arrangements as being "in limbo." I wrote to both women with my concerns, but, as expected, was completely ignored. Perhaps the police should be called, but not to deal with KC; it is my view that his behaviour is a symptom, not the problem.

Orla once asserted that biology didn't matter in LGBT families, but she's obviously wrong! KC is now living full-time with Titi, his biological mother, and May is now seeking to reduce her contact with Titi and KC; wishing to live full-time with Orla, her biological mother. Of late, the only quality time that the children share together is when they are with me. It's all pathetically sad, especially for KC, and I genuinely fear for his future. Through their selfishness, the two women have created yet another angry young (black) man. They had denied him his biological father – Orla's brother, and after inviting me to step into the vacancy and 'bond' with him, they then ripped me out of his life without any concern about the harm they would cause him; they didn't care. Yes, KC has genuine reason to be angry, but I hope he won't go through life hating on women because of his mothers' mistakes.

As for my own relationship with KC, it is apparent that our fortnightly contact over the years has been inadequate to mend what's been broken between us; our bond is increasingly tenuous. He is understandably fiercely loyal to Titi, who constantly reminds him that I am not his real father. As a result, he seems anxious at our 'handovers'; fearful of being seen to be too warm towards me. Frankly, our time together is more akin to a fun day out rather than anything father/son related, and that's fine with me. I'm just pleased that he and May get to see each other and that I facilitate this. The children didn't ask for this mess and I wish all the adults in this situation would remember that fact. The women had succeeded in damaging us all, but I hope it won't be permanent, for the children's sake.

I wish my woeful experience of gay-parenting with a lesbian couple was a one-off, but I am not at all alone. Many well-intentioned gay men have experienced the same and worse as me; ending up being discarded and in expensive legal battles. Once the bundle of joy arrives, its packaging soon starts to stink when the baby is treated as the personal property of the lesbian couple concerned. The mortified gay dad is then left struggling to keep in touch with his child for years to come. The bias of the family courts towards women doesn't help dads, and this is readily exploited by malicious-minded mothers, both lesbian and straight. This vile selfish behaviour will reap its just reward in time, but for the interim the children and father have to suffer, as I did.

My message to fathers, gay and straight, is simple: your children did not choose to be fatherless, so don't give up on them, ever! They will come knocking one day, and you must be able to show evidence that you tried to see them. Even better, don't have children with desperate women in the first place; don't walk away, run! Take a train, boat or plane, but get your ass out of there. That said and meant, I do of course love the kids in my life, but would I willingly repeat my experience? Hell no, and certainly not with Orla and Titi. If I could turn back time... but we can't.

Given everything that we'd been through, I thought it was high time that the kids and I had our first international holiday together, and Disney World was the unanimous destination of choice. Together with a long-time friend of mine - a fellow gay dad, also forced to win his parental rights in family court - and his two similarly aged kids, we jetted off to sun-kissed Florida in the summer of 2013, leaving all the stress behind us. The private and generously sized luxury villa, with its games room, BBQ, Jacuzzi, and swimming pool, was everything we deserved. Intrusive phone calls from both mothers were quickly curtailed; not by me, but by the children themselves, who had 'do not disturb!' all over their happy faces. It was indeed a very happy holiday and a fantastic time was had by each of us.

Tragically, as I suspected, the ongoing hostility by the mothers' in the years' ahead would result in the children and me eventually becoming estranged, perhaps permanently so. After all my efforts I was to be the ultimate loser and have no option but to resume my pre-children gay life as if the whole fatherhood adventure had been a nightmarish dream. In truth, that's exactly what it had become.

There would be no further court applications initiated by me, but I would forever be a dad; of the foolish, sperm-donating, unintendedly-estranged variety. How very very different the last few years would have been if only I had disposed of my semen into a tissue and down the loo like most men do, and not handed it over to two abhorrent deceitful liars. A terrifically horrible lesson learnt!

As the year ends, I once again find myself exiting from family court, but this time it's for a very different reason than on previous occasions. I was there in my newly adopted capacity as a 'McKenzie Friend', representing a distressed (gay) father who had not been allowed to see his two beautiful children for many months. He was signposted to me by a mutual friend, and I was happy to represent him. He chose well. Not only was I committed to supporting fathers in his position, whether gay or not, and mothers too, but it was an opportunity to build upon my basic qualification as a paralegal. I intend to be the best McKenzie Friend that the family courts had ever experienced.

Although this was my first case I had no intention of leaving court with a disappointed tearful father on my hands.

Failure to reconnect this man with his children was not an option. The respondent lesbian mothers had a very competent QC on their side, but my extensive experience of family court, coupled with my very capable communication skills, meant that I was not at all disadvantaged; indeed, I rose to the challenge with great relish. The happy father left court with a contact order in his hand and a smile on his face, but I secretly pondered whether he was as happy as me. Result!

I got rather lost after my work during the height of the HIV/AIDS crisis, but my commitment to the people affected will continue, at least until there is a permanent memorial to them in London. The outstanding equality issues raised in my prologue also require action, as do family courts. I intend to act. Yes, Vernal Scott still has work to do!

53. AHH MEN: THE CIRCUMCISION OF RELIGION

Leviticus 20:13: *"If a man has sexual relations with a man as one does with a woman, both of them have done what is detestable. They are to be put to death; their blood will be on their own heads."*

Amazing grace: I once was blind but now believe that the original spelling of the Bible must have been Babble or even Buybull. Be warned, this add-on chapter is my unholy rant which would afford me life for only another few minutes if shared in the wrong place. It is my long overdue exorcism of the corrosive Holy Spirit, which, from my youth into adulthood, tarnished my self-esteem and riddled me with suicidal guilt and shame for the 'sin' of being who and what I am; a gay man. Having cleansed myself of its damaging effects, my life has become a statement of graceful acceptance and self-love. I have eyes for a reason; to see for myself, and I now see that blind faith is no faith at all; it's just being blind. I am now willing to ask the hard questions and see the answers, or lack of them, for what they are. I reject the biblical lie that I was born a defective sinner and that I should spend my life trying to correct myself to avoid the wrath of a pissed-off invisible god. News alert: I am good and correct as I am and that holy mind-shit no longer works on me. I have flushed it down the toilet, together with the obscene guilt-trip that Jesus Christ, if he ever existed, died on the cross for my sins; even though my birth was some two thousand years after his alleged passing. But hey, didn't he rise again only to remain out of sight ever since? Hmm, if he did rise again, doesn't that mean he didn't "die" for me in the first place?

The bad 'good book' promotes:

- Indoctrination and fear
- Human sacrifice
- Self-loathing
- Terror in children and adults
- War genocide and execution
- Suicide and depression
- Shaming of innocence
- Entrapment and conformity through guilt
- Oppression and suppression of women, children and gay people
- Incest, slavery and gang rape
- Homophobia and anti-gay hate
- Irrationality over reason
- Hell fire for the 'sinner'
- Heavenly tyrannical domination for 'the good'

I believe life is about love, and to love is why we exist; everything else is dust waiting to happen. The Bible's 'love with threats' isn't love at all; its approach is foreign to me and the genuine love that I feel towards my fellow human beings.

Although the Bible, written before science, refers to homosexuality, it does not refer to same-sex LOVE, and that's what is manifestly missing in scripture. To reiterate its hate dressed up as morals, the Bible refers to people of my sexuality with distinctly unloving terms, such as abomination, vile affection, defilers, effeminate, sodomite, violating nature, etc. It and other holy works provided the ammunition that has led to countless murder and suicides of my LGBTQ brothers and sisters over the years. This holy curse, coupled with society's incessant hetero-centric lies about gays as paedophiles, agents of disease, destroyers of the family, and sex-crazed deviants, make the closet an essential refuge for millions of perfectly good people. Our self-imposed prison was often the safest place to be. It doubled as an improvised classroom in which to rehearse our skilful lies to family, friends and co-workers about our true sexuality. We've seen lots of hysteria from some religious quarters in the UK and America about same-sex marriage, and Bible scripture was often cited as sufficient reason to deny gays the ultimate public symbol of a committed loving union. Same-sex marriages are no threat to heterosexual marriages, nor are they a threat to churches or other religious institutions that do not want to conduct them. The answer is simple: if you don't approve of gay weddings then simply do not conduct or attend them (unless you are employed to provide a related service) or let your prejudice or ignorance prevent others from entering into the union they wish to commit to. Let's face it, this world needs more love, not less, and no one should seek to prevent it, especially not citing "a loving God" as their reason.

Some people, religious and not, regard gay sex as unnatural, but I can confirm that it's very natural, if you are gay. I don't have sexual relations with women because it isn't natural for me, as a gay man, to do so. Hating on me or bashing me with Bible scripture or baseball bats will not change me and my natural state of sexuality. Heterosexuals are not meant to enjoy gay sex, but they are not ordained to oppose, condemn, or prevent it. It is irrational to expect gay people to turn away from our essential nature as sexual beings and enjoy the gift of our sexuality; either through marriage, in a partnership, or as single people. One's sexuality, whether gay or heterosexual, cannot be suppressed without serious self-destructive consequences. My sexuality is not a choice and I refuse to suppress it or accept that I was born gay just to test whether I could successfully restrain myself. That would make God, if he existed, stupid, and if not that, then he is intrusively obsessed with our sex lives when he should be preventing the nine million childhood deaths which occur each year due to one thing or another. To restrain myself would serve no purpose other than to appease the ignorant haters out there and obey parts of Bible scripture that are as inhumane as slavery or the stoning of children, which it encourages. Consensual sex is a gift to be enjoyed with a sense of fun, but also, of course, with responsibility.

A self-propagating parasitical mind-robbing curse, Religious Compulsion Disorder (RCD) is patently characterized by the believer's willingness to embrace irrationality over reason, even when their beliefs are demolished by cogent argument and compelling opposing evidence. I was personally afflicted for many years and perhaps you still are. Other common symptoms include appearing to be frighteningly oblivious to one's own self-righteous fever and frothing at the mouth with nonsensical assertions that would see someone who isn't similarly diagnosed committed to the nearest mental health facility. OK, I confess that RCD is a disorder of my own creation, but it has greater cogency than the fiction spouted by the infuriating nuisances I describe. But that's the tainting viral effect of religion; it enters the mind and then re-programmes it to make us feel shame and guilt about who we are and how we live. It specifically corrupts our liking of things that we find naturally pleasurable, such as sex and attraction to others, personal wealth, and, of course, non-obedience to Holy Scriptures. As you saw in an earlier chapter, my sense of shame about my sexuality nearly cost me my teenage life. With the same replicating characteristics as HIV, the religious virus is determined to own its host and infect as many new hosts as possible. Passed on by those who are mostly unaware of their own infection, it has no respect for age, wealth, education, gender, sexuality, or race, and it's not at all interested in cats, dogs, apes or plant life; to thrive it simply needs gullible human beings, like I once was. We now know how to protect ourselves from HIV, and I offer similar advice regarding religion: protect yourself with the sheath of cogent reality and the super-lube of authenticated hard evidence. You've been duly warned!

Anyone seeking to sell religion to me will regret their efforts, so annoying Jehovah's Witnesses be warned! I can see through the camouflage of your dark spell and find it hypocritical of self-righteous fanatics like you that the freedom which allows you to preach is the same freedom that you would deny me to love. My sermon to you is simple: I did not free myself from the prison of the closet only to allow you to shackle me to the walls of your life-sapping holy dungeon. I honestly have no patience for you, but I might have an ounce of sympathy, because your delusion was once mine.

Fact: when you have evidence you don't need to have faith. Claims such as the existence of God require extraordinarily credible and conclusive evidence, but this has eluded us over the past two thousand years. Science is the intelligent method used to obtain facts through observation, experimentation, research and logical reasoning regarding the world and universe around us. Blatantly ignoring all of that, religious folk say faith is the justification for their belief in a God, but their faith is just self-deception. We are all born faithless or non-believers until our minds are stolen by the indoctrination that is religion. In preparing to write this chapter, I decided to finally read the King James Bible that had occupied prime position on my bedside table since it was given to me on my 40th birthday by Gloria Gaynor, the 'born again' Godmother of Disco. The reality of what it says had a truly profound effect on me, and I am certain, the opposite of what its legendary gift-giver had envisaged. My eyes were opened to my hitherto gross denial, bordering on dishonesty, about the Bible's darker content, and the realization that it is utterly ghastly in places, with enough indiscriminate killing carried out by God himself or men acting in his name to make the last two world wars look like unfortunate warm-up acts. I would conclude that religion's prevailing influence in the form of the Bible, Koran, and other established holy works, is evidence of a formidable contamination affecting our world. Having started its reign in the early centuries, manifesting in the depraved sacrifice of animals and then fellow human beings in the name of one invisible God or another, modern-day manifestations are no less obscene. Just watch tonight's news for the latest 'inspired' atrocity.

According to science, the universe is estimated to be about fourteen billion years old. The Earth and its solar system are about four or five billion – forming after the evolution-inducing big bang. The writing of the Bible started around two and half thousand years ago – about 300 BC. Each book within it was written over a number of subsequent centuries by men, not a God. There are of course writings older than the Bible in existence, just as there are older man-made constructions, including those in Egypt. Therefore, to say the Bible and other Holy books were written by a God is clearly false, as are the assertions that the Earth is only six thousand years old. Dinosaur bones and ancient relics put paid that nonsense, but many Christians refuse to be moved by such evidence. There are now numerous iterations and translations of the Bible, which in turn influence the plethora of different denominations which make up the disparate Christian faith.

Religion and identity are one and the same to many people and are intrinsically linked to ethnicity, nationality, culture, gender and even sexual orientation. Religious indoctrination is a powerful imprisoner and programmer of the mind and a common symptom is disengagement with reality and cogent reasoning. The forceful preaching (selling!) of God is all it takes for the susceptible to fall under religion's spell; inspiring many to do good but others to commit unbelievably wicked acts, as above. We need to look no further than the verbal incontinence of the average Jehovah's Witness, or the impact of Islamic State upon previously peaceful people turned deadly jihadists, to see how charismatic recruiters successfully use murderous modern interpretations of ancient holy books to stun and then intoxicate their prey; usually society's marginalized, ostracized or Mr and Ms Angry about something. Suddenly they are being invited to join a club for like-minded aggrieved people; a holy brotherhood of death-politics disguised as religious adherence. Hunted in places of worship, education, prisons, or via the web, the smitten are soon involuntarily compelled to spout contradictory religious nonsense or carry out heinous acts that they believe secures them a place in a fictitious heavenly paradise. Once afflicted by their impenetrable delusion, no Political rhetoric or cajoling by concerned family or friends, however impassioned, will get through to them. Some will go on to become 'sleeper death cells' or 'lone wolf' assassins; 'inspired' to kill others along with themselves, as seen in the recent past and will undoubtedly be seen in the months and years ahead, with sporadic bloody reminders at home and abroad. The paradise-hungry death-seeking suicide killer appears to be the ultimate foe, and they are indeed as lethal as they are unpredictable, but it's their unseen recruiters who are the original demons from religion's earthly hell.

This is a different kind of war involving bombs and bullets, planned and opportunistic bloody mayhem, psychological terror, and perhaps the most lethal weapon of all, the dark seduction of the vulnerable mind using the World Wide Web with the objective of crafting and triggering *the enemy within*. The radicalized extremist is a foot soldier representing an international menace and the common arch enemy of even the most marginally democratic country and countries distracted by petty feuds with others. An attack today in Paris or Amsterdam could very well happen next in London, Moscow, New York, Madrid, or on a plane, at a beach, or a sports stadium anywhere in the world. Therefore, it is in the interest of all advocates of freedom to work together in a robust seamless coalition, within and across borders, to foil and defeat, as best as possible, both planned and opportunistic terror attacks. An effective response here in the UK will require sophisticated leadership characterized by vision, agile judgement, active listening, and the courage to be 'politically incorrect' where necessary. Praying won't do it! There must also be a willingness to act 'outside of the box' or risk being damned to a corpse-friendly pine box of your own; this is an acknowledgement that getting the advantage over the extremist may mean abandoning compliance with established stringent rules and laws of combat, which the enemy gleefully defecate on. The right leader will know this and possess the fortitude to deal with the Political, legal, and psychological consequences of acting accordingly, or they must release their position to someone else with the necessary aptitude and resilience. Crucially, the solution must also involve an inclusive community-led counter-narrative involving all schools; and yes, I have an issue with 'faith schools', which, by their very nature, separate rather than unite communities. In fact, I believe that there should be a gradual but deliberate neutralization of the influence of religion in the everyday functioning of society as a whole. The crux or essence of this challenge has to do with winning the war of ideas and beliefs, and specifically, peaceful vs violent interpretations of religion. Dropping bombs on Islamic State in Iraq or Syria might generate vote-winning headlines for our politicians at home, but it also has the potential to validate and bolster the polluted mind-set of the home-grown terrorist-to-be; born and residing in London, Paris, Sydney or New York and who share the same bloody (!) warped beliefs. Islamic State's deadly ideology doesn't need a passport to reach, radicalize and recruit new foot soldiers; the convenience of the web will do. We know that sex education is too late when you are first learning about it as a frightened pregnant teen, and the same principal should apply to the counter-terror narrative; school is the correct intervention point, not an interrogation unit in a high security police station in the wake of the latest atrocity. The interventional learning should be less about God and more to do with how the learner can contribute to the welfare and betterment of his/her fellow human beings, especially where those human beings are or appear to be 'different' from them. The goal should be to enable and enhance empathy and respect for all aspects of human 'difference'; it's easier to kill those with whom we have no empathy. A capable leader will also seek to address the festering complex issue of segregated communities, where dangerous narratives are able to propagate unchallenged; but I fear that the leader has yet to be born who can persuade the mindset of residents of Chelsea in London to live, share, and exchange experiences, aspirations, and similarities with the residents of Bury Park in Luton. Yes, their similarities! This should all be part of a permanent multi-facetted effort that is strategically joined-up in its thinking and proactive on the ground in implementing practical measures to try and thwart a cunningly slithery doorstep enemy. As for the rest of us, we must banish any hope that the terror threat as horribly experienced on 9/11 and 7/7 will disappear by itself; it is destined to be a lingering menace for as long as the Trojan horse of corrupted religion remains an active conduit for fanatical hate. The vile architects of our next terror attack are always at work and a major challenge, whether their plans succeed or fail, will be to remain mindful that extremism is the actual enemy and not any particular faith or adherents of a particular faith. If we look back over recent history we will see that people of different faiths and none have been both the victims and perpetrators of catastrophic terror and evil; future deadly events must be seen in that wider context in order to fully understand them; but the context will never in any way justify the wrong that is terror; it has no justification, especially where totally innocent people become its victims. That said, we must be brave and honest enough to ask ourselves why we are being attacked. Is it just about an interpretation of a religion or something else? Without that question we cannot hope for lasting solutions.

To show that we all share the same revulsion about their grotesque crusade of holy carnage, it would be encouraging to see more of the thus far disappointingly few 'Not in Our Name' anti-Islamic State rallies. Where are they? Their scarcity in our streets could have many interpretations, including some that might be quite worrying. Silence often speaks louder than words.

The knowledge-stunted writers of the Bible *created* an intrinsically flawed concept of 'God' that could only fail when seen against scientific facts and all that is wrong and challenging in the world. Their God is invisible for logical reason; he doesn't exist and never did. The anointment of the Jewish people as God's 'chosen ones' was dictated by the race of the authors. If the writers had been Black African, then the Bible would have reflected that; Blacks would have been the chosen ones and Jesus would have been portrayed as an African all these years, but I wonder if the (White) Christian world would have worshipped him in the same way. Hmm, let me guess...

From our stalls as infants to our graves as adults, we are expected to live our lives to please God; a complicated and conveniently invisible deity whom we cannot witness with our own eyes, ears, or hands; only the imagination, fuelled by suspect stories from ancient scriptures. The geo-centric authors of the Bible had no appreciation of science, physics, biology, or the wider world beyond their own patch. They could not understand that the moon was a rock and that the sun was another star, much less anything else in the universe.

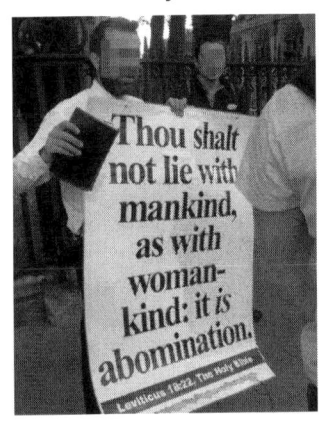

What they've given the world in the form of the Bible is an inhumane morally defective and very toxic product, with despicable supernatural messages that have caused the undeserved shaming of billions of perfectly good people; boys and girls, men and women, who must live our lives in submission to its assertions that we are born sinners; irredeemably bad, wrong, unworthy, and unclean. In fact, it is the Bible itself that are those things, and worse.

True to its grotesque form, the Bible says unruly children should be stoned to death, sanctions gang rape (Lot offered his virgin daughters to a mob, but in an equally abhorrent incestuous twist, they later become pregnant by him) and states that women are to learn submissively and not teach or have authority over men. Further, it instructs that a woman be stoned to death if she isn't a virgin come wedding night; there is no such gory fate for her non-virgin husband. Indeed, the Bible blatantly promotes men over women at every opportunity, just as it promotes heterosexuals over homosexuals. You will find yourself doomed if you commit nonsensical sins such as wear garments of mixed materials or eat shell fish. Even the inane act of gossiping will mean punishment of death. Strangely, amongst the mass slayings, incessant cruelty, and curtailment of basic freedoms that make life worthwhile as seen in Exodus, Leviticus, Deuteronomy, there are instructions that are kind, such as 'Love thy neighbour as yourself.' Of course, the vast majority of us will fall short because we naturally love our families and ourselves more than strangers, including neighbours. So an unreasonable bar has been set that makes us feel bad about ourselves because we cannot possibly live up to it. Hey God, have you met our neighbours?! Of course, 'Thou shalt not kill' is a very worthy commandment, although the *hidden* text is: 'but go right ahead if your victim is homosexual or a woman of independent mind. In such instances, he is perverted and must die and she is a witch and must die also. This is further evidence, if needed, that the Bible is incapable of offering a humane gesture without swiftly sabotaging its own status as the 'good book' with its wielding of the bloody sword.

With tainting notions of sin and threats of posthumous Hell fire, the Bible's deliberate installation of fear-based mind control seeks to reduce us to an emotionally damaged and mentally dependent sheep-like state. Its agents, smiling charlatan leech-like prosperity preachers, readily suck cash from their guilt-captive praying prey and use it to buy lavish houses and the latest luxury suit, car, boat or plane, aided by their portrayal of a contradictory God; who, on one hand, is loving and merciful, but on the other, genocidal and sadistically vengeful with it. He saved Noah and the animals on his Ark but murdered everyone else on Earth whilst displaying something of a human peculiarity usually seen in insecure spouses and perpetrators of domestic violence; he describes himself as "jealous". Now, if there was ever a clue that ordinary men wrote the Bible then the revelation of that particular human flaw is it.

My Bible was a much appreciated 40th birthday gift from Gloria Gaynor. Her hand written dedication reads: "To Vernal, I pray that with this Bible the Lord will lead you into the truth that sets you free. Love, Gloria."

Despite his strict conditional love, God's blind believers bestow much praise on him, and in seeking to win his divine favour, they exempt his monstrous tendencies, just in case an honest objection attracts his wrath. He is the *supposed* author of morality and yet lacks any when he threatens to cast us into an eternity of excruciating Hell fire. No loving father would do that, or even threaten it. If an ordinary man was to threaten such barbarism we would quite rightly avoid him, but because the hideous threat comes from God, his petrified followers avoid confronting the issue. So, caught up in the trance of the Holy Pied Piper, followers dance to his fear-inspiring tune without really listening to or questioning the lyrics of his song, and without a shred of tangible evidence to support his alleged existence, they continue to believe in him, come what may. However, some of us, the ones with the courage to open our eyes and see reality for what it is, can see that the eternally silent supernatural daddy in the sky has less substance than a passing cloud. Believers will ultimately find themselves in the sordid predicament of an eternity in torturous Hell for 'the sinner', or an eternity of tyrannical domination in Heaven for 'the good'. Well, I confidently predict *'Limbo' (if it exists)* to be forever plagued by keen over-stayers.

To live up to the expectations of the Bible would be akin to living (and dying!) in a Christian iteration of what Islamic State and Boko Haram offer in Syria, Iraq, and Northern Nigeria; a world of fear and grotesque cruelty, dished out with unflinching savagery to men, women and children alike by rabid extremists, who have convinced themselves that they are their God's personally appointed foot soldiers on a mission of justified holy carnage. Their sickening narcissistic delusion promises them a posthumous heavenly reward if the carnage they cause brings about their own earthly demise. Jesus may have died on the cross thousands of years ago, but at the behest of evil men like these, the crucifixion of children as young as thirteen still happens today. God, where were you then and where oh where are you now?

About thirty-eight thousand different denominations make up Christianity and the billions of people involved rarely consider other religious perspectives. However, the eight hundred million Hindus in the world, for example, have a completely different take on religion and God, and the same goes for adherents of Islam, the world's second largest religion. Adherents all believe that their personal religion is the right one. Location, culture, and religious association are intrinsically linked and we tend to follow that which is adhered to by our parents, who label us like the hot-iron branding of cattle: 'Muslim Child'; 'Christian Child'; 'Jewish Child', 'Hindu Child', etc. If we were not told or taught (indoctrinated) to believe in their God, then we would have no reason to even imagine him. This hideously divisive branding marks us as the property of our parents' God and sets us apart from other children for life: physically (by dress), mentally and socially. Thus, as well as sowing the seeds for inter-faith conflict when the children become adults, our branding also sows the seed for inner turmoil in the form of self-loathing, guilt and shame when the former child, now an adult, finds they cannot conform to what is expected of them. In seeking inner peace, authenticity, and bespoke identity, the adult may feel it necessary to ditch not only his uncomfortable religion, but also the related cultural 'trappings' which curtail or inhibit key components of his identity, such as his sexuality. He may cope by deciding to give the illusion of conformity, and, in so doing, hope that he will not lose himself and reap difficulties further down the line. Another coping strategy is to consciously embrace multiple identities, depending on the context of the given setting e.g. when with family, in the community, at worship, or with a lover or peers/friends, etc. Some may even marry the opposite sex to convince themselves and others that they can live up to expectations. This is how many lesbian and gay people cope in the journey of their lives, but many are increasingly 'coming out' and finding the courage and integrity to be who they really are. They know that the on-going denial of their true sexuality is a disastrous strategy and only unhappiness will come of it.

When I was in my bleakest internalized-homophobic moments as a youngster, and later as an adult, Bible-touting preachers compounded the situation by making me feel that my life wasn't worth living. I prayed hard and long about my sexuality and was still gay at the end of it. Of course I was! I am clear; God doesn't discriminate, people do! Surely if we can move on regarding the Bible's nonsense about shell fish and the wearing of mixed garments, then why can't we move on regarding homosexuality? I am eternally grateful to Archbishop Carl Bean in LA for helping me to appreciate that I was simply born this way. If only all men of the cloth were as kind as he is. The idea that God is more concerned with my sexual activity than he is about earthquakes, war, or cancer makes no sense at all. Sexual intimacy involving consenting adults is nobody else's business and only a voyeuristic God would concern himself with them. The Bible's other nonsense needs attention too, including that to do with Eve being created from Adam's rib and the two of them then causing sin to come into the world by the daft act of eating an apple. Rules and laws are useful, but sins are emotionally damaging garbage designed to taint, intimidate and control the minds of the gullible and those loathed by the authors of those sins. As for Noah's ark, please, already! Desmond Tutu is another inspiration. He is a rare example of a faith leader with the courage and readiness to think with his heart, and acknowledge that the love for his fellow man is his over-arching priority. He does not make wounding judgments based upon ancient scriptures about involuntary issues such as one's sexuality, for example. The Bible, its portrayal of God, and outcomes for the world, would have been very different if it had been penned by the likes of Desmond Tutu or Carl Bean.

As well as causing internal strife, Holy works have been used as justification for the oppression of countless people over the centuries. Black Africans, for example, suffered five centuries of abuse as slaves. Women and gay men continue to suffer grotesque religious-based inequalities and deadly barbarism today.

In the alleged presence of a loving, all-knowing, all-powerful, perfect God, we live in a world plagued by natural disasters, horrible illnesses, insane wars, barbaric crime – including genital mutilation and 'honour killings' – unrelenting greed, unnecessary starvation and poverty, abuse of the vulnerable and countless other injustices wherever we look. Ready expressions of love, God's most revered (and much needed!) characteristic, are plainly absent, as are his solutions to the above problems. What is God's plan for the children who will die of disease, war and starvation by this time tomorrow?

The Catholic Church brings religion into further disrepute with its thoroughly reprehensible conduct regarding sexual abuse perpetrated by hundreds of its own paedophile priests, who used innocent children as holy sex club fodder and behind the pulpit birth control substitutes. Going into self-protection lock-down, instead of enabling their prosecution, the church colluded, schemed, and strategized to ensure their escape from justice. Concurrent to this, the church affirmed its inhumane and incompetent decision-making by adopting a genocidal stance regarding HIV prevention. It saw AIDS as a catastrophe, but saw condom use as even worse and banned their use. This resulted in the loss of many millions of lives, especially in Africa. Then, cementing its facilitation of genocidal outcomes, the church remained silent during the bloody Rwandan slaughter, which filled our TV screens every night two decades ago. It was hard to believe that this was Africa's most prominent Catholic country, but it was. Its own personnel – depraved bishops, priests and nuns – would later find themselves in the dock charged with crimes against humanity. The world is looking to Jorge Bergoglio of Argentina, now Pope Francis, to make changes on many fronts, including the treatment of gay people, divorcees, victims of abuse, and, of course, disease prevention. He is said to be more pragmatic than his predecessors on matters of sexual morality, but action speaks louder than words. He should start with a grovelling apology for his church's criminal behaviour and misjudgements that caused immeasurable suffering and the ruin of too many lives over the years. The Catholic Church's support and dissemination of so much evil could only find acceptance and protection behind the detestable cloak of religion, supported in complicit complacency by their 'good members', who colluded with the evil by failing to leave the church in their droves. Indeed, notables such as Tony Blair, the former British Prime Minster, famously joined the church. Such outrageous wrongs cannot be for the church or Pope to forgive; it has forfeited the right to do so. The victims and their loved ones are the only voices who can remain Catholic and utter the word 'forgive' without shame. But then again, if it had any concept of what shame is, then the church would have long ago voluntarily and permanently closed its doors.

Just a scant look at events around the world and we can see how religion undermines the potential of love between diverse members of human kind, whom, if it were not for religion, would embrace rather than kill each other: from Northern Ireland and Bosnia, to Iraq, Rwanda, and Kenya. And there is nothing godly or rational either about murdering people because they 'imagined' God as a cartoon or 'portrayed' him in fiction novels. All decent people know this, however, in a disgraceful demonstration of collective gutless cowardice, instead of standing up for the much lauded principle of a 'free press' and print such images, the world's media shamelessly prostrate themselves at the mere thought of possible repercussions for carrying out their profession with integrity, thus enabling religious madness to thwart journalism's most heroic characteristic: courage. Further, the indiscriminate bombing from war planes of thousands of innocent people in Iraq is no less awful than flying planes into office buildings in America. These acts can only find justification in the name of sick religion – or in revenge for politicians' bruised egos; the same politicians who indirectly engineered the removal of the monsters we knew in the form of Gaddafi and Hussein, and by so doing, enabled their blood-gushing successors: the rampaging nightmare of Islamic State (I.S.). Either way, innocent people of faith, or none, die in their many many thousands. Emphatic religious belief can lead seemingly good people to do the most terrible things, and the above are just a couple of examples from the thousands available. As stated in my prologue, we don't need religion as a context for love. The principal purpose of our existence on Earth, our gift, is to love one another, without conditions or prerequisites. It really is that simple, but instead, we take destructive comfort in dividing ourselves from each other based on race, nationality, colour, sexuality, age, gender, disability, wealth, education, land, location, politics, and the biggest divider of them all, religion. Oppressed and abused women can also trace their plight to religion and the warped superiority complex derived from it by their abusers. In its favour, religion can do some good, for example, when it influences individuals to turn from crime, or brings people together for charitable purposes, or even just to lay down some roof shaking gospel music. So whilst I have pointed out religion's flaws, I am willing to acknowledge the love and compassion that it inspires in many people. However, people with sadistic intentions can also insert their values into religion and interpret (manipulate) Holy Scriptures to suit their own sordid ends. The result is the catastrophic blood-letting that religion has caused throughout the centuries, and looking at today's news, the madness will undoubtedly continue into the future.

Religious confusion is emphatically neutralized by naturalism and science, not the other way around. Theism – Christianity, Islam, Judaism, and Hinduism, etc. – lacks cogency, consistency, and common sense. It relies on the existence of and belief in an external supernatural God, Devil, Heaven, Hell, angels and demons etc. Naturalism, on the other hand, as implied by the name, is an acceptance of naturally occurring events e.g. homosexuality, heterosexuality, earthquakes, meteors, life, ageing, and death etc. Our beloved Judge Judy famously says, "If it doesn't make sense then it isn't true!" That's the case with theism; who's God(s) was never humanoid, caused tsunamis and earthquakes, punished sinners, or lived above the clouds sporting a white beard, of course not! He could not and did not prevent the Holocaust or AIDS, and was never capable of miracles, acted as an intervening unseen force, or created you, me, this world or anything in or external to it. His silence in the face of the frequent world-wide tragedies that affect our lives is explained by naturalism; he isn't there. Men and women are capable of good and evil intent as individuals or groups, but there are no good or evil 'forces', even if it may seem that way. So, what's the evidence of the last two thousand years? God and the Devil don't exist. If God does exist then he either does not care to intervene or possesses no such powers, so why call him God? And there is no evidence of a Heaven or a Hell, other than the physical and emotional experience of both on this very Earth. And how did the universe or our planet come into being? Science is constantly working on it, but it seems nonsense to attribute it to a supernatural God that there is no evidence of over the much more likelihood of naturally occurring phenomenon; especially as humans can only (naturally!) occupy a portion of our own planet and none of the rest of the universe. It is only human and religious arrogance that could lead us to believe that everything was 'created' just for us to exist in the equivalent of a speck of dust of what's out there. What is the demonstrable difference between a universe and planet created by a God over the same that has naturally occurred? Without the manifested conclusive determining evidence of God himself to show otherwise, we must go with the evidence of what we currently have: no God! We evolved as we did because events affecting our planet were conducive to that outcome, nothing more. We obviously had a beginning of some sort, and, scarily, will probably have an end point, too. Remember the mighty dinosaurs? Well, their God sent them to dinosaur hell, or maybe the indifferent planet Earth simply stopped being conducive to their existence here. Now, which is more plausible to your rational mind? I do accept that the universe and earthly life cannot have come from nothing (basic: nothing produces nothing!), and appear too fantastically complex and meticulously 'designed' to be the outcome of a freak 'big bang'; but complexity doesn't always allude to intelligence, and even if it did, it doesn't mean a God is behind it. It makes perfect sense to me to assume that there has always been a 'something'. If we assume a God created everything, then who created God, God Mama? Some would argue that if we were to throw a grenade into a paint shop the result would produce messy colourful destruction, not a pristine, well-framed Picasso; that's unless our work of art, the universe, is the result of billions of evolving and conducive years and not an overnight big bang explosion. Wait!!! Did I say pristine? Our world and universe are riddled with hazards to human health and wellbeing, from cancers to earthquakes. There is nothing meticulous or perfect about them because they 'naturally' occur and kill. If we give God credit for creating the lovely things, we must also credit him with the horrors that threaten us and bring about our demise. Further to my earlier point, the universe may continue to evolve for billions of years, with or without planet Earth and human life. For now, at least, we have to accept that the universe and time just 'are', and that the how or why will remain unobtainable to inconsequential spots of cosmic dust like you and me. We are here due to yet unknown natural universal causes. We weren't always here in the past, and we won't always be here in the future. We are here, for now.

Having evolved as the species we've become from a process of natural selection and random mutation over many millions of years following the big bang, we have to acknowledge that we're now living in a truly amazing, if imperfect, reality: bespoke men and women of all colours, sexualities, and smiles; countless varieties of wonderful animals; the magnificent seas and mountains; thrilling plants and trees; the glistening sun, moon, stars and possibly billions of planets and galaxies; and everything seemingly placed exactly where it needs to be to promote and sustain life on Earth; at least that's how selfish humans wish to perceive it; it's all about us, matey! In truth, 99.9 percent of the earth's known species or life forms have become extinct, so our continued existence is really a galactic lottery win when seen through the lens of the cosmic millisecond that is human life and the estimated lifespan of planet Earth. Even if our jackpot were to last for millions of years after the publication of this very book, it can't and won't last forever. The universe and what lies beyond it is the vehicle on an unknown evolving journey to a somewhere or a nowhere, and we are mere dust on its tyres. Perhaps there is no destiny, just an endless evolvement. If there is a destiny then it is currently beyond our limited intelligence, but you and I will probably be long gone before these things are known and fully understood. Science can't answer all of our questions today, but this doesn't mean they won't be answered tomorrow, or in a thousand years from now. Significant new discoveries are being made every other decade or so, such as the recently discovered Gravitational Waves caused by the merger of two black holes over a billion years ago; yes, before God didn't write the Bible, ha ha! This event was alluded to by Albert Einstein a hundred years ago. I am confident that when the answers to our outstanding questions do come, they will come via science, not a God or ancient scriptures. Science is the God of knowledge and every new discovery is a nail in the coffin of religious nonsense and the people who propagate it. Thanks to science, modern man knows that the sacrifice of babies will not influence whether we have rainfall and a whole lot more besides. The idea that God created everything just to ensure that you and I live our lives as Christians is man-conceived nonsense. Our journey of discovery of scientific facts is incremental. President Lincoln didn't live to even conceive of man landing on the moon and had he no concept of the smartphone either. President Obama did see those things. So progress comes with time and the pursuit of knowledge. Future generations will probably look back through history and acknowledge that my generation knew so much but still so little. When I find myself puzzled by the things I don't yet know, I simply file them away in my 'I Don't Know' folder. It is mightily empowering to admit that I don't know something, and I wish more of us would do that instead of deceiving ourselves with works of supernatural fiction.

The belief in an afterlife is a popular fantasy, but this life is it, baby! At a date and time that most of us are not privileged or unfortunate to know in advance, death will become us, and our beliefs or none will cease with our last heartbeat. Only a fool will waste this life hoping for the next. The laws of physics and biology tell me that Jesus, if he ever existed at all, died like all living beings ultimately do, and wasn't up and walking around three days later. Fact: corpses don't walk unless they are on the set of The Walking Dead television series. However, if I choose to believe otherwise, and knowingly go against common truth (reality!), then I would be engaging in a crazy dance of self-deception. I occasionally see people who strongly resemble friends who are long dead, and I can believe all I like that it is them, but my belief won't change the reality; it isn't them! Despite what the Bible says, we know that the deceased do not rise up to catch the latest sale at Harrods, they really don't! Jesus didn't rise from the dead either, and that's okay. His time on Earth, like yours and mine, was limited to a beginning, middle and end. The world will continue to spin after we're gone, as it did before we arrived, and that's okay, too.

Regarding Heaven, that much hyped glorious address for the reconstituted undead of privilege. Well, if it exists, we have to remember that its architect is the same God who believes children and woman should be stoned to death and advocates the keeping of slaves, so his wondrous paradise should generate suspicion among all wannabe dwellers. Jesus 'believers' seek to convince the rest of us that Heaven is indeed real, but they can't possibly know. That said, I would concede that before birth introduced each of us to our magnificent planet of extraordinary contrasts called Earth, pre-life non-believers could very well have argued that such a place was just a bizarre fantasy for over-imaginative dreamers. 'Hahaha', they may have laughed; 'You mean a world of land and sea, and people with physical bodies of different colours and genders who have lots of something called sex and dance to composed nonsense called music. Give me a break, mate! You're going tell me that they eat, shit, reproduce and fly planes next. Ha ha!!' In truth, if we were not here to experience it in person, then we would be most challenged to imagine and believe it. Hey, what if there's an afterlife but no God, or a God but no afterlife? Hmm... Well, whatever, if anything, that exists pre-life or post-death, I think it's crass insanity to fail to live (and love!) our earthly lives by maximizing the gift of each precious moment because we hope to one day reside in a gold-paved place of eternal pleasure after death, while people we once knew and loved (in life) burn in eternal hell because the Bible's concept of God judged them fitting for such a dreadful fate. Could we really enjoy heaven under such mental agony? But heaven and hell aside, the very certainty of our inevitable death, should, by itself, be sufficient incentive to ensure that every morsel of our physical life time is used consciously and constructively; it would be an insult to the gift of life to do otherwise. I'm reminded at this point of the millions of children who never live to see their teenage years because of war, starvation, disease, abuse, and other catastrophes. If it was not for our lucky chance of birth, then our fate could easily have been the same as theirs. They should be reminders to us all of just how fortunate we are to have the gift of life in the first place, and cause us to dismiss the almost selfish fantasy of a heaven as a preoccupation for those who are perhaps least deserving of such a grand posthumous abode. There is no evidence or guarantee of a heaven, or even of a tomorrow. What we do have is the evidence, guarantee, and opportunity afforded by today and this very moment, and if we are wise, we will use it to love, learn, work, and give to others who are less fortunate than ourselves; in other words, put goodness out into the universe. Every new day should be greeted and utilized as if it could be our last on Earth, and accept that we will know about the reality or not of a heaven in due course; but right now let's live in the present; the gift of right now. It is in the present that all things are possible. What is also certain is that upon death our body decays and I believe that our inner spirit becomes reacquainted with the universe, as it was before physical life (birth) became our reality. The creepy idea that billions of dead people from over the centuries suddenly become the undead and rise from their graves at the behest of a returning Jesus Christ is the stuff of oh so tired zombie movies. Anyway, do we really want to rise again, as we were, with our strange noses, odd ears, elephant thighs, disappointing adult baby-sized penises, no-pack instead of a six-pack, breasts lower than our knees, and bare scalp where there should be thick hair? Er, Jesus, can we talk?

The difference between theism and science is that for events that we weren't personally present to witness, science seeks evidence to substantiate or dismiss the related theories and alleged facts. It is because of science that we have been able to dismiss much of what religion promotes as truth. As intelligent beings, we are born with a natural intrinsic curiosity, and therefore, a need to question the world around us. This promotes growth and maturity, and enables the development of a personal perspective of the world, based upon a healthy on-going learning experience. Religion, however, has been stunted in growth for many centuries, and demands that we comply with it as it is and never question, probe, or analyze its credibility. This is an unnatural demand which goes against our instinct to learn through questioning; so much so that it yields chaos and turmoil within us as individuals, and in the world as a whole. I would argue that it is religion that is unnatural, not our adverse reaction to it. We would not ask a class of keen students to never ask logical questions or utilize the tool of science to better understand the world in which they live, and yet that's exactly what we do when it comes to the too long considered untouchable subject of religion and its arch works, the Bible and Koran. This ghastly act of self-deception leads to the wilful imprisonment of the naturally inquisitive mind through indoctrination and insane conformity, and promotes the heinous self-delusion that can lead a man or woman to strap a bomb to their body and detonate it, killing themselves and the innocent people around them; justified in doing so by their interpretation of and adherence to a religion that they never sought to question, although I do accept that a sense of injustice (social and economic), may be a co factor. These extremists are very different from yesterday's terror groups, such as the politically-driven IRA. To the religious extremist, one's mere non-compliance with the beliefs that they have never questioned is enough to justify the curtailment of our lives. Going against her infamous reticence, Mrs Thatcher's successors were ultimately able to negotiate peace with the IRA, but no such outcome is likely with the fanatical religious extremist, who feels justified, due to his unwavering indoctrination, to take innocent lives and joyously lose his own in the process; buoyed on by an emphatic belief that his martyrdom will be rewarded with a place in Heaven or Paradise. The UK's 7/7 bombers, and more recently, the young British-born Muslims who leave the UK to fight with the I.S in Iraq and Syria, or marry their members, is irrefutable evidence that extremist indoctrination is able to propagate here in the UK. These tragic young people have forgotten the thousands-strong anti-Iraq war protests that took place in the UK, which should be sufficient evidence that the UK is not an anti-Islamic enemy; we were all victims of our then political leadership. Instead of building upon that legacy of protesting for truth and peace, I.S-bound young Muslims have given in to the poisonous indoctrinated promise that earthly life in a caliphate, and later, in afterlife's Paradise, is unequivocally better than life here in the UK with family and friends. In order to stem the doomed exodus, families and loved ones must become more vocal. Where are the demonstrations against the morbid seductive pull of I.S. and their recruiters? Silence on these matters will be perceived by some as tacit approval for what I.S. is doing. Their evil spell can only be broken by vigilant, proactive, and vocal parents and wider community, at worship and educational level, but also in the home. Our government should be proactive and adopt a national and international strategic response to identify the ATM (Arms, Training and Money) trail, which, if followed, should lead to the head of the terror snake. The government should also support local communities in their efforts at combatting the indoctrination of children and young people. To be clear, I am not advocating the singling out of Islam; this will feed the idea that that particular faith is 'the problem' and needs special attention; no, it's extremism that needs our shared attention; therefore leaders of Islam and all other faiths and none should play an active role in identifying and implementing solutions – together! All faiths rely on indoctrination to some extent, even if this is never admitted, but not all of them, or all members of any specific religion, encourage or celebrate martyrdom. Islam, like Christianity, is not homogenous in how it is followed or practiced; adherents are diverse individuals, not one big mass.

It is clear to me that the indoctrinated (learned) hatred of homosexuality is cut from the same vile cloth as the teachings that promote extremist terror, and must be countered with equal determination. The preaching of hate is always wrong, whether it is faith, colour, gender, or sexuality based. The self-loathing caused by religious hate is responsible for countless suicides and destructive lifestyles.

I say all that I have knowing that I probably come across as a rabid atheist, but I'm no Sam Harris, Christopher Hitchens, or Richard Dawkins. Together with Laurence Krauss, these highly educated gentlemen, branded 'New Atheists', are right to question the fallacy of religious inconsistency and the madness of its extremism, as I do, however, their form of uncompromising atheism won't heal the world either. The men come across to some like verbal jihadists; mercilessly cutting down anything or anyone associated with religion and disregarding the fact that it is an emotional crutch for billions of people. In my experience, indoctrinated believers should be gently encouraged, where possible, to see the contradictions in religion for themselves, as I ultimately did. That said, I think atheists and religious folk alike should enjoy equal freedom to speak as they see fit, but sensitively, responsibly and without promoting conflict and hate. Our famous atheists have never, to my knowledge, used the spoken word to promote hate or violence against believers or anyone else, unlike the copious number of vile preachers of religious hate, such as American pastors James David Manning and Steven 'Lucifer' Anderson. From his pulpit, Anderson, a gun touting father of nine, was filmed saying that "the cure for AIDS is the execution of all homos by Christmas, in line with God's written word". The idiotic and painfully stupid Manning, on the other hand, has called for the stoning of "sodomite" gays and even asserted that Starbucks sells coffee containing gay men's semen "to improve the taste". No atheist could come close to being as totally repugnant as these two examples of holy excrement, and I sincerely hope that they don't follow fellow pastors such as Eddie Long and Ted Haggard and later 'come out' as gay themselves after spending their lives condemning other gays from the pulpit. The gay community deserves better company than people who are now infamous hypocrites. But being atheist, agnostic, or a humanist doesn't mean that you've dealt with your own racism, sexism, or homophobia, and I won't mention Mr. Harris' perceived bias in the Israeli/Palestinian conflict, either. Whoops, I just did! In other words, people in glass houses should keep their stones to themselves. Er, hang on just a moment while I put my own stones away.

Earlier in my book you would have read about my evangelical mother, 'Sister Scott', who was a proud megaphone-touting, Christian woman. On any inspired day you'd find her at Jubilee Clock on Harlesden High Street, or Brent Cross Shopping Centre, deafening passing "sinners," by calling them to Christ. Like most of her brethren in black (and white) churches here and abroad, my mother was taught and remained committed to a completely anti-gay interpretation of the Bible. So, my homosexuality, even though she would later acknowledge that I was born this way, was a massive disappointment to her. Indeed, on the day I came out to her, she wept and wailed as if I had suddenly died before her eyes. I can hear her now: "Man must not lay with man. The Bible says it's a sin, an abomination!" I wrote about the Sunday afternoon she came home from church in tears, having denied, out of shame, that I was her (very public gay) son. She prayed and begged God to forgive her. Conjuring up a visual akin to the Bible 'God's voice in the head' story of Abraham and Isaac, shame-filled Christian parents appear ready to sacrifice their children for no other reason than that child's homosexuality. Their child hasn't committed mass murder, robbed a bank, or contaminated baby food; she/he, like millions of others, is simply gay. These otherwise very capable parents have been misled by the pulpit and/or their own personal prejudices to the point that they cannot see the corrupt error of their ways and immense damage they will do to their child. Their child was born in their image, and by rejecting him/her, they are trying to erase the shame that they feel about themselves, but only education, acceptance and love can deliver that outcome. If my mother was still here today, given her beliefs, she might pray and ask God why her two heterosexual-born sons were taken, while her only gay son lives on, and why AIDS was visited upon the heterosexuals in her family while the homosexual was unaffected. But it is my belief that my dear mother, like so many other Christians, misunderstood or didn't fully consider the context of the scripture that she was referring to. She didn't appreciate that at the time it was written the goal of society was to grow itself as a nation; so procreation was the objective of the passage rather than an objection to homosexuality per se. At least that's my interpretation of it. Either way, Jesus Christ said nothing about homosexuality in his lifetime, which is powerful evidence that his God/father isn't preoccupied by sexuality; there are many hundreds of scriptures in the Bible, but less than eight make reference to homosexuality, although, as mentioned before, the ones that do aren't kind to us.

The above would be big uncomfortable questions for someone like my mother, and she may have to conclude that one's sexuality doesn't afford preference in God's eyes, and more to the point, AIDS and God have nothing to do with each other, end of! Even more challenging than this, she would have to accept that her long-held interpretation of the Bible was wrong, and that whilst churches regularly preach against gay people, Jesus Christ, the earthly manifestation of God, never uttered a single anti-homosexual word, not once.

London-based Reverend Paul Bailey, a black, happily married, heterosexual father of two, was mercilessly vilified by readers of the black press when he dared to suggest the Bible had been misinterpreted in respect of gay people. His remarks were honest and brave, and they reaffirmed a belief held by gay Christians that they too are loved by God, despite the Bible and ignorance and hate from the pulpit. I decided to look at Bible scripture where it makes reference to homosexuality, to see whether I could somehow correlate it to my actual experience as a gay Christian and retain my Christianity with integrity. I didn't find much to be happy about; hence my departure from the faith. The following is what I did find.

Genesis 19 gives the account of Lot in Sodom and Gomorrah, from which the derogatory term 'sodomite' is derived. The context of the passage is that God has sent two angels, who appear as men, to execute judgment on Sodom and Gomorrah. They are invited to reside with Lot, and are then subsequently subject to threats of 'sex' by an all-male mob with a dislike for foreigners. The manner of the threat is not about homosexual love or homosexuality per se; sex was threatened as weapon of humiliation, denigration, domination and coercive power, as we sometimes see in today's prisons. Lot was threatened with "worse" if he did not hand the men (the angels) over. God did not condemn these cities for homosexuality, contrary to common belief; these cities where condemned for their wickedness prior to the attempted attack on Lot's visitors.

The full account in Genesis 19 reads:

"Before they had gone to bed, all the men from every part of the city of Sodom—both young and old—surrounded the house. They called to Lot, "Where are the men who came to you tonight? Bring them out to us so that we can have sex with them." Lot went outside to meet them and shut the door behind him and said, "No, my friends. Don't do this wicked thing. Look, I have two daughters who have never slept with a man. Let me bring them out to you, and you can do what you like with them. But don't do anything to these men, for they have come under the protection of my roof." "Get out of our way," they replied. "This fellow came here as a foreigner, and now he wants to play the judge! We'll treat you worse than them."

What got my attention was Lot's plea that the mob does as they wish with his two virgin daughters. I know of no decent father, myself included, who would make such a repugnant offer, and yet very few Christians ever refer to this element of the story; preferring instead to stick to their unhealthy obsession with and prejudice against (perceived) homosexuality. Frankly, it is passages like the one cited that fuel scepticism and Atheism. But it is what it is.

The mob of Sodom and Gomorrah were a xenophobic bunch of thugs seeking to dominate and abuse foreign visitors to their city. They were not attracted to these men as homosexual lovers; they wanted to hurt and abuse them by committing gross acts of (sexual) violence. The same scripture has been misused for centuries by homophobic 'Christians' and prejudicial others to justify the oppression of loving, law-abiding gay people. Again, this scripture describes a vile scene that has nothing to do with consensual, loving homosexual relationships.

The Old Testament passages found in Leviticus 18.22 and Leviticus 20.13 have long been cited as unequivocal condemnations of homosexual behaviour. Leviticus 18 condemns a man having sex with another man as if he were a woman. Leviticus 20.13 expands on this by saying "If a man has sexual relations with a man as one does with a woman, both of them have done what is detestable. They are to be put to death; their blood will be on their own heads."

The entire premise is of course flawed, because male couples do not act as 'women' when they have sexual relations, even if penetration is involved (and it often isn't!); they are still men/male. In other words, it isn't possible to have sex as a woman if you are male. And if the 'unspoken' issue here is anal sex, then this is not at all exclusive to gay men. The truth is some men, both gay and heterosexual, engage in anal sex, and it is therefore irrational and unfair to single out gay men regarding this activity – not that it's anybody else's business!

Perhaps the authors of Leviticus perceived penetrative intercourse between men as a feminizing assault against masculinity and manhood, and that to do so is somehow letting the macho side down. It is clear that the authors were not themselves homosexual, because if they were, they wouldn't think of male on male intimacy in such a base and poorly informed way. What's blatantly missing, is any notion of an emotional context; that same-sex couples can and do form committed loving relationships, and what they do behind closed doors is in line with that quite beautiful reality. Yes, there, I said it!

Paul, in Romans and again in Timothy, like the editors of Leviticus, considered homosexuals to be a sinful abomination, and a wilful deviation from God's created order. He says: The men, instead of having normal sexual relationships with women, burned with lust for each other. Men did shameful things with other men and, as a result, suffered within themselves the penalty they so richly deserved". He goes on to say, "They are fully aware of God's death penalty for those who do these things (including gossip), and yet they go ahead and do them anyway". They would, because it's their nature.

Claims of "lust" aside, Paul assumed, wrongly, that sexuality was a matter of will or choice, but we now know that it is not; it is a natural involuntary occurrence (not an accident!) of birth. If he had been aware of this then I'd like to believe he would have acknowledged it. He also doesn't appear to have a concept of the possibility of same-gender love. If Paul were here today, then I hope he'd educate himself with the facts in order to gain a better understanding of the psychology and actual experience of same gender loving men and women. I would also hope that he would do the same in respect of women in general. His apparent ignorance has been the cause of centuries of discrimination and abuse. Modern day followers seized upon Paul's words during the modern day AIDS crisis, claiming it to be God's punishment for the 'sin' of homosexuality. But, of course, the millions of non-gay people affected were just a hard-to-hide inconvenient truth in the midst of a big lie. Intelligent people knew that AIDS was caused by a virus called HIV and that a non-existent God had nothing to do with it.

Blacks of African and Caribbean descent heroically freed themselves from centuries of dehumanizing slavery only to then shackle themselves to the mental prison of their former owners' dire religion. Dressed to the nines in hypocrisy, they spout religion-based anti-gay hate as if it flowed from a tap, whilst conveniently forgetting that their amazing-sounding choir is largely made up of closet gays who bring in the punters and the cash. And we won't talk about the heavenly chemistry between the choir director and the head usher. I tell you, those two men... Shhhh, now! To their own duplicitous detriment, traditional Christians, particularly rural fundamentalist whites and roaring city Baptist blacks, are consistent in their condemnation of gay men (much more so than lesbians), but are intensely inconsistent (dishonest!) in how they apply the Bible to their own lives. For example, many re-marry after divorce, which is viewed as adultery in the Bible and punishable by death, but they'll skip past that part and jump in the aisles instead to their pastor's venomous condemnation of gays in the same tone once used by slave owners to condemn blacks. It is cowardly convenient for him to adhere to the 'word of God' where it supports his prejudices, hatred, and bigotry rather than the parts which might expose his own sins and hypocrisy. But isn't there a line in the Bible which says, 'Let he who is without sin cast the first stone'? Oh yes, that's something else for the pastor to ignore, even if the protruding lump in the front of his pants is proof that he cannot yet ignore cute Mrs Betty Jones, who religiously (!) gets his attention every Sunday. Perhaps someone should remind Pastor Smith, who is now on his second wife, that adultery is forbidden by the Ten Commandments while homosexuality is not. Which reminds me; we can all agree with the 6th Commandment – thou shall not murder, but I have a personal issue with the 10th, which states that we shouldn't covet our neighbour's ass. God, can we please talk about this? Oh, you mean donkey? Phew! OK, back to our pastor. Someone should whisper in his ear that his gay brother, who's currently dying in hospital of brain cancer, still loves him and hopes for a visit before it's too late to say a final goodbye and 'I love you, brother', in person. Perhaps his dying brother, coincidentally a former brain surgeon, will remind the pastor that love should come out of his mouth easier than condemnation. Yes pastor, instead of your weekly rant about Sodom and Gomorrah, how about love and compassion for your brother and the people who share the same sexuality as him? Ultimately, if you cannot allow love to overcome your sickening hatred of gays, then stop singing songs written by them in your church and dressing in elaborate suits designed and created by them. You'll soon be standing there half naked with nothing to sing or say apart from your hate. Then again, you'll still have your shrimp and lobster sandwich to look forward to. Whoops! Lesson for all the hypocritical pastors out there: you can't insult and inspire the same people at the same time.

If God exists then he evidently has no objection to gay people, because aided by our parents he creates millions of new gay people each year; in every culture and all parts of the world. The exclusion of LGBTQ people from established or traditional places of worship is un-Christ-like; he is supposed to have showed love and compassion towards all kinds of people, but today's church has mostly forgotten this, and instead of behaving like their idol, they ridicule and condemn everything and everybody but themselves. They preach that everyone is made in God's image, but somehow this does not extend to LGBT people. Further, they preach that they love the sinner but not the sin. Well, I hope they will find it in their hearts to forgive me for telling them where they can shove their BS. Our nature is not a sin; it's a fact and needs no explanation or apology. Despite their plight and fight for acceptance, LGBTQ Christians won't give up on Jesus, because they believe he hasn't given up on them. They'll continue to seek to be included, but will survive on the outside, if they must. Come to think of it, some of those buildings and ornaments of gold should be sold to feed the hungry and house the homeless. Now that's what Jesus would do, but he would never be allowed in some of today's out of touch, self-serving congregations; he's too 'different', too queer. He's much more acceptable to them as part of Christian mythology; nailed to the cross and bound within the pages of the New Testament. Jesus in person would be just another of God's excluded children.

I am heartened that the shackles of rigid religious authority are being broken with each passing day by scientific progress and a shared sense about what's morally right in a modern world. The recent willingness to 'modernize' itself is evidence of the church's uncertain footing in a modern world and an acknowledgement too that the wellbeing and happiness of society no longer need them or their works. Gay people (and others) have been fighting back against their brand of 'right', 'wrong', 'good', and 'bad' for some decades now, and that fight will continue; both inside and outside of religious circles, and in every culture and country. The faithful, if they possess an ounce of integrity, should be increasingly willing to admit that some of what the Bible says falls below their own moral standards, but I won't hold my breath. I am willing to admit that in all that I have said, I am not saying that all people of faith are corrupt or unfortunate beings, or that without religion we would have no wrongs in the world.

Countries where religion is most prominent are also where intolerance of homosexuality is greatest, so it isn't a mystery why gay people feel alienated from it. The Bible, for example, has been used for centuries as a weapon by the bigoted and ignorant, dressed up as men of the cloth and supposed messengers of God. These are the same people who proclaimed the arrival of AIDS as God's punishment for homosexuality, and who abandoned the dying and bereft when their need for love and compassion was at its greatest. It is due to these preachers of intolerance and hate that the blood of too many gay people soils the Bible's pages, and that people flee in their millions to embrace atheism.

In America, so-called 'Christians' stoke fear with talk of 'the homosexual agenda.' They support the murderers of gays with signs depicting messages such as *Fags Belong in Hell* and *God Hates Queers*. All over the world, there are killings of gay people who are hanged, burnt, stabbed, and bludgeoned to death, often in the name of religion. In my parents' homeland of Jamaica, there have been shootings, stoning and knife attacks. Hundreds of gay men are executed in the Muslim world; some beheaded, whilst others have had their heads crushed by concrete blocks, or been thrown to their deaths from roof tops.

The Cameroon is one of the worst places to live if you are homosexual. As I write this chapter, there are reports of a native gay activist, whose neck, hands, and feet were broken and a hot iron used to disfigure his face. Torture-death victim, Eric Ohena Lembembe, his homosexuality his only crime, was killed in his own home. His grotesque murder was quickly followed by that of sixteen-year old Dwayne Jones, who was hacked, stabbed and shot to death by a frenzied anti-gay/trans mob in Jamaica. When I posted a video condemning his murder, one menacing response was: "It died of natural causes". Another said: "All batty bwoy fi dead". Someone else wrote: "Vernal Scott, you are an inspiration to lots of little shits." My response to him was simple: "I'm pleased to have inspired you." To date, nearly two hundred thousand people have viewed the said video on my You Tube channel. Dwayne's slaughter was followed by many others, including that of Dexter 'face of JA Pride' Pottinger in August 2017. His courageous visibility attracted his killer, whom, I am sure, will go unpunished.

I could fill this book with the names of similar victims of homophobic hate from most parts of the world: Russia, Uganda, Nigeria, Zimbabwe etc. The Jamaican Prime Minister and the other so-called 'leaders' of countries where these hate-induced atrocities continue unabated, undoubtedly have the blood of innocent people on their hands. Inaction is not leadership; it is incompetence and collusion with murder. Effective leadership involves taking protective action for all citizens, not just those born heterosexual. So, I plead to the Jamaican Prime Minister, and her counterparts elsewhere; please lead for everybody, or relinquish your position to someone who can. The world is in no doubt that your leadership is directly enabling the wanton killing of your gay countrymen. Meaningful change starts with the repeal of ancient anti-sodomy laws, which serve as the underpinning foundation of anti-gay hate. Stop the killing now, show leadership, and show hate the gate once and for all!

While terrorism and world economics continue to dominate mainstream press real estate, together with the birth of the latest royal baby, the aforementioned victims of anti-gay hate go unmentioned; which supports the perception that they led undeserving or disposable lives. It will therefore be up to all decent people everywhere to make sure their deaths were not in vain, by speaking out against all forms of hate. These and similar barbaric slayings are often the result of ignorance or the manipulation of cooked up religious dogma; they are hateful homophobic acts which have nothing to do with a 'loving God'. Every decent human being, especially those who claim communion with God, should want to stop such attacks, and not condone them in any way. Every time a religious leader preaches hate against homosexuals, he or she colludes with, and is directly or indirectly responsible for, attacks upon gay people. It is important that congregations of the faithful challenge such twisted perversions masquerading as God's message.

On the 30th October 2013 I met with the Jamaican High Commissioner to the UK to explore my ideas about how, working together, we might put a stop to anti-gay violence in her country. I presented my 15-page discussion document, which included the following Vison Equality Statement:

Aloun Ndombet-Assamba, Jamaican High Commissioner to the UK

"A healthy, wealthy, educated, and confident Jamaica, where every child, woman and man, regardless of age, colour, disability, gender, identity, marital status, religion, or sexuality, experiences freedom, dignity and equal life chances. A modern, forward-looking Jamaica will promote dignity for all, and embrace and celebrate our diversity as an

asset, not a problem; discrimination of any kind will be committed to the past. Our ambition to achieve and deliver excellence under the sun, means every Jamaican will be judged by the character of our heart, and personal contribution to making our beloved country the ideal place in which to live, visit, do business, and thrive. Self-discipline will ensure prosperous outcomes, and in the process, draw us closer together as one Jamaica."

My discussion paper recommends the drafting of a fifteen-year Equality and Life Chances action plan, intended to complement and run as an integral component of Vision 2030 Jamaica, the country's ambitious National Development Plan. The opening paragraph reads:

'Jamaica's diversity is a strength, and failure to embrace it as such could seriously undermine our very worthy ambitions as set out in Vision 2030 Jamaica. The world is moving towards greater diversity and people will increasingly want to live, work and visit places where they experience freedom, equality, and respect, regardless of their personal identity. Jamaica (and her Commonwealth sister countries) should not risk being left behind.'

My paper received a warm but cautious reception but was later forwarded by Her Excellency to the Jamaican government for consideration and possible action. We will see in due course whether my effort was worthwhile.

Writing this chapter has freed me from the twisted umbilical cord of irrational religious dogma, and revealed it to be one of the world's greatest self-destructive traits, next to greed and nuclear weaponry. It coerces the innocent and gullible, suppresses and oppresses the weak, intimidates justified critics, inspires good people to do wicked things, makes intelligent people plain stupid and worse. I encourage my readers to remove their own blinkers and shackles, and question established holy works for themselves. I also hope you will join me in rejecting the notion that we are born sinners (bad). We are in fact born untarnished into the world's human family; to love and act out of equality and dignity towards each other; whatever our birth or chosen identity. Together, we can be the example of love that religion isn't. Together, we can also stand up for an authentic and honest relationship with life and God; be he the God of the Bible, Koran, Tipitaka, Torah, or the universe.

Religious compulsion is a sign that there is something wrong in our lives; it's a symptom rather than a cure. If we face and consciously seek to heal our inner pain, insecurity and brokenness, then our need for the camouflage of religion, like excess alcohol and drug use, will be healed too. Blind religion is yet another addiction to contain our demons rather than exorcise them. In my experience, self-love and authenticity are the greatest healers of all. We should strive to love and celebrate our lives as we really are, and shine a bright light of reality on everything that makes us who we are; starting on the inside. Self-love and integrity will heal, nurture, free and enable us to become our full potential. We don't have to dream it, we can live it!

Courageous authenticity leads to amazing grace: I once was lost, but now I am found. I declare that I have shed the guilt and shame that held me bound, and with my eyes wide open and feet firmly on the ground, I have seen the truth that has set me free. I am out of the closet and living in the light: the light of reality. I am undoubtedly worthy of life and love, as I am, as are my LGBTQ brothers and sisters. We are the children of a most distinctive and beautiful rainbow, and it is with brazen pride that we sing: "Life's not worth a damn, 'til you can shout out, I AM WHAT I AM!"

Rant over. Ahh men, Amen! Peace, love and disco! V x

54. WORDS OF LOVE & LIGHT FOR MY DAUGHTER

1. "Invest in love, life's most precious gift. To love is why we exist and everything else is dust waiting to happen."
2. "Choose your life's destination and take responsibility to get there. Start with a plan, get in the driver's seat, stay focused, and cast your past to the rear view mirror."
3. "You are a unique gift to the world; born to be your authentic self. A denial of *your truth* will tarnish life's joy."
4. "Be bold! Fear is a frame of mind, change it to courage."
5. "Being powerless is a choice. Reclaim your power every day: it's in your knowledge, voice, hands, and feet."
6. "Nurture relationships that respect and celebrate you. Count your blessings, learn daily, be kind, and have fun."
7. "The heart often has better vision than the eyes. 'Bling' is pretty, but never ever become blinded by it."
8. "It's a new day! Yesterday is a prison for fools. Never let its mistakes rob you of today's opportunities. Move on."
9. "The truth will always be the truth, even if we wish it to be otherwise. Let love, truth, and integrity shape you."
10. "A bad chapter (in life) doesn't make a bad book."
11. "It may be on your plate, but you don't have to eat it! Bin what doesn't work, and embrace what does. This may have to include negative or destructive people."
12. "You have both a physical body and an inner spirit. Take the most precious care of both."
13. "You can manipulate the mind but not the heart."
14. "Time is precious, so use it well and use it now... now!"
15. "Forgiveness is about setting yourself free, not the other person... and be sure to forgive yourself."
16. "There's always a solution, even if it isn't ideal."
17. "Pressure makes diamonds. Shine (smile), baby!"
18. "Death is incapable of destroying (a father's) love."
19. "You love me by loving yourself." Love always, Dad x

55. CONTACT THE AUTHOR VERNAL W. SCOTT

London men whispering sweet nothings in my ear. Typical!

Book Vernal as a keynote for your conference/workshop or other events: Black History; LGBT History; World AIDS Day; Fathers and Family Courts; Equality and Diversity advice, training and policy development; eLearning; Sexuality and Parenting/Gay Dads; Community Consultation; Staff Support; Sexuality, Equality and Commonwealth Countries; Sexuality and Christianity; Creating gay-friendly communities at home and abroad. He also offers private readings in your home. The perfect private dinner guest, book him today!

Vernal provides **confidential support** to public and private individuals dealing with sexuality, 'coming out' and HIV issues. He's also a McKenzie Friend (nominal fee/expenses charged) in Family Court.

Link with Vernal on Facebook, You Tube, LinkedIn, or Twitter. You can email him directly at: vernalscott@gmail.com or www.vernalscott.com

Vernal Scott is the media commentator you've been looking for. Catch him on Arise TV News and other media sources.

Visit marshallacm.com for all your eLearning needs. Mention Vernal.

Check out Vernal's reviews on Amazon UK.

God's Other Children: A London Memoir   573

Find out what Vernal Scott is doing now. Google him!

Connect on Facebook, Twitter, Linked In, and You Tube.

Obamaland

Sizzling Sydney

I love New York

God's Other Children: A London Memoir 576

North Wales

Key West

God's Other Children: A London Memoir   577

2008: Chicago by night - waiting for the election of Barack Obama

God's Other Children: A London Memoir   578

Zillions of black gay men at the annual Atlanta 'White Party'

God's Other Children: A London Memoir 580

Wales

Miami. I love the beach, the Pink Café, and the Nexxt restaurant. Yummy!

Barcelona

Legendary ladies: Thelma Houston and Marlena Shaw in London

Peter Andre

John Prescott

KC at the steering wheel and May (aged five!) at the camera

Hampstead Heath walkies with lil' Miss May Scott

56. GOD'S BACKROOM DISCO CLASSICS: BURN BABY, BURN!
Heaven and Hell's eternal flame foot movers:

1. Never Can Say Goodbye LP/Experience LP/I've Got You LP/Glorious/This Love Affair/Kidnapped/I Will Survive/Love Tracks LP/Tonight/Tease Me/Mackside/I Am What I Am/The Last Night (w Giorgio Moroder) – Gloria Gaynor

2. If My Friends Could See Me Now/Gypsy Lady/Red Light/I'll Keep On Loving You/Shoot Your Best Shot/You Are You Are/Runaway Love/The Heat In Me/Hold Me Close – Linda Clifford

3. Hit and Run/Love Sensation/Dreamin/Runaway/We're Getting Stronger/Shout It To The Top/Ripped Off/Good Good Feeling/Catch Me/Relight My Fire/Seconds – Loleatta Holloway

4. Hot Stuff/Bad Girls LP/I Feel Love/Wasted/I Need You/Rumour Has It/McArthur Park Suite/Last Dance/Love's Unkind/Love's About To Change My Heart/Melody of Love – Donna Summer

5. I Was Born This Way – (Archbishop) Carl Bean

6. Midnight Love Affair suite/I Wanna Stay With You/Night Fever/Crime Don't Pay/Headline News/Life Time Guarantee/Doctor's Orders/Burnin' – Carol Douglas

7. Dr Buzzard's Original Savannah Band LP

8. You Make Me Feel Mighty Real/Do You Wanna Funk/Give It Up/Sex/Take Me To Heaven/Dance Disco Heat/Over and Over/I Need You/Down Down Down – Sylvester

9. Turn The Beat Around/Hold Tight/Daylight/Hot Summer Night – Vicki Sue Robinson

10. And The Beat Goes On/It's A Love Thing – The Whispers

11. Hot Shot/Bring On The Boys/You Ain't Nothing – Karen Young

12. I Want Your Love (Dimitri mix)/Le Freak/Everybody Dance/Good Times/Dance Dance Dance/Why - Chic

13. La Vie En Rose/Pull Up To The Bumper/Need a Man/Tomorrow/Don't Mess/Saved/Below the Belt/Fame/Use Me – Grace Jones

14. Hold Your Horses/Let No Man Put Assunder/Let Me Down Easy/Love Thang/Sittin Pretty – First Choice

15. What A Diff'rence A Day Makes LP/Ooop Ooop Ooop/Mr Magic/We've Got A Good Thing Going/Turn Me Out – Esther Phillips

16. Fire Island/Village People/Hollywood/YMCA/Go West/5 O'Clock In The Morning/Do You Wanna Spend The Night – Village People

17. I Love Music/ Now That We Found Love/Darling Darling Baby/Living For The Weekend/Message in Our Music/For The Love of Money – The O'Jays

18. We Are Family/Thinking Of You (Dimitri mix)/Lost In Music – Sister Sledge

19. Gonna Get Over You/Come To Me/Wanna Take A Chance On Love/Can We Fall In Love Again – France Joli

20. Like An Eagle – Dennis Parker

21. Got To Be Real/Star Love/Shake It Up Tonight/Encore - Cheryl Lynn

22. Shame/I'm In Love/Love Come Down – Evelyn 'Champagne' King

23. Carry On/Fantasy/I Don't Know Anybody Else/Everybody Everybody/Just Us/No One Can Love You/It's Raining Men - Martha Wash/Two Tons O' Fun/Weather Girls

24. Knock On Wood/Get Your Love Back/Friends – Amii Stewart

25. This Time Baby/How's Your Love Life Baby/Walk Away/Don't Knock My Love – Jackie Moore

26. Feed The Flame/The More I Get – Lorraine Johnson

27. Love In C Minor/Supernature /You Are The One/Midnight Lady/Black is Black/Music of Life/Give Me Love - Cerrone

28. Most Of All/On A Rien Perdre/Hold On To Love/Fill My Life With Love/La Symphony Africaine/One More Minute – Saint Tropez

29. Was That All It Was/If You Wanna Go Back/Don't Let It Go To Your Head/Time Waits For No One/Sweet and Wonderful – Jean Carn

30. This Is It/Free/Standing Right Here/You Stepped Into My Life/Read My Lips/Promised Land/Play Boy Scout/Pick Me Up I'll Dance – Melba Moore

31. In The Name Of Love/Can You Handle It/You're A Winner/Beat The Street – Sharon Redd

32. Love Hangover/Who/The Boss LP/I'm Coming Out/Upside Down/You Were The One/Sweet Summertime Lovin' - Diana Ross

33. K-jee – MFSB

34. Easy Money/I Love You Anyway/Happy 'Bout The Whole Thing – Dee Dee Sharpe Gamble

35. The Love I Lost/Bad Luck/The More I Get The More I Want/You Can't Hide Form Yourself – Teddy Pendergrass and Harold Melvin

36. Helplessly/Loving You Is Killing Me/So Much – Moment of Truth

37. Can't Fake The Feeling/It Doesn't Only Happen At Night/Ne Me Dis Pas Adiev/J'ai Mal – Geraldine Hunt

38. Watcha Gonna Do With My Lovin/You Can Get Over/Put Your Body In It/Stand Back/Try My Love/Medicine Song – Stephanie Mills

39. Take Me I'm Yours – Mary Clark

40. I Got A Thing For You remix – Silver, Platinum and Gold

41. Don't Leave Me This Way/You Used to Hold Me So Tight/If You Feel It/Make It Last/Never Gonna Be Another One – Thelma Houston

42. Am I Dreamin/Small Circle of Friends – Tom Moulton/TJM

43. Touch and Go/Ask Me/We Can Do It Too – Ecstasy, Passion and Pain

44. You Gave Me Love/Galaxy of Love – Crown Heights Affair

45. Could Heaven Ever Be Like This – Idris Muhammed

46. I Want Us Back Together/Funtime/Shake Your Groove Thing – Peaches and Herb

47. Nights On Broadway/Young Hearts Run Free/When You Wake Up Tomorrow/Victim/Chance – Candi Staton

48. Since I Fell For You/One More Love Song/Don't Take Away Your Love – Hodges James and Smith

49. You're Gonna Get Next To Me – Bo Kirkland and Ruth Davis

50. Don't Stop Me Now/Malory – Skip Mahoney

51. All About The Paper/Face To Face/Changed Man – The Dells

52. Summer Love/In The Bush/Keep On Jumpin – Musique

53. Golden Eldorado/Souvenirs/ Fly Away/Tahiti Tahiti/From East To West/Scotch Machine/Point Zero - Voyage

54. Sweet Beginnings/It's Better Than Walking Out/Pictures and Memories/Touch Me In The Morning/Love Dancing – Marlena Shaw

55. Boys Will Be Boys/You Give Me Such A Feeling/Outside Love/Sadness In My Eyes – Duncan Sisters

56. When I'm Dancing/Choosing You/Please Don't Tempt Me – Lenny Williams

57. How High – Cognac

58. Love No Longer Has A Hold/Hang on in There – Johnny Bristol

59. Rio de Janeiro (Morales extended mix)/Brazilian Nights – Gary Criss

60. Disco Inferno/Where The Happy People Go/Stop and Think/Zing – The Trammps

61. Move On Up Suite – Destination

62. Do It To The Music/Just In Time – Raw Silk

63. I've Got The Next Dance – Deniece Williams

64. You're The One For Me/Music/Keep Giving Me Love – D Train

65. Take Me Home/Wasn't It Good/Believe/Strong Enough - Cher

66. Cocomotion/I'm Mad As Hell/Love to The World – El Coco

67. Found A Cure/Dance Forever/Flashback/It Seems To Hang On – Ashford and Simpson

68. Love Machine – Tempest Trio

69. Deliverance/Carry On Turn Me On/Prison/Save Your love – Space featuring Madeline Bell

70. Get Down – Gene Chandler

71. In The Socket/A Night To Remember/There It Is/Uptown Festival/Second Time Around/I Can Make You Feel Good/Over and Over - Shalamar
72. Dancer/Dance To Dance/Try It Out – Gino Soccio
73. Is It It/The Louder/Dance On Music/One Two Three – Peter Jaques Band
74. Changin – Sharon Ridley
75. Heaven Must Be Missing An Angel/Don't Take Away The Music/More Than A Woman/Make It Soon (with Freda Payne) – Tavares
76. Can't Live Without Your Love/Creepin/Let It Flow – Tamiko Jones
77. Love Shook/Let's Make Love To The Music/Don't Make Me Wait/After Dark – Patti Brooks
78. Get Off/You - Foxy
79. Let's Have A Party/Listen To The Music/I'm On Fire – Danielle
80. Love and Desire/Runaway/Let The Music Play – Arpeggio
81. Think It Over/Warning-Danger/Somebody Should've Told Me/It Doesn't Only Happen At Night – Cissy Houston
82. It Must Be Love/Crazy Love/99.5 Percent – Alton McClain and Destiny
83. I Thought It Was You/You Bet Your Love – Herbie Hancock
84. Don't You Want My Love/New York Eyes/Why You Take My Love – Nicole J. McCloud

85. African Queens LP/Give Me A Break/Life is Music/All Night All Right/Brazil/Put Your Feet To The Beat/American Generation – Ritchie Family

86. We Got The Power – Ron Green

87. Fall Down/In The Morning Time/The Rock – Tramaine Hawkins

88. Manhatten Love Song – King Errison

89. Number Onederful – Jay and the Techniques

90. 24 Hours A Day/You Are The Music Within Me/Spend A Little Time With Me – Barbara Pennington

91. Let The Music Play/Give Me Tonight/Sweet Somebody – Shannon

92. I Specialize In Love – Sharon Brown

93. Night Fever/Staying Alive/You Should Be Dancing – Bee Gees

94. Where Is The Love/Clean Up Woman/Shoorah Shoorah – Betty Wright

95. Sweet Dynamite/Why Must A Girl Like Me – Claudja Barry

96. Queen Of Fools/Love Masterpiece/I Close My Eyes and Count to Ten – Jessica Williams

97. I Like You/Don't Stop The Train/Land of Make Believe – Phyllis Nelson

98. If You Could Read My Mind/Up On The Roof/Your Love/Stormy Weather – Viola Wills

99. Ou Sont Les Femmes/Got A Feeling/I Love America – Patrick Juvet

100. Which Way Is Up/Wear It Out - Starguard

101. I'll Take You There/Slippery People/If You're Ready – Staple Singers
102. Singing In The Rain/Spacer – Sheila B Devotion
103. I'll Always Love My Mama – The Intruders
104. Ten Percent/My Love Is Free – Double Exposure
105. I'm Gonna Let Ya/Car Of Love/Love and Harmony/Take My Love – Nancy Wilson
106. I Like It/Disco Inferno/Turn The Music Up – Players Association
107. Me And My Baby Brother/Low Rider – War
108. Party On – Pure Energy
109. Never – The Body Shop
110. Gone Gone Gone/Begin the Beguine – Johnny Mathis
111. Walk Away From Love/I Can't Stop The Rain/You're My Peace Of Mind – David Ruffin
112. The Magic Is You/Ain't That Enough For You/Holler – John Davis and the Monster Orchestra
113. Shake Your Body Down To The Ground/Can You Feel It – The Jacksons
114. Another Star/As/Sir Duke/Superstition – Stevie Wonder
115. Hit and Run Lover/Mercy/Touch and Go Lover/All The People Of The World – Carol Jiani
116. Stuff Like That/Love I Never It So Good/Bethca Wouldn't Hurt Me – Quincy Jones
117. In The Evening – Sheryl Lee Ralph

118. Dance With You/Street Corner Symphony – Carrie Lucas
119. Heat You Up – Shirley Lites
120. Sinner Man/Lucky Tonight – Sarah Dash
121. Disco Dance/Can You Feel It – Michelle
122. Hot For You/Lovin Is Really My Game – Brainstorm
123. Get On Floor/Don't Stop Til You Get Enough/Rock With You – Michael Jackson
124. Glow Of Love/Searching/Miracles/On Top – Change featuring Luther Vandross
125. What Can I Say/Lowdown – Boz Scaggs
126. Ain't Nothing Going On But The Rent/Padlock – Gwen Guthrie
127. Your Love - Lime
128. Disco Lady/What About My Love/Just Ain't Good Enough/ Mister Melody Maker – Johnny Taylor
129. When Love Is New/I Want'cha Baby/You Can Do It – Arthur Prysock
130. Shaft/Shaft II/Stranger In Paradise – Isaac Hayes
131. You're The Best/Rising To The Top/Let Somebody Love You – Keni Burke
132. Secret Rendezvous/I Love You More/Banging – Rene and Angela
133. Night Fever/Spanish Hustle – Fatback Band
134. Rock Steady/Jump To It/Get It Right/Who's Zoomin Who? – Aretha Franklin
135. Give Me The Night/Love Ballad/Love X Love – George Benson

136. Ooh La La/Harmony – Suzi Lane

137. One of These Nights – The Eagles

138. Jump To The Beat/Dynamite – Stacy Lattisaw

139. Strawberry Letter 23/Stomp/Real Thing – Brothers Johnson

140. Til You Take My Love – Harvey Mason featuring Merry Clayton

141. Another Man/Don't I Ever Cross Your Mind – Barbara Mason

142. Star Wars – Meco Monardo

143. Trying To Get Next To You – Arnold Blair

144. Love Goes Deeper Than That/Number One/1000 Laughs – Eloise Laws

145. You're My Man/Baby Come On – Sex O'Clock USA OST

146. Crazy Water/Are You Ready – Elton John

147. You're My Driving Wheel/I'm Gonna Let My Heart Do The Walking/Stoned Love (Tom Moulton mix) – The Supremes

148. Running Away/Can't You See Me – Roy Ayers

149. Love Is In The Air – Jean Paul Young

150. Don't Let Me Be Misunderstood – Santa Esmeralda and Leroy Gomez

151. You Know How To Love Me/Loving You, Losing You – Phyllis Hyman

152. Let's Stay Together/Love Explosion/Disco Inferno – Tina Turner

153. That'll Be Johnny/I Need You More Than Ever Now/Makes Me Wanna Holla – Sarah Vaughan

154. Best Of My Love/Flowers/I Don't Want To Lose Your Love – The Emotions

155. Thunder In My Heart/You Make Me Feel Like Dancing – Leo Sayer

156. It's In His Kiss/Baby I'm Yours – Linda Lewis

157. I'm Always In The Mood/Love Be With You/Love is All We Need/Things That I Could Do/Love Formula 69 – Randy Brown

158. Keep The Fire Burning/Funky Sensation/Love I'm Giving – Gwen McCrae

159. Somebody Else's Guy/I Wish You Would – Jocelyn Brown

160. Everybody Needs Somebody – Ann Margaret

161. Nice and Slow/Flip – Jesse Green

162. The Bull/Cosmic Wind /Disco People – Mike Theodore Orchestra

163. Garden Of Love/Got Have Loving/Standing in The Rain/My Desire – Don Ray

164. Heaven must Have Sent You/Jump For My Love/Automatic – Pointer Sisters

165. You're A Star – Aquarian Dream

166. Self-Control/Solitaire/Gloria – Laura Branigan

167. You + Me = Love - Undisputed Truth

168. Sweet Rain remix/Lonely Disco Dancer/One In A Million – Dee Bridgewater

169. Car Wash/Is It Love You're After/Still in Love/Magic Touch/Rose Royce Express – Rose Royce

170. Inside Out/Use It Up Wear It Out/Hang Together/Native NY - Odyssey

171. Let the Night Take the Blame – Lorraine McKane

172. There But For The Grace Of God - Machine

173. Giving My Love/Smack Dab In the Middle/Passion and Pain – Janice McClain

174. Giving Up, Giving In/The Runner/Dirty Ol Man – Three Degrees

175. Classic/I Wouldn't Give You Up – Chatelaine

176. Come On Dance Dance – Saturday Night Band

177. Baby I'm Burning – Dolly Parton

178. Hit and Run/Unyielding/I Come To Party/Second Best – Jeannie Reynolds

179. Déjà vu – Paulinho Da Costa with Philip Bailey

180. Sunny - Boney M

181. Casanova/I Wanna Be With You - Coffee

182. Six Million Steps – Rhani Harris

183. Saturday(Dimitri mix)/I Like Love/Sorcerer – Norma Jean

184. I'm Every Woman/Ain't Nobody – Chaka Khan

185. Just Keep Thinking About You, Baby/Get It Up For Love/Been On My Own Too Long/Full Speed Ahead/Reachin Around My Love – Tata Vega

186. Haven't You Heard/Forget Me Nots/Look Up/Don't Blame Me – Patrice Rushen

187. Highwire/Philly Hound – Linda Carr

188. Peter Gunn/Whistle Bump - Deodato

189. Ain't No Stopping Us Now/I Heard It In A Love Song – McFadden and Whitehead

190. You See The Trouble With Me/You're The First – Barry White

191. Party Line/More More More/What's Your Name – Andrea True

192. Tonight I Feel Like Dancing – Toulouse

193. The Beat Goes On – Ripple

194. Let's Go Round Again/Pick Up The Pieces – Average White Band

195. Do You Wanna Get Funky With Me/Dance With Me – Peter Brown

196. It's in Your Blood – Linda Hopkins

197. I'm On Fire/I Love To Love – 5000 Volts and Tina Charles

198. Touch and Go/Count The Days/Earthquake – Al Wilson

199. Spring Rain – Silvetti

200. Streetlife – The Crusaders with Randy Crawford

201. Bonus cut 1: Dancing Queen/Gimme/Voulez-Vous/Lay Your Love On Me – Abba

202. Bonus cut 2: Do You Want The Real Thing/Cathedrals - DC LaRue

203. Bonus cut 3 Get Ready – Ella Fitzgerald:

Acknowledgements and appreciation continued:

Stephen Maglott, Reverend Paul Bailey, Stian Amadeus Antonsen, Thierry Henry, Ash Kotak, Danni Gee, Viv Brosnahan, Malik Mohammad, Helen Cox, Lewis Rae, Colin Grant, Eugene Scott, Jonathan Capehart, Van Jones, Roger Collins, Maajid Nawaz, Johnny Soutan, Topher Campbell, Victoria Beckham, Dean Atta, Wayne Herbert, Dr Martin Patrick, Dana West, Ruby Turner, Clare Summerskill, Ajamu X, Andre Lloyd, Bidisha, Suzi Feay, Rachel Holmes, Brian Fillis, Assaad Samara, Tony Williams, Paul Newton, Jay Shah, Jason Latty, Michael Cadette, Keith Norman, Ian Clifford, Ammana Shaka, Annie Lennox, Dean Hamilton, Cordelle Sailsman, KG Lester, Paul Egbers-Kane, Dan Savage, David Wailing, Rod Shields, Terry Joe, William 'Bill' Wilcox, Lorne Burrell, Patrick Vernon, Linda Bellos OBE, Tony 'Diva Radio' Messera, Stephen Morris, Wayne Mertins-Brown, Peter Davey, Matt Moore, Daniel Abrahamovitch, Pam St Clement, Ertanch Hidayettin, Ian Poitier, Lord Chris Smith, Jason Jones, Jonathan Buxton, Kristofer David, David Embleton, Kofi Nyero, Denise Wellington, Christine Ricketts, Patrick Lewis, Gary Henson, James Barrett, Philippe Talavera, Hans Spaarney, Huub Van Tol, Stafford Scott, Pim Scraven, Ellen Pendersen, Brian Ellis, Thierry Giunta, Patrick 'Queer Nation' Lilley, Steve Swindells, DJ Mel, Danilo Agusto, Astrid Zimmermann, Carlos Herrera, Jet Kording, Keith Boykin, James Thompson, Dario Rolandi, Kenneth Sylvia, John Halsall, Andrew Sherwood, Pavlos Mastiki, Hazel Taylor, Ann Allcock, Peter Hughes, Jeoffrey Watson, Sir Alan Duncan MP, Thomas J. Ryan, Sharon McFarlane, Amelia Lawrence, Steve Farragher, Aaron Sokell, John Amaechi OBE, Michael Joseph Anderson, Will Sawney, Neil Sitges, Kamran Saeed, David 'Yes' Mcalmont, David Morrison, Rod De Souza, Juan Walter, Junior Hamer, Russell E. Thornhill, Calvin 'DJ' Dawkins, Jeremy Joseph, NAZ: Khaiser, Munira, Maureen, Carlos, Jose, Zahra, Ivana, Harvey, Louise the caterer, Matt, Winnie, Daniel Thomas and the Joyful Noise Choir, Menno Kuijper, Phil 'Givin It Back' Hurtt, Roderick Earle Young, Keiran Williams, Derrick Prwtch Leblanc, Justin Rudzki,

Turner Miranda, Andy Gee, Danni Gee, Stephanie Gold, Matt Mostyn, Martin Wilcox, Nicki Alade, Clara Arokiasamy, Matt 'Funkytown', Yanni Tsekas, Frank Booth, Vincent Gil Jacome, Carrol Thompson, Lisandro Caffaratto, Tim Smith, Vivia and Winsome Pinnock, Carol 'Hit and Run' Jiani, Jem Dairo-Bowen, Joey Luciano, Sly Scarbough, Shirland Aird, Nick Savva, Cajjmere 'DJ' Wray, Ahmed Abdel Hady, Chuka Umanna MP, Diane Abbott MP, Colin Moon, Francesca Okosi, Rajendra P Joshi, Franc Hayes, Andras 'Vital Europe' Gyorfi, Rev TJ Royal, David DK Soomarie, Or Regev, Bill Pearce, David Cubbin, Kashy 'the voice' Keegan, Steven Hitchens, Roland Nedd, Robert Shaw, Jeremy Ward, Scott Whittaker, Pavel Pietrzak, Sally Moss, Karim Karim, Richard Kirker, Robbie Blackhall-Miles, Sally Hall-Jones, David Lammy MP, Lee Lockhart Mure, Elias Vigneswaren, Mhairi Dunlop, Graham Wilkinson, Anthony Carter, Barry Myers, Ariel Morel, Rembrandt Peralta, Carl Hodson, Sam Harvey, Victor 'Stephanie Mills' Antonio, Rudy Calvo, Rev Simon Buckley, Neville Fleming, Richard Hill, Meco 'Star Wars' Monardo, Waleed Walid, Herro Johnson, Gary L. Tracy, Calvin Stovell, Trevor Dunn, Dane McGregor, Ernest Owens, Mohammed Salim, Lee Jasper, Yvonne Wilson, Shirley Stephenson, Dorethea Smartt, David G. Benjamin, Neil Meron, Kyle Wagner, Ralph Tee, Guy Berger, Larrio Ekson, Robert Maragh, Jason B Moore, Kay Phelps, David Truswell, Luca Benzoni, Vijay Puri, Ken Goppy, Leroy Morgan, Pascoe Sawyers, Tai Newsome, David VanDalfsen, Steve Paulden, Albert Dixon Cunningham III, Xabier Oiarbide Bargos, Nevin Powell, Ron Weinberg, David Kassa, Anton Phillips, Mark Blake, Michael Frederick, Mikel Scott-Makin, Roger Spencer, Arnold Gordon, Andrew Francis, Matthew Christiansen, Michael Head, Dominic Hunt, Don 'Talk Talk Talk' Oriolo, Ngosi Fulani, Jordan Gabriel, Kevin Ford, Yvonne Taylor, Mhairi Dunlop, Richard Knight, Fabian Cataldo, Nick O'Neil, Dr Rusi Jaspal, James Wright, Darren Brady, Guy Ivie, Finn Reygan, Omar Arizmendi, Pauline Asgarali Gomez, Milly 'Cakes' Carew, Robert Shemin, Robert Freeman, Andy Davies, Oscar Watson, Daniel Corten, Ivan Berger, Maxwell Charles, Jose De Pablo Deco, Spencer Carter, Arick Messer,

Richard Blake, Dinesh Ragawala, David Baker, Jack Flavell, Innocent Chidzero, Goran Kay, Jerome Francois, Daniel Tietz, Shareef Khatib, Shepard Smith, Tony Warr, Jay Wilson, Jonathan Richardson, David Whitmore, Barry Honeyman, Gustav Andersson, Wayne 'Big Break' Dickson, Tom Moulton, Jotham Annan, Michael Brown, Kingsley Jordan Wells, Maarten Verhaegen, Mario Ledesma.

To organisations: Terrence Higgins Trust, London Lighthouse, 56 Dean St, Black Communities AIDS Team, The People's Group, the Brent HIV Centre, Peter Tatchell Foundation, Blackliners, BHAN, UK Black Pride, Sue Sanders and Tony Fenwick (LGBT History Month), GMFA, ACT-UP, Polari, all the men of Tongues, Gay's the Word, Prowler, WH Smith, Bertrams, Gay Dads UK/Support, House of Rainbow, SHAKA, The Atheist Experience, Stonewall, and all at (David) Marshall E-Learning.

Providers of the soundtrack to my typing: Nancy Wilson, Sarah Vaughan, Tramaine Hawkins, Tina Turner, Esther Phillips, Gloria Gaynor, Linda Clifford, Loleatta Holloway, Donna Summer, Scott Walker, Four Tops, the O'Jays, Dionne Warwick, Shirley Bassey, George Benson, Aretha Franklin, Stephanie Mills, Merry Clayton, The Eagles, George Michael, Elton John, Luther Vandross, Barbra Streisand, Cher, Jennifer Holliday, Cissy Houston, Whitney Houston, Regina Belle, Jackie Moore, Jean Carne, Diana Ross, Gregorian Masters of Chant, Keni Burke, Louisa Mark, Hodges James and Smith, Philadelphia International Classics, Grace Jones, Michael Jackson, Marlena Shaw, Stevie Wonder, Sylvester, Martha Wash, Tata Vega, Randy Crawford, Evelyn 'Champagne' King, Eloise Laws, Roberta Flack, Dee Dee Sharp Gamble, Saint Tropez, Sandra Feva, Dorothy Moore, Simon and Garfunkel, Earth Wind and Fire, Madeline Bell, Pointer Sisters, Odyssey, Lillie Nicole J. McCloud, Miki Howard, Rose Royce, Seal, Thelma Houston, Viola Wills, Vicki Sue Robinson, The Carpenters, Sam Smith, Randy Brown, The Dells, and Diva Radio – *Disco Music Paradise!*

www.VernalScott.com and Facebook

God's Other Children: A London Memoir   602

www.VernalScott.com and Facebook

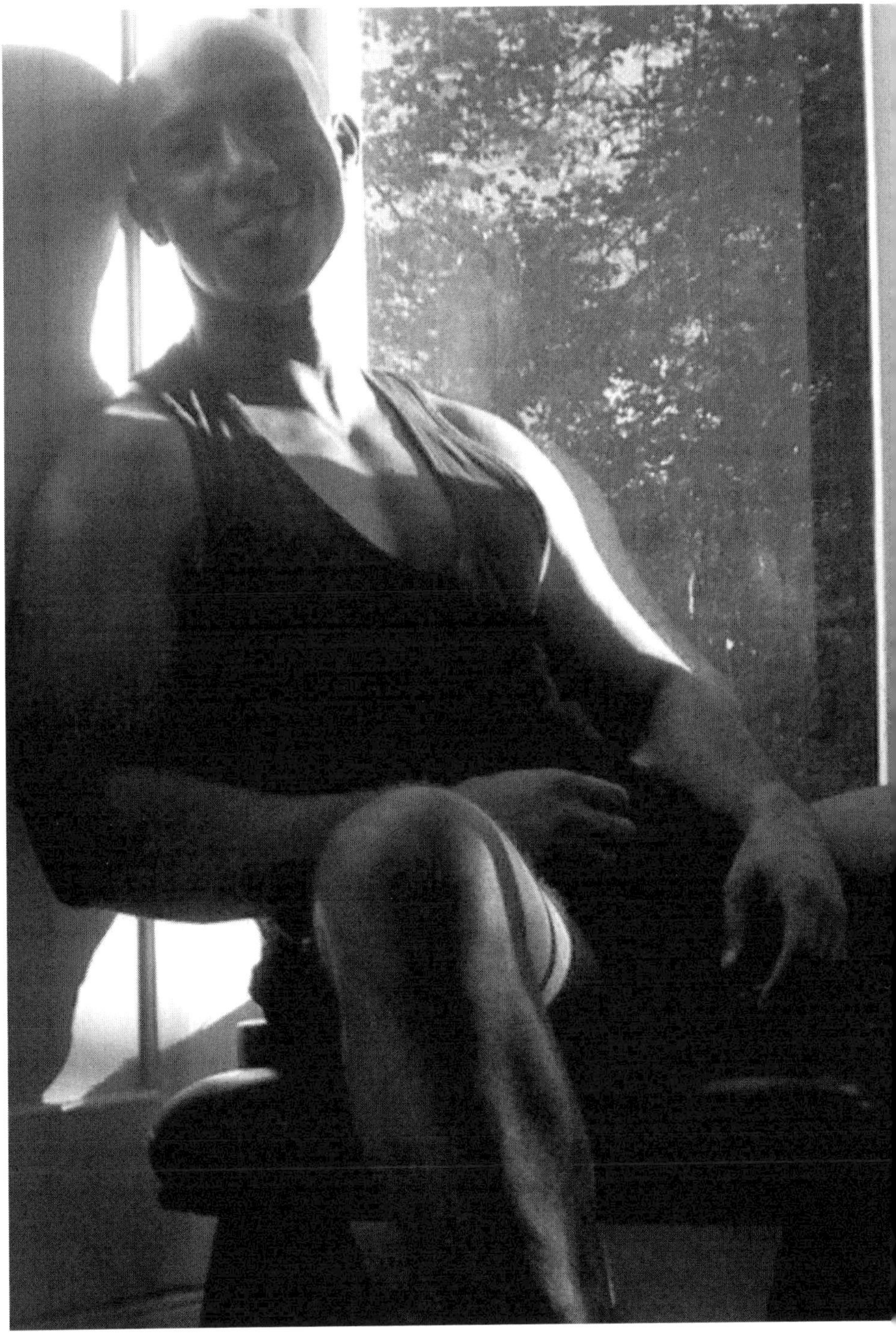

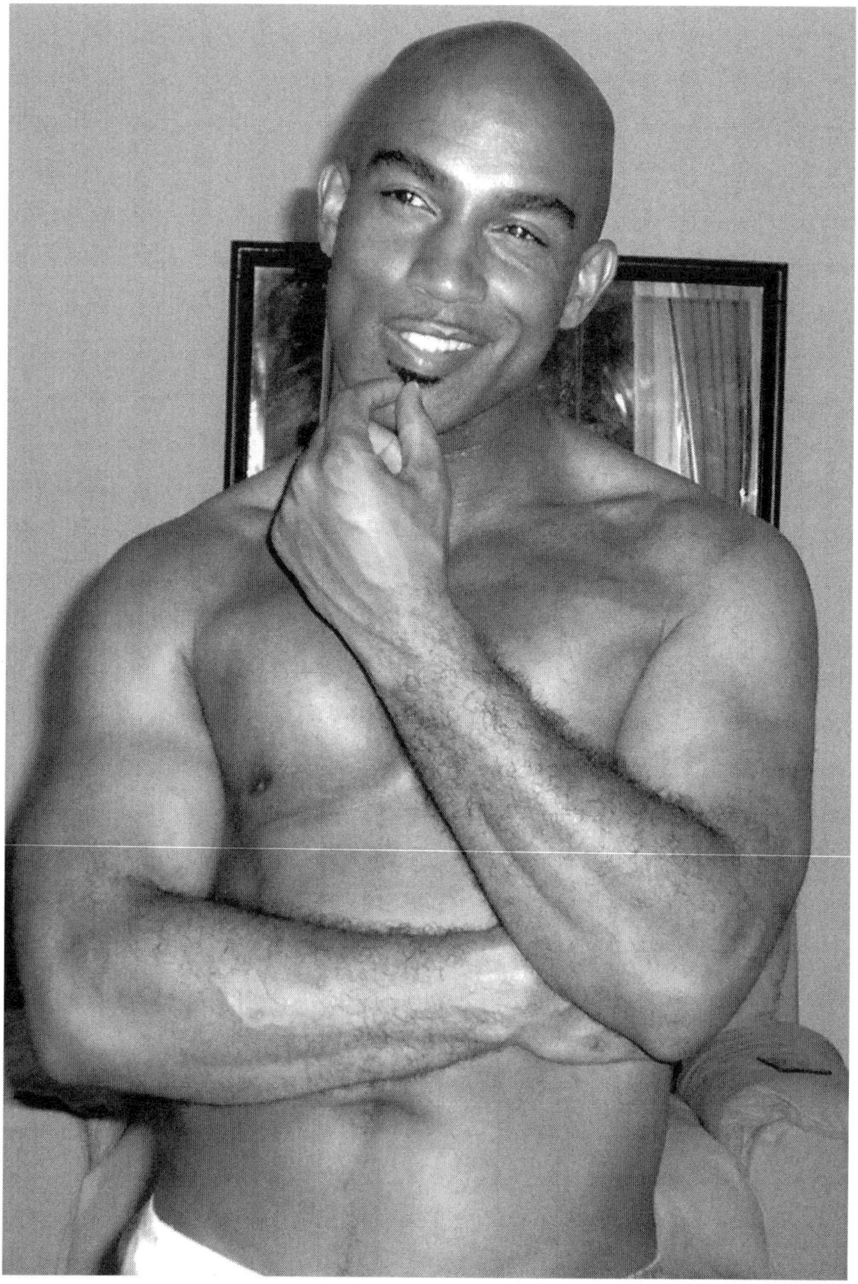

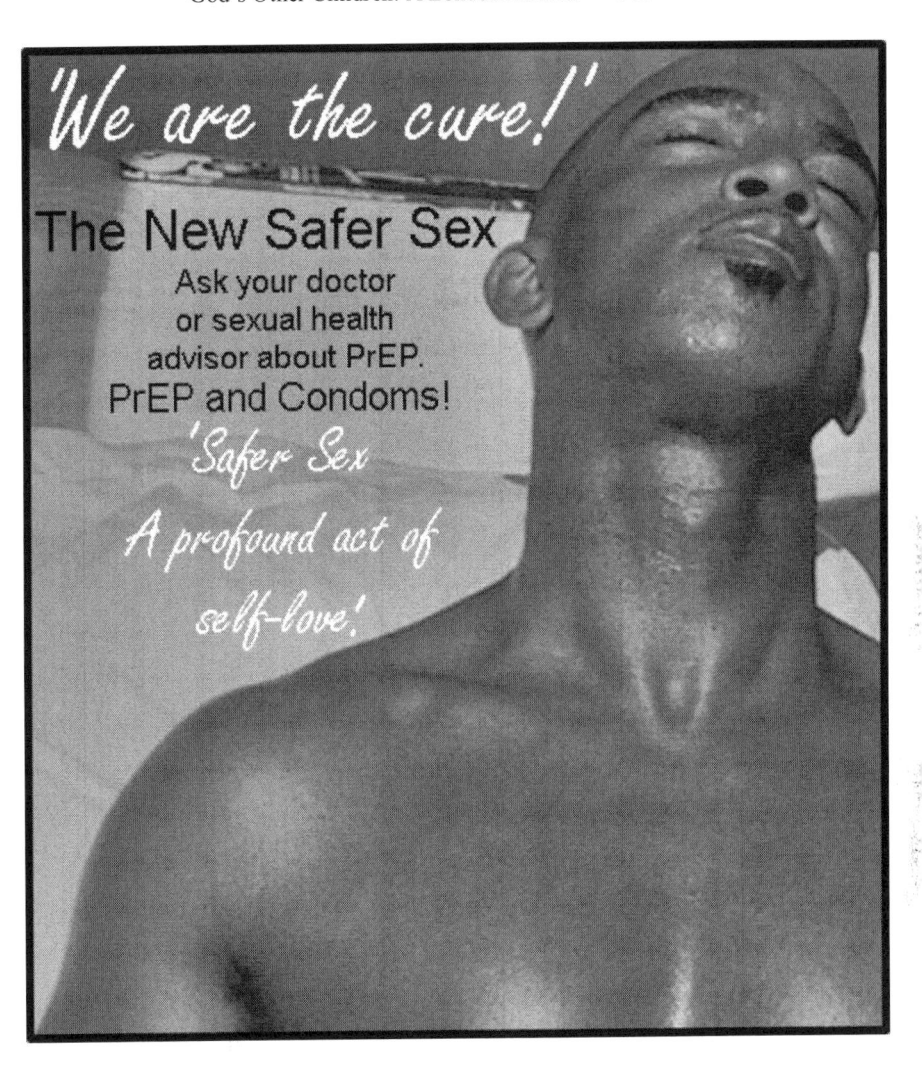

"Enjoying safer sex is a profound act of self-love. Let's do it!" - Vernal Scott.

Using PrEP and condoms mean we can enjoy a great sex life with confidence and reduced risk. While we're doing it, we'll be helping to make new HIV infections a thing of the past. Find out more about PrEP from your local sexual health advisor or GP. We are the cure! Vx

www.VernalScott.com, Facebook, Twitter and Amazon

On sale at WH Smith across the UK:

LIVERPOOL STREET   GATWICK SOUTH   EUSTON   YORK RAIL
LUTON AIRPORT   NINEWELLS HOSPITAL   BIRMINGHAM AIR
GLASGOW CENTRAL   NEWCASTLE AIR   CARDIFF CENTRAL
BRISTOL RAIL   MANCHESTER PICCADILLY   READING RAIL
DONCASTER   DERBY RAIL   STRATFORD   HULL RAIL   LONDON CITY AIRPORT   MANCHESTER AIR T1   HEATHROW T5
KINGS CROSS WESTERN   VICTORIA   WATERLOO
BRISTOL AIR   BIRMINGHAM NEW STREET   EAST MIDLANDS AIRPORT   HEATHROW T3.

Also at Amazon, Foyles, Gay's the Word, Prowler, Barnes and Noble

Printed in Great Britain
by Amazon